HOT FEET
AND
SOCIAL
CHANGE

HOT FEET
AND
SOCIAL
CHANGE

AFRICAN DANCE AND
DIASPORA COMMUNITIES

EDITED BY
KARIAMU WELSH, ESAILAMA G. A. DIOUF,
AND YVONNE DANIEL

FOREWORD BY THOMAS F. DEFRANTZ
PREFACE BY DANNY GLOVER, HARRY BELAFONTE,
AND JAMES COUNTS EARLY

**UNIVERSITY OF
ILLINOIS PRESS**
Urbana, Chicago, and Springfield

Publication of this book was supported in part by the University of Illinois Press Fund for Anthropology.

Library of Congress Cataloging-in-Publication Data
Names: Welsh-Asante, Kariamu, editor. | Diouf, Esailama G.A., editor. | Daniel, Yvonne, 1940– editor.
Title: Hot feet and social change: African dance and diaspora communities / Edited by Kariamu Welsh, Esailama G. A. Diouf, and Yvonne Daniel.
Description: Urbana : University of Illinois Press, [2019] | Includes bibliographical references and index. | Summary: "African dance has a long history in the United States: Asadata Dafora, a Sierra Leonean, had a successful run on Broadway with "Kykunkor" in 1934, and he was one of many artists who, in the 1920s to 1940s, concertized and stylized what we have come to know as African dance. Many African dance specialists remained in the States and taught dance, which began a renaissance in African Dance across the Americas in the 1960s, particularly in the U.S. As a result, the last fifty years have seen an explosion of African performances, choreography and courses in academic institutions and cities across North America, South America, and Europe. Still, there is little information available on African dance per se and some artists and teachers, while well intentioned, disseminate within performative information, myths and falsehoods that continue to characterize African dance as undisciplined, ahistorical, and with scant technical skills. This collection brings indelible stories of African dance as it exists within major cities across the United States, demonstrating the power and considerable influence it has in awakening identity, self-worth, and diverse community respect. It alerts readers to the revealing research that dance investigators have completed and are pursuing—for example, analyses of the aesthetic components within African dance movement, the relationships between the musical and movement elements of African performance practices, or the differences between African and Diaspora usage of improvisation. And it represents traditionalists, neo-traditionalists, artists, teachers and scholars as they tell their stories"— Provided by publisher.
Identifiers: LCCN 2019019862 (print) | LCCN 2019980573 (ebook) | ISBN 9780252084775 (paperback) | ISBN 9780252042959 (cloth) | ISBN 9780252051814 (ebook)
Subjects: LCSH: Dance—Africa—History. | Dance—United States—History. | Classification: LCC GV1705 .H68 2019 (print) | LCC GV1705 (ebook) | DDC 793.3196—dc23
LC record available at https://lccn.loc.gov/2019019862
LC ebook record available at https://lccn.loc.gov/2019980573

CONTENTS

Foreword: The *Bantaba*! Initiation of Purpose
Thomas F. DeFrantz   vii

Preface
Danny Glover, Harry Belafonte, and James Counts Early   xi

Introduction: When, Where, and How We Enter
Kariamu Welsh, Esailama G. A. Diouf, and Yvonne Daniel   1

PART I. HOT FEET AND LOCAL HISTORIES

SAUCE!: Conjuring the African Dream in America
through Dance
Esailama G. A. Diouf   21

Dance Rooted in the Movements of Bedford-Stuyvesant:
Two Choreographers, One Aesthetic Tradition
Indira Etwaroo   37

From Warm-up to *Dobale* in Philadelphia: Embodying
"Community" Meaning in a West African Dance Class
Julie B. Johnson   56

PART II. THE ELDERS' WORK AND WORDS

Ago! Ame! Baba Chuck Speaks!
Charles "Chuck" Davis with C. Kemal Nance   75

The "Gospel" of Memory: Inscribed Bodies in the
African Diaspora
Kariamu Welsh   84

Kankouran West African Dance Company,
Washington, D.C.
William Serrano-Franklin   104

Muntu Dance Theatre of Chicago: 1972–2018
and Still Thriving
Amaniyea Payne   114

Kumbuka African Drum and Dance Collective:
In the City and a Prison of New Orleans
Ausettua Amor Amenkum   123

"The Fierce Freedom of Their Souls": Activism of
African Dance in the Oakland Bay Area
Halifu Osumare   143

The African Choreographer's Envisioning
Naomi Gedo Johnson Diouf   166

Mentoring Notes on African Diaspora Dance
Styles and Continuity
Yvonne Daniel   180

PART III. PERPETUAL MOTION IN THE
AESTHETICS OF AFRICA

Embodying Rhythm: Improvisation as Agency in
African Dance
Abby Carlozzo   205

From Village to International Stage: *Baamaaya* and
the Politics of Adaptation
Steven Cornelius and Habib Iddrisu   228

Men Walk in Parallel! Dancing in Chuck Davis's "Paths"
C. Kemal Nance   249

Bibliography   263

Contributors   279

Index   285

FOREWORD

The *Bantaba*! Initiation of Purpose

Thomas F. DeFrantz

When I was in high school in San Francisco, I was lucky enough to take African dance class with Nontsizi (Delores) Cayou. I was beyond lucky, actually, to be allowed into such a space where Black lives and loves could be explored through moving alongside others. Dancing together, we learned to account for rhythm, timing, and ancestral memory through our gestures. The classes I took were offered in a community center in an odd part of town: not in either of the traditionally Black neighborhoods of San Francisco (Hunter's Point and Western Addition) but in Laurel Heights, across the street from the bus terminal. We gathered on the weekend in this unusual space, fully aware that Cayou also taught other places when she could: at San Francisco State and sometimes at City College; in Oakland, in Berkeley, and all around the East Bay.

In my memory, Cayou dances as a reasoned intellectual, clear in her directions, and forceful in her leadership. She called us as a group toward our shared destinies as dancers and musicians, helping us manage time through our shaping of rhythm. She was, like many who claim the identity of dancer, majestic and glamorous in her delivery of ideas, whether physical or verbal. She was gorgeous and inspiring; committed, vibrant, and eminently accomplished. She helped me imagine a purpose through dance

Cayou's classes were nothing like the *jazz* and *tap dance* lessons we might have taken sporadically in other studios around town. In Cayou's class, we learned history and the philosophical underpinnings to particular steps and their rhythms. We learned to recognize beauty as gestures we could share through our creative labor. We learned to vibrate alongside the drums to imagine an enlivened Black possibility. Cayou motioned us toward this possibility engaged by direct practice in embodied musicianship shared among each other toward an end of our collective achievement. She moved us toward the spiritual circle of the Bantaba—the place, in West African dance cosmologies, of community affirmation that initiates self-purpose.

My adolescent anecdote frames how I understand the importance of the volume you now read. In African dance, we learn of the group's history, told through participation in the arts, and usually led by a visionary activist who works well beyond the terms of everyday dance teaching. We learn to imagine toward a speculative future of engaged activity, responding in real time toward ancient activities of collective action. And we learn that African dance and music *move* across space and time, sharing amazing capacities to the many different audiences who grow as they partake of its embodied bounties.

To write about African dance and musicality is to engage the source. African dance: the animated, bubbling wellspring where life emerges and shapes itself toward creative possibility. So many people around the globe engage in African dance as practitioners and audiences that it seems criminal how little has been written about its contours. This volume remedies that absence in the urgent direction of a diasporic accounting of influences and legacies of African dance in the Americas. Here, we find stories too long denied or passed over: stories of African dancing in Chicago, Washington, D.C., New Orleans, Philadelphia, Oakland, Brooklyn, N.Y. The authors tell us how dancers experience moving in rhythm, across geographies, and through time. Smartly, and with particularity, the volume focuses on the ways that African dance has become constituted in the Americas.

African dancing and musicianship have held a crucial place in Black Power and freedom struggles in the Americas as the dancing demonstration of affiliation with an ancestral legacy of direct participation in the arts. The formation of many African dance companies and theatrical experiments in African dance in the United States coincided with the migration of outstanding artists to the United States (as in Asadata Dafora), a generative interest in aesthetic transformations precipitated by the Middle Passage into the Caribbean (as in Katherine Dunham), and a desire to return to the place of unknown and unknowable ancestors on the African continent (as in Pearl Primus). These three celebrity ancestors of dance created space for thousands of other Black dancers and encouraged us to dance to the collective rather than an audience. Of course, this would be an entirely necessary aspect of Black political organizing: that we move ourselves toward a powerful assembly, encompassing our differences through gestures that honor the group and its diverse histories.

By 2019, when we try to account for how Black popular culture drives the planet toward its rhythmic destinies, we turn, inevitably, to the innovations and engineering of African dance. African dance, inevitably intertwined with its music, generates the source code of rhythmic innovation. To understand popular culture is to think through an engagement with rhythm and the beat; African dance constantly explores the creation and transformation of rhythm into motion. Here, in this volume, authors contend with the myriad ways African dance has shaped lives and inspired urgent creative activity.

When Dr. Takiyah Nur Amin and I connected in 2011 to think together about what we might contribute to the field of Black Dance Studies, we focused on the need for more writing. There is nowhere near enough translation of the exquisite subtleties of African-based musicality and dance into literary form. Text matters, especially in these times of continued uncertainty for Black people all over the planet. As we gathered to consider how to move the Collegium for African Diaspora Dance (CADD) toward a shared usefulness, we began with the desire to center considerations of Africa in as much of its diversity as possible. North, South, East, West, and Central African musicality would be part of our call to action. In our conferences and our writings, we intended to feature discussions of the rich legacies of African dance that feed into our understandings of Black life and global Blackness.

A group of twelve researchers agreed to form the first executive committee for the Collegium alongside Amin and myself: Shireen Dickson, Nadine George-Graves, Jasmine Johnson, Raquel Monroe, C. Kemal Nance, Carl Paris, John O. Perpener III, Makeda Thomas, Andrea E. Woods Valdés, and Ava LaVonne Vinesett. (*n.b.* Calling forth by name is an important aspect of Africanist communication.) We were blessed that Mama Kariamu Welsh agreed to be a keynote speaker at our first conference in 2014. Baba Chuck Davis still lived in Durham at the time, and he agreed to attend and consecrate the event. We worked to spread the word that our considerations of Black dance in its complex variety would arrive alongside a thinking through of African expressions as a source. We invited elders and youngsters alongside all of the in-between folx and set workshops and paper presentations throughout the conference, alongside discussions of women in *tap dance*, *capoeira*, experimental live art, trans and queer identities in ballet, afrofuturism in dance, and on and on and on.

How happy are we all that the call is answered! The 2014 CADD conference, "Dancing the African Diaspora: Theories of Black Performance," brought ongoing research to light, resulting in two journal editions and a forthcoming anthology.[1] Now we are graced by this present volume, an exciting, rich compendium of original research. The dancing ground calls, and we answer with our assembly in the circle of the Bantaba!: remembering our past lives and honoring the ancestors; telling the crucial histories of where and how we danced; and fashioning the textual analyses of African dance that will aid in the global advancement of Black people as truth-tellers who dance in the spirit to demonstrate the possibility of a moving, caring, politically engaged humanity. To the editors, the authors, and to all of us who find ourselves called to purpose through African dance, we exclaim, *AXE!*

Note

1. "Black Moves: New Research in Black Dance Studies," co-edited with Tara Aisha Willis, *Black Scholar* 46, no. 1 (Spring 2016): 1–3; "Black Dance Inside Out / Outside In," co-edited with Takiyah Nur Amin, *Conversations across the Field of Dance Studies* (Fall 2016): 8–11; *Dancing the African Diaspora*, edited by Thomas F. DeFrantz (Durham, N.C.: Duke University Press, forthcoming).

PREFACE

Danny Glover, Harry Belafonte,
and James Counts Early

In American and European media, Africa is most often represented through tropes: a place of abundant wildlife and of quaint, backward, isolated, and uncivilized people, unrelated to the modern world and the ideas that animate it. Modern-day Africans—those on the continent, those dispersed across the Americas through the transatlantic slave trade, and those who have migrated in the worldwide African Diaspora—descend from the people who populated once-thriving empires like Ghana, Mali, Songhai, Kanem-Bornu, Kongo, Oyo, Dahomey, and Asante, as well as from smaller civilizations typified by decentralized, nonhierarchical self-governance. Each of these civilizations has not only a chronological history and folkloric legacy but also a rich, formal intellectual history that bridges the tangible and intangible domains of its respective culture, that performs a presumed impossible feat of alchemy with the elements of mind, body, and spirit.

When the United Nations declared the International Decade for People of African Descent in 2015, it initiated an epoch of global reflection on and engagement with Africa and the African Diaspora that centers on its diverse peoples—highlighting their accomplishments in the contexts of discriminatory limitations imposed on them and earnestly listening to their voices in view of the opportunities they choose or create to pursue for their own wellbeing and for the enrichment of humankind. For those of us outside of the continent to truly listen to and appreciate all people of African origin, it is incumbent upon us to overcome the intellectual horizons imposed by the transatlantic slave trade, colonialism, and the continued economic subjugation of the Global South. By casting aside our illusions of cultural supremacy,

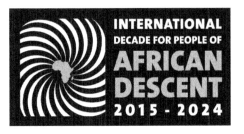

FIGURE 0.1. United Nations
Decade for People of African
Descent Logo

those of us in the Diaspora—of African descent and otherwise—can begin to engage with and benefit from the philosophical depth of African cultures.

Hot Feet and Social Change: African Dance and Diaspora Communities thus frames African dance, specifically West African dance, as a practice of actively embodying philosophical thought through a communitarian art form: a practice that demonstrates the values and ideologies of cultures through bodily movement. From an African philosophical orientation, the American and European traditions of disjoining the mind and body and valuing the mind over the body are inappropriate. Instead, the body, with its choreographed and improvised movements, is a tangible manifestation of the mind; body/mind interactions account for the philosophical inquiry that drives human civilization.

The International Decade for People of African Descent provides an important global invitation, a specific cultural policy lens, and a dedicated time-frame to release and highlight this important collection. These essays provide the reader with scholarly and practice-oriented insights on what African dance means in the context of the International Decade for People of African Descent, as well as what it means to dance from an African philosophical orientation in the present day. Most of the volume conveys an historical account of the development—or, properly speaking, the reintroduction and re-development—of continental West African dance forms in the United States, tracing the founding and successes of West African dance companies across the United States from the 1950s onward. The remainder, including one case each from the Caribbean, Ghana, and Burkino Faso, further explicate issues raised within U.S. cases and represent, as well as provide comparisons to, African dance styles and aesthetics found in the United States or in another American Diaspora site.

Africa is indeed a major contributor to human development and civilization. African art forms and the human beings who create and steward them have transformed societies around the world for the better through the intrinsic appeal of African cultural heritages. African dance, in particular, bridges otherwise intractable social, aesthetic, economic, and political divides, and ignites and reveals a passion for justice and equality.

HOT FEET
AND
SOCIAL
CHANGE

INTRODUCTION

When, Where, and How We Enter

Kariamu Welsh, Esailama G. A. Diouf, and Yvonne Daniel

African dance has become a distinct genre that traces its lineage across a worldwide Diaspora to the dances of Africa. Thereby, African dances are found on six of seven continents: Africa, Asia, Australia, Europe, and North and South America; however, our concern here is the "American African Diaspora," which ultimately extends from Canada to Chile, the Caribbean to the Hawaiian Islands. In these sites the term "African dance" includes social and popular dances, sacred rituals, folkloric traditions, concert forms, and tourist displays as well.

In the United States, African dance has emerged among those who called field hollers on southern plantations, in Pinkster festivals of the Midwest and Northeast, and in circuses, World Fairs, and trade expositions all across the country. Asadata Dafora, a Sierra Leonean, had the first successful run of an African-inspired Broadway show, *Kykunkor*, in 1934; he was one of many black artists who, in the 1920s to 1940s, concertized and stylized what we have come to know as African dance. From the *charleston* and the *dab* to hip-hop's *b-boying*, *turfing*, and other contemporary dance forms, African-based dances have been the bedrock of many American social dance practices. Regionally, nationally, and internationally acclaimed and accredited African music and dance ensembles have been performing in universities and colleges across the United States for decades. More than sixty-two professional dance companies, operating within the past twenty years, identify themselves as teaching and performing "African Dance." These companies are composed mostly of people of African descent who teach dance and music techniques that are rooted in the cultural traditions of Western, Central, and Southern Africa. In addition to performing, these companies also carry out extensive education programs that offer weekly and daily arts-in-education community classes to thousands of adults and youth throughout at least fifty-five cities in the United States. Some of the companies are teaching and performing dances that are in danger of being forgotten in their countries of origin. This is often due to wars, gentrification, generational disinterest, and/or economic hardships. Though not as widely known as it should be, the work of African performing artists permeates the entirety of American culture, addressing social conditions, affirming identity, and encouraging a distinct narrative of African Diaspora experience. This is the deeply rooted goal, the undercurrent of African dance in the United States.[1]

Beyond the United States in other parts of the American African Diaspora, African dance has also made significant national inroads. In the Caribbean, for example, specific distinctions among African dance traditions have been retained over centuries without the boost of fresh African input from strong African dance masters and despite environmental and cultural variations that were different from their sites of origin on the continent. These African dances have been maintained and/or reconstituted and are routinely recognized and performed as distinct West and Central African heritage, often in modified or Creolized forms. For example, Haiti's *yenvalú*, *Mayí,* and *Congo* dances, as well as Suriname's dances of the Winti religion, are differentiated from more Europeanized, but also popularly deemed "African," dances, such as Haiti's *affranchi* or Cuba's *tumba francesa.* In the Caribbean in particular, the dances are venerated (and sometimes rejected) as "African dances" that are attached to major religious systems (like Haiti's Vodou or Cuba's Lukumí) or as linkages to widely acclaimed social dance fads of the past (like *rumba,* *mereng/merengue,* and *mambo*). While these dances have not thoroughly permeated the educational systems of these relatively small, postcolonial islands, they are indelible cores of ordinary Caribbean life and are formally recognized folkloric traditions that signal national and regional identity.

In one of the farthest expanses of the American African Diaspora—that is, in South America, where Africanity has routinely been denied—African dances have recently become more public. For example, an African dance called *candombe* has been named one of Uruguay's national dances (2003);[2] elsewhere, books are appearing with titles like *Se dicen que no existo, pero estoy aquí* (They say that I do not exist, but I am here). These public declarations often point to the use of African regional dances as proof of national

African heritage.[3] In Bolivia, Chile, Ecuador, and other nation-states, African descendants have been reported parading and dancing with their drums in the halls of their nations' capitals.[4] African dance has been noticeably important to African descendants throughout history, even including those marginalized Africans of Mexico and Central America.

When African nations became independent from colonial rule, starting in the mid-1950s and early 1960s, West and Central Africans began to migrate to other continents, but especially to the United States. Many African dance specialists, who began to tour the United States with their respective national dance companies, decided to remain in the States and initiated a renaissance of African dance. The students, dancers, and choreographers who emerged out of this period are aging now, and many have passed on already; for example, Baba Chuck Davis transitioned in May 2017.[5] Many of the African dance pioneers living in the United States, as well as the courageous and defiant African dance proponents of the Caribbean and Afro-Latin America, are unknown outside of their local circles, yet their contributions have been invaluable. Many of them have left moving legacies, but there is scant trace of them in the current literature on African dance. Thus, the genesis of this book, a collection, was born.

It was at the first CADD (Council of African Diaspora Dance) conference at Duke University in Durham, North Carolina (2014), under the aegis of conference co-chair Thomas F. DeFrantz, that artist/scholar Kariamu Welsh realized that it was time to hear the voices of African dance elders, of which she is one. She envisioned a book that would be inclusive in that it would present voices that represented different regions and different perspectives on the important African dances that have spread across the American African Diaspora. She knew she could not do this alone and reached out to Esailama G. A. Diouf, a younger-generation artist/scholar in Performance Studies who is intimately connected to African dance, and asked her to be a co-editor. Esailama agreed to work bi-coastally, as Kariamu lived in Philadelphia, Pennsylvania, and she lived in Oakland, California. They sent out a call for papers and knew that chapter drafts would come from scholars in academe, but they simultaneously planned for written interviews with the older generation of dance artists and community scholars in order to access the oratory of African dance elders. Additionally, the two recognized that pictorial essays might document even further the histories they were after. The envisioned collection would reflect different approaches to telling dance and culture stories; they did not expect their collection to conform to a conventional model.

In 2016 they convened a panel at the 2nd CADD conference that included Baba Chuck, Naomi Diouf, Yvonne Daniel, Assane Konte, Ausettua Amen-

PHOTO I.1. CADD Elder Panel at Duke University, 2016 (left to right: Ausettua Amenkum, Naomi Diouf, Assane Konte, Kariamu Welsh, Yvonne Daniel, and Baba Chuck Davis).

kum, and Kariamu Welsh, with Esailama Diouf as the moderator. The panel only affirmed the need for documentation, and the original editors were energized to continue moving forward. Not long after convening at Duke University, they asked dance anthropologist/dance educator Yvonne Daniel to join as another co-editor and assist in bringing this major project to fruition. As the ancestors would have it, Yvonne is a neighbor of Esailama in Oakland, and thereby, we, now three co-editors, were able to make quicker strides toward publication.

This collection represents a small number of the hundreds of artists and scholars in African dance with thousands of stories to tell. The knowledge shared in this collection encompasses different ways of knowing and different diasporic experiences. For the book editors and each contributor in the volume, "African Diaspora" refers generally to the path or journey of African descendants as they remembered, retained, reconstituted, or created African-derived cultures in relation to treasured African heritage, passed on to them by elders from the African continent or their descendants. For us, "Africa" is a complex and continuously reconstituted idea based on race, colonization, economies, nationhood, and ethnicities; it is more than a location or even a continent. Therefore, what constitutes the location, scale, and temporal boundaries of what is commonly referred to as "the African Diaspora" is not always a shared agreement—especially colloquially in dance communities. Finite definitions of African Diaspora(s) shift when unconsciously referencing the United States as the only site of an African Diaspora. There have been other African Diasporas, and all have *not* been the result of the transatlantic trade in humans.[6] Accordingly, with regard to African dance in the Diaspora, current scholarship attempts to be inclusive and acknowledge the worldwide dispersal of Africans by using precise locations and time periods for specific dance examples.

This volume actually centers on the United States, where it shows pointedly that African dance, especially West African dance from present-day Senegal, Mali, the Gambia, and Guinea, has had its own "internal diaspora" within and among communities that have emerged in the United States over the past four decades. In the following chapters, we concentrate on dance communities where West African dance, in particular, has had pronounced social impact; indelible stories of local histories document this wave of African input and influence. We also include research findings for African dance in the Caribbean, as well as dance on the African continent; in these latter stories, contributors represent hundreds of other storytellers of African retention, creativity, and influence who are found from one end of the American African Diaspora to the other.

What the editors have privileged is, first, the recognition that dance is part of a large artistic whole. Music, theater/drama, visual and sculptural art, media, and bodily movement are ultimately interdependent parts of a huge dance phenomenon that seeks to mirror or reflect upon the cosmos, society's belief systems, human communities, and human relationships with nature and, additionally, seeks to speak to future generations. Traditionalists, neo-traditionalists, and contemporary artists, teachers, and scholars are represented here—all telling their stories of living African dance traditions, how they entered into and continue their practices, and what the teaching of African-based dance has meant to them and their communities. In telling these stories, this collection privileges the oral tradition relating to dance and archives its trajectory and development in writing (with dance names italicized).

We honor artistic voices of experience as well as research dialogues that are accessible; that is, we honor both academic and artistically driven communication in this collection. While we respect most of the individual preferences of our contributors, as well as the integrity of historic disciplines of knowledge, we also attempt to educate readers concerning pervasive Eurocentrism and lingering, undeserved (literal and figurative) capitalization of references to former colonial and paternalistic canons, institutions, and perspectives. We therefore avoid the terms "Western" and "the West" generally, and we communicate more directly as to what those terms really mean, which, in most cases, is "European and/or North American" canons, institutions, and perspectives. Within these communication processes, our contributors have revealed findings with integrity, and we, the editors, have confidence that readers will come away with accurate and thorough understanding.

As we discuss African dance within its varied Diaspora communities, we must also speak to the conceptual importance of establishing and claiming people of African descent in the Americas as Africans and critical stakeholders in conversations around social change. In the Americas, especially the United States, Africa is still largely represented as a place of misfortune, disease, and backwardness. We must lend symmetry to Africa and the Diaspora in our discourses and pinpoint how African dance reminds us of our past and positively affects the people we are and will become. In many continental African societies, dance is not simply motion set to music but rather a mechanism for cementing ongoing familial-like relationships, building cooperating communities, and communicating value systems that prioritize cohesion and consensus. Dance is not merely for performance, but rather a participatory means through which communities are able to embody and demonstrate their values in physical space. African dance is thus a social institution predicated on mobility, an institution established to reward innovation and "tradition," to revere generosity and inclusion, and to value respect for the elders, ancestors, and cosmological spirits. By centering Africa in our identities and discourses here, we empower ourselves and affirm the reality of the African continent, with its more than fifty countries. It is a mammoth site of creative, intellectual, spiritual, and artistic brilliance, as well as historically and maliciously targeted productivity.

Many of the contributors in this collection are activating this consciousness of "traditional" African dance in increasingly diverse ways that engage and build their local communities and address the root causes of persistent social problems, including issues of economic, educational, and environmental injustice as well as inequalities in civil and human rights. This collection represents cultural workers who are leading anchoring arts organizations at the intersections of artistic excellence, community access, and social justice. More than just teachers and performers, African dance cultural leaders have created viable jobs in the arts and have become critical stakeholders in policy conversations around cultural economies, creative placemaking, gentrification, and belonging. African dance cultural artists nationwide are working harder with policymakers and philanthropists to engage in decision-making processes about employment, housing, healthcare, and community service, mastering both the language of policy as well as the civic-engagement process from the municipal level up. At a philosophical level, African dance has much to contribute to recent political discussions about restorative justice, economic mobility, and intractable social divides in American societies. For the editors and contributors of this collection, social change is integral to the ideas, beliefs, and goals that are woven throughout the process, practice, and performance of African dance.

Our collection is divided into three sections: Hot Feet and Local Histories; The Elders' Work and Words; and Perpetual Motion in the Aesthetics of Africa. These tell impressive stories of African-based dance that exist within eight major cities across the United States and demonstrate the power and considerable influence dance practices have in awakening identity, self-worth, and community respect. Our collection alerts readers to revealing research that dance investigators have completed and are pursuing—for example, analyses of the aesthetic and educational components within dance companies and among artistic directors of professional African-based dance companies, the relationships between the musical and movement elements of African performance practices, the differences between African and Diaspora usage of improvisation, and gender reading of black dancing bodies. Additionally, our collection acknowledges the critical contributions of current African and Caribbean dance research; in these additional sites, African dance has been honorifically conserved as it has simultaneously continued to change and influence change.

In the first section, Hot Feet and Local Histories, performance scholar/ artist Esailama G. A. Diouf delves deeply into history and genealogy to detail the significant politico-cultural figures, dance artists, institutions, and social conditions that allowed for a reclaimed connection between African Diaspora dance forms and spirit knowing. Dismantling still lingering European and North American notions of Africa, African dance, and African drumming, which permeate the early history of dance in the Americas, Diouf points to restoring notions of genetic birthrights and culture transmission for African Americans through a renaissance of West African dance and music on the West Coast, specifically in California. Her findings give dancers more awareness and understanding and thereby the chance to embody their claim to spirit and SAUCE.

In a chapter focusing on the East Coast—Brooklyn, New York, specifically—arts administrator/educator Indira Etwaroo situates two bodies of artistic work shaped by the Great Migration, the Black Arts and Black Power Movements, and the daily realities of mid- and late-twentieth-century African American urban life. She explores how Kariamu Welsh and Ron Brown, proponents of "neotraditional African dance," have recalibrated traditional African dance aesthetics for use in North American and European performance contexts that are quite distinct from those rooted in traditional African societies. Etwaroo looks at how Welsh's and Brown's artistic expressions have secured a contemporary relevance for the historically rooted dance aesthetics they pioneered.

Last in this section, dance artist/educator Julie B. Johnson charts the five main components found in West African dance classes. Johnson uses the organization of a West African dance class as a lens through which she explores the varied understandings of community that can emerge through engagement with African dance traditions. She describes each component from an experiential perspective—the warm up, the lesson, dancing down the floor, the circle, and the concluding ritual, or *dobale*, to honor the musicians—and thereby outlines a narrative through which students construct shared understandings of community at each phase of the class's procedural structure. Employing poetry and vignettes, Johnson provides a participatory ethnography of African dance classes that is rooted in scholarship and firsthand experience. Together, these three chapters give readers comfortable familiarity with African dance characteristics and their basic shared goals.

In the second section, The Elders' Work and Words, we chronicle the stories of many legendary African-based performers and researchers: founders of dance companies, choreographers, scholars, and pioneers of African dance in the Americas. As many members of these older generations are passing on, this section of the collection archives the influence and wisdom of African and African American dance elders and seniors. It uses interviews, reflections, poetry, photographs, charts, songs, and performance analyses of important African dance specialists and some of their long-term students. Overall, this section's emphasis on the dance elders simultaneously continues to map important African dance centers across the United States and alerts readers to other formidable dance artists and dance centers across the American African Diaspora. By this section's end, readers understand how dancers comprehend the history of African dance in the Diaspora and how extensive, diverse, and, most important, how instrumental African dance has been and continues to be in the Americas.

In this section's first chapter, dance artist/educator C. Kemal Nance has captured the legendary perspective of Baba Chuck in a 2016 interview regarding the seminal words Davis spoke, the history he preached of African descendants in the African Diaspora, and his vision of the state of African heritage traditions in the Americas today. Discussions include the history, business practices, and dancer-management style Baba Chuck employed within the Chuck Davis Dance Company; they also reveal Baba Chuck's pathway from New York to North Carolina, his connections to African dance contemporaries, such as Kariamu Welsh, and his understandings of what the future holds for his dancers and his company. This interview has become even more poignant since Baba Chuck's recent death. When asked how he would want his legacy to be remembered, Baba Chuck answered simply, "He danced," but the legacy he left will have him remembered for so much more and for many decades to come.

Following this chapter, artist/scholar/educator Kariamu Welsh presents the foundational understandings of African dance in the United States. She dissects and analyzes with emphases that straddle two objectives, one historical and one theoretical. Welsh unpacks terminology for African dance from her long-term, dual perspective of both researcher and performer; she names and records the African dance/music masters who contributed to the implantation and dispersal of African dance and gives her explanations regarding notions of Africa and its Diaspora. She then proceeds philosophically to offer a "Gospel of African dance"—that is, she sets out concrete reasons and understandings for memory and "trace" in their crucial positions, which affects both the past and the future of African dance.

Next, business-management analyst and former youth dancer William Serrano-Franklin presents an interview with Assane Konte, the co-founder of a Washington, D.C., dance institution, Kankouran West African Dance Company (KWADC). Accompanied by a series of historical photographs, Serrano-Franklin's contribution documents Konte's desire to reintroduce black Americans to West African culture through the medium of dance. Konte's personal direction and the spirit of Kankouran have guided the development of dynamic community-engagement practices with benefits beyond dance as an art form.

Thereafter, Amaniyea Payne, dancer/choreographer and artistic director of Muntu Dance Theatre, offers her reflections on Muntu's more than four decades of work in Chicago, Illinois. There, in the Midwest, Muntu shines a bright and powerful light on African dance, due in large part to its artistic and educational vision, which has been influenced by Payne's artistry, research, and global dance connections. Her research and artistic experiences display the seminal connections among Diaspora dance artists and their similar concerns regarding education of African, Diaspora, and other cultural groups. Payne and Muntu exemplify the characteristic duality of professional African-based dance companies in the United States: on the one hand, she and the company develop and present fascinating, contemporary choreographies using traditional African vocabularies; on the other hand, they are enmeshed in educational projects and neighborhood and community development through dance.

Shifting the focus to New Orleans, Louisiana, dance artist/educator Ausettua Amor Amenkum provides an experiential account of the formation of the Kumbuka African Drum and Dance Collective, which is not only a performance troupe but also a community institution. Utilizing poetry and the engaging tone of the American South, Amenkum situates the emergence of African dance companies founded by African Americans in the mid-twentieth century. She chronicles both the company's impact over forty years on local culture and her personal work, which uses what she has learned and gained from African dance as a holistic approach to the healing of incarcerated women at the Louisiana Correctional Institute for Women.

Next, our collection features the social and political history of African dance in the Oakland–San Francisco Bay Area by American Studies scholar/dance educator Halifu Osumare, who tells a detailed story of African dance development from the 1960s to the second decade of the twenty-first century. Beginning with the first cohort of local Katherine Dunham–trained dance instructors in the 1950s and 1960s and then moving on to more contemporary instructors hailing directly from the African continent, Osumare recounts how African and African Diaspora dance traditions became fixtures in the California Bay Area. She reveals how these dances have become powerful tools in teaching social values through various community programs and during protest eras.

Also based in California, the Liberian dancer/choreographer/educator Naomi Diouf highlights the inadequacies of the vocabulary that many American and European dance critics use in reviewing African dance choreographies and presentations. In her chapter, Diouf introduces a set of stylistic descriptors to help choreographers and critics alike in discussing African dance performances in a more culturally specific, sound manner. Additionally, she links her philosophical discussion to the physical demands of African dance traditions, describing dance movements as demonstrative of aspects in daily traditional life. To further address this linkage of philosophy and physicality, Diouf analyzes a choreographed production, *Jusat*, which portrays past and current events such as birth, initiatory rituals, warfare, and death, which are the foundations of African dance drama.

Ending our elders section, dance anthropologist/dance educator Yvonne Daniel provides a historical and stylistic analysis of African dance in the

Caribbean and parts of Latin America, an anthropological view beyond the United States but still within the American African Diaspora. She bridges standardized Afro-Cuban dance categorizations to similar traditions found throughout the Caribbean and along Atlantic and Pacific shorelines. Daniel encourages employing carefully analyzed terminology when discussing African dance—terminology that distinguishes dance forms based on their history, geography, social context, and characteristic style. Using a continuum that encompasses both the multicultural nature of a colonialist aftermath and the huge diversity of African ethnic groups transported involuntarily to the Americas, Daniel offers a pluralistic typography of African origins dance forms that allows a more precise representation with respect to African historical and ethnic legacies. Ultimately, Daniel shifts her discussion of dance forms to recommendations for all practitioners and researchers in African dance communities. While she speaks throughout as an elder sharing her knowledge, her chapter simultaneously represents the voices and dance behaviors coming from Diaspora dance communities outside of the United States, setting up the next section, which examines cases from the continent and the United States.

The third and final section, Perpetual Motion in the Aesthetics of Africa, examines, compares, and evaluates Africanist approaches to improvisation, the significance of African music and dance movement, and danced gender and sexuality—on the continent and in the United States. Dance educator/ researcher Abby Carlozzo compares insights on improvisation gained from her fieldwork in Burkina Faso and from the European and North American understandings of improvisation in which she has previously trained. The philosophical and ideological tensions that arise as a discrete creative practice in standardized European and American perspectives are critiqued from an "Africanist" point of view, in which improvisation is inextricably linked to the parameters of living and ever-evolving dance traditions. Carlozzo aligns her analysis with scholarship on improvisatory dance approaches and aesthetics in the African Diaspora; she uses her analysis as a lens through which to explore continental African dance forms, arguing that "improvisation" in African dance contexts is better described as "stylistic innovation within form."

In the chapter that follows Carlozzo's, percussionist/dance and music critic and ethnomusicologist Steven Cornelius and dancer/choreographer and ethnomusicologist Habib Iddrisu explore the role of traditional music and dance within the *baamaaya* genre of the Dagamba people during and resulting from Ghana's independence movement. Cornelius and Iddrisu focus on how those art forms were transformed into folkloric patrimony as policymakers staged performances and established national performance troupes to mitigate regional and ethnic tensions in a newly independent, postcolonial nation. Through their insights into the changing social contexts and national significance of *baamaaya*, Cornelius and Iddrisu address questions of identity, cultural values, nationalism, and the politicization of traditional arts, particularly when these forms are performed in different situations within the nation-state and, later, in the American African Diaspora.

Our final chapter is an ending homage to our most recent and beloved dance ancestor, Baba Chuck Davis, one that highlights the critical analyses of dancer/choreographer/cultural theorist C. Kemal Nance. Nance examines a male duet from Baba Chuck's choreographic repertoire and provides a collective discourse on African American men who employ African dance vocabularies in their creative work. Through his own experiences as an African dance performer, as well as through the analyses of several interviews with Stafford C. Berry Jr., Nance's male dance partner, and Baba Chuck, his dance mentor, Nance reflects on the ways in which African American men utilize dance vocabularies in artistic and academic works. Centering an analysis of gender and sexuality, Nance explores the scripted nature of these discourses while addressing the ideological implications of historical representations of the black male body, masculinity, and heteronormativity in the field of African dance.

As co-editors, we have solicited and selected these contributed works in terms of the need for firsthand and/or documented history and research about African dance, mainly from those who dance the dances of African heritage themselves. Then we organized and shaped these intergenerational perspectives with our overriding desire to make a contribution to UNESCO's dedication to the International Decade for People of African Descent, 2015–2024. As we commemorate this assigned decade, we offer our dance collection as a historic heralding of the latest phase in the excavation of African dance and the recognition of dance artists of African descent who have contributed and continue to contribute in significant ways to global and African societies. Yet, despite the past fifty years of African dance performance explosions—choreographies, artists, professional dance companies, and academic courses—all across North America, South America, and Europe, there is little information available on African dance per se, and some artists and teachers, while well intentioned, disseminate myths and falsehoods within performative information, which continue to define and characterize African dance as undisciplined, ahistorical, and as having scant technical skills.

Thus, there are many questions that need to be asked, now that African dance is in centers of learning around the world. For example, here we have dealt with the questions "What is African dance?" and "What does African dance do in dancing Diaspora communities?" but these questions are mostly answered as we understand African dance in the most prominent and influential center of the African Diaspora—the United States. Within our collection, we offer a couple of responses apart from the context of the United States, but to what extent does U.S. American understanding differ from definitions and understandings in other Diaspora sites? How is African dance taught in the academy? How is documentation of African dance rehearsal processes and performance productions related to the cultural certitude of African peoples in the Diaspora? How can the younger generation remain involved with African and other Diaspora dance/music practices in the context of the present technology-based world? How can African performing arts have a stronger presence within conversations of cultural economy, creative place-making, restorative justice, and community belonging?

Despite the fact that African dance is a huge category and is problematic as a term, it is, for now, identifiable and therefore useful as a named dance genre. Written documentation on the dances of Africa in the Diaspora is fairly recent and concentrates on the earliest descriptions by plantation owners, traders, and missionaries; however, only a few early chroniclers of African dance in the Diaspora were dancers or music specialists.[7] Another wave of dance research came from or focused on descriptions from the Jim Crow era, where researchers revealed the masked resilience, camouflaged resistance, and courageous agency of African descendent performers across the Diaspora.[8] Eventually, several dance histories and ethnographies have documented African descendent concert artists, choreographic forms, and ritual practices, as well as African-derived popular and social dances.[9] However, many of these studies feature formidable African descendent innovation, dance creations that were based on African elements and values but often do not retain specific African dance traditions; that is, they are influenced heavily by both African and European heritages. Thus, our collection is vital and relevant as a source of reliable twenty-first-century information about African dance material thriving in the Diaspora.

These chapters reframe the too-often negative or patronizing view of African dance and drumming. The historical stories found within our case-study commentary fortify dance as resistance. This type of resistance does not involve immobility, laying barriers, boycotting, or ending certain practices; it concentrates on continuing, producing, and documenting practices of memory. This type of resistance connects memory across centuries and generations; it addresses the potential for change, artistic change in the form of innovation, creativity, and purpose, as well as social change in the form of new relations within and among Diaspora communities, and between outside communities and Diaspora communities. Our collection shows that resistant continuity brings forth continuity (Daniel, chapter 11 in this volume) and, in effect, fathoms, reveals, and produces social change.

This book also points out that despite the colonial European distaste for and banning of African dance styles across the Diaspora, Africans responded not only with resistant continuity but also with resilience, constantly seeping in and invading the boundaries of racism, colorism, classism, and postcolonial coloniality. Africans and their descendants continued African dance styles in segregated performance spaces or camouflaged their African dance practices within imitative and/or ridiculing performances in full sight of oppressive power against them. Their historical agency was adopted not only by the revolutionary dance artists of the 1930 through the 1950s (such as the well-known Asadata Dafora, Katherine Dunham, and Pearl Primus) but also by dance artists within the Black Arts and Black Liberation Movements of the 1960s and 1970s, whom we identify here.

Our collection inserts into dance history the stories of a generation, now elders, who stood on the principles of earlier black artists and amazingly and immeasurably shaped the relationship of African dance and Diaspora communities. In Bed-Stuy-Brooklyn, Philadelphia, Washington, D.C., Chicago, New Orleans, Oakland/Berkeley/San Francisco Bay Area, New York, and Durham, the dance component of the Black Power Movement proceeded and matured within a Black Arts Movement that affected both community and concert dance. For two examples, the first African dance technique emerged in Philadelphia with Kariamu Welsh's creation of *Umfundalai* technique (see Etwaroo, chapter 2 in this volume) and Oakland struggled successfully in political efforts to usurp dance spaces and marginalize African dance as well as majority/minority communities (see Osumare, chapter 10 in this volume).

Additionally, our collection projects African-based artistry on the concert stage in a different light. It adds to the well-known list of African American dance treasures since the 1960s (including Janet Collins, Arthur Mitchell, Alvin Ailey, Judith Jamison, Bill T. Jones, Bebe Miller, Jawole Willa Jo Zolar, etc.), the names of African and Diaspora immigrant dancers working and effecting change *inside* the United States. By naming African dance masters, African dance styles, African dance institutions, and African dance researchers, our work here reconstitutes notions of "American" dance history and dance artistry. It includes West African dance teachers and West and Central African dance forms as significant parts of "American" dance performance and dance practice. Thus our collection traces changes that have come about. It documents the invaluable perspectives of those who do the dancing and the valiant continuity and indelible and consequential practices of African dance.

Ultimately, this book is a humble attempt on the part of three women who have been involved in African dance in the Diaspora for decades, as we pay a deep respectful, prostrating bow—a *dobale* in writing—to honor and revere first those who came before us (in alphabetical order): Ruth Beckford, Chief Bey, Abdoulaye Camara, Ladji Camara, Malonga Casquelourd, Asadata Dafora, Baba Chuck Davis, Baba Dinizulu, Katherine Dunham, Kwame Ishangi, Djimo Kouyate, Charles Moore, Ella Moore, Nahgeree Sutton-Silas, Baba Olatunji, Pearl Primus, Meshach Silas, Alyo Tolbert, Camille Yarborough, Lavinia Williams Yarborough; and Mothers Ivy Baxter, Sylvia del Villard, Elise Ifel, Beryle McBurnie, Nereyda Rodrigues and Fathers Percival Borde, Jean León Destiné, Sir Rex Nettleford, Eduardo Rivera; and Mercedes Baptista and Mestre King.

We also make our *dobale* to those who are marching forward with us (also in alphabetical order): Germaine Acogny, Molly Ahye, Ausettua Amor Amenkum, Marie Basse-Wiles, Bobby Crowder, Mariama Curry, Melvin Deal, Thomas F. DeFrantz, Souleymane Diop, SuQuan Diop, Naomi Diouf, Zakarya Diouf, Inaicyra Falco Dos Santos, Fatou Gittens, Brenda Dixon Gottschild, Doris Green, Ramiro Guerra, Marcia Heard, Zohar Israel, Linda Faye Johnson, Assane Konte, Youssouf Koumbassa, C. K. Ladzekpo, Moshe Milon, Amaniyea Payne, John Perpener, Ramon Sila, Sterling Stuckey, Robert Farris Thompson, Giovanni Washington, Angela Watson, Dorothy Wilkes, and the hundreds of dance companies that are keeping African-based dance alive within our theaters and concert halls, schools, community centers, churches, prison systems, and senior centers.

We are referencing and discussing a great deal of literature within this publication, but much more is needed: African and African Diaspora dance history, creative processes, education efforts, social justice missions, and studies confronting continuing coloniality, as well as ecological, economic, and humane survival in the dance arts. We begin, however, with the efforts of this collection's fiercely dedicated contributors.

Notes

1. Brenda Gottschild, *Digging the Africanist Presence in American Performance: Dance and Other Contexts* (Westport, Conn.: Greenwood, 1996).

2. In 2003, UNESCO sponsored a conference on African dance heritage in Montevideo and helped the nation-state of Uruguay to publicly acknowledge *candombe* as one of its national dances. Before this, *candombe* was understood as an African heritage dance/music in the Rio Plata area of both Argentina and Uruguay. *Candombe* became a viable, formally listed dance on UNESCO's Intangible Culture list in 2009; see https://ich.unesco.org/en/RL/candombe-and-its-socio-cultural-space-a-community

-practice-00182 and https://en.wikipedia.org/wiki/List_of_national_dances. For *candombe* dance details, see Tomás Olivera Chirimini, "Candombe, African Nations, and the Africanity of Uruguay," in *African Roots/American Cultures: Africa in the Creation of the Americas*, ed. Sheila S. Walker (Lanham, Md.: Rowman and Littlefield, 2001), 256–74.

3. Margot P. Loyola and Osvaldo V. Cádiz, *Me niegan pero existo* (recording and pamphlet, Santiago, Chile: Consejo Nacional de la Cultura y las Artes, 2013); Lucía Dominga Molina and Mario Luis López, "Afro-Argentineans: 'Forgotten' and 'Disappeared'—Yet Still Present," in Walker, *African Roots/American Cultures*, 332–47; Romero Jorge Rodriguez, "The Afro Populations of America's Southern Cone: Organization, Development, and Culture in Argentina, Bolivia, Paraguay, and Uruguay," in Walker, *African Roots/American Cultures*, 314–31.

4. See Juan Angola Maconde, "Las raíces africanas en la historia de Bolivia," in *Conocimiento desde adentro: Los afrosudamericanos hablan de sus pueblos y sus historias*, ed. Sheila Walker (La Paz: PIEB [Programa de Investigación Estratégica en Bolivia], 2010), 1:145–222; Marta Salgado Henriquez, "El legado africano en Chile," in Walker, *Conocimiento desde adentro*, 1:223–70; José F. Chalá Cruz, "Los afrochoteños: Legítimos guardianes de la memoria histórica y del conocimiento," in Walker, *Conocimiento desde adentro*, 2:1–32.

5. "Baba" in West African societies means "Father"; it is also an endearment title, a sign of deep respect that is used as a cultural practice to publicly acknowledge elders in African-descended communities but particularly in African dance communities in the United States.

6. See ASWAD, the Association for the Study of the Worldwide African Diaspora, at aswadiaspora.org, where European, Asian, and Oceanic African Diasporas are acknowledged, in addition to the more well-known American African Diaspora; also see Joseph E. Harris, "The African Diaspora in World History and Politics," as well as Joseph E. Inikori, "Africans and Economic Development in the Atlantic," both in Walker, *African Roots/American Cultures*, 104–17 and 123–38, respectively.

7. For examples of those who are/were dancers or musicians writing on early forms of African dance, see Zora Neal Hurston, *Tell My Horse* (Philadelphia: Lippincott, 1938); Katherine Dunham, *Journey to Accompong* (New York: Holt, 1946); Katherine Dunham, *Dances of Haiti* (Los Angeles: Center for Afro-American Studies, University of California, 1984 [originally published in *Acta Antropologica* 2, no. 4 (1947): manuscript copy, 1-64]); Katherine Dunham, *Island Possessed* (Garden City, N.Y.: Doubleday, 1969); Lynne F. Emery, *Black Dance in the U.S., 1619 to 1970* (Hightstown, N.J.: Dance Horizon, 1988 [1972]); Julian Gerstin, "Tangled Roots: Kalenda and Other Neo-African Dances in the Circum-Caribbean," *New West Indies Guide* 78, nos. 1 and 2 (2004): 5–41 (updated reprint in *Making Caribbean Dance*, ed. Susanna Sloat [Gainesville: University of Florida Press, 2010], 11–34).

8. See for example, Jacqui Malone, *Steppin' on the Blues: The Visible Rhythms of African American Dance* (Urbana: University of Illinois Press, 1996); Brenda Gottschild, *Waltzing in the Dark: African American Vaudeville and Race Politics in the*

Swing Era (New York: St. Martin's, 2000); Brenda Gottschild, *The Black Dancing Body: A Geography from Coon to Cool* (New York: Palgrave MacMillan, 2003); Thomas F. DeFrantz, ed., *Dancing Many Drums: Excavations in African American Dance* (Madison: University of Wisconsin Press, 2002); and Richard A. Long, *The Black Tradition in American Dance* (New York: Rizzoli International, 1989).

9. See, for example, Rex Nettleford, *Roots and Rhythms: Jamaica's National Dance Theatre* (New York: Hill and Wang, 1970); Rex Nettleford, *Dance Jamaica: Cultural Definition and Artistic Discovery; National Dance Theater Company of Jamaica, 1962–1983* (New York: Grove, 1985); Kariamu Welsh Asante, "Commonalities in African Dance: An Aesthetic Foundation," in *African Culture: Rhythms of Unity*, ed. Molefi Asante and Kariamu Asante (Westport, Conn.: Greenwood, 1985), 71–82; Kariamu Welsh Asante, *The African Aesthetic: Keeper of the Traditions* (Westport: Praeger, 1994); Yvonne Daniel, *Rumba: Dance and Social Change in Contemporary Cuba* (Bloomington: Indiana University Press, 1995); Yvonne Daniel, *Dancing Wisdom: Embodied Knowledge in Haitian Vodou, Cuban Yoruba, and Bahian Candomblé* (Urbana: University of Illinois Press, 2005); Anita Gonzalez, *Jarocho's Soul: Cultural Identity and Afro-Mexican Dance* (Lanham, Md.: University Press of America, 2004); Umi Vaughan, *Rebel Dance, Renegade Stance: Timba Music and Black Identity in Cuba* (Ann Arbor: University of Michigan Press, 2012); and several others.

PART I

Hot Feet and
Local Histories

SAUCE!

Conjuring the African Dream
in America through Dance

Esailama G. A. Diouf

While generalized categories such as "African dance" neglect the diversity
within African continental and diasporic traditions by assuming a cultural
homogeneity among Africans and Afro-descendants globally, the manifold
"spirit(s)" of dance have rarely been interrogated. Beyond the bodily techniques that all dances encompass, a dance harbors a spirit that manifests
and produces meaning through embodiment. Cultural policymakers, like
Leopold Senghor, and cultural artists, such as Katherine Dunham and Pearl
Primus, spoke of dance as a vital force, one that "can take you out." The dancer
both loses and finds her-/him-/themselves when mounted by the spirit of the
dance, and it is through the dancer that the spirit of the dance—sometimes
multiple spirits—"lives in the world." What both continental West African
and African Diaspora dancers have generally called "spirit"—and which is
called *ase*[1] in Yoruba-based Diaspora traditions and *espri* in Fon-based Diaspora traditions[2]—facilitates transcendence within performance and enables
what dancer/choreographer M. Jacqui Alexander refers to as *spirit knowing*,
a mechanism for making the world and the meta-worlds intelligible.[3] For
most Europeans and North Americans, despite formal religious beliefs and
practices sometimes expressed in their dance, their experience is largely
understood in secular materialist terms, divested of spiritual aspects. As
a result, *spirit*, as a way of knowing, is not generally believed to have the
capacity to bodily instruct on dance, performance, or the African diasporic
experience. However, in its true essence, dance, like music, transcends mate-

rial, cultural and geographical borders; it involves rhythm; it depends not on, nor is it dictated by, time; and it requires no special clothing. Dance needs only to connect with the spirit of the performer through a form of communication that I refer to as *spirit talk*. Transcending materiality and discourses on authenticity, aesthetics, or cultural production, the spirit of the dance interlocks with the spirit of the dancer. Beyond verbal dialogue, two spirits enter a dialogic and dialectic conversation that alters the dancer's entire being and existence in the world, exposing her/him/them to a kaleidoscope of colors, shapes, textures, and sounds. In these liminal moments the spirit of the dancer is fortified and the spirit of the dance persists, and both are raised at a meta-level of creative expression.

SAUCE!

After meeting in California in the 1970s, my parents, Naomi (from Liberia) and Zakarya (from Senegal), joined together in the development of a U.S.-based West African Dance Company.[4] Their mission was to educate U.S. Americans, particularly African Americans, regarding Africa's—mostly West Africa's—rich cultural heritages through the practice and performance of traditional music and dance. Our two-bedroom apartment served most often as a studio space for workshops, rehearsals, and the making of costumes and drums, as well as for the learning of new songs and creation of new choreographies. In our small apartment, sometimes for weeks at a time, my parents hosted five to ten visiting artists from the national dance companies of Senegal, Guinea, Mali, or Liberia. Back then, U.S.-based dancers and musicians, both West African and African American, not only came together in whatever space they could find to rehearse, but they also ate and lived together. Engaging under the same roof in day-to-day exchanges, they learned about each other, along with the history, culture, language, and spiritual contexts of the music and dances they were practicing and performing—transforming themselves and their new social relations and environments. This was an era in which the performance of West African–derived (WA-derived) dance was at its height in California, during the late 1970s and early 1980s. However, few formal WA-derived dance companies existed then. Nevertheless, it was a time when Africans and African Americans joined together in intense cultural exchanges that broke through stereotypes and invited dialogue and discovery.

In our home, the practice of music and dance was also a regular occurrence, particularly in the kitchen. The kitchen, specifically, served not only as a venue for preparing West African dishes, such as *ceebu jen* (Senegalese fish and rice), but also for singing, sewing costumes, rehearsing movements and choreography, learning the folklore—traditional beliefs, stories, and knowledge systems—associated with dances, and debating current events. As such, it became an important place for forging offstage relationships between West Africans and African Americans. It was from these settings that the idiomatic expression "SAUCE!" was created.

In many West African cooking traditions, soups and sauces, such as *mafaa* (peanut stew) or palm butter (popular Liberian palm nut sauce[5])—whether red or clear, cooked with palm oil or peanuts, or served over rice, *fufu*, or cassava—are a mainstay of daily meals. As a child, I would watch as continental West African women taught teams of African American women how to make these dishes. One West African woman would direct a group of African American women in preparing the base of the sauce, while other West African women directed other groups of African American women in preparing the ingredients that would go into the pot. As food preparation was underway, other members of our community of dance students and teachers formed male and female clusters around the small kitchen table, where they monitored everything that was occurring while either sewing costumes for the next show, learning new songs, or analyzing movements. The activities—whether in the form of singing a song, stirring a pot, or tapping on the table—always fell into a shared rhythm with no clear beginning or end. For us, the kitchen became a metaphoric context for the synergy created by the interplay of our company's creativity and the power inherent to the transmission of tradition and culture.

The role of the "kitchenspace"[6] as a binding element was reflected in the emergence of "SAUCE!" as an exclamatory idiom in the company's internal jargon. Shouting "SAUCE!" on the dance floor signaled that the performance of a dancer, drummer, or group had reached a certain spiritual climax, a point at which creativity and tradition combined to yield something greater than the sum of their parts. It was at this point that all structured choreography would be abandoned, leaving the dance to pure improvisation—the point at which interpretation and spiritual connection prevailed. It was through this practice that great artists were revealed.

Among most groups of West African and African American dancers in the United States, a shout of "SAUCE!" is used to indicate moments of high or exquisite WA-derived performance. Just as most sauces maximize flavor and jazz up a meal, "SAUCE!" was shouted on the dance floor when a dancer has discovered how to balance the technique of the dance form with his or her own style, while maximizing the varying flavors within the rhythm. Taking the execution of the dance "up a notch," this dancer's performance exudes the varying textures of the rhythm and "speaks in tongues" within movement to a congregation of fellow dancers, who in turn are spiritually uplifted. "SAUCE!" was thus spirit talk, vernacularly rooted in the phenomenological experiences of a local, yet global, community of artists and students of WA-derived cultural productions. Through such childhood experiences, I learned early in my life as a dancer that achievement in dance does not depend primarily on how well you *copy* a *movement* or learn a choreographic phrase, but how well you *understand* and *embody* the dance's *spirit*. It is through this spirit that many African Americans came to know African dance.

My Africa

While the dynamic within my parents' dance company was one of appreciation, exchange, and learning, we also came to know the many obstacles our African American members had to overcome to become receptive to African culture. In effect, they had to *un*-learn the many falsehoods they had been taught about Africa in order to allow themselves to embody its many cultures and traditions. Arthur Moore, a former Katherine Dunham drummer, noted: "My first impressions of Africa and African rhythms were influenced by movies like *Mogambo* and that garbage out of *Tarzan*. In school, there was no curriculum that involved African history; world history was European history. And I had no idea, because in this diaspora the farthest I ever thought I would go was East St. Louis."[7]

Moore's statement reflects the experience many musicians and dancers had during the late 1960s regarding the image of Africa presented by Hollywood: one of "jungles, wild animals, 'primitive' or 'savage' blacks, and thundering drums."[8] Referring to films such as *Tarzan of the Apes* (1918), *The African Queen* (1951), *The Snows of Kilimanjaro* (1952), and *Mogambo* (1953), actor Danny Glover noted that regardless of whether a film was about Africa or was dominated by African scenes, filmmakers tended to use Africa as merely an exotic background for love and adventure stories that did not concern Africa in any fundamental sense.[9]

In *The Invention of Africa*, African philosopher V. Y. Mudimbe surveys how the "Western" construction of Africa shaped the way in which Africa and Africans were imagined. Mudimbe argues that this ideological campaign involved setting the European and North American intellectual configuration of knowledge as the epitome of European power, against which all others would be compared and judged. Mudimbe hypothesizes that, while first despised, works of "primitivism" became integrated into the "Western" tradition during the twentieth century through what he calls the "ethnologization" and "aestheticization" processes. According to Mudimbe, ethnologization is the process of isolating a datum from its real context in order to analyze and classify its attributes, identify its model, and, finally, assign it a label that allows for its location/categorization, such as a degree of latitude or the name of a tribe. In early ethnographic studies, a product is granted or denied the status of art based on external criteria; in effect, a work must have visible characteristics and constraints that can, technically, be localized along the timeline of European and/or North American intellectual and aesthetic history in order to belong to the realm of artistic achievements.[10]

Mudimbe's theory is referenced here to help describe how performances of expressive culture have also undergone ethnologization. Like "art objects" or "ethnographic artifacts," many WA-derived dances were developed in specific indigenous spaces, which means that the original or local dances often differ from their reproductions in festivals, theaters, and studio spaces. Bearing traces of "the folk" while developing the characteristics of new bodies and new spaces, WA-derived dance performances became live elements of a "material stock," representing the "everyday life" of African people. Indeed, "traditional" dance had to move and change through performers, space, and time, simply in order to survive. Hence, it is certain that change would have emerged, regardless of whether the dancer, producer, or choreographer had attempted to apply Mudimbe's three-pronged approach to account for the origins of the dances and transcend the "shortcomings of anthropologists' ethnologization and aestheticization of the objects."[11]

Nevertheless, when traditional dances are passed down to contemporary performers, the formal, historicized transmission of customs and beliefs—while surviving—also assume contemporary meanings because of their assimilation into new spaces and contexts and the cultural frames of new performers. African Americans, just like many of the African dancers in Le Ballet National de Senegal, for example, were not born into the cultures from which the dances had emerged. Many of the resources used to make the musical instruments, ritual artifacts, and costumes in the areas of dance origins were absent or not available in new American spaces. Therefore, it was not, nor should it have been, expected that the "new" traditional or folk dances—dances that were performed in new spaces by new dancers—would be performed in exactly the same manner or function as they did in their indigenous settings. Thus, the newly arrived African immigrants and local African Americans who performed these dances created a creole performance culture that, although indebted to its continental African origins, still had its own unique character.

In his keen examination of the difference between "preservation," "conservation," and "urgent anthropology" in the 1950s, anthropologist Robert

W. Nicholls urged cultural workers to adopt a "conservationist agenda."[12] Nicholls argued that the trouble with "preservation" is that its focus was just that, "guarding" or "maintaining something in a constant or unaltered state"; its activities are disciplined based, limited by archival considerations, and oriented toward the academic community rather than the indigenous imaginative art-producing community. In contrast, "conservation" focuses on maintaining continuity, as in this case study, within a living tradition.

African American performance of WA-derived dance contravenes the false binary of "contemporary versus traditional" by placing the contemporary (the dance as it is practiced and performed by Africans and African Americans in the United States) in constant dialogue with the traditional (the dance's indigenous context and people). Hence, the ways in which the dances were once defined and categorized are no longer fixed. Although the structural DNA—the nuances that identify the core technique of dances—may have remained consistent with the traditions of the dances, the performance and even the cultural environment of the dances have changed because they were and are being performed by different performers in different locales and across successive generations. Each dance bares an identifying kinesthetic signature and phraseology that readily marks them as the dance names they are most popularly known by (for example, *lenjeng* performed by the Mandinka people or *sabar* performed by the Wolof people); but performers of varying backgrounds and in varying contexts can harness those signatures and phraseologies to write new dance narratives.

Although greatly indebted to Western and Central African origins, the creole performance culture, which formed in the United States through the bi-continental experiences of African artists and African American dancers and choreographers in the 1960s, differed from the styles of its predecessors in several respects. As creolized forms, WA-derived dance performances served as a way for both African Americans and newly immigrated West Africans to revise or re-envision their Diaspora relationships with Africa and the United States.

"Gettin' Down with the Cause"

The desire of African Americans to connect culturally with Africa was complex and loaded with deep sentiments, especially in terms of participating in African dance and gaining an understanding of dance as a transmitter of culture. Together with their desire to perform, African Americans brought the conviction of their genetic birthright to African culture, a particular sense of kinship within the music, distinct patterns of visual aesthetics, and social behaviors. As the late eminent dancer/choreographer Chuck Davis recalled in a personal interview:

> Yes, in the sixties, we were doing some of the movements, we were doing some of them, BUT, it began to get to the point where we wanted to know; yes, this is my heritage, but how does my heritage compare to yours? How does my Mende compare to Yoruba? How does Yoruba compare to Congolese? How does Congolese compare to Burundi? And it goes on and on and on, the Tutsi, it goes on and on and on, the Jola, it goes on and on and on, into Egypt.[13]

Former Dunham dancer Luisah Teish affirmed:

> That's the work that needed to be done to bridge the gap between, "Oh, we ain't African, we don't want to be African," to "This is who we are and we are Africans being impacted by our experience of being in America." I could take it a step further and talk about racial consciousness, and say that I have seen African American children when we taught during the '60s—and now—who had never seen African dance in their life, hear a rhythm, start to move, and then I can identify for them which of the African dances they were doing. It's in us, it's in us, and nothing is going to drive it out. It is the same as when you see the second lines or churches where I grew up in New Orleans, before coming to St. Louis.[14]

These artists recognized that, for the African American dancing body, dance and music act as instruments of transmission and doorways into West African culture. In his study on the formation of dance traditions in immigrant communities, dance historian and performer Anthony Shay explains:

> During the 1960s, a rising wave of ethnic identity crisis arose in North America. This was largely fueled by the sense that third, fourth and fifth generations of children of European immigrants were losing their ethnic identity through the process of assimilation into Anglo American and Canadian societies. (...) [An] interest in a return to ethnic identity intersected with the Civil Rights movement and the explosion of ethnic pride in African American, Latino, and Asian communities, spurred on in some communities by the appearance of state-sponsored national folk dance companies like Ballet Folklórico of México, Les Ballets Africains of Guinea and LADO of Croatia that enjoyed enormous popularity in the 1960s and 1970s.[15]

While living "American" experiences, many African Americans underwent "a cultural awakening" through the learning and performance of WA-derived dance. Through dancing in a community with other self-identified Americans of African descent and drawing on what dance scholar/performer Kariamu Welsh (as she is known today) refers to as *epic memory*—in other words, the ability to have a kinesthetic and empathic connection to an African identity—WA-derived dance practitioners acquired a deep connection with their "roots."[16]

In the 1960s the immigration of Senegalese artists such as Ladji Camara, Mor Thiam, and Zakarya Diouf allowed many African Americans to deepen their understanding of WA-derived dance via a holistic learning process that transcended the process of studio rehearsal, presentational staging, and choreographed performance.[17] In addition to learning movement techniques, performing students learned how an ethnic dance that symbolized traditional activities, such as hunting, wrestling, war, harvest, or rites of passage, functioned within the belief system of the society, as well as how the reiterative performance of certain gestures within the dance portrayed multiple meanings. Mastering a particular folk dance, like mastering a language, became an embodied process, opening a portal into a new understanding of, and relationship to, being in the world.

Dunham drummer Arthur Moore provides an in-depth example:

Now we were using these African rhythms for Dunham technique, but there was something that was missing, something that wasn't meshing. When Zak came in, I started to understand how that down beat came into play. In hearing it, I heard it with that European ear, yet when I saw Zak dance to the rhythm, it added a whole different inflection on the rhythm. Because before we were using the *Afro Negro* rhythm for progressions and Dunham pieces, and the count was going 1-2-3-4/1-2-3-4, that European count. But once Zak got here and Mor started to play it and we started to do "African" dance classes, it changed everything. There was one rhythm in particular that I noticed it profoundly in, and that was *Wolosodon*. Now, I knew the rhythm, but I didn't understand the rhythm. When Zak got here, he started to sing the song, *Ma kine/Ma kine/Ma kine*, and the way he would dance to it. Now when I first heard him sing it, it was like a dirge to me, but it wasn't a dirge [*begins to sing the rhythm*], and then the bass line in it, the way that it changes and then when it speeds up and slows down, and then to watch the movements. I learned that different parts of the rhythm would dictate different parts of the body. I said Wow! Now at fifteen–sixteen years old, you know, this is blowing my mind because I'm trying to digest this stuff. [. . .] And then I got to a point and said well, I might just be overcomplicating things, trying to solve problems when really it's not about solving, it's about opening up to the emotional aspect and spiritual aspect of the dance and receiving it. And once I started to do that and started to feel this rhythm, it gave me a whole other understanding of the relationship between rhythm and dance.[18]

While African American cultural forms, including blues and jazz music and *tap dance*, usually contain elements of polyrhythm, Moore's understanding comes not out of his own experience with African American culture but through witnessing and studying West African–derived music and dance. Baba Chuck Davis also described the moment he began to understand:

> I had sessions with Geoffrey Holder from Trinidad, and Geoffrey Holder forced us to go inside ourselves. And that was picked up from Mama Syvilla Forte, who forced us to go inside ourselves as we studied Dunham. And that was picked up also by Mama Pearl Primus. But it really started to take hold when I was living with the Ntoris, with the Watutsi East Africans, because everything they did was coming from the inside. Because you become that heritage where you're honoring the cows and your arms must be like the horns, and the power you get from the earth, and all of that has to be internalized as in order for it to come back out.[19]

Learning WA-derived music and dance inspired many African American dancers to travel to Africa to expand their learning of certain dances and to witness dances in their original environment as participatory practices. By studying WA-derived music and dance, many African Americans also began seeing and understanding African aesthetics in everyday African American cultural expressions. One of these, Darlene Blackburn, recalled her experience in Ghana:

> Right then when I went [to Africa] and was at the University of Ghana—like I said I'm not timid, I'm not a timid sister—and I saw the Ghana Dance Ensemble and they were up there dancing, and I am sure I'm telling you, they were doing the "mash potatoes." I jumped up on that stage like girl that ain't nothing. I GOT that. I saw the connection right away! I choreographed a dance from that when I came back called "Coming to America," where we did eight bars of African dance and eight bars of the social dances here in America. 'Cause I saw all the different connections, and so did the African dancers in the dance ensemble. Me and that girl became like this. We were just dancing back and forth. You would have thought I was her sister or something.[20]

Through their bi-continental experiences in West Africa and the United States and their embodiment of WA-derived movements, African Americans consciously constructed their own on- and offstage choreographed performances of *Africanité*/Africanness. Examination of this relationship between individual African American performers and embodied African practices confirms what performance theorist Susan Foster has suggested: that performers are not only objects written upon by others but also subjects capable of writing, generating ideas, and, through practice, theorizing on their own.[21] As such, Foster sees not only who choreographs, sponsors, or views the dance, or the kinds of narrative themes that the dance embraces as significant, but also the social aspect imbedded in the choreographing and training of dancers.

Africanness was quickly recognized and embodied through very specific, stylized movements and aesthetics, mostly from Sene-Gambian, Malian, Ghanaian, and Nigerian ethnic groups; this was repeated through space, time, and generations. West African dancers provided average African Americans with a *social choreography* that, over time, came to be viewed as *the* cultural norm of Africanness. This process became particularly evident with the spread of *Afrocentricity*, the ideology that was inspired by political scientist Maulana (Ron) Karenga, popularized by communications theorist Molefi Kete Asante, and included in Black Liberation politics and socioeconomic activities of the 1960s. These leaders, in turn, stimulated many African Americans to consciously integrate certain regalia, foods, languages, and mannerisms into their everyday lives as materials for learning and practicing WA-derived dance.[22]

For example, Dunham dancer Daryl Braddix recalled how "because of the exchange, we had some of the Willie's over here changing their names to Fila or Sila—until they get their paycheck and they still got Willie on it."[23] Also, Teish pointed out that such a practice reflected an understanding that "the person who names is the one with authority. It is a pull between domination and identity. When you rename yourself, you redefine yourself and put the power back in your own hands."[24] Additionally, performance theorist E. Patrick Johnson explained his motives for consciously integrating West African elements into his everyday life as follows:

> Blackness is not something one necessarily wears on the outside (through skin or clothing) but something more ephemeral and processual—a performative that calls attention to the slippages among biology, culture, ideology, and politics. Thus, wearing kente or acquiring an African name is one kind of Black performance, but it is a no less authentic performance of Blackness than wearing blue jeans or being named John or Mary.[25]

To African Americans who performed WA-derived music and dance, claims of links to the past—a history beyond that of enslavement heritage, legitimized by institutions such as national museums, cultural centers, and festivals—were fundamental to the politics of cultural and self-revisionism. These claims laid the foundation for their present and future claims. For the Black Liberation Movements of the 1960s and among the many African Americans who practiced WA-derived music and dance, authenticity was vital for both constructing self-identity and "ethnologizing" and "aestheticizing" the practice of WA-derived music and dance. Initial attempts to recapture "authentic" African cultural heritage focused on the collection of customs deemed "traditional" by continental Africans and revolved around the reconstruction and collection of traditions that had been brought to the United States by immigrant Africans or African Americans who had visited Africa or studied African music and dance forms. Nevertheless, while some African Americans revered continental Africans as exemplars of Africanité, others were more cautious. They were aware that by employing critical tools from precolonial traditions, it would eventually become necessary to discern how these traditions had changed over time in accordance with changing material conditions and the perceptions of their adherents.

Probing further into the dialogic/dialectic relationships between African immigrants and African Americans, artists of WA-derived performances have highlighted instances where the performance of Africanness proved risky yet offered a platform from which to examine the shaping of diasporic relationships and identities. For African immigrants and African-identifying Americans, dance performance became not only a medium through which social realities were translated into movement but also where provocative encounters of embodied knowledge and agency could be discussed.

Inspired by the work of ethnomusicologist Paulla Ebron, I consider the West African immigrant dancers and musicians of the 1960s, and still in 2018, as entering a transnational circuit and negotiating different histories, traditional values, and storytelling in order to shape "African" identities.[26] This shift in dynamics between the interpersonal and the institutional, interspersed with travel and tourism, has led to the emergence of new forms of both cultural production and politics among West African performers on the continent and in the United States.

In discussing the ways that authenticity, cultural commodification, and tensions concerning cultural protectionism affect the creation of identity, Ebron argues that by engaging in an act of self-representation for foreign audiences, West African artists assume the role of a "trickster." By presenting diverse symbolic meanings depending on whether the performance was in a West African or international space, and by presenting themselves to international communities with the titles of "master" of their craft or producers of "village life," West African artists orchestrated a particular kind of experience, juggling a multiplicity of worlds and, in the process, destabilized a range of meanings. Local (living in the United States) West African musicians and dancers, like Mor Thiam and Zak Diouf, have eagerly strived to become "tricksters" in order to embark on international careers, while both international and African American audiences have eagerly aspired to "go native." As Diouf notes, "Our experience in the national dance company in Senegal taught us about marketing ourselves."[27]

Being able to traverse between indigenous practices and performances that contain stereotypical aspects of Africa for foreigners requires the acquisition of certain kinds of knowledge and skills and an understanding of the grammar of placement through which various practices facilitate different modes of perception. In the 1960s, West African artists-turned-international-celebrities quickly learned that these classifications must not only appeal to a broader audience but should also alter local cultural practices in order to meet the demands of "global aesthetics." Concurrently, they remained keenly aware of their need to maintain their social, economic, and emotional connections with the people and events of their homeland and to bequeath the cultural values, beliefs, and knowledge of their ethnic origins to their American-born children.

African-immigrant artists also recognized the need to present a more informed and positive representation of Africa and Africans to African Americans, with whom they invariably felt strong cultural and historical bonds and desired closer dialogue.[28] Diouf noted that when he and Thiam first arrived in the United States, they soon became aware of both the negative images of Africans within U.S. society and the civil rights struggles of African Americans living in inner cities, such as East St. Louis and Chicago:

> We had some differences and sometimes the Black Americans thought they were better than us and sometimes we thought we were better than them. But when it all came down to both me and Daryl walking down the street in East St. Louis at night, we both had to think about whether we were going to get arrested because it was late and we were Black—it didn't matter whether I was from Senegal or he was from East St. Louis, we were just Black men.[29]

Conclusion

In this chapter I have focused on several significant people, institutions, and conditions under which African Americans came to learn of, claim, and perform African culture. The practices and performances of WA-derived dance have conveyed both varying social processes and the (re)imagining of West African Diaspora communities within a transnational context. Thus, a critical space has been carved in which dance can be further analyzed as a collective re-imagination of history and genealogy, as a repository of individual and communal identities, and as an archive. Through the production of WA-derived dance in the United States, African immigrants and African Americans have become active agents—as artists, producers, and consumers. They have created both normative discourses and counter-discourses, which in turn have permitted them to formulate interpretations of their identities, interests, and needs. Thus, performances of WA-derived dance have established not only a space for entertainment and spectatorship but also a venue for artistic depiction, symbolism, and representation.

For many of the dancers described in this study, the body continues to be a key vehicle through which Africa (whether imagined or actual) has been experienced, sustained, and (re)created. Furthermore, embodiment, a technique for positioning the body in time (history) and space (place), has become a means of converting Africa from an idea into a way of seeing and being in the world. Emerging in the 1960s, the concept of embodied Africanness, or what Senghor referred to as Africanité, remains relevant to many West African dancers today. Additionally, in searching for their roots, African Diaspora dancers have uncovered the Pan-Africanist foundation of dance in the Diaspora, as is apparent in the choreographic and research works of Zora Neale Hurston, Katherine Dunham, Pearl Primus, Ruth Beckford, Lula Washington, Chuck Davis, Alvin Ailey, Brenda Dixon-Gottschild, Kariamu Welsh, Ron Brown, Clayola Brown, and Yvonne Daniel, among many others. Concurrently, the transfer and performance of African-derived heritage in the United States have resulted in new creolized performances that later have become "traditions."

At play underneath the factors that shaped the emergence of a creolized WA-derived dance milieu were broader intellectual movements throughout the African Diaspora and twentieth-century geopolitical developments. The emergence of decolonized African nations on the global political stage, the overturning of racially discriminatory immigration laws in the United States as a direct result of the Civil Rights Movement, and the rise of globalization as the dominant means through which nations and peoples interact in political space created a world in which Africans and African Americans—populations that had lived in forced isolation from one another for several centuries—could renegotiate the terms of their relationship through dance.

The West African artists who immigrated to the United States were empowered and inspired by the Negritude movement and the political significance of their own folk arts in gaining their independence. They brought not only the songs and movement sequences of West African dance to the United States but also a way of drawing power from the artistic traditions that were enthralling many African Americans. In the cultural aftermath of the Harlem Renaissance and the Civil Rights Movement, African Americans were creating their own Black Arts Movement to theorize and operationalize a new Black aesthetic. Indeed, the development of WA-derived dance became the major vehicle through which African and African American performers could hash out the details of globalization's impact. The postmodern world continues, as communication technologies like the internet and social media have facilitated exchanges of ideas, values, and culture. WA-derived dance, then and today, has an enhanced ability to serve as a conduit through which African and African-descendent communities can continue to articulate resistance in the face of persistent marginalization and oppression.

Beyond the direct purview of politics, activism, and resistance, the American WA-derived dance world has had a broad effect on the African American cultural topography since the 1970s. The children of some West African artists who immigrated to the United States in the 1970s have been significant contributors to African American popular culture, particularly *hip hop dancing* with rapping. Multiplatinum recording artist Akon, for example, is the son of Mor Thiam and is well versed in traditional African music and dance. Madiou Diouf, son of Zak Diouf, became a music producer working with well-known artists such as Aloe Blac and specializes in creating beats that infuse stylized *sabar* and *djembe* drumming within hip-hop rhythms. Also, Weedie Braimah and Amadou Kouyate (son of famous kora player Djimbo Kouyaté) have gone on to travel the world, record with international music artists, and release their own world music albums. Rappers with recent West African roots, like Blitz the Ambassador, Wale, and Jidenna, have also found success in the U.S. hip-hop industry.

As African American popular culture globalized in the late twentieth and early twenty-first centuries, West African participation has been key. Indeed, many African American recording artists have begun drawing more heavily upon African dance and aesthetic imagery in creating their art and including African locales in their world tours (Beyoncé, most notably). In the postmodern world, new forms of cultural collaboration and exchange can emerge among Africans and people of African descent around the globe. Spirit talk can now progress to spirit conversation and spirit discourse on an unprecedented scale. Nevertheless, "SAUCE!" is still needed in kitchenspaces, on stages, and in the minds of Africans and African Americans alike—to imagine new possibilities for themselves and their communities and to craft victorious responses to their circumstances for the betterment of humankind.

Notes

1. *Ase* (also spelled *ache*, *ashe*, or *axe*) is a Yoruba-derived word generally defined as "the power to make things happen" and also refers to the spiritual life force that flows through all things and beings.

2. A parallel word in Central African traditions is *simbi*; however, in this chapter I concentrate only on West Africa and West African transnational communities in the Diaspora.

3. M. Jacqui Alexander, *Pedagogies of Crossing: Meditations on Feminism, Sexual Politics, Memory, and the Sacred* (Durham, N.C.: Duke University Press, 2005), 15–16.

4. In this chapter, West African traditions, trends, and dances refer to those originating from present-day Senegal, Gambia, and Mali. Such trends also reflect cultural nationalism, national dance company formation, and the development of dance companies during the late 1950s and 1960s in Liberia, Ghana, Sierra Leone, and Nigeria. The terms "West African" or "continental West African" are used here to refer to "Black" Africans born and reared in a West African country—in other words, those who are *not* descendants of enslaved Africans taken to the Americas. Therefore, West Africans are presumed not to have had the same experience of enslavement as African Americans. However, West Africans and African Americans share the experience of being colonized and the conditions related to colonization.

5. Palm nuts are crushed into a creamy consistency and cooked with meats and seafood, and then served over rice or farina.

6. In my usage and understanding of the landscape of the kitchen, I follow geographer Maria Elisa Christie, who coined and defined the *kitchenspace* as a complex of spaces, both indoors and out, associated with the preparation of food. According to Christie, activities and relationships delineate the kitchenspace as much as physical structures do. See Maria Elisa Christie, *Kitchenspace: Women, Fiestas, and Everyday Life in Central Mexico* (Austin: University of Texas Press, 2008).

7. Arthur Moore, personal interview, East St. Louis, Ill., July 5, 2009.

8. Luisah Teish, personal interview, Oakland, Calif., October 11, 2010.

9. Danny Glover, telephone interviews and conversations, Berkeley, Calif., 2002–2016.

10. V. Y. Mudimbe, *The Idea of Africa* (Bloomington: Indiana University Press, 1994), 57.

11. Mudimbe, *Idea of Africa*, 57.

12. Robert W. Nicholls, "African Dance: Transition and Continuity," in *African Dance: An Artistic, Historical and Philosophical Inquiry*, ed. Kariamu Welsh-Asante (Trenton, N.J.: African World Press, 1996), 41.

13. Chuck Davis, workshop at Muntu Dance Theatre, Chicago, Ill., 2006.

14. Luisah Teish, personal interview, Oakland, Calif., October 11, 2010.

15. Anthony Shay, *Choreographing Identities: Folk Dance, Ethnicity and Festival in the United States and Canada* (Jefferson, N.C.: McFarland, 2006), 45–46.

16. Kariamu Welsh-Asante, "Commonalities in African Dance: An Aesthetic Foundation," in *Moving Histories/Dancing Cultures: A Dance History Reader*, ed. Ann Dils and Ann Cooper Albright (Middletown, Conn.: Wesleyan University Press, 2001), 144–51.

17. A former member of Les Ballets Africaines de Keïta Fodéba, Ladji Camara was one of the first West African artists to settle in the United States and teach djembe-based traditions that originated from Francophone Africa (for example, Mali, Guinea, and Senegal). Camara, known as the father of the djembe movement, particularly

in New York, was invited to California and East St. Louis by Katherine Dunham to work with her company and community students.

18. Arthur Moore, personal interview, East St. Louis, Ill., July 5, 2009.

19. Chuck Davis, workshop at Muntu Dance Theatre, Chicago, Ill., 2006.

20. Darlene Blackburn, personal interview, Chicago, Ill., July 31, 2009.

21. Susan Foster, "Choreographies of Gender," *Signs: Journal of Women and Culture and Society* 24, no. 1 (1998).

22. Luisah Teish, personal interview, Oakland, Calif., October 11, 2010; Arthur Moore, personal interview, East St. Louis, Ill., July 5, 2009; Darlene Blackburn, personal interview, Chicago, Ill., July 31, 2009; Najwa Soyini I, personal interview, Chicago, Ill., July 31, 2009.

23. Daryl Braddix, personal interview, St. Louis, Mo., July 3, 2009.

24. See also Mark Ellis Sunkett, *Mandiani Drum and Dance: Djembe Performance and Black Aesthetics from Africa to the New World* (Tempe, Ariz.: White Cliffs, 1995).

25. Patrick E. Johnson, *Appropriating Blackness: Performance and the Politics of Authenticity* (Durham, N.C.: Duke University Press, 2003), 27.

26. Paulla Ebron, *Performing Africa* (Princeton, N.J.: Princeton University Press, 2002).

27. Zakarya Sao Diouf, personal interviews, Dakar, Senegal and Oakland, Calif., 2006–2010.

28. Abdoulaye "Papa" Camara, personal interview, New Orleans, La., November 14, 2004.

29. Zakarya S. Diouf, personal interviews, Dakar, Senegal and Oakland, California, November 28, 2009.

Dance Rooted in the Movements of Bedford-Stuyvesant

Two Choreographers, One Aesthetic Tradition

Indira Etwaroo

We know who we are by the stories we tell about
    ourselves and the world.
We know who we are through the family and community
    of whose stories we are a part.
We make our own stories and our stories make us.
—Wendell Pierce, *The Wind in the Reeds*

I am forged in the stories of a past that began on another continent and that moved across waters that became both transport and burial ground.[1] It is, ultimately, a journey toward freedom, and the narratives, the stories "we tell about ourselves and the world," have unfolded across centuries.

In 1619, shackled feet stepped onto foreign soil and shackled hands shielded eyes from the sun lighting a place that was no longer "home." A narrative of freedom had already begun, as captive Africans jumped overboard to escape the cruel novelty of bondage. It continued with every runaway slave, every enslaved child who secretly learned to read and write by the dim light of a candle, and every passenger on an underground railroad.

This narrative of freedom strained under a proclamation that emerged out of the bloodiest battle on American soil some 150 years ago, and it grew faint as the laws of Jim Crow produced a strange fruit that filled the air with an aroma not soon to be forgotten. The stories sparked a renaissance in Harlem after birthing the blues, an art form reinvented time and time again as a visceral resistance to terror in one's own country. This narrative marched on Washington, even as warriors of justice would never see the narrative of history rewritten. This narrative of freedom has many authors. It is a living document that has been edited, amended, and revised, time and time again. It has been tested, challenged, downtrodden, and it has been shored up with countless whispered prayers and hallelujah shouts.

The dance from the shores and soil of Africa became a conduit, bringing the pulse, rhythm, and culture of different tribes to a "new world." Two choreographers have given us an ethnography of a people, chronicling the African American experience as this narrative of freedom stepped onto global stages from the asphalt of a place that has most famously become known as "Bed-Stuy do or die,"[2] a bustling, diverse, and creative area of Brooklyn, New York. My reflection here spotlights two choreographers, whom I have worked with and whose work is critical to understanding the role of African dance in the United States in the late twentieth and early twenty-first centuries. Dr. Kariamu Welsh[3] and Ronald K. Brown[4] are globally renowned dancers, choreographers, activists, educators, and scholars. They both grew up in Bedford-Stuyvesant and they both bring with them the spirit of the African ancestors that speaks of intellectual and corporeal wisdom, understanding, and inventiveness. Welsh and Brown move through many of the same professional dance circles, and Brown refers to Welsh as "Mama," a term of endearment and respect for an elder, teacher, and mentor in African and African American communities.

This chapter is filtered through my own lens and my experiences as a Black woman who is a member of the Bed-Stuy community, which is where I live and work. To me, Bed-Stuy sounds and feels like home: the *djembe* drumming whose rhythms float through my open window during the summer nights, the laughter and shouts of Black folks on a street corner, cars with the latest in music blasting from rolled-down car windows, ambulance or police sirens, and other sights and sounds that remind me of downtown Newport News, Virginia, where I grew up . . . a neighborhood of Black folks working, living, and just "trying to make it." There are also sights and sounds that are different from what I have known as home, like the demographic shifts in Brooklyn: white-owned and -run coffee houses and brownstones, ethnically diverse families traveling up and down the streets and avenues, and construction happening everywhere. Construction often speaks of progress, but the question remains . . . for whom?

I am an arts administrator, a minority in the arts-and-culture nonprofit sector of New York City, yet I have discovered that there is nothing "minor" about representing and curating a specific point of view that presents the heterogeneous and dynamic diversity of the African Diaspora and all of its ever-evolving stories in a field that has mostly presented art forms by, for, and about Eurocentric cultures and communities.[5] I have lived, studied, and taught dance and dance research in the studio, lecture hall, and "the field" in the United States; Tegucigalpa, Honduras; and Addis Ababa, Ethiopia. I have choreographed and directed works that used aesthetic idioms that are rooted in West African, East African, and North and Central American cultures and countries. There is a common belief among dance historians and anthropologists that "to understand the culture, study the dance. To understand the dance, study the people."

My written exploration here articulates in writing what isn't always observable by the human eye or even capable of being captured linearly with the English language. Welsh and Brown—from two different generations— embody the essence of "blood memory," as renowned choreographer Alvin Ailey called it; a remembering, a re-conjuring of a past that one may not remember cognitively but viscerally recalls.[6] These two choreographers have not achieved global prominence in spite of growing up in Bed-Stuy but *because* of it. Bedford-Stuyvesant, a place of seemingly never-ending concrete and asphalt, has been fertile ground for great dance innovation. My written reflection moves through the methodologies of oral histories, thick movement description, and memory. It explores the dynamic and evolving culture of Bed-Stuy through the lens of these two choreographers and the unifying principles of African aesthetics.

Bedford Stuyvesant

A walk through Bed-Stuy in 2019 reveals a community of divergences with $2 million brownstones across from public-housing units, dilapidated storefronts next to stylish new bistros, high-income households alongside 33 percent of residents who live in poverty, and, despite an influx of young professionals drawn to Bed-Stuy's proximity to Manhattan and relatively affordable housing, 17 percent of residents are unemployed. This three-square-mile area, home to 154,332 residents (64 percent Black)[7], boasts a historical landscape that has been a cultural mecca for people of African descent for decades. It has been home to such luminaries as Lena Horne, Jay-Z, Max Roach, Eubie Blake, Stephanie Mills, Notorious B.I.G., and Yasiin Bey (formerly known as Mos Def).

First settled in 1662 and named by 1667, the town of Bedford was formally purchased in 1670 from the Canarsee—the indigenous nation from whom the Europeans acquired land. Bedford was initially much larger than it is today. Even in the late 1960s, it encompassed much of Clinton Hill (including

Pratt Institute), most of today's Crown Heights, and some of Ocean Hill. It also included Weeksville and the Hunterfly Road Houses. After the Revolutionary War, Bedford was a small community: the 1790 census records 132 free African descendants and seventy-two enslaved people. Rapid growth would follow major improvements to public transportation. The first phase of growth can be dated to 1836, when the Brooklyn and Jamaica Railroad connected the area to the Atlantic Avenue ferry. The second phase of growth was in 1936 with the inauguration of the IND Fulton Street Subway Line. Both projects created an increased interest in Bed-Stuy, but for different reasons. In the first case, it made the area convenient for those with jobs in Manhattan. By 1873 the (mostly white) population was fourteen thousand. In the second case, it connected the neighborhood to Harlem, the residents of which could take the A train to Bed-Stuy as a means to escape the saturated housing market of Harlem and remain accessible to family and friends. The population exploded from forty-five thousand in 1920 (the great majority white) to sixty-five thousand in 1940 (counting just Blacks).[8]

At the turn of the twentieth century, six million people of African descent voted with their feet and fled a terrorist South in the United States, migrating to western and northern states.[9] Harlem is famous as a hotspot destination for the "Great Migration";[10] however, Bedford-Stuyvesant became one of the most prominent communities for the city's Black population. African Americans first moved there in large numbers during the 1920s and 1930s. This significant ethnic shift resulted in at least one positive change for the Black community: access to property. Housing discrimination was still rampant in the early twentieth century, but the concentration led to increased purchasing power. It was around this time that locals began to call Bedford and Stuyvesant Heights by the combined name.[11]

Kariamu Welsh and Bed-Stuy

Kariamu Welsh was born in Chester, South Carolina, in 1949 and moved to Bedford-Stuyvesant at age five. Her recollection of Bed-Stuy in the mid-1950s was:

> Once the whites moved out and then the blacks moved in, the brownstones were a source of pride. Seeing blacks like us own those homes that were so beautiful! I lived in what was called a tenement, but it didn't seem so cramped because the space where things happened was on the sidewalk and on the stoop. You know, we played jump rope or jacks . . . lots of activities on the street. There were a cappella singing groups, generally young men, but that was also a part of the rhythm, the texture of the neighborhood. For me, those sounds would just come in and out the apartments because we didn't have air conditioners

then and so you would open your window and hear those sounds and they could lull you to sleep or they could just stay with you throughout the night. You know people make surprising noises. It was relatively safe to me. It was a community. I'm not saying there weren't dangers as there would be in any community, but nothing like you see in the last thirty years.[12]

By the 1960s the outlook of Bed-Stuy was bleak. Bed-Stuy was an urban stage—a microcosm—that played out the burden of racial inequities combined with economic disinvestments across the United States, particularly urban spaces. Between 1965 and 1968, 329 urban rebellions took place in 257 U.S. cities, resulting in nearly 300 deaths, 60,000 arrests, and hundreds of millions of dollars in property loss. On July 9, 1966, the *New York Times* ran an article with the headline: "400 Youths Join Brooklyn Brawl: Police Break Up Fighting in Bedford-Stuyvesant." They reported:

> A crowd of 400 Negroes and Puerto Ricans threw bottles and trash-can covers at each other last night at crowded intersection in the Bedford-Stuyvesant section of Brooklyn. The disorder was quelled quickly, but not before a police sergeant was struck on the head by a bottle and an angry throng rocked a patrol car, attempting to turn it over. There were two arrests. By 11 P.M. the four square blocks around the intersection of Throop Avenue and Hart Street were saturated with 100 policemen, many of them members of the elite Tactical Patrol Force. They had been called in from duty in Manhattan and the Bronx. The disorder started, the police said, as an outgrowth of recent hostilities and skirmishes between Negroes and Puerto Ricans in the area. One resident, a Puerto Rican, said the fight started after a Puerto Rican boy called a Negro boy a "nigger."

A population of 450,000 residents occupied just 653 blocks, making it the second-largest black community in the country.[13] The area's high schools had a 70 percent dropout rate. Infant-mortality, delinquency, and unemployment rates were twice the city average. Underemployment was at 28 percent—astounding even today, but especially so when you consider the city's unemployment rate was just 3.7 percent. Many of Bed-Stuy's brownstones had fallen into disrepair. Crime was high; race riots broke out.[14]

Senator Robert F. Kennedy visited on February 4, 1966, to walk the streets of Bed-Stuy. While Kennedy was meeting with community members, he "was challenged by neighborhood activists to go beyond speeches and help produce something tangible."[15] Ten months later, in December 1966, Kennedy, along with Mayor Lindsay and Senator Javits, presented a plan for the Bedford-Stuyvesant Development and Service Corporation. Kennedy told residents, "The program for the development of Bedford Stuyvesant will combine the best of community action with the best of the private enterprise system. Neither by itself is enough, but in their combination lies our hope for the future."[16] This has been the guiding principle and strategic ethos for the development of the community by the Bedford Stuyvesant Restoration Corporation over the past fifty-one years.

Ronald K. Brown and Bed-Stuy

While 1966 birthed an idea that manifested itself a year later as the first community-development corporation in the nation, Bedford Stuyvesant Restoration Corporation (Restoration), it was also the birth year and birthplace of Ronald K. Brown.

Brown was born at Albany Hospital on the corner of Albany and Atlantic Avenues. He grew up first on Summer Avenue between Fulton and Decatur. Brown lived with his maternal great-grandmother. Brown explains, "My sensibility and approach to choreography show that I'm a Brooklyn-born black man with roots in the South. The ideas that inspire me are informed by all that has been poured into me by my teachers, family, and ancestors."[17]

The artistic, cultural, and environmental sensibilities of Bedford-Stuyvesant, as a unique community where the African aesthetic survived and thrived on American soil with, as Brown states, "roots in the South"—notwithstanding the current threat of gentrification—became the home place that seeded the aesthetic sensibilities within the choreographic works of both Welsh and Brown. Dance historian and critic Brenda Dixon-Gottschild explains:

> Like the ordinary/extraordinary of the black dancing body, traditional African dance utilizes the ordinary imagery of home and community (whether mortar, pestle, scythe, animal imagery, or moral tenets of good and evil) to reach for the extraordinary—these ineffable flights that can be expressed only in the medium of the dancing body and are not necessarily translatable into words or the verbal telling of a story. The real story in the African dance is the manifestation and presence of the dancing body. It doesn't mean something else: It is what it is![18]

This exploration aligns with the premise that Welsh and Brown, while choreographers deeply informed by African aesthetics, are not choreographers of traditional African dance, but rather, as Welsh puts forward in much of her scholarship, they are creating from neotraditional African dance forms.[19]

Neotraditional also includes the dances and movement forms that come from Christian churches (mainly Pentecostal and Baptist) across the United States that in this case Bedford-Stuyvesant, also influence the works of Welsh and Brown. For example, "shouting," which is a transcendent spiritual ritual, was first practiced by enslaved Africans in the Caribbean Islands and the United States. Worshippers stomp their feet and clap their hands, often bow-ing forward at the waist. Shouting is still practiced in some African American churches into the twenty-first century. Shouting loses its traditional context once it moves from a sacred place of worship to the concert stage, as these traditional worship sessions may go on for hours. Just walk down Tompkins Street in Bed-Stuy and hear the organ music, the singing, and the shouting still coming out of the open doors of the church at 4 o'clock on Sunday afternoon for a church service that started hours earlier. "The dances become proscenium which means that it's no longer in the round, it's no longer fluid between the audience. I understand the people who are wedded to the traditional dance but what they are doing is neotraditional."[20]

Choreographic Aesthetics and Bed-Stuy

There are aesthetic principles from the continent of Africa that, while they do not address the specificity of tribal groups, villages, or nation-state borders, speak to fundamental aesthetic principles that are shared across the continent. I have relied on the works of both Robert Farris Thompson[21] and Kariamu Welsh-Asante[22] as a guidepost for this reflection. Their aesthetic paradigms, combined, provide a pathway, a substantive and clear trajectory to proceed through the choreographic works of Brown and Welsh as manifestation of their rootedness in Bedford-Stuyvesant. From the work of Thompson and Welsh-Asante, I utilize eight African aesthetic principles: oral tradition, polyrhythm, polycentrism, repetition, get-down quality, multiple meter, correct entrance and exit, and call and response.

The keen focus on these aesthetic principles applies a unifying element to complex danced narratives, community spaces, and bodies of knowledge that, at first glance to the unqualified eye, may seem chaotic, simplistic, and/or lacking organizing values. In fact, these dance works, these communities, and these bodies of knowledge that apply African aesthetics on American soil bring with them the intersections that connect to one path, which is fundamentally a journey toward equity, a journey toward freedom. While these principles serve as a through line for deepening our understanding of the lives, choreographic processes, and artistic works of Welsh and Brown, these two reside as peers to other artists/activists who were also forged in the sociocultural and aesthetic kiln of the Civil Rights, Black Power, and Black Arts Movements: Sonia Sanchez, Eleo Pomare, Ruby Dee, Chuck Davis, August Wilson, Amiri Baraka, Geoffrey Holder, and countless others.

Additionally, Black Nationalism in Brooklyn was central, as the Brooklyn Chapter of CORE (Congress on Racial Equality) continuously challenged the inequities that were playing out in Bed-Stuy neighborhoods in the mid to late 1960s. Bedford-Stuyvesant was a community shaped by social movements that advocated for the rights of community members to control local public schools, government investment in antipoverty programs, and political fear of urban riots and unrest.[23] In October 1969, a small group of Brooklyn community activists, including several who had been involved in the city's recent school decentralization controversy, joined together to publish a modest monthly newssheet aimed at the local black community. Initially consisting of a handful of 8½ x 11" pages stapled together, *Black News* combined strident political commentary with tales of black and poor people's encounters with the police, public schools, welfare system, and other oppressive municipal institutions. One Bedford-Stuyvesant resident stated in 1964, "Things are moving, but the whites have got to understand that we are flesh and blood and we want our rights now, and through protest is the only way we are going to get it."[24]

Welsh and Brown, throughout their choreographic careers, have tackled issues of social injustice, inequality, and the search for individual and global freedom and peace. Kariamu Welsh's *RAAAAHMONA REVISITED* is a group choreographic work that features a black woman soloist inspired by the MOVE event on May 13, 1985, in Philadelphia, Pennsylvania.[25] A house was targeted at 6221 Osage Avenue, battered by police bullets, and eventually brought down by a makeshift bomb. The bomb was dropped from a police helicopter due to a standoff between members of MOVE and the City of Philadelphia. Subsequently, eleven people died in the resulting fire and more than 250 people in the neighborhood were left homeless. Ramona Africa, the only surviving adult MOVE member, was charged and incarcerated for seven years on riot and conspiracy charges.[26] Welsh states, "I am an 'artivist,' meaning that one of my responsibilities as an artist is to tell the stories, myths, legends and histories of the marginalized, the invisible, the forgotten and the oppressed."[27]

Ronald K. Brown created "March," a movement excerpt from the multi-movement choreographic work titled "Lessons"; it was "a duet between two male dancers to the speech, entitled 'The Quest for Peace and Justice,' given by Dr. Martin Luther King Jr. during the Nobel Prize lecture on December 11, 1964."[28] This speech, hence choreographic work, explores the technological progression of mankind that is contrary to a lack of moral character. Brown's "March" features a black male soloist, as well as a duet. I explore these two choreographies through the lens of eight African aesthetic principles, which are rooted within the context of Bed-Stuy.

PHOTO 2.1. (Opposite page) *Raaahmonaaah Revisited!* Kariamu Welsh, choreographer; Tamara Thomas, dancer; Bill T. Herbert, photographer, 2012.

PHOTO 2.2. *March*. Ronald K. Brown, choreographer; Arcell Cabuag and Ronald K. Brown, dancers; Julieta Cervantes, photographer.

Choreographic Analyses

The oral tradition is, in fact, a significant part of African aesthetics, which were transported to the Americas. In many ways, the oral tradition is also a key distinction between the work of Welsh and Brown and between the work of choreographers of African descent and that of European or European-influenced choreographers. This orality is a communication style that is rich in allusion, metaphor, and imagery; it is also prolific in the use of body gestures and nonverbal nuances.[29]

In Welsh's 2013 *RAAAAHMONA REVISITED*[30] we see a solo woman dancer onstage, draped in a white dress that covers her torso (but leaves her shoulders bare except for thin shoulder straps) and has a split front, allowing free movement of the legs. A downstage solo light projects upstage against a darkened scrim and creates a halo of light with a bigger-than-life-size silhouette of the solo dancer in the center. Every movement is enlarged against this backdrop, creating a visual repetition of the real solo form, but intensified. We hear a full alto voice of the woman soloist that trumpets the title name "Raaaahmona"; in a sing-song-like rhythm, the audience hears: "Rahmona mona babona, fee fi Rahmona. Rahmōōōna. Rahmōōōna. Rahmōōōna!"

The dancer's movements are minimal as she commands the attention of the audience with her full voice; she takes a few small steps forward to stage left, leaning toward the audience, then a few steps to stage right, then stage left again, leaning forward as her arms drape naturally at her sides and her feet remain parallel to each other, positioned underneath her hips. Her call is delivered in a strong 4/4 meter, followed by a spoken-word piece that is free flowing and not within a set meter. The spoken-word piece unfolds the history of the title figure, "Rahmona," using the oral tradition. We are led through her pain, as well as her power, with phrases like "locked away in your steel castle," "cast your lot towards Africa," and "as you sway, we'll move with you." The phrases are full of the imagery of the character's experiences. The use of the oral tradition to open this piece, which is presented in a concert-stage setting, signifies to the audience to listen up, pay attention. Something very important is about to be conveyed.

I shift to analyze the solo excerpt from Ronald K. Brown's "March" and his use of the oral tradition.[31] The stage is black with a single spotlight and one male dancer. He is dressed in loose black trousers with a waistline that extends right below the pectoral muscles and high on the abdomen and is held up by inch-wide black suspenders. The recorded voice of Dr. Martin Luther King Jr. resonates out with words from the English poet John Donne laced throughout: "No man is an island, entire of itself; every man is a piece of the continent, a part of the main . . . any man's death diminishes me because I am involved in Mankind; and therefore, never send to know for whom the bell tolls, it tolls for thee."[32]

Brown presents the oral tradition through the historical pioneer Dr. King, both orator and oral historian, as the soundscape to his piece. The words are in partnership with the movement yet create a complex polyrhythm of both meter and thought. We hear the words of King in soulful rhyme and cadence that are emphatically juxtaposed against the frenetic movement of the dancer. What we also witness in "March" is the elevated language of the great orator Dr. King juxtaposed against the get-down quality that is present in Brown's movement. We see, but also feel, a pulsing internal rhythm, a rootedness, yet all within a spirit of corporeal celebration. In addition to being influenced by African, Caribbean, and American dance forms, Brown is influenced by dance-club moves and the House Music Movement that emerged in the 1980s, which epitomizes the African aesthetic of the "get-down quality" that is evident in Brown's work.[33]

During the spoken-word section of Welsh's *RAAAAHMONA REVISITED*, the solo dancer begins movements that emanate from many bodily centers. She exhibits polycentrism[34] with undulations of the torso, with knees bent and arms that slice forward and then are drawn back sharply by the elbows, and with arms drawing a circle around the dancer's head, even as the torso of the dancer continues its circular undulations in a clockwise pattern. The dancer draws one knee after the other up to her chest and steps forward with an almost military-like precision, pushing the weight of the foot down as it pushes the weight of the body up. The fingers on her hands are tightly closed and straight, as the hands serve to carve out space in exacting ways.

One movement draws her upstage, as her entire body seems to inhale sharply, creating a strong contraction in the torso and deeply arched back that draws the head and shoulders of the dancer forward as she backs up with small, fast, and light demi-steps led by the weight of her hips with softened knees. Her arms are stretched out to the sides. I am reminded of Welsh's words: "The representation of the cosmos in the body is a goal. The myriad possibilities in the universe also exist in the body for the African dancer";[35] and of dance scholar Matthew Nelson's words: "connect[ing] polycentric movements to a belief that there is no singular reality or truth."[36] Hence, polycentrism in a philosophical and ideological realm reveals a polyperspective, a complexity that becomes most significant for people of African descent on American soil as we work through the double-consciousness that is our reality.[37]

This polyperspective or polycentrism is also evident in the lighting design at the opening of the piece. Again, we see a petite and lean-in-stature black woman dancer presented to us onstage against a backdrop that makes her larger than life, powerful, strong, and almost goddess-like visually. Within the hierarchy of political, social, cultural, and economic realities, both nationally and globally, it can be argued that the black woman remains most vulnerable, most underpaid, and most ill-recognized for her historical achievements. This reality is layered with the projection of the woman dancer. Welsh presents these polyrealities with polycentric ideas through movements that emanate from many central points of the dancer's body: her torso, her shoulders, her legs, and her head.

Welsh's spoken-word piece, which grows in intensity and volume until the dancer is shouting at full voice, ends with the words "You are Rahmona. Reflections to set your people free. Rahmona mona babona, fee fi Rahmona. Rahmōōōna. Rahmōōōna. Rahmōōōna." After each "Rahmona," we hear ululations from performers offstage, vocal responses that are loud and piercing in both volume and pitch, which are a response to the call of "Ramōōōna!" Coming from offstage, these vocal responses speak to an encouragement, an affirmation, a holding up of this woman in challenging times. Call-and-response, as an African aesthetic principle, is a powerful connector between the individual and the community. The separation between performer-audience, musician or rhythm-keeper, and dancer, which are often observed in Eurocentric or Eurocentric-influenced dance works, are applied uniquely within this African and Afro-descendent aesthetic canon. Fundamentally, the soloist is reassured: "I am because we are."

Intensification develops with the repetition of each "Rahmona," which speaks to the aesthetic principle of repetition, often inaccurately perceived as a movement, a rhythm, or a sound identical to the one that proceeds it. Those who observe dance performance may even go so far as to think that repetition might suggest a lack of inventiveness on the part of the choreographer. Dance critic Anna Kisselgoff asserts:

> The issue of repetition is one that choreographers do not like to discuss. It is common to evade the whole problem by taking a Heraclitean stance—by quoting a pre-Socratic philosopher without even knowing his name and declaring, "You cannot bathe in the same river twice." In translation, this means that the dancer who seems to repeat the same step is different from the dancer he was a second ago—that the step cannot possibly be the same as it was then since it is already "different." None of this will really wash.[38]

The criticism of neotraditional dances that use repetition, which is formed by and through the aesthetic principles of continental Africa, overlooks the nuance and importance of when a word or a movement is repeated beyond the traditional, ritualistic spaces where movements can be repeated for hours or even days. Repetition provides emphasis, as well as a sense of intensification.

> Repetition highlights an accountability for every note/sound in the sense that each [word] could represent centuries of pain and perseverance, or breaking cycles of psychological bondage, or picking away at the locks that shackle the minds of many Black[s]. . . . Repetition serves to intensify the effect and leads to a climax.[39]

Repetition is also a clear aesthetic element used in the dancer's arms in Brown's March excerpt. The arms are bent at the elbow and held in a fixed position with fists closed at the sides of his face. He turns his torso right, left, right, left in a repetitive rhythmic pose. This movement shows a repetition of the movement with an intensification, not in size or spatial usage, but rather in intention. The dancer's head drops forward and the weight of his head drops forward as his right hand touches the ground followed by his left—it is in the visceral sensibility of a *dobale*, a sign of respect for one's elders that is expressed in many African cultures. As he bends at the waist, his knees bend softly and then slowly return to a standing position facing forward.

The dancer whips to the side, facing stage left and then begins to whip loose arms around his body. His arms wrap around one side of his body torso and then the other, imitating an African spin drum from the western region of Africa, as he walks forward. A polyrhythm of multiple meters take place in his feet and in his arms. Instead of the drumming accompanying the work, the body becomes the drum. We see a repetition of the spin drum motif and, each time, it grows in intensification. The movement of the dancing body accents the words, yet it never supersedes the words. Each—the word and the movement—is partner to one other.

As Welsh's *RAAAAHMONA REVISITED* moves through multiple meters toward a driving 4/4 polyrhythm[40] of many drums and the sounds of many rhythms from the feet of the dancers, its greatest balance is the seemingly off-balance-ness of multiple meters. Welsh explains:

> Nothing escapes my palette; and images—of my mother singing in her bra and half-slip in the sticky humid August evenings in Brooklyn as she ironed, washed, and cleaned—resonate with me not only as memory but as movement. Jumping Double Dutch as a young girl until it was so dark that I couldn't see the rope and reluctantly had to come in for the night gave me a polyrhythmic foundation that taught me how to enter and exit a rhythm.[41]

As the first section of *RAAAAHMONA REVISITED* ends with the solo performer, we hear the ululations crescendo and blend into dembe drum roll, and as that increases in intensity and speed, approximately twelve dancers run onto the stage. They appear in seconds and form a triangle with the solo female dancer as the point. The space—based on this entrance—within seconds becomes a developed ensemble section. The lights then fade to black, and when the lights come up, the stage is empty. Yet, a driving polyrhythm beats out first from a steady percussive cow bell rhythm; djembe drums are being played with a stick to maintain a resounding bass pattern and drive the syncopated hand beats and rhythms of the other djembe drums.

In "March," the black male soloist moves through a series of movements, applying the aesthetic principles of repetition, polyrhythm, and polycentrism on multiple spatial levels simultaneously, which involves a thrust of the leg through an extension, a turn of the body with a knee bent, which brings the weight of the dancer to the ground into a still position, as the voice of Dr. King reverberates—the oral tradition rings out. Brown tells us that "the impulse was to create work that would be a reflection of the human condition. For audiences to see themselves in the movement and the stories told through music and text."[42]

The use of African aesthetic principles within choreography is the major shared element of both Welsh's and Brown's artistic creation. The influence of Welsh on Brown's work, as well as their shared influences from black dance legacies (Alvin Ailey, Pearl Primus, Katherine Dunham) and Welsh's contemporaries (Pearl Reynolds, Diane McIntyre, Donald McKayle) on Brown's work are seen in their shared ethos not only to speak out against injustice but also to present Black lives onstage through the dance. These shared characteristics are seen in their consistent and steady use of African aesthetic principles in their work.

Conclusion

The principles that govern that which we value, hold up as beautiful, as art, as African aesthetics, are deeply meaningful, affecting, and part of the landscape and soundscape that is Bed-Stuy. From the 1930s, when people of African descent began moving from Harlem to Bed-Stuy, establishing it as the second-largest black community in New York City, to the 1960s, when almost 90 percent of the community was of African descent, the Bed-Stuy community was and is still performing African and Afro-descendent aesthetics. Anthropologist and folklorist Zora Neale Hurston, in *The Sanctified Church*, has written, "It is said that Negroes keep nothing secret, that they have no reserve. This ought not to seem strange when one considers that we are an outdoor people accustomed to communal life."[43] Life, as it plays out on the streets of Bed-Stuy, embodies what we hold dear: community—the many versus the one; equity, as balance; our stories, our culture, our families; and circles, continuums, looking back in order to move forward.

The streets of Bed-Stuy are the closest thing to walking the streets of an African country that I have experienced. The oral tradition is alive and well in Bed-Stuy—from the conversations and stories being shared on the stoops and from speeches of Malcolm and Martin, two of the greatest orators of our time, blasting from storefronts to the rhythmic poetry spouted by young

Black men who saunter down the streets and are heard rapping or singing over recorded music. Black folks in Bed-Stuy don't greet each other with a nod or a handshake; it is most common to hear a call from across a busy street with a response that is echoed by a group who might be standing on a corner. Any phenomenon—from the smallest occurrence to a larger event—solicits the response of the community, "I know that's right!" And the sounds—they all come at once: the multiple rhythms, the polyrhythm of the day, djembe drums or a marching drumline sound against the rhythm of the A train, reverberating a steady percussive beat from beneath the pavement, the passing of cars and the crescendo and decrescendo of music coming and then fading away as it blasts through open car windows. You see and hear the polyrhythm of children running or riding over the cracked pavement, making a popping sound with each crack on bikes and scooters. Correct entrance and exit couldn't be more important on the streets of Bed-Stuy. It is an unspoken rule—the rules of the street—about when and where to enter. Welsh explains:

> And that is what has stayed with me and stayed with my work all this time . . . the sounds and rhythms of Bed-Stuy. When we skipped Double Dutch, [it] was a skill, a key asset in both turning and jumping. It was in the Double Dutch that I learned the correct way to enter and to leave. You continue turning into the rope in a way that connects you to the world and then you have to be able to leave the rope while it is still turning, and that's really quite a skill.[44]

In Bed-Stuy, there are constant epicenters of activity that spring into place and then disperse—groups on a corner, lines of people waiting for something to open or to start, a performance of song, music, or rap with people encircling the performer, and all of these centered occurrences happening simultaneously—a polycentrism of culture. It is not atypical to see a group marching in protest, groups as small as a handful of people to hundreds, still speaking out about injustices and inequalities, all adding to the soundscape and movement of Bed-Stuy. Brown stated: "Most of my work is about liberation and perseverance. This is one of the invaluable gifts that Bed-Stuy has given me as inspiration."[45]

Welsh and Brown manifest a quote from the Ghanaian Nationalist leader Kwame Nkrumah, who led Ghana's drive to independence from Britain in 1957: "I am not African because I was born in Africa, but because Africa was born in me."[46] The African aesthetic has survived across centuries. It has survived a transatlantic slave trade. It has survived the enslavement of more than twelve million Africans. It has survived and thrived as new ways of being of African descent on American soil have manifested new art forms, time and time again, such as the blues, jazz, gospel, and hip hop's artistic combinations. The same aesthetic principles found on the continent are also on the streets and in communities across the world in which the descendants of Africans continue to perform them. Welsh and Brown have brought the streets of Bed-Stuy to stages across the globe, and they have affirmed, through the dance, the cultural beauty and richness of this place, this community that I and so many others from the African Diaspora call home.

Notes

1. David Eltis, Stephen D. Behrendt, David Richardson, and Herbert S. Klein, *The Trans-Atlantic Slave Trade: A Database on CD-ROM* (electronic resource) (Cambridge: Cambridge University Press, 1999). According to the database, 12.5 million Africans were shipped to the New World; 10.7 million survived the dreaded Middle Passage, disembarking in North America, the Caribbean, and South America. Out of these 10.7 million Africans, 388,000 were shipped directly to North America.

2. The terms "Bedford-Stuyvesant" (formal) and "Bed-Stuy" (colloquial) are used interchangeably by longstanding and new residents. To use the colloquial term is quite acceptable, but longstanding residents have voiced disapproval at the use of just "Stuyvesant," which they believe aligns with the gentrification of the area.

3. Kariamu Welsh is widely published in both scholarly journals and book-length studies and is a scholar of cultural studies, including performance and culture within Africa and the African Diaspora. Welsh serves as the director of the Institute for African Research and Performance and as artistic director of Kariamu & Co.: Traditions. She is the recipient of numerous fellowships, grants and awards, including a National Endowment for the Arts Choreography Fellowship, the Creative Public Service Award of New York, a Pew Fellowship, and three Senior Fulbright Scholar Awards. She is the founding artistic director of the National Dance Company of Zimbabwe and is also the creator of the Umfundalai dance technique, a Pan-African contemporary technique that has been in existence for more than three decades. Kariamu Welsh is also referenced as Kariamu Welsh-Asante in her earlier academic work.

4. Ronald K. Brown founded Evidence, a Dance Company in 1985. Brown has set works on Alvin Ailey American Dance Theater, Cleo Parker Robinson Ensemble, Dayton Contemporary Dance Company, Jeune Ballet d'Afrique Noire, Ko-Thi Dance Company, Philadanco, Ballet Hispanico, and others. He has collaborated with such artists as composer/designer Omotayo Wunmi Olaiya, Craig G. Harris, and Ernie McClintock. Brown has been awarded an AUDELCO Award for his work on Regina Taylor's *Crowns* and the Fred and Adele Astaire Award for Outstanding Choreography in Gershwin's Tony Award–winning *Porgy and Bess* on Broadway. He has been awarded a Guggenheim Fellowship, National Endowment for the Arts Choreographers Fellowship, New York Foundation for the Arts Fellowship, and United States Artists Fellowship. Brown's Evidence has made Bedford Stuyvesant Restoration Corporation its artistic home, where he conducts rehearsals and workshops, as well as develops new works.

5. Robin Pogrebin, "New York Arts Organizations Lack the Diversity of Their City," *New York Times,* January 28, 2016.

6. See Martha Graham's *Blood Memory: An Autobiography (New York: Doubleday,* 1991) and Yvonne Daniel's *Dancing Wisdom: Embodied Knowledge in Haitian Voudou, Cuban Yoruba and Bahian Candomblé.* (Chicago: University of Illinois, 2005).

7. "Brooklyn Community District 3: Bedford Stuyvesant, 2015," New York City Community Health Profiles 2015, https://www1.nyc.gov/assets/doh/downloads/pdf /data/2015chp-bk3.pdf.

8. "Bed-Stuy: A Very Brief History," June 23, 2012, *Weekly Nabe Publication*, http:// www.theweeklynabe.com/2012/06/23/bed-stuy.

9. Isabel Wilkerson, *The Warmth of Other Suns: The Epic Story of America's Great Migration* (New York: First Vintage, 2010).

10. Terry Gross, "The Great Migration: The African American Exodus North," interview with Isabel Wilkerson, *Fresh Air*, NPR, September 13, 2010, http://www.npr .org/templates/story/story.php?storyId=129827444.

11. "Bed-Stuy: A Very Brief History."

12. Kariamu Welsh, interview by Indira Etwaroo, May 2016, Glenside, Penn.

13. Chicago's South Side was the largest Black community in the nation, 82 percent African American and 12 percent Puerto Rican.

14. "400 Youth Join Brooklyn Brawl."

15. Jake Mooney, "Star Power, Still Shining 40 Years On: In Bedford-Stuyvesant, Robert F. Kennedy's Work Lives On," *New York Times*, January 29, 2009,

16. History of Bedford Stuyvesant Restoration Corporation, http://www.restoration plaza.org/about/history.

17. Ronald K. Brown, interview by Indira Etwaroo, August 2016, Bedford-Stuyvesant, Brooklyn, N.Y.

18. Brenda Dixon Gottschild, *The Black Dancing Body: A Geography from Coon to Cool* (New York: Palgrave Macmillian, 2003), 15.

19. Kariamu Welsh explains that "Traditional [dance] would not be for the concert stage; traditional dance would be traditional within the context of the tradition. The [traditional] dances go from half an hour to three hours a day; [while neotraditional dances [are] twelve minutes, fifteen minutes, twenty minutes . . ., which takes [them] out of the tradition. There is [also] an idea of presentation." Kariamu Welsh, interview by Laura Katz Rizzo, August 8, 2012, published on https://movementresearch.org /publications/critical-correspondence/kariamu-welsh-in-conversation-with-laura -katz—.

20. Rizzo interview, 2012.

21. Robert Farris Thompson, *African Art in Motion: Icon and Act* (Los Angeles: University of California Press, 1974).

22. Kariamu Welsh Asante, *The African Aesthetic: Keeper of the Traditions* (Westport, Conn.: Praeger, 1994).

23. Brian Purnell, *Fighting Jim Crow in the County of Kings: The Congress of Racial Equality in Brooklyn* (Lexington: University Press of Kentucky, 2013).

24. Gene Demby, "I'm from Philly: 30 Years Later, I'm Still Trying to Make Sense of the MOVE Bombing," May 13, 2015, https://www.npr.org/sections/codeswitch /2015/05/13/406243272/im-from-philly-30-years-later-im-still-trying-to-make-sense -of-the-move-bombing.

25. Ibid.

26. Ibid.

27. Mama Kariamu | Umfundalai, http://www.mamakariamu.com.

28. Nobel lecture by Dr. Martin Luther King Jr., December 11, 1964, https://www .nobelprize.org/prizes/peace/1964/king/lecture.

29. Janice D. Hamlet, "Word! The African American Oral Tradition and Its Rhetorical Impact on American Popular Culture," *Black History Bulletin* 74, no. 1 (2011): 271–89.

30. Mama Kariamu | Umfundalai, "Raaahmona Revisited," http://mamakariamu .com/portfolio.

31. Ronald K. Brown/Evidence, "March: An Excerpt from *Lessons*," https://www .youtube.com/watch?v=wabf31OC6vY.

32. This poem, "Meditation 17," is one in a series that the English poet John Donne wrote in 1623; see http://www.online-literature.com/donne/409.

33. Brown interview, August 2016.

34. Polycentrism is many movement patterns happening at once throughout the body and coexisting together.

35. Kariamu Welsh Asante, *Zimbabwe Dance: Rhythmic Forces, Ancestral Voices, and Aesthetic Analysis* (Trenton, N.J.: Africa World, 2000), 146.

36. Matthew Nelson, "Polycentrism in Contemporary Dance," accessed July 26, 2016. http://mail.bodysensate.com/bodysensation.

37. W. E. B. Du Bois, *The Souls of Black Folks* (New York: Signet Classic, 1994 [1903]).

38. Anna Kisselgoff, "Dance View: What Is Repetition Doing to Choreography?" *New York Times*, October 19, 1986, http://www.nytimes.com/1986/10/19/arts/dance -view-what-is-repetition-doing-to-choreography.html?pagewanted=all.

39. Melanie Batcher, "Song and Dance Nexus in the Africana Aesthetic: My Approach," in *African American Studies*, ed. Jeanette R. Davidson (Edinburgh: Edinburgh University Press, 2010), 232.

40. Polyrhythm is expressed as many meters and/or rhythms happening in concert all at once.

41. Kariamu Welsh, interview by Indira Etwaroo, May 2016, unpublished interview, Glenside, PA.

42. Brown interview, August 2016.

43. Zora Neale Hurston, *The Sanctified Church* (Berkeley, Calif.: Turtle Island, 1981), 60.

44. Welsh interview, May 2016.

45. Brown interview, August 2016.

46. Nkruhma qtd. in Godfrey Mwakikagile, *The People of Ghana: Ethnic Diversity and National Unity* (Dar es Salaam, Tanzania: New Africa, 2017), 14.

From Warm-up to
Dobale in Philadelphia

Embodying "Community" Meaning
in a West African Dance Class

Julie B. Johnson

My knees are bent. My torso is pitched forward with my chest almost parallel to the floor. A rhythmic pulse is riding up my spine like a wave. I shift my weight side to side with a slight shuffle step from right foot to left. I dip my head and, as each foot returns from its shuffle, I thrust my hips back. My arms push out over each step, as if shooing away some invisible nuisance. The air is thick; I feel immersed in the musty dampness collectively created by the moving bodies in the room. Our effort generates heat that opens my pores, I feel the sweat beading on the surface of my skin. Effort in this moment doesn't feel like hard work. Instead, I am swimming in a sensation of aliveness. In my periphery, I see classmates dipping their heads, pushing their arms, riding the same wave. The dim floodlights cast a golden hue around this old dance space. Splashes of bright colors and patterns enter my view as I turn my head and see all the lapas, the wrap skirts we usually wear to this West African dance class, tied around the waists of the women bobbing along with me. Syncopated movement of colors—greens, golds, pinks, deep indigos, and corals—offer visual layers of rhythm driving our dance. Dancers of various shapes, sizes, ages, and skin tones fill the space, uniquely riding the same rhythmic wave.

The instructor tells us that this dance, "n'gri," is meant to evoke the feeling and image of a jumping gazelle. I hear the "break" in the music that gives us the cue to change to the next step. I lift my torso slightly; my spine continues to undulate as my shuffling feet propel me further side to side. My hands are now held against the small of my back. I see the drummers in front of me, their arm and chest muscles contracting with each strike and release. Their heads tilt back, sideways, or forward, as if in response to some secret surge of energy emitted from their drums that only they can comprehend. They play the break again. My shuffle instantly changes to a lift of the knee with each step. I spiral my torso alternately right and left, opening my chest and arms wide. "Ay!!!" the instructor yells out, providing guidance and encouragement through one powerful intonation. The rhythmic pulse is constant; it now feels less like a wave and more like explosive bursts launching me upward. I am jumping! I feel the wooden floor under my bare feet, the grooves between the slats rub against the skin on the balls of my feet upon takeoff and landing. Every push off the floor releases pent up energy and somehow recharges me. I feel a synchrony with the dancers, our bodies create new rhythms to add to the already intricate percussive pattern that fills the air . . .

This moment, documented in a reflective journal entry, still so vivid, lives in my body such that I can conjure it at any moment. It reflects a phenomenon that I have experienced time and time again—the feeling that through the practice of dance, I have become part of (or created with others) something larger and deeper than the dance movement, something that I identify as "community." I perceive an intrinsic relationship between dance and community, and my participation in this West African dance class in West Philadelphia, which I first attended in the fall of 2012, has made this even more evident.

"Community" is a multivalent concept, subject to a plurality of contexts and constructs that can alter and shift its meaning. As a dance artist, I have encountered myriad understandings and manifestations of community through dance practice. This particular West African dance class, designated as a "community-based" class by the instructor, provides a rich opportunity to excavate community as a concept and a practice. Not intending to fix a universal definition, examining this class brings to light a collection of understandings and experiences that can illuminate the ways in which community operates in a particular dance setting—our shared and divergent experiences and the ways these inform us individually and as a collective.

The class, one of several offered throughout the city, is an intergenerational class attended by a diverse demographic of participants (race/ethnicity, gender, profession, class, age, ability, and so on) with an array of motivations and goals for participating in class (as made evident through conversations and interviews). All are welcome to attend, regardless of previous experience or skill level.

I refer to the class as West African dance to acknowledge that the majority of the material taught in class is associated with countries, ethnic groups, and cultural practices of West Africa. While some dance classes in the United States take the name of one particular form (like *sabar* dance, a genre of social dances from Senegal, for example) focusing on one specific dance style or technique, this particular class in West Philadelphia covers a wide range of dances and rhythms. The label "West African dance," in this sense, is not intended to diminish, homogenize, or overlook the rich diversity of dance forms that have emerged (and continue to emerge) from the region but rather to acknowledge the vast repertory of work addressed in the class.

Philadelphia has a long and rich history of African Diaspora movement arts, a realm of practice that includes West African dance, Cuban and Brazilian *Orisha* dances, *capoeira*, *hip-hop* body moves, fraternity *stepping*, *modern dance*, and more.[1] This particular West African dance class is offered on Monday nights; therefore, many of us simply refer to it as "the Monday night class." It is held at the Community Education Center (CEC) in West Philadelphia, a nonprofit arts incubator for a diverse range of artistic practices, established in 1973. This class builds on a lineage of West African dance classes, workshops, and rehearsals for performing groups housed in this particular space, stemming from 1989.

For many who have participated in the Monday night class, this simple moniker alludes to something much more than the time designation. Our experiences work to affirm, create, manifest, or contest our individual and collective understandings of "community," a term that often emerges when participants discuss the class, as in, "it is community-oriented," "it is about community," or "I feel community there." Ethnomusicologist John Miller Chernoff explains: "In the African context, performance in music and dance responds ultimately to a single aesthetic concern, the realization of community."[2]

Here, I offer a glimpse of collective experiences by profiling the five main components that make up the Monday night class: the warm-up, the lesson, dancing down the floor, the circle, and the concluding ritual of honoring the musicians, known by some as *dobale*. Throughout, I illuminate some of the ways in which lived experiences and understandings of community operate, particularly with regard to utopian notions of working together to achieve a common ideal.[3] This collectively constructed ideal is centered on shared practice, family, support, and musician/dancer reciprocity. At the surface, these attributes may not always account for the political dynamics, power differentials, and tensions of identity and belonging that are integral to the construct of "community."[4] It remains, though, that while the imagining of the ideal does not necessarily actualize utopia, it inspires actions toward its potential. These "inspired actions"—striving together toward an ideal—undergird the "community" dialogue that is the focus of this chapter.

As a member of this particular West African dance class, I situate my own experiences within that of the collective, migrating inward and outward between personal reflection and poetic narratives (set in italics) that further illuminate our sensory engagement and our "shapes of intersubjectivity," the ways in which our individual perspectives and experiences intersect, entangle, or depart.[5] Throughout, I weave theoretical discourse around sociocultural and historical contexts of African dance, particularly of West African dance practice as it has developed in the United States. As such, this investigation lies at the intersection of subjective, intersubjective, and cultural knowledge.

The instructor, Cachet Ivey, has designated the class as "open" or "mixed level," geared toward intermediate/advanced adult dancers, though anyone is welcome to attend. Cachet is a Philadelphia-based dance artist, choreographer, and educator focusing on dances of West Africa and Yoruba-based Orisha dances. She is also a performer and choreographer with Kulu Mele African Dance and Drum Ensemble, one of Philadelphia's longest-running dance companies, founded in 1969 by Baba Robert Crowder. Participants in Cachet's class include dance students and musical accompanists, from the very young to the elderly, whose attendance ranges from regular to sporadic. Regardless of the inconsistency in each participants' attendance pattern, the class has a strong following and rarely has fewer than fifteen to twenty dancers and musicians in attendance (and often upwards of thirty). With the exception of some holidays, the class runs weekly all year long and is one of the most well-attended ongoing African dance classes in the city.

Though there are participants who have been consistently involved in the class for many years, the demographic makeup is difficult to discern, complicated by the unpredictable flow of participation and attendance. To generalize, the population includes men, most of whom play percussion for the class, and women, most of whom dance. While I do not know how every participant self-identifies in terms of race and/or ethnicity, the class primarily consists of people of color, along with several nonblack people of color and white participants in attendance on a regular basis. Among the participants, I also include the random visitors and invited guests who often observe the class. "Visitor/spectator" and "participant" categorizations are porous, since it is not uncommon for visitors to spontaneously join in, and for active participants to stop and observe.

Within the structure of the class, from the warm-up to dobale, there are multiple access points for engagement. Whether through physical and/or technical rigor, creative immersion, stress relief, camaraderie, or all (or none) of the above, dancers and musicians who choose to continuously participate in the Monday night class have identified ways to connect that are meaningful to them. Likewise, there are barriers to engagement; some folks who have come to class choose to not continue. While these perspectives are also important to understanding community, here I focus on intentional participation. Investigating the nature of our individual and collective experiences in class illuminates the ways in which our particular understandings of community operate within the class. The research demonstrates a collective mode of embodied engagement with the Monday night class that includes sensory, social, and cultural interaction—the attention to our bodies, our space, and each other.[6]

The Warm-Up: Moving into Shared Practice

I sit on the wooden floor, moving through some gentle stretches while waiting for class to begin. A few women enter the studio, take off their shoes, and wrap their lapas around their waists. Through the windows I can barely see the Center City skyline behind the recently erected Drexel University buildings, looming manifestations of a rapidly changing cityscape. Cachet begins the warm-up with head and shoulder isolations. As I turn my head from side to side, I let my eyes scan the room. I see a couple of men, musicians who have just arrived, setting up their drums. More women enter the room, not in any particular hurry, though the class has already begun. They put their belongings down, put on their lapas, and join in. I see young children, perhaps as young as four or five, orbiting their mother like little planets as she rotates her shoulders and ribcage, they pause their orbit occasionally to join in the movement of the warm-up.

Jogging around the perimeter of the studio, I feel the sweat running down my face as Cachet commands, "Knees up!! Knees up!!" I lift my knees higher, trying to remember to breathe. At this

*point, many more students have joined in the class, as well as a
few more musicians. We jog back to the center of the room, reach
to the ceiling taking a deep inhalation. On the exhale, we drop
our heads, roll downward through our spines, reaching toward our
toes, then slowly roll back up to a standing position as the music
ends. I take a few gulps of water and I'm ready for more.*

The warm-up gets our bodies physically ready for rigorous movement. It
shifts our consciousness from the concerns of our daily grind to the task of
taking in the music and movement over the next hour and a half. Moving
in unison, following Cachet's sequence of exercises and stretches, gets us
acclimated to the rhythms, to each other, and to the space.

When I enter the CEC and join the warm-up, hear the *dunduns* and *djem-
bes* (drums) reverberate around me, and see my fellow classmates moving
through the space, I feel a local/global and micro/macro connection in my
body. The CEC is a physical space with a deep history of social interaction through artistic pursuits. This history is embedded in every nook and
cranny; its presence is uttered in each creak and groan of the wood. In this
space, on this particular day and time each week, my fellow classmates and I
gather together, driven by a commitment to West African dance practice. This
practice in Philadelphia is rooted in dance and music that has been retained
through the transatlantic slave trade and passed on through generations; it
was adapted through social interaction and encounters in its new environment. It is tacitly understood through epic memory and invented and re-
created daily through lived experiences. It is a practice that is continuously
supported and re/learned through travel and the availability of technology,
such as social media and YouTube.[7]

African and African American dance pioneers promulgated West African
dance in the United States, and specifically in Philadelphia. The emergence
of national ballets throughout Africa in the 1950s and 1960s, particularly
those of Guinea and Senegal, helped promote West African dance around the
world. These companies toured internationally with the aim of repairing the
damage of colonial views of Africa, dispelling negative stereotypes of African
culture, and promoting positive images.[8] As the Black Power and Black Arts
Movements of the 1960s and 1970s developed in the United States, they, too,
helped establish West African dance practice as a means of cultural empowerment. These, in conjunction with the dedicated Philadelphia artists working
prior to, during, and after these social justice movements, have helped shape
the current field of Philadelphia-based West African dance into a "powerful
validation of the imaginations, visions, sacrifices, and labors of countless local

people, going back sixty years," as documented in the Philadelphia Folklore Project.[9]

This history of collectivity upon which the Monday night class is built helps me to understand the class as what folklorists Paul Jordan-Smith and Laurel Horton call a "community of practice" based on "shared enjoyment and participation in traditional music and/or dance" in which participants "self-consciously construct themselves as 'community.'"[10] Our shared practice promotes the feeling of interconnection within a "whole" or through individual participation in a collective entity.

While shared practice alone does not necessarily engender friendships or social networks outside of the studio or guarantee that participants will feel an affinity for one another, it does serve as a point of interpersonal connection within, or extending from, the dance space. Communities of practice "develop a stable network of interpersonal relationships and a common body of semantically important resources for producing meaning."[11] Dancing communities are composed of what performance theorist Judith Hamera calls "interpersonal micro-practices" that construct and organize relationships, open communication, and produce opportunities for interaction and social formation within and beyond the dance space.[12]

In this sense, shared practice foregrounds an understanding of community that requires relationships as its core, rather than a single activity. It needs the interchange of attitudes and/or feelings toward self and between members, a concern for the well-being of the whole. In the Monday night class, this begins as soon as Cachet enters the space and begins the warm-up, and it continues throughout and beyond the class's spatial and temporal location at the CEC.

The Lesson: Empathic Connection through Experience and Culture

Power! Power! Power!
My power stance way down low,
grounded with feet far apart and thighs parallel to the floor.
Pelvis east, torso north. I could go anywhere from here.
Polyrhythmic arms thrash amid the constant pulse of ribs and
*   shoulders.*
Hips stir the air, dust particles whip in a twirling frenzy.
Rapid-fire foot stomps like a drum roll, open palms toward the
*   drummers as their palms strike the skin.*

My own skin dances atop muscle and bone, another layer of rhythm.
Dancers' feet depart from the ground inducing a moment of
airborne togetherness.
I am infected. . . . addicted before my feet even return to the
   floor.

I wrote this poem almost immediately after I took my first Monday night class in 2012. As I read it, I can sense it all again—what I saw, heard, touched, how I moved, what I *felt*. In the Monday night class we learn a particular dance, hailing from a specific region or ethnic group in West Africa and associated with a particular musical rhythm(s). Cachet demonstrates the technique of each movement and discusses the various historical, geographical, and cultural contexts of the dances, including the name of the dance, its region and/or community of origin and the dance's purpose (a male or female initiation ceremony, for example). Her conversations around these components are often centered on the genealogical complexity of music and movement within the African Diaspora, the implications of colonization, cultural exchange and appropriation, and the variation between dances performed in social/community settings and concert stage settings. Contextual information about the dance is offered to us throughout the series of weeks that the dance is taught. This knowledge not only connects us to African and African Diaspora cultures, it deepens the connection among participants in the class.

Our embodied movement experiences serve as an empathic tool—a means to relate to and reflect on the movement experiences of those who came before us and those dancing alongside us on the dance floor. I cannot truly *know* the experiences of others, but when I, for example, talk to classmates about *n'gri,* a dance associated with the image of a gazelle, I can find connections to my own experiences while dancing it in class. I can recall how the movement began low to the floor with our torsos pitched forward, and how the rhythm evoked a wavelike head bob and undulation of my spine. The movement gradually progressed into an explosive jumping step and I recall seeing my classmates' bodies propelled vertically into the air. I can remember how my feet felt against the floor as I pushed off to jump, how the sweat poured from my skin, how our unified undulations to the rhythm made me feel part of a collective—how I felt happy and fulfilled in that moment.

These experiences open up opportunities to find connections; embodied participation makes possible the ability to ask questions and generate dialogue based on having danced this dance. In turn, sharing our experiences with each other allows us to recall, reflect, and re-imagine the moments—and re-create the meanings we associate with them. Our experiences are not merely juxtaposed but intertwined, overlapping, and co-relational. Together, we engage in West African dance as a cultural and artistic practice that provides the material for participation in the Monday night class.

Down the Floor: Music, Dance, and Family

We're going down the floor . . .
riding our rhythms to the other end of the room . . . where they are.
Though their sounds fill every inch of this space, their bodies at first
*   seem a mile away.*
My feet hit the floor in an alternating down-to-the-ground triplet
*   step.*
Shoulders propel forward, shimmy and shake . . . arms extend out as
*   if to clear the way ahead.*
I am traveling forward, getting closer to them.
Torso pitched forward, knees bent. Fleshy reverberations signal con-
*   tact between soles and wooden floor.*
Halfway across the room now.
The women before me have had their fleeting encounters and have
*   since dispersed . . . did they look, I wonder?*
Only a few bodies occupy the space between me and the end of the
*   line where I will have to decide.*
The intricate layers of slaps and tones intensify as I draw near.
I can feel their eyes on me now.
I see my feet zigzagging . . . driving me onward.
I see a whir of hands moving too fast to match the sounds they create.
I see pulses of contracting muscles and beads of sweat.
I can see blurred faces that might become clear if only I would just
*   look.*
Close enough to touch . . . I cannot meet their eyes.

Once we have learned a movement sequence in the lesson, we then take it "down the floor" executing specific steps of the dance while traveling linearly from one end of the room to the other in rows of two or three. Always progressing toward the musicians, we travel closer and closer until dancers and musicians are eventually face-to-face. Some classmates have mentioned an awareness of the musicians' gaze but suggest the possibility that it may be imagined, or it may be a "soft gaze" in which they are looking at the dance as an object rather than at the dancer as an individual.

Reflecting on Sondra Fraleigh's assertion that the dance cannot be separated from the dancer, I have asked musicians about their perspectives on this dancer/musician encounter.[13] Several conversations from the Monday night class centered on the concept of dancers as the visual aesthetic and drummers as the aural aesthetic. An inherent exchange occurs when drummers watch dancers and dancers listen to drummers. Both musicians and dancers have expressed the reciprocal and intrinsically linked nature of music and movement and its impact on their experience. One musician suggested that at the heart of the awkwardness in the meeting of the gaze is a fear of the intense intimacy within the shared sensorial relationship. Social anthropologist Franca Tamisari uses the term "intercorporeality," in which "the performer, and with her, the spectators enter into an empathic space where the other person is encountered at a deeper level of intensity" than what is routine or ordinary.[14]

The understanding that dance and music are inseparable in African-derived dance practice is widely accepted in Africanist scholarship.[15] This has been referred to by several participants, particularly musicians, as a "marriage." Embedded in this marriage is a dialogue. For example, with a drum "break" or signaling pattern, the drummer communicates to the dancer when to start the specific movement pattern, when to transition to a new phrase, when and how to change tempo or rhythm, and when to stop. The dancer responds to the musical cues, and, in turn, the musicians can reflect or respond to what they are seeing in the dancing body. The interaction between musician and dancer can be a sort of mirroring or a call-and-response dialogue.[16]

My classmates and I have experienced an embodied/internalization of this dialogue, describing the ways in which we *feel* the music somatically and energetically. Our own bodies signal to us, for example, if the music is "off" (in other words, the musicians haven't yet found their groove together); it can hurt physically. The marriage is then on the rocks. Or, when the music is "fire," a togetherness creates a heightened collective energy and euphoric feeling in the body. This connection of inner/outer experience suggests a blurring of the boundary between dancer and musician, between self and other.[17] This process is reciprocal; the level and character of the dancers' energy affect how musicians play. Likewise, musicians can influence the dancing with their own energy.

Dancing down the floor provides opportunities to utilize this reciprocal relationship and to contribute to the well-being of the class. This includes communal connections, such as keeping up with our line partners, being aware if someone is ahead, falling behind or struggling with the movement, and then responding accordingly. Reciprocity is exhibited among classmates while waiting on the sidelines for our turn to dance; we clap, shout, and smile to motivate and encourage others dancing down the floor; touching the floor or kneeling near a dancer or musician who is really "in the zone" or joining in the movement of someone who is struggling to get down the floor are mutually felt expressions.

This collective show of support, physically and/or in attitude or spirit, all require individual contribution and effort toward being together. Our labor, through dance and music, is given; it is "worked" on the floor. We give what we have and work together every Monday night, bound together, however briefly, through shared practice. It seems, then, not so alien to work for each other outside of this space. Or we seek to expand this space, to continue to experience what we feel on the dance floor. We are able to extend the temporal bonds experienced within class to moments off the floor.[18] We attend performances, parties, and educational or political events together. We come to each other's aid with financial support, advice, or volunteer labor when needed. We support each other's careers and business ventures.

We extend these bonds through expressions of "family," such as our use of familial titles in the class ("Sister," "Brother," "Mama," and "Baba," for example), an established cultural practice within West African dance and music in the United States.[19] We sit and eat family-style at the table on the first floor of the CEC to celebrate special occasions. We care for participants' children in the class. When I hear a fellow participant say, "Goodnight, dance family!" after class, I feel a part of this constructed family, and I carry that feeling with me outside of the dance space. African diasporic experience and wisdom are embodied in music and dance practices that have been used by Africans in the Americas to "save and protect their individual spirits, their dignity as humans, and their sense of a cosmic family."[20]

The Circle: Manifesting the "Whole"

After dancing down the floor, we sometimes gather in a circle. Known as a *Bantaba* circle,[21] this spatial formation is typically reserved for acknowledging a community member's achievement or milestone—a birthday, a new job, a graduation—or to pay homage to ancestors. Standing body to body around the circle's edge we can see and interact with each other, providing encouragement and affirmation, as folks enter the circle to improvise, either alone or in groups. The thought of entering the circle and being completely exposed to the gaze of the collective can induce great anxiety for some. For others, it can be perceived as a cathartic shedding of inhibition or release of emotion;

Improvisation

Elation   Energy

Release   Anxiety

Milestones   Homage

Hesitance   Protection

Witnessing   Motivation

Ancestors   Affirmation

Experience   Uncertainty

Acceptance   Wholeness

Exposure   Spirituality

Judgement   Gratitude

Lifecycle   Power

Conversation

an opportunity to exchange energy with fellow classmates or convene with ancestors; or a chance to further develop skills through improvisation. The circle, for these reasons (among others), provides opportunities to deepen our engagement with each other and understand ourselves as a "whole."

The circle in African Diaspora dance in the United States is rooted in the *ring shout*, a sacred dance created on plantations by enslaved Africans.[22] It retained and conjured elements of African ancestral ceremony and was a means of forming a "cultural oneness," which suggests a "certain wholeness that encouraged the spirit of community."[23] Our circle in the Monday night class makes the collective (and our role within it) visible. The relationship between individuality and collectivity, or the role of individuals toward creating and supporting community, is an important element of African dance and music aesthetics—everyone plays a part.[24]

Dance as a celebration of life is a circular element of African Diaspora cultural and artistic expression. It is a medium between life and death, rooted in African cosmology that understands humanity as existing in four stages: youth, adult, elder, and ancestor/deceased.[25] Each stage plays a role in community life. Ancestors, though no longer physically present on earth, guide us and pass along wisdom, and so we honor them and show our gratitude in a multitude of ways, including music and dance in the Bantaba circle. In doing so, we are affirming our personal relationships with our ancestors and with each other.

Dobale: Practicing Gratitude

Learning kassa, *a* Malinke *dance from Guinea connecting rhythm and movement to the labor of harvest . . . Cachet reflects, "Support the people that you want to harvest for you." I contemplate how I/we can encourage and support laborers and leaders doing the hard work that benefits us all. I wonder how I can share the load, remembering how my dad would sing, "we mow the hay, and we rake the hay, and we carry it away together." I feel thankful for the dancers, musicians, teachers, friends, and family who inspire, challenge, and motivate me.*

I wrote this reflective journal entry in December 2014 after first learning *kassa* and listening to Cachet describe how this rhythm and movement work to unite members of a community. She explained that everyone has a role in the harvest; whether collecting crops or supporting and encouraging the farmers by accompanying their labor with music and dance. Each role contributes to the collective effort to sustain a community. She alluded that this effort can also include those working to serve their community in the midst of systemic injustices. At the time of this conversation, protests were springing up throughout the country, centered on the killings of unarmed black people by police. Just as there are a multitude of ways community members can support the harvest, there are a multitude of roles in resisting oppression. Whether we choose to put our bodies on the line by blocking traffic in the street or we engage in efforts to decolonize education, whether we document state and street violence or create art, whether we uphold and build upon cultural practices or facilitate critical dialogue, whether we create safe spaces for communities to gather or participate in the political process, there are individual entry points to working toward the whole. And we can acknowledge and support the ways in which everyone does the work. This, I believe, is at the heart of the ritual of dobale.

Before leaving the dance floor, we honor the musicians, either symbolically with a gesture (which might include lowering down, placing the hand to the heart, then to the floor near the feet of each drummer) or monetarily (with a donation of a few dollars, if we are able), or both. Some participants offer the same gesture to Cachet or give her a hug before leaving and say "thank you." This is referred to by some as dobale, a Yoruba term for "gesture of respect."

More than a gesture, dobale is a form of spiritual exchange between dancer and drummer. It is the dancer's acknowledgement of the musicians' work, their skills, and their humanity. On and off the dance floor, musicians and dancers work to contribute their individual effort, skill, and energy toward that of the "whole."[26] We participate in the rituals of this weekly encounter from the warm-up through to dobale, and this ongoing participation and personal investment in the rituals—the mechanics of the class—are generative of communal meaning making.[27] The particulars of these rituals are all determined by whomever attends on a given day. The experience of every Monday night class is shaped by intersubjectivity, grounded in practice, to create a collective embodiment of the "whole." Off the floor, group interactions are microcosms of the whole, reflecting through social behaviors that which has manifested in the dance, and vice versa.[28]

Elements of "Community" Meaning

The collective embodiment, which is achieved through engagement in the Monday night class, creates opportunities for experiencing shared somatic states. Through these, we learn about ourselves, each other, and the world.[29] Expressions of community centered on shared dance and music practices stem from sense perception and bodily knowing—our individual embodiment informs and is informed by the collective. When we engage in the practices of the Monday night class, we are forging a path in an ever-changing urban landscape that has, at its roots, the rich cultural traditions established by pioneers of West African dance and music in Philadelphia. Outside of Monday night class, African cultural traditions have been, and continue to be, marginalized. When we affirm these practices, we are also affirming ourselves, individually and collectively, regardless of how we self-identify. Through cultural/artistic practices, we galvanize our human rights to survive and thrive (as one elder *mama* in the Monday night class says).

Through examining the collective experiences in the Monday night class, I have found community as a multivalent concept, much like the Bantaba circle. It can be improvisational; it can shift and change; it can be a mode to process information, to affirm and celebrate, or to work through tension and discomfort. Individuals can enter the class or the circle, contributing a unique self-ness, while participating in collectivity. The actual process can feel isolating, exposing, and anxiety inducing; however, in the Monday night class, the Bantaba circle is a place where we strive to support and lift each other up. Still, for some of us it is a place to work through our fears in order to be able to dance in the center, alone or with others.

Considering this complex duality of harmony and conflict, I am reminded of anthropologist Kate Crehan's assertion that romantic notions of community are commonplace yet ill-defined.[30] Vacuous community narratives in which tensions or conflicts go unexamined can be divisive, laden with false assumptions about the social realities that constitute the communities at the center of said narratives. Alternatively, community conversations can shift hegemonic assumptions, make space for marginalized voices, and challenge oppressive practices.[31] Reflecting on this, as well as on the aforementioned assertion that the manifestation of community is a central aesthetic concern of African dance, I believe the consideration of community experiences and understandings within African Diaspora dance practices can illuminate how these operate within given dance settings. This, in turn, may point to ways in which community potential might be fulfilled.

In the Philadelphia Monday night class, our collage of meanings and experiences has affirmed and enlivened my passion for community inquiry. It has confirmed the infinite and inexhaustible depth of the notion of community; there is a deep well of knowledge and experiences to be tapped. I am inspired by the work of Philadelphia-based artists who have cultivated and sustained African Diaspora practices, and I am thankful for the space to continue exploring community through embodied practice and generative conversations with fellow classmates in the Monday night class. This is often on my mind at the end of class as I join in our collective *dobale* gesture. Sweat-soaked, exhausted, yet totally fulfilled by the dance, the music, and my classmates, I touch my hands to my heart, to the floor, and back to my heart.

Notes

1. Benita B. Brown-Danquah, "African Diaspora Movement Arts in Philadelphia: A Beginning Resource List," *Philadelphia Folklore Project Working Papers* (1994), 1–41.

2. John M. Chernoff, *African Rhythm and African Sensibility: Aesthetics and Social Action in African Musical Idioms* (Chicago: University of Chicago Press, 1981), 149–50.

3. Jill Dolan, "Utopia, and the 'Utopian Performative,'" *Theatre Journal* 53, no. 3 (2001): 455–79.

4. Audre Lorde, *Sister Outsider: Essays and Speeches by Audre Lorde* (Berkeley: Crossing, 1984), 112.

5. Corrine Glesne, "That Rare Feeling: Re-presenting Research through Poetic Transcription," *Qualitative Inquiry* 3, no. 2 (1997): 204.

6. Deidre Sklar, *Dancing with the Virgin: Body and Faith in the Fiesta of Tortugas, New Mexico* (Berkeley: University of California Press, 2001), 100.

7. Giovanna Washington, *Performing Africa: Memory, Tradition, and Resistance in the Leimert Park Drum Circle* (PhD diss., University of California, Los Angeles, 2008), 71–82.

8. Francesca Castaldi, *Choreographies of African Identities: Négritude, Dance, and the National Ballet of Senegal* (Chicago: University of Illinois Press, 2006), 49–52;

Sarah Sandri, *Performance, Politics, and Identity in African Dance Communities in the United States* (PhD diss., Eugene: University of Oregon, 2012), 42–45.

9. Philadelphia Folklore Project, "Honoring Ancestors: Notes from an Exhibition," *Works in Progress*, 26 (Summer 2014): 1–2, 4–7, 23–25.

10. Paul Jordan-Smith and Laurel Horton, "Communities of Practice: Traditional Music and Dance," *Western Folklore* 60, no. 2–3 (2001): 103–9.

11. Ibid., 105.

12. Judith Hamera, *Dancing Communities: Performance, Difference, and Connection in the Global City* (New York: Palgrave Macmillan, 2011): 17.

13. Sondra Fraleigh, *Dance and the Lived Body: A Descriptive Aesthetics* (Pittsburgh: University of Pittsburgh Press, 1996), 22–42.

14. Francesca Tamisari, "The Responsibility of Performance: The Interweaving of Politics and Aesthetics in Intercultural Contexts," *Visual Anthropology Review* 21, nos. 1–2 (2005): 49.

15. Castaldi, *Choreographies of African Identities*, 6; Robert Farris Thompson, "An Aesthetic of the Cool: West African Dance," in *Signifyin(g), Sanctifyin' and Slam Dunking: A Reader in African American Expressive Culture*, ed. Gena Caponi (Amherst: University of Massachusetts Press, 1999), 72–86.

16. Thompson, "Aesthetic of the Cool," 72–86.

17. Rebecca Norris, "Embodiment and Community," *Western Folklore* 60, nos. 2–3 (2001): 111–24.

18. Anita Gonzalez, "Urban Bush Women: Finding *Shelter* in the Utopian Ensemble," *Modern Drama* 47, no. 2 (2004): 249–68.

19. Patricia H. Collins, *Black Feminist Thought: Knowledge, Consciousness, and the Politics of Empowerment* (New York: Routledge, 2000), 59; Efia N. Dalili, *"More than a Sisterhood": Traditional West African Dance in a Contemporary Urban Setting* (PhD diss., Philadelphia: University of Pennsylvania, 1999), 207; Yvonne Daniel, *Dancing Wisdom: Embodied Knowledge in Haitian Vodou, Cuban Yoruba, and Bahian Candomblé* (Urbana: University of Illinois Press, 2005), 64.

20. Daniel, *Dancing Wisdom*, 64.

21. *Bantaba* is a Malinke-derived word that refers to social gatherings or communal meeting places. The colloquial translation among West African dance communities in the United States is "dancing ground," perpetuated by renowned elders such as former choreographer and director of DanceAfrica, Baba Chuck Davis, and dance scholar/choreographer Kariamu Welsh.

22. Lynne F. Emery, *Black Dance: From 1619 to Today* (Princeton, N.J.: Princeton Book, 1989), 62, 120–26; P. Sterling Stuckey, "Christian Conversion, and the Challenge of Dance," *Dancing Many Drums: Excavations in African American Dance*, ed. Thomas F. DeFrantz (Madison: University of Wisconsin Press, 2002), 39–58.

23. Stuckey, "Christian Conversion," 44.

24. Chernoff, *African Rhythm*, 149–50; Thompson, "An Aesthetic of the Cool," 72–86.

25. Tracy Snipe, "African Dance: Bridges to Humanity" in *African Dance: An Artistic, Historical and Philosophical Inquiry*, ed. Kariamu Welsh Asante (Trenton: Africa World, 1994), 63.

26. Chernoff, *African Rhythm*, 149–50; Thompson, "An Aesthetic of the Cool," 72–86.

27. Karen Bond, "The Human Nature of Dance: Toward a Theory of Aesthetic Community," *Communicative Musicality: Exploring the Basis of Human Companionship*, ed. Stephen Malloch (Oxford: Oxford University Press, 2008), 401–22.

28. Dorothea Hast, "Performance, Transformation, and Community: Contra Dance in New England," *Dance Research Journal* 25, no.1 (1993): 21–32.

29. Norris, "Embodiment and Community," 111–24.

30. Kate Crehan, *Community Art: An Anthropological Perspective* (New York: Berg, 2011), 38–40.

31. Crehan, *Community Art*, 38–40.

PART II

The Elders' Work and Words

Ago! Ame!

Baba Chuck Speaks!

Charles "Chuck" Davis
with C. Kemal Nance

During one of our weekly Thursday morning conversations, I mentioned to Mama Kariamu that I had intended to spend some time in Durham in order to conduct interviews, hopefully for a book project.[1] She and I have an ongoing dialogue about my research interests in examining African American men's lived experiences in studying and performing the dances of Africa. I told her that I had intended to interview Chuck Davis not only to explore some of his thoughts about gender performativity in dances of Africa but also to generate a contact list of dancing black men who have danced with him over the years—men who could potentially serve as subjects for my study. In her soft, melodic voice, she replied, "That's good, Sweetheart! You know? There are some questions that we, Esailama and I, have about Baba's work for this book we're working on. I'll email them to you. Maybe you can get his responses when you talk to him." I replied, "Okay, *Amai!*[2] I will probably head down to Durham around the 4th. I want to see AADE[3] at the Eno River Festival. I love Eno!" A few days later, I received a battery of interview questions and immediately incorporated them into the script for my conversation with Chuck Davis.

It was a hot, humid day in July when I arrived in Durham. I traveled after the "Fourth" so that I could secure more seasonable hotel rates. Prior to my arrival, I had heard rumors from various dancers and musicians from around the country that Baba Chuck had been having some health challenges. I had suspected that something was awry because his response time to my phone calls over the past few months had gotten significantly longer than the one to two days to which I was accustomed. While Chuck Davis and I had agreed on a specific time for our interview, I thought it would be nice to pay him an impromptu social visit before we commenced with our academic business. I just wanted to give him a hug and say "Hey!" before I checked in at my hotel.

I rang the doorbell. He opened the first door. With his shoulders hung forward, he shuffled his way to the main door of the building. He greeted me with his usual grin that seemed to stretch the length of the universe and welcomed me in. He explained that he just had "some work done" at the hospital and was a bit tired and cold. "Kemal, I just can't get warm. I think I need some soup." As sweat poured from my forehead from what I felt was the unbearable heat of his apartment, I replied, "Okay Baba, I'll get it. What kind you want?" As he sat on the bed with a blanket over his shoulder, he lifted his head and turned it slightly to the right to look at me and said, "Chicken noodle."

I quickly left his apartment and drove to the Whole Foods Market on Main street to retrieve the biggest container of chicken noodle soup I could find. I raced back to his apartment and was met by Ivy Birch who, like me, had brought Baba Chuck chicken noodle soup. She opened the door with delight in her eyes, her classic blonde micro braids pulled in a ponytail and her smile that epitomizes Southern comfort. After Ivy and I exchanged our usual pleasantries, replete with firm hugs, chuckles, and child-like slaps on each other's shoulders, she quickly took the soup from my hands and poured it into a bowl. She gently placed it in Davis's hands and then walked the remaining soup to the back of the apartment in the kitchen and placed it in the refrigerator. Chuck Davis shivered as he slowly drank the soup. When Ivy returned to Davis's bedroom, with a uniquely Southern and motherly tone, she peppered him with questions: "How's that Baba? You got enough? Is it hot enough?" Davis just nodded and shivered. This moment felt like it should have been a private one. In my own awkwardness, I engaged Ivy in small talk and quickly took my leave under the guise of "allowing Baba to get his rest."

I left Baba's apartment with feelings of confusion. I was alarmed by seeing him so vulnerable and weak, yet concurrently I was optimistic, convinced that what I saw was not as bad as my gut suggested. I repeatedly told myself not to overact. "Everything was going to be all right." I checked in at the La Quinta hotel on Chapel Hill Road. Sporadically throughout the rest of the afternoon, I would call Baba Chuck's apartment to inquire about his health. Each time I called, I was greeted by a different voice. Each person who answered the phone during my attempts sounded as if he/she worked for the loan department in a bank. Each person sounded elated by the sound of my voice. Each person inquired about my location and state of being. Each person in his or her own way confirmed that Baba Chuck was indisposed and was not available to take any calls.

The following morning when my cell phone rang, I could feel my spirit lift as I realized that it was Baba Chuck calling me. I answered, "Hey Baba! How are you feeling?" In his usual ominous voice, the one that sounds like Mufasa from *The Lion King*, the one with which I am most familiar, he replied, "I feel much better today. I have a few meetings this afternoon so let's meet tomorrow morning for breakfast. You can come here and I can drive us to get food." I responded, "You got it! I'll see you then." Then, in a classic black grandfather tone, he closed the conversation with "Oh, kaybe!" and hung up.

The next morning, during another hot and humid day in Durham, we piled into his navy-blue minivan. He drove us to the IHOP, where we talked about dance, his company and my career. I was relieved because he seemed more like himself to me, like my Baba, with his multicolored pants, baseball cap, self-designed T-shirt, and pouch. Baba always has a bag. We talked and laughed the morning away as we ate pancakes, eggs, turkey sausage, toast. Finally, we drove back to his apartment and sat down in his kitchen to conduct the "official" interview. Like a nervous graduate student, I checked to ensure that each of my devices was functioning properly. He leaned back in the chair at his kitchen table, awaiting my readiness as he ran his hand over the scruffiness of his unshaven face. In the loud silence of his apartment, in what would become the last time I saw my Baba Chuck alive, we had the following conversation.

■ ■ ■

Baba Chuck Davis could arguably be called the "Father" of African Dance in the United States. He first danced with Babatunde Olatunji, BeBe Miller, and Eleo Pomare and then, in 1984, he returned to his home in Durham, North Carolina, and started the African American Dance Ensemble (AADE). Baba Chuck Davis was also the founder and artistic director until 2015 of DanceAfrica, a performance and teaching laboratory within the Brooklyn Academy of Music (BAM). At the time of his transition, Baba Davis served as artistic director emeritus of DanceAfrica, BAM; his company, the AADE, continues to the present day as a formidable dance institution for the performance and instruction of African Diaspora dance.

The following interview outlines Baba Davis's career as a choreographer and as a visionary in the practice of West African dance in the United States. Baba Davis's career spanned several decades and sociocultural contexts, making his insights into the longevity of West African dance forms, in the United

States particularly, instructive for students of both history and the arts, as well as for those interested in the behind-the-scenes dynamics that arise in most artistic endeavors. As a luminary in the expansion of West African dance traditions in the United States, Baba Chuck Davis became a national treasure. His words and perspective spoke, and continue to speak here, not only to the history of people of African descent in the Americas but also to the present state of heritage traditions relative to their contemporary circumstances.

Fortunately, as one of Baba Davis's esteemed "godsons" and also as a dance artist working for years in the vocabularies of West African dance, I am able to share some of the underpinnings of his legacy, here—in his own words. I interviewed him on July 13, 2016, in his Durham, North Carolina, home.

NANCE: So today is the thirteenth of July, Wednesday. I am in Durham, North Carolina, talking to Baba Chuck Davis, "Emperor" of the African Dances of America and the globe. [*Chuckles.*]

DAVIS: And give thanks.

NANCE: And give thanks. So Baba, as I explained to you over breakfast, there are a couple of questions that the editors of [this important collection on African Diaspora Dance in Perpetual Motion . . .] have about your work—that wrap up the contributions to the historical study. I may have a question or two about the research I'm doing. The questions are pretty straightforward, so I'll go ahead and get started.

So CDDC was around in the early '80s, late '70s. Right?

DAVIS: The Chuck Davis Dance Company started in 1968.

NANCE: That's right.

DAVIS: And then, as time moved on, we've been in residency for the American Dance Festival and at the end of the seventies and met dancers here.

NANCE: Here, meaning North Carolina?

DAVIS: Here meaning Durham, North Carolina, and at that time my parents were still with us and I said I wanted to be a little bit closer to them. So, I decided to start a second unit so it'd been the Chuck Davis Company 2. But when we got here, we figured it would be better to have our own 501(c) 3 et cetera; you know, all the business and the political stuff, and as a result the AADE was formed.

NANCE: And that was like in 1983 or 1984?

DAVIS: No, that was in 1979 when we first came together because I was at ADF [the American Dance Festival] and they were all students in the community—and Ava and then of course was Jimmy and Thad and Sherone—all were in college, North Carolina Central. And it was meant to be through the works of the good Lord.

NANCE: So the question then is how have you been able to sustain a company all of these years since 1968? How did you do it? I know that's a loaded question.

DAVIS: Right, blood, sweat, tears, gut, and sheer determination—because at that point, I wanted to be the only African-based dance company that had dancers and musicians on salary, year-round, with insurance benefits. And we had Pam Martin Green, who is now the manager for Ron Brown and others who worked getting grants—and through ADF projects because the AADE was responsible for ADF's huge grant to preserve the black traditions in dance and because of that then, that helped spread the name around. And then when people saw us and they saw the unbridled energy . . . I insisted on being beyond professional. That's the whole thing about time. You can ask anybody who works with me—about Baba Chuck and time. They will tell you when it comes to being in a theater, I believe in arriving two hours before, et cetera, et cetera. Others picked up on what I was trying to do. We were getting grants and good bookings, we had a nice booking agent and everything, and as we got into the nineties the funds began to creep away. You know, so I wasn't able to maintain; so then we went on naturally, paid per,[4] which is at the point where we are now. [. . .] And we aren't accepting huge concert grants 'cause we don't have the personnel. We have a core for "lec dems"[5] and small things, and I was pulled away because in order to eat and to maintain I was getting paid. So, I had to rely on my DanceAfrica and my teaching here and there, and choreographing over there, and things like that. So, that took a toll on the body, mind, soul, and spirit because I would look and see the works I was setting on other people. My piece, "And the Children Are Watching," that I set on Denver Dance Theater? It won award after award and it is fabulous. It's work I would like to set on ADF. Can't do it because number one, don't have the personnel to follow through and other works that are out there. So, to pick up and carry on the name, Abdel is doing [this] because he knows my technique.

NANCE: So, and I think you have told me this a thousand and one times that I can name, but I've never asked a question this way, and that is: What facilitated your move from New York to North Carolina? Like you had CDDC in New York and then you moved to North Carolina.

DAVIS: Right. That was it. We were in a residency. We were offered a residency with the ADF and then once I got here and met the young dancers who were eager, Sherone, Jimmy, and all of them, we would rehearse and have class until one and two in the morning.

NANCE: I remember you telling me that.

DAVIS: So, you see? That was what facilitated the move here, the fact that there was young talent ready to be tapped.

NANCE: And so did you find that there was any difficulty in reestablishing yourself in North Carolina since you had been away in New York for those years?

DAVIS: I used what I learned in New York; but don't forget, I wasn't limited because I was traveling back and forth in the beginning. I was traveling and would be here for a while and then I would travel back to CDDC [Chuck

Davis Dance Company] and I was still doing things with BAM and other places. And I am really fortunate because I think I am one of the few people that do not have a problem in saying, "I don't know. Let me learn. Teach me."

NANCE: What were some of the major challenges that you faced running a fully salaried company that toured every year?

DAVIS: Personnel was a major problem.

NANCE: What do you mean by personnel?

DAVIS: Personnel was because even though they were on salary, their salary was not that great. And there were these small things they would have to do on the side, which means rehearsals would be missed. So, you had to deal with that. Then, you had to learn how to deal with personalities. There were eight people in the core, but you had to learn to deal with forty personalities because each one of them had six different personalities. You see? Do you know the old adage, "Eyes open, ears open, mouth shut?" It took a long time to learn that because I'm quick you know and I'm volatile and I know it. So, I would know that, okay yeah, I had to learn to curtail and put the lid on.

NANCE: Well, I admit I've never experienced the volatile Chuck Davis, but I know he's there.

DAVIS: Oh, I have thrown chairs, books, record players. It used to get to the point where I would say something in this tone of voice and if you didn't move, somebody had better grab you because I would throw things. I was from the streets, so I would fight.

NANCE: So, was there ever a point in all these years when you were just like "I'm not running a company anymore; I'm just done with it."

DAVIS: Every morning.

NANCE: What's your Peter Principle? What sends you over the edge? What's the thing that makes you say to yourself, "I'm not dealing with this anymore?"

DAVIS: Well, I can't really say until it happens because it might be one thing today, and you just sort of brush it off, and then tomorrow, before you even get anywhere close to it, [it] is World War 6. So, it has to be right there, but one thing I can't tolerate—I go crazy—is lateness. [And] I cannot tolerate disrespect to the elders; I cannot.

NANCE: Have you seen any of that over the years, among the company?

DAVIS: As years have gone by, there have been several clashes. I mean several clashes. We've had to deal with some issues of a personal nature and some of a group nature. We were getting ready at the American Dance Festival, standing room only because it was the AADE, and I fired all of the musicians right there; we went out with hand clappers and one drum. Thank God for Khalid, because the musicians were out in the back—smoking pot. I said, "You ain't hitting my stage. Bye!" You see? Some said it was impulsive, but I didn't give a shit because, as I said, I don't want this anywhere near me— because the smell in your clothes and everything and we doing all this work with children. Oh no no no, you will not bring it around me!

NANCE: So what's the counterpositive? So what keeps you going? You've been doing this a long time. So what keeps you getting up at it every day?

DAVIS: Knowing that somewhere down the road, there will come a point like what has happened with DanceAfrica. I pass the baton over to Abdel. You see? As we go along, there will be moments like I'm getting ready to do *Porgy and Bess*. You see? It is going to be *Porgy and Bess* done with African Dance style. But [it has to be] worthwhile; but this, as you can see, . . . there's not that much I can do. But I have Courtney; I have Rochelle; and I have Ivan, who are there—who know my technique and . . . they stand just . . . like Marilyn Banks used to do. Marilyn Banks used to stand with her thumb in her mouth and just listen to what I wanted, and then two seconds later, she's twirling across the stage. She and Marshall Romaine. . . . You know? You look to that. (I am not going to cry.) That's the way I had looked at Stafford. You see? But, in hindsight, you look and you see that the best decision was made. The one he made was the best one—because now look at his career. It's just going and going and he's establishing Stafford Berry, like you're establishing C. Kemal Nance.

NANCE: I've got to start saying it the way you say it. Nunz.

DAVIS: [*Chuckles.*] And, it hurts for a minute? It hurts for a minute. But . . . the way I am? I don't want to put any shackles, any type of shackles on, to keep you from *your* destiny. You see? I want to be right there.

NANCE: What makes the Baba Chuck Davis get up and do it? You talked some about passing the baton; you talked about some love and loss in terms of people you've trained. But what makes you get up every day?

DAVIS: I've got to pay the rent. Shit!

NANCE: [*Chuckles.*] Okay! Well, that's practical enough.

DAVIS: Right? I need to work on these different projects because we aren't on salary to salary. Right? If you don't do a performance, you don't get paid; plus, that interferes with the rehearsals. You want to come to rehearsals, but you can't come to rehearsals because you got three kids and those kids got to have milk. You know? . . . and clothes and so forth and so on. And with me? Getting up just like I'm sitting here? I have to figure out the program that I'm going to do in November and looking ahead and trying to make sure that I've been out here for a minute. So I do try to have a good reputation. But, I have to make sure that I follow through on that reputation.

NANCE: So how do you want your legacy to be remembered?

DAVIS: He danced. If I put it this way, it says . . . Kemal, go in there and look over on that side of the—where the lamp is and on top there's a plaque. Just pick it up; it's carved out of wood and you can take a picture of that.

[NANCE *walks into* DAVIS'*s bedroom to retrieve a wooden plaque.*]

Now isn't that a beautiful piece?

NANCE: Yes, delicate too. So how do you feel about the decrease in funding from the state and federal levels for the arts and things?

DAVIS: Well . . . just like with everybody else, it hurts! I want to be sustained. Even with a small educational core, I want to be able to go into the schools and share *real* history of the dance and the music. I don't want to go in just doing routines. Right? If you're standing there and you have on a grand *bubu*. . . . What is a grand bubu? Why do you wear a *babush* with a grand bubu? What does this move mean? Where is it from—with that simple grand bubu hanging right there? That's ten sessions right there. You talk about the embroidery that brings it into modern day, but in the old days, they used to sit and have to do all that by hand. You have the symbols. What do they mean? There are some symbols that you can use that I can't. So, that's the type of thing I want to continue doing because many of these African teachers coming over here now come over with a set routine. They do all of these different conferences and it's the same combination at every conference. Marie Basse is the only one that really starts out with, "This is what you were doing; this is where it's from," et cetera, et cetera, et cetera. That's why I love her so much.

NANCE: You've done a lot; I mean you've done everything, Baba.

DAVIS: No, I ain't done nothing yet.

NANCE: Really.

DAVIS: I won't be satisfied until every one of these books . . . I'll be able to tell the name of the book and I quote it word for word.

NANCE: Do you think young people are prepared now to run companies?

DAVIS: No.

NANCE: [*Laughs.*] What do you think they lack, generally speaking?

DAVIS: Everything.

NANCE: Can you be a little bit more specific than "everything"? [*Laughs.*]

DAVIS: Because I am sitting here with you and sit with my Stafford because there's that quest—that almost unquenchable quest for wanting to know. No, y'all are just plain nosey.

NANCE: You're probably right. [*Laughs.*]

DAVIS: But most of them are missing because we still are suffering from the plague. We are suffering from the plague. At the point when those young ones should have had more guidance, they were thrown into leadership positions. So they had to learn by rote due to AIDS, due to an onset of many of the mental and physical diseases that took away the elders. There're not many Mama Kariamu's left. You see? Fortunately, Mama Kariamu was a wise woman and she . . . developed the technique, *Umfundalai*. . . . And then, there are young folks who are able to take it and develop their path. And as they are developing the path, then of course, thank God, she is still here. You can get on the phone and call and then because Mama Kariamu, being Mama Kariamu, two seconds after that curtain closes, she gone. [*Laughs.*] I have picked up on that. When we are finished, I'm ready to go! As we are finishing the concert, I am packing my bag. We were in D.C. doing DanceAfrica! By the time that curtain came down, my bag was packed and Ngoma [Ngoma Woolbright, long-time affiliate of AADE], out the back door; Norma out the side door; people coming to Norma so that I can slip around the side way and I'm gone. You see? That's all Mama Kariamu [*laughs*].

NANCE: [*Laughs.*] Yup! That's my Mama. That's how she rolls. She don't play. So, here is my last question, Baba. If you had to do it all over again, what would you do differently?

DAVIS: Nothing, not one blessed thing, Kemal, because I look upon everything that happens as a period for growth. If I cut that out, then we wouldn't be sitting here. Who knows what it would be, but it wouldn't be this. And there are ups; there are downs; and all of us—you, me, and everybody, "Oh! Let me hit the lotto so I can do this, do that and do the other!" If we were rich, we wouldn't be doing this. You see? If I were rich, I would be having this—but it wouldn't be here. It would be somewhere and there would be six black Nubians. All I would have to say is "Ready!" Then, they would come and pick me up and carry [me] everywhere I needed to go. [*Laughs.*] You hear statements like that on TV and what not, but one thing I would try to do is: I would try to find some way to buy one hundred yards of duct tape and duct tape Donald Trump's ass to a light pole or something. But seriously, there is good and there is bad.

Notes

1. Foreign but commonly understood phrases for certain dance communities appear in the title: *Ago! Ame!* These are call-and-response expressions in the Twi language of Ghana, West Africa. *Ago* means "Call to attention" or "Knock, knock." *Ame* is a response to the call or the knocking. The meaning of *Ago* has been extended to mean "I am asking for your attention" and *Ame* has evolved into "I am or we are listening" in African American Kwanzaa celebrations.

2. In the Umfundalai tradition of African dance, *Amai* is a term of endearment that only dancers who have reached a high level of virtuosity and maturity can employ. Umfundalai's progenitor or female dance master must grant her student permission to call her "*Amai.*" Doing so without permission is deemed disrespectful.

3. The African American Dance Ensemble, Chuck Davis's dance company.

4. "Paid per" is a term that members of Chuck Davis's AADE use to refer to company members who do not receive a full-time salary for dancing with the company. These members are not compensated for rehearsal, nor are they expected to travel with the company and dance in every concert during a given season. Rather, these dancers function more like apprentices and are "paid per" performance.

5. Lecture demonstrations.

The "Gospel" of Memory

Inscribed Bodies in the African Diaspora

Kariamu Welsh

Introduction—African Dance

Discussions about "traditional African dance" or "African dance" in general come from a variety of perspectives found in the records and logs of anthropologists, missionaries, early ships' captains, and explorers.[1] Anthropologists Hélène Neveu-Kringelbach and Jonathan Skinner state that "dance does not simply 'reflect' what happens in society or serve a particular 'function,' but that it is often central to social life [along with] . . . music and other forms of expression."[2] They go on to say, "It is not fixed outside the bodies of performers and is therefore malleable enough to be manipulated according to context, ideology, and purpose."[3] African dance as a genre suggests that African traditional dances are, in fact, encapsulations, resources, like cultural informants that inform and portray historical, religious, and ethical beliefs about the societies in which they are found. Yet African dance continues to be linked to an irreconcilable past in the public imagination, afloat with a prescribed aesthetic that acts as a "tyranny of expectations." That "tyranny" anticipates a certain kind of performativity, one that privileges fast, propulsive movements, the *djembe* drums, acrobatics, and nostalgic village scenes as "authentic" staging. This expectation often thwarts appreciation of the huge diversity among African dance and music traditions, many of which do not always include the elements just mentioned.

When used without careful attention, the term "African dance" subsumes not only the ancient past, recent past, and present, but it also takes on the name of, and potentially represents, an entire continent. This is problematic given that there are fifty-four countries and thousands of ethnic groups on the African continent, and this becomes even more complex when African dance is contextualized and re-contextualized within the African Diaspora. Speaking more directly, there is no such entity as "African dance." In reality, there are Malinke dances, Serer, Ewe, and Ashanti dances, as well as Shona, Zulu, Makonde, Massai, and Chewa dances, to name a few more accurate dance names. African dance as a corporeal mass that encompasses all the dances of Africa does not exist; still, the term or label lingers and persists.[4]

Thus, in the following discussion, while acknowledging the aforementioned issues, I present some key features of both African dance and African aesthetics to balance long-standing misconceptions and provide commonalities for discussion. I first differentiate and situate traditional, neotraditional, and contemporary African dance as genres that have developed and are understood in the Diaspora. This route of inquiry points to identity, memory, and "trace" as important concepts or keys that I reference to the "inscribed" or embodied Diaspora dancers who perform African dance. Discussion follows regarding two overlapping generations of artistic directors, choreographers, and performers who have promoted stellar performances and distinguished themselves as teachers of African dance. Finally, I summarize what is essentially a "Gospel" of African Dance, that is, the "good news" that carries forth the foundation and goals of African dance in the Diaspora.

African Traditional Dance

It can be argued that dance has a particular propensity to foreground cultural memory as embodied practice by virtue of its predominately somatic modes of transmission. Indeed, in traditional forms of danced display, it could be argued that longevity of human memory is publicly enacted, demonstrating the ethereality of longevity of human experience as successive generations re-present the dancing.[5]

African dance was part of a whole until European interventions and disruptions caused a shift toward an isolated type of dance. After all, dance had existed in Africa long before contact with missionaries, colonial governors, traders, and explorers.[6] Colonial Europeans wrote their impressions of the dances they observed. This motley group of men, at different times and places, viewed and wrote about the dances enslaved Africans performed from the perspective of Christian beliefs during that period. Their written documents would eventually establish African dances as portrayals of one huge uncivilized society and, as another consequence, provided additional rationale for enslavement of Africans.[7] Their commentary on the dances was often negative; because of this, I offer an understanding and definition of what "traditional dance" implies.

In this collection and, generally, African traditional dance refers to dances that have been performed for at least three generations and in the context of communal living, both in rural and urban areas. Traditional dance is performed within the prism of ritual and ceremony, as well as within other recurring social situations of ongoing social and cultural communities. The dance is part of a larger system than movement alone; that system includes music, song, and drama with masked dancing, and it serves many functions (for example, to celebrate marriages, births, and religious events, to provide assistance in economic tasks, or to underscore prestige and authority). The past can extend back fifty, seventy, or hundreds of years, depending on the efficacy of the oral tradition and the extent of colonialism in a particular region.[8] Belief systems are ensconced in traditional dance, music, visual and sculptural art as well as theater, and the beauty and power of traditional art forms are an integral part of African heritage. Anthropologist and dance studies scholar Yvonne Daniel posits it this way:

> Traditional dance is not static, therefore, but part of a dynamic process. This process is an ongoing one of selection, presentation, elimination, augmentation and manipulation. Specific esteemed elements of movement, which are recognized within a given group from a given location and which characterize a style, complex, or tradition, are identified and given social value.[9]

Great care is taken to preserve and honor those dance traditions that have been repeated for specific purposes such that they reach a certain level of remembrance and understanding. This does not preclude change that was always occurring in villages and among neighboring groups, but this nomenclature permits a distinction between dances as they were and are performed in their site of origin and dances that have been transformed as they were performed elsewhere under new or different conditions.

Neotraditional African Dance

Neotraditional dances have developed from many dance traditions within continental Africa; they are, and hold, the "traces" of African memory, history, and identity that have been inscribed on dancing bodies on the continent and in the Diaspora. These neotraditional dances have been stylized and/or reshaped for the proscenium stage. They may continue to be described by their functions (courting dances, harvest dances, rites-of-passage dances, and so on), but in actuality they rarely function in those capacities. In rural areas of many African countries, it is possible to see traditional dances in context; but in this technological age, it is more difficult to maintain these traditions. As people access the internet and smartphones, they are exposed to the dancing of other groups, to new ideas, and to abundant creativity. With that exposure comes influence and mimetic renditions, as well as change and appropriation.

Usually, neotraditional dances have a fixed time and other venue constraints requiring a stage and specialized technicians for their performances. They may honor the spirit of a traditional dance, but they do not replicate the religious or social ceremony from which the dance has been taken. There are many reasons for this: a ceremony may take too long for the expense of a theatrical presentation; an actual ritual may call upon a spirit or force that is not conducive to the stage; many contemporary performers are not prepared or equipped to handle the complexities of a tradition-based ritual. For example, neotraditional dances may refer to or indicate a deity, but they rarely invoke the deity during performance, as is expected in a traditional setting.

Additionally, costumes, lighting, recorded sound, and a proscenium perspective are in contrast with ritually baptized drums and specified animal or bird materials in costumes within the dance drama space, and there is a definite beginning and ending in neotraditional dances. This is in opposition to what happens in traditional settings where the dance is not separate from the elaborate and often labor-intensive preparations and celebratory rituals or ceremonies, which end only when the event has run its course. In many cases, this can be for days. Also, staging neo-traditional dances must shift the spacing of instruments, musicians, and dancers to make a compact semi-circle. This allows an advantageous sightline for both the audience and the drummers, who need to see both the dancers and the audience.

On the other hand, neotraditional dance presentations permit dances of different ethnic groups, nations, languages, and belief systems to converge in a neutral site—the stage. There, previous conflicts, historical animosities, and taboos are disregarded for the sake of national or international camaraderie.

Neotraditional dances are widely performed in the African Diaspora, and although they are some of the most popular dances, they come from distinct villages within separate, national boundaries. For a few examples, *lindjien/ lenjengo/lindjiang/lindjien* is a dance of the Mandingo/Mandinka people in what is now Sierra Leone; it is primarily recreational, performed by females, and followed by singing.[10] *Mandiani/Mendiani/Majani* is a dance of the Bamana people in Mali; it is now in the repertories of the national dance companies of Guinea, Mali, and Senegal. A *mandiani* is " . . . the girl who is the best dancer in the village. When she reaches puberty, the mandiani relinquishes her title and chooses her successor."[11] *Sabaar/Sabar* refers to both a Senegalese dance and a Senegalese drum. The rhythms and their correlating dances have more than a dozen variations or distinct versions; they also have intricate legwork and footwork, and several have undergone many transformations. Presently, in one of its social-dance variants, called *leumbeul*, the dance features women using hip-circling and pelvic thrusting to challenge one another and men regarding their opinions about political issues and family life.[12] *Fanga/funga* is a welcoming dance that comes from the Vai people in Liberia, and it is also a specific rhythm. It was brought to the United States in 1949 by Pearl Primus and has become the dance to know, teach, and perform for thousands of African Americans.[13] *Patakato* is a Nigerian political dance that mimicked and satirized European style as an outlet for frustrations with colonization. It is a heel-and-toe dance representative of African satire or commentary in movement.[14] Originally, *adowa* was a funeral dance, but it is performed today as a symbol of Asante ethnic identity.[15] *Wolofsodung/Wolosodon* is a Malian dance traditionally performed by non-nobles—that is, it cannot be performed before chiefs and other dignitaries. It was thought to be a dance for those who were enslaved, and although many Malians perform this dance, it is restricted to certain venues.[16] *Kete* is dance/drumming of the Akan people in present-day Ghana. The dances used to be performed in the royal courts of traditional chiefs; they are presently performed at chief enstoolments and high official activities.[17] *Gahu* is a dance of the Ewe people in southeastern Ghana. It is danced at weddings, funerals, political events, and on other celebratory occasions.[18] *Odunde* is derived from Yoruba heritage; it is prominent in the South Street *Odunde* Festival of Philadelphia, where it is part of New Year traditions.[19]

In most of the mentioned dances above, songs are sung in local languages, but usually all performers do not speak or understand the lyrics, especially if they come from another part of the country or represent a different ethnic group from dances included within the performing company's repertory. The structural changes in the dances noted above have changed the spatial and emotional dynamics. Thus, the neotraditional dancer's context is "performance" and the actual performance becomes the new ritual or ceremony with its own set of aesthetics and rules for neotraditional African dance.

Last, many dances that have been transplanted and adapted by dance practitioners in the Americas or Europe lend themselves to a performance dynamic that is amenable to a particular North American and European aesthetic appetite. Many dance companies from the continent and across the

Diaspora capitulate, often for financial needs, and design programs to please such international audiences. These audiences have often been primed to attend to what they perceive as "authentic African dance," and authenticity is then tied to stereotypes. Thereafter, stereotypes have functioned to privilege continental Africans over their diasporan counterparts, and African artistic agency is often held at bay.

Africa's population is tremendously diverse, and among its thousands of represented cultures there has been constant migration intracontinentally since the time of the ancient Kemet kingdoms and intercontinentally mainly since the transatlantic trade in humans. Consequently, one dancer cannot know all of the dances from the continent or know all the dances of the major ethnic groups. Besides, the same dance can be claimed by several ethnic groups, as well as different countries, because of the artificial boundaries drawn for African nations at a European conference in Berlin in 1884.[20]

Contemporary African Dance

Contemporary African dances are choreographed by one or more individuals using the movement vocabulary of both traditional and neotraditional dances and extending that movement vocabulary with new meanings. Contemporary African dances have been influenced generally by current trends, attitudes, and beliefs, both local and global. Performance Studies scholar Esailama G. A. Diouf connects contemporary dance to the ever-present past. The present and ever-present past are interdependent and reflect changes in movement and music styles, but they also reveal changes in approaches to the dance and how those changes are articulated. She states:

> As contemporary dance is always in dialogue with tradition, the definition of "folk" or "traditional" dance is not fixed. While the structural DNA—the nuances that identify the core technique of the dance—may stay consistent, the performance and even cultural environment of the dance must change as bodies that carry "folk traditions" travel through varying locales and across generations. Each true climactic moment within the dance of contemporary times springs from a contest in which each artist challenges tradition; each solo flight or improvisation represents a definition of the identity of an individual who, as a member of a collective, is a link in the chain of tradition. Thus, because dance finds its very life in an endless improvisation upon traditional materials, the dancer/choreographer's identity must be lost as it is simultaneously found.[21]

In my words, contemporary African dance also relies on African "traces," cultural memories, genealogical heritages, and genuine and imagined histories that interrogate and intervene in traditional dances with respect and honor. Contemporary artists locate themselves in the now, the complex and often disruptive present, making use of many movement sources, as well as technological advances. Contemporary African dance finds its roots in the Black Arts Movement of the 1960s and 1970s within the United States, which was the impetus for many African descendent choreographers across the Americas and Europe to connect with their African heritage. Artists like Ron Pratt (d. 1987), Eleo Pomare (d. 2008), Dianne McIntyre, Baba Chuck Davis (d. 2017), and, later, Jawole Jo Willa Zollar, Abdel Salaam, Ron Brown, Camille Brown, and others—all created works that incorporated their African heritage into their movement vocabulary and artistic content. The Black Arts and the Black Power Movements (re)claimed the term "Black" and contemporary Black artists say it in the present with a capital B!

African Dance Aesthetics

Dance in African contexts is woven intrinsically with music so that both are inseparable and feed off each other's energy, creating a union that is distinct by way of its wholeness. The whole, in most cases, is not separated into the parts, except for those African dance forms and traditions that have migrated to Europe and the Americas. The inseparable and interdependent quality of the dance and musical rhythms of Africa signify a philosophical approach toward life that many African traditions embody. This union exhibits a poly-rhythmic, sensory, and visual display of dance.

Traditional music (dance) can be defined as a repository of rhythms (dances) that encapsulates belief systems that have their origins in ancient societies. Tradition in the modern world is variable rather than constant, precarious rather than fixed, always responsive to contemporary challenges.[22] I substituted "dance" for "music" as I paraphrased ethnomusicologist Kofi Agawu's statement, but this did not change the meaning of either aesthetic or expressive element. Memory is the connecting fiber between traditional, neotraditional, and contemporary dances in the African Diaspora. Accessing memory from the past is part of the process of preserving and documenting the multilayered treasures of song, instrumental music, rhythms, and dance movements that constitute what is known as African and African Diaspora dance. Memory is fluid and porous, yielding varying accounts according to who does the remembering and for what purposes.

> Tradition has age and a mythical grounding on its side. For some people, it indexes the precolonial. Traditional music is wedded to those things that traditional people do in traditional life, and so it may include court music, ritual drumming at festivals and healing ceremonies, and funeral dirges.[23]

Traditional dances rely on memories as guardians of cultural history so that knowledge is forwarded to the next generation in a kinesthetic and inscribed mode. "Body movement in dance may be understood as the embodiment of history, of existential givens, of social value systems, and/or thought per se."[24] Traditional dances also serve as media in their societies: heralding the news, praising the praiseworthy, and mocking the status quo. Therefore, there are relevant moments in both the past and the present when traditional dances have played significant roles, and it is helpful to know the time frame of the performance. For example, it would be interesting to know about dance fifty or more years ago as Africa was in constant upheaval: What were the traditional dances of Zimbabwe around the outbreak of smallpox in the early twentieth century or the *ngoma* dances of Kenya right after the Mau Mau wars?[25] One could also ask about the traditional dance in Malawi that celebrated the late President Kamazu Banda's coronation or the performance of the *sabaar* dance right after Senegal's independence.

Historical events frame and influence African aesthetics, and both colonial and precolonial histories have informed African aesthetics. In the following section, I insert a contextualized and brief account of pertinent events that shaped the structure and content of many African dances.

Precolonial and Colonial History

I now present a broad historical sweep that is important for dancers of African-based dance to know. It is an overview of African and colonial history that forms the background for many African dances. Here, it frames notions of African aesthetics; and because history is so important for memory and heritage, I include it as part of my "Gospel" of African dance.

In 1884 the continent of Africa was apportioned and divided by political leaders in specific European nation-states to create new nations and borders.[26] Fourteen nations were initially involved in the carving of Africa: Austria-Hungary, Belgium, Denmark, France, Germany, Great Britain, Italy, the Netherlands, Portugal, Russia, Spain, Sweden-Norway (unified from 1814–1905), Turkey, and the United States of America. Of these fourteen nations, four—France, Germany, Great Britain, and Portugal—were the major players in the conference, controlling most of colonized Africa at the time. Before the conference, 80 percent of Africa still remained under native, traditional, and local control. By 1914, however, Africa had been divided into fifty or more "Un-natural States." Ethnic and regional dances, therefore, had to be deliberately designed to appease the European governor or ruling magistrate of a particular territory or, alternatively, dances would be performed secretly. These dances—masked, stilt, ceremonial, recreational, courtship, and religious dances—retained repeated rhythms and movements that ensured a degree of continuity; in fact, most can be identified today.[27]

The colonial period was characterized by great changes; however, the pre-colonial period involved a broad set of distinct conditions that affected not only coastal areas but also inland regions across the entirety of Africa. Prior to 1540, for example, there was trade between China and Africa, Portugal and Africa, and India and Africa.[28] Some of these historical events are worth mentioning in a brief overview.

Arab peoples invaded Tunis and Carthage in 698–700 AD and soon controlled all of coastal North Africa. These were Muslims, and most of North Africa converted to Islam; Christian Ethiopia was the exception.[29] Soon kingdoms developed across sub-Saharan Africa, which permitted sub-Saharan Africans to trade with northern Arab Africans—using gold plus the increasingly valuable commodity: enslaved peoples.[30] One of the first kingdoms to develop was Ghana, which was located in what is now southeastern Mauritania and western Mali.[31] The Ghanaian empire grew rich from the trans-Saharan trade in gold and salt but then lost its power in the eleventh century.[32] Additional kingdoms developed across the continent, including those in Benin and Mali.[33]

Empire development was not limited to the north and west. In eastern Africa, Mogadishu, the largest city in Somalia, was settled by Arabs also, and their reach extended south to Zanzibar in Tanzania, which was used as a base for voyages between the Middle East and India.[34] As other organized kingdoms were formed in central and southern Africa, the Portuguese began to explore the entire western coast of Africa. By 1445 they reached the Cape Verde Islands, the coast of Senegal, and the mouth of the River Congo in 1482. They even sailed around the Cape of Good Hope in southern Africa.[35]

The continent-changing sixteenth century began with Europeans transporting enslaved Africans for profit. From the sixteenth century to the nineteenth century, an estimated ten million people were taken captive and brought to the Americas and parts of Europe.[36] Thereafter, because of the difficulties surrounding declining profits from human trafficking over time, as well as the eventual backlash against human enslavement, several colonial powers began to look elsewhere for economic gains. France became one of the first countries to abolish slavery, in 1794.[37] Britain banned the slave trade in 1807, but it was not officially abolished in all British colonial sites until 1848.[38] The Abolition movement surged in the United States and initiated the Civil War with the institution of slavery abolished officially in 1863. The last national territories to declare an end to slavery were Cuba in 1886 and Brazil in 1888.[39] Enslaved Africans transported their dances to the Americas for at least three hundred years, with fresh input continuing from at least the early seventeenth century until the late nineteenth century.

On the other hand, wholesale colonization of Africa by European countries began in 1814, when the British snatched the Dutch colony of South Africa.[40] After the continent was carved among the British, Dutch, French, Germans, and Portuguese by the end of the nineteenth century and the continent was all but controlled by European powers,[41] the land grab continued into the first decades of the twentieth century, as the British took control of Egypt. By 1920 the forced occupation of African lands began to sour in Europe.[42] Change was in the wind; as well, Africans were driven by their ongoing desire for independence. The movement became unstoppable, and just past midcentury most of the continent was proclaimed independent. Sudan and Ghana were among the first sub-Saharan African nations to be liberated from colonialism in 1956 and 1957 respectively; Angola was the last nation to be freed, in 1975.

There is scant information, however, on the extent of the Atlantic slave trade's impact on dance. Many traditions were disrupted and obliterated, given the enormity of the expanse of time in which the trade took place and the millions of Africans who were uprooted and taken away. It was in the Gullah Sea Islands of the Carolina coasts, in the early outskirts of New Orleans, Louisiana and Mobile, Alabama, and in the former Danish, Dutch, English, French, and Spanish islands of the Caribbean where African dances continued and were more easily developed. Fortunately, dancing African descendants were isolated by geography, and, consequently, their memories kept the dances for both secret and public performances.

The Unified Body

Basic to an African aesthetic is the use and display of the body. African dances are integrative or holistic in that they use the entire body and do not privilege one body part in favor of another. The entire body is central to the memory process, but the head, of course, is significant for direction, stabilization, and creativity. The head is used in vigorous and subtle ways while dancing because it situates and centers the dancer in the universe. It establishes directions for dancers in relationship with other dancers, musicians, and participants. The head can swing from side to side, make a complete circle, and can be vibratory or tremulous, indicating the inner pulse of rhythms within the body.

Sometimes, the head may be hidden beneath a mask, but the movements of the head are visible and facilitate the expressivity of the dance by serving as a focal point that engages the audience.

The torso in African dance is accentuated and venerated, as it houses the heart, the womb, and the sex organs. These three are all life giving and define the essence of what constitutes a human being. In many African sculptures, the torso is elongated and the limbs are shortened to demonstrate the significance of the torso to life-giving properties.[43] Within the torso, the pelvis is a particular signifier, and in many African cultures the pelvis is freely expressed through "hip isolations" or emphasized hip movement in every possible direction, speed, or quality of motion. Early settlers, colonialists, missionaries, and explorers often misunderstood this body expression and regarded the use of the hips as an indication of vulgarity, improper sexual behavior, and/or a lack of moral values. In fact, the use of the pelvic area is another tribute to the torso's life-giving properties. Africans celebrate life and procreation and the pelvic area symbolizes life. In fact, women in African art and aesthetic forms are equivalent to life.

Many dances are directed toward the earth, acknowledging its function as a food source, but also as the resting site of their ancestors. Both nourishing food and wise ancestor knowledge feed the individual and the group; accordingly, the feet are used to maximize and emphasize the relationship between humans and the earth. Flat feet are used to shuffle, stomp, brush, graze, or otherwise embrace the ground with the entire foot. Many times, when the foot is lifted, the emphasis is to return the foot to the ground as quickly as possible, maintaining contact with the earth. The ground, that plane on which we all walk, functions and continues to be the foundation for all that we do as human beings.

Spirit

Also basic to African aesthetics is the reach or journey toward the spiritual plane of existence. Transcendence to a spiritual or extraordinary realm is a key component in African aesthetics and especially in traditional dances. In the following section, I briefly outline concepts that I have devised for understanding the manifestation of spirit in African cultures; these guide the performance of traditional, neotraditional, and contemporary African dance.

- The first concept is "Carry," which is the ability of the rhythms to take the body on a journey and then return it to its former state.
- The second concept is "Transference," which is the exchange of energy and dynamics between participants (in a dance performance, a social event, or

a ritual practice) that empowers individuals to draw from and give to one another, so as to make transformation possible.

- The third concept is "Transformation," which is a changed and charged state of existence. The dancer, initiate, or participant no longer exists in the same state (or spiritual plane) as that in which he/she/they entered the dance, the ritual, or celebratory event.
- The fourth concept in this quadrant of agents is "Transcendence," which has been commonly referred to as "possession," but it is more precisely (and less pejoratively) a fully altered state of awareness. It is the complete immersion into the dance, the ritual, or the ceremony, to the extent that the body is given over to extraordinary phenomena and is under the control of a particular energy, spirit, or deity until such time that the music, chants, rhythms, and songs in tandem give the signal for the person to be "let down," "eased," or returned to the earthly, ordinary realm.

In sum, African dance aesthetics appear in both precolonial and colonial history, as well as in current trends within local and global situations, and involve the entire body and spirit. These culminate in tight musical and danced interchanges encompassing traditional social life, along with the performance environment of the proscenium stage. African dance aesthetics involve cultural perspectives that rely on memories and the ancestor spirits who influence contemporary societies as artists and visionaries.

African Dance Visionaries in the Diaspora

As cultural phenomena in the United States, especially, and in other parts of the African Diaspora, African dances are artistic, nationalistic, and political. They have been linked historically to the struggles of African peoples in the Diaspora, and as such, the dances represent ancestral heritage for millions of Black people. Each generation brings to the present stellar examples of African aesthetics through African and African Diaspora artists. Here, I document and honor an important historical series of African dance and music masters who have created and influenced the development and appreciation of African dance in the Diaspora.

According to dancer/scholar Marcia Heard and drummer/dancer Mansa K. Mussa, the history of African dance as concert art begins in the 1920s and 1930s when Efrom Odok, Asadata Dafora, and Momudu Johnson founded groups in the United States that taught dances mainly from Nigeria and Sierra Leone.[44] There have been hundreds of African dance companies across the United States ever since. For example, Asadata Dafora (1890–1965) came to the States from Sierra Leone in 1929 and presented his first dance concert in 1933. Following the success of the 1934 work "Kykunkor," Dafora created several more operas that were performed on Broadway. He also toured throughout the southern and western United States and served as a choreographer for Orson Welles's production of *Voodoo Macbeth* (1936).[45]

The Dinizulu's Dancers, Drummers and Singers drew heavily on the influence of Asadata Dafora. Nana Yao Opare Dinizulu and Alice Dinizulu formed a school of dance in 1948, which, since 1970, has been called "The Aims of Modzawe," in Queens, New York. This institution still serves as the center for information on Akan culture and religion in the United States.[46]

Another African master artist, Babatunde (Michael) Olatunji (1927–2003), came from Nigeria to Morehouse College in Atlanta, Georgia, as a scholarship student. Upon graduation he moved to New York, where he began to perform with Asadata Dafora. Soon after, he formed Olatunji's Drums of Passion and made the classic recording "Drums of Passion" (1956). Olatunji played with many jazz musician giants, including John Coltrane, Canonball Aderley, Max Roach, Horace Silver, and Quincy Jones. He was recognized for inserting the African bass and creating other contributions to "World Music"; he collaborated in interdependent musical projects with Carlos Santana, Bob Dylan, Bob Marley, and others. He toured the U.S. South with Dr. Martin Luther King and was an impassioned activist for social justice using African drumming for peace.[47]

In the 1960s Ladji Camara came to the States while performing with Les Ballets Africains of Guinea. On his second tour, he decided to stay and teach, introducing the djembe drum and especially Manding culture. Camera performed in the company of dancer/choreographer/activist Katherine Dunham and then joined Olatunji and his Drums of Passion. He later formed the Ladji Camara African Drum and Dance Company, becoming a major force among the increasingly popular West African artists who migrated as African nations became independent.[48]

In addition to the aforementioned African visionaries was an African American dance master, Baba Chuck Davis, who was born in 1937 in Raleigh, North Carolina, and who made his transition in May 2017. He danced in the companies of Olatunji, Raymond Sawyer, Bernice Johnson, Joan Miller, and Eleo Pomare before forming his own company in 1968. The Chuck Davis Dance Company of New York was the first African dance company from the United States to tour Europe under the auspices of the U.S. State Department. In 1977 he created DanceAfrica, an annual festival dedicated to the dances of Africa and the Diaspora at the Brooklyn Academy of Music (BAM). In 1982 he returned to his North Carolina roots to create the African American Dance Ensemble (AADE) in Durham.[49]

The dance artists named above were the first to establish the idea of "African Dance as concert dance." They placed African dance in professional settings and set examples for another generation of African and Diaspora artists whose passion was contemporary African dance. Thereafter, a plethora of African dance companies and individual artists came on the dance scene, influenced by the U.S. Black Arts Movement of the 1960s. There are too many to name here, but a few must be mentioned for their significant contributions to the African dance traditions in the United States.

I mention Melvin Deal first within this generation because of his sustained work over almost sixty years. Deal is the artistic director of the Washington, D.C.–based African Heritage Drummers and Dancers and was its founding executive director in 1959. Deal continues today as a veteran artist, working to educate and preserve the dance history of Africa and its descendants.

Assane Konte, who is the artistic director, choreographer, and costume designer of Kankouran West African Dance Company in Washington, D.C., started professional dance at age fifteen in Dakar, Senegal. With his childhood friend Abdou Kounta, a master drummer, he co-created this African dance company in 1983. He has taught dance and music at Howard University for almost thirty-five years.

Since 1987 Amaniyea Payne has directed Muntu Theater in Chicago, although it was founded in 1972 by Alyo Tolbert. As a talented African American dancer, she studied extensively in Senegal and Guinea. She is now a dancer/choreographer and teacher who displays all that African dance symbolizes.

Zakarya S. Diouf and Naomi Diouf are co–artistic directors of Diamano Coura ("Those Who Bring the Message" in Wolof), a West African Dance Company in Oakland, California. Since 1975 they have contributed not only their mastery of Senegalese and Liberian dance and music heritages but also their collaborative skills and generosity among all African dancers and musicians in the United States. They have produced an annual festival of African and Diaspora dance—Collages des Cultures Africaines—for more than twenty years.

Ausettua Amor Amenkum in New Orleans, Louisiana, is an African American who has been seminal to community-based learning and teaching of African dance. She is recognized for her commitment to what African dance can do, especially among women who are incarcerated.

One of the first two Senegalese drummers who came to the United States came at the invitation of the late choreographer/dancer/anthropologist/activist Katherine Dunham. Mor Thiam was one; the other was Zakarya Diouf. Among Thiam's Senegalese people, his family holds the position of representative drummers who tell the history and genealogies of their people through the talking drum. Thus, Thiam and his students have made considerable contributions to the world of West African dance in the States.

Through these particular and pivotal dance/music artists—their performances, teaching, and personal stories—millions of people have learned much about African histories, cultures, religions, and dances. These are the dance visionaries who have simultaneously contributed to the foundation and the development of African dance in the Diaspora.

Conclusion—Dynamic Cultural Memory and an African Dance Gospel

In order to address all elements—beyond definitions, African, European and Diaspora histories, and key founding artists in the Diaspora—I conclude with a further explication of cultural memory and "trace" and their critical importance to African Dance.

African dance as "trace" represents an homage to that which existed before millions of Africans were brought to this hemisphere as chattel, property, or commodities. "Trace" is manifested throughout continental Africa, and memory facilitates "trace" across the American African Diaspora. As this chapter has delineated, dance traditions of many different ethnic groups were operationalized and improvised during the Middle Passage and over time to create reconfigured and new dances of survival. The forced performances onboard ships were "stagings" and proved a metaphor for things to come. The Black body would be the inscribed site of inhuman labor, whippings, lynchings, medical experiments, mass incarcerations, segregation, and the ever-present colonial gaze. Simultaneously, however, the Black dancing body has become the inscribed site of proud heritage, unearthed honorific history, and bodily and philosophical inspiration. The Black dancing body in African dance is a center of integrity, strength, and persistence—that is, a center of values from "the high road." The Black dancing body in the Americas has been the conduit of many "traces" that honor ongoing life and vitality. African dances have been and continue to be "traces" that represent a continuity that empowers millions of people in the Diaspora.

Traditional African dances serve as keepers of social mores and the values of a particular society in which tradition can change swiftly and radically or it can gradually absorb local and outside influences.

> Traditions can change through responses of their bearers to features of the traditions themselves in accordance with the standards of judgment, which their bearers apply to them. These standards of judgment may derive from newly

presented traditions, from traditions previously unknown in society although well developed in alien [sic] societies. The confrontation of a tradition internal to a particular society and an alien [sic] tradition is usually a consequence of demographic, political, military, or economic changes in the relations between the societies. Traditions may change in response to changed circumstances of action, themselves products of changes recurring with the society in which they were previously practiced.[50]

Traditions reflect the creative will of a community that seeks change and innovation while evidencing "trace." Communities and dance companies that are heavily vested in tradition, however advantageous, may be resisted or challenged. Changes, perceived as coming from the "outside," are suspect and subject to rejection without consideration of potential value.

> But what do traditions yield? Why do recollections defer to the ideas and reflec-tions that society opposes to them? The ideas present, if you will, the conscious-ness that society has of itself in its present situation. They result from a collective reflection detached from any set of opinions that takes into account only what exists, not what has once been. It is the present. It is undoubtedly difficult to modify the present, but is it not much more difficult in certain respects to transform the image of the past that is also—at least virtually—in the present, since society always carries within its thought the frameworks of memory?[51]

Change can be challenging, and changing a perceived past is difficult if one must answer to the living elders who are attached to a particular, seemingly unchanging past.

Anthropologist Michael Herzfeld hones the discussion when he states:

> There is a possibility of the subtle re-castings of official discourses that we might call counter interventions of tradition, in which local and minority groups vari-ously and (often discordantly) propose a host of alternative pasts.[52]

In many African Diaspora communities, memory with its many "alterna-tive pasts" is contested territory. Seniority, rank, prestige, and position all play a role in who determines the outcome(s) of this discordant discussion. Dance performances balance all views by displaying, on the one hand, rep-licas based on memories of older rural and urban, neotraditional versions on stage and on the other, creative imaginings of contemporary situations and understandings. Both versions reveal core cultural memories, stories handed down generation after generation and imaginative futuristic visions. Regard-less, memories guide creativity, as well as speak to present-day communities and audiences.

Technology has produced dramatic changes in African dance performance while it also archives quantities of diverse dance traditions. Changes in the dance occur because as dancers and choreographers have access to advancing technologies, they are exposed to and influenced by a diverse array of dances and boundless creativity, regardless of geography, time zones, and terrains. The seeping in of the "outside" should be expected at times, especially when it is embraced by the young (and often dismissed by the elders). However, the same technology permits exposure to recordings of dances that, perhaps, are no longer performed or have been forgotten.

Those African dances that are remembered and are performed regularly in several contexts become "classical" dances. They evolve from traditional dances and often take on national significance. They can be relegated to special occasions and performed only on a few occasions, perhaps years apart, but these "classical" dances represent the best of what the group or nation has to offer. In the moment of performance, they act as cultural ambassadors and can be exported, even though they are often stylized forms from regional traditional dances that are embedded in ritual, ceremony, and social events, all of which could reflect only one or perhaps a few ethnic groups or one village.

Memory and "traces" are gospel when addressing African dance, although they are not absolute. As stated early in this chapter, memory is the connecting fiber between traditional, neotraditional, and contemporary dances in the African Diaspora, and "trace" lingers from memory. The past is ever present, and both memory and the past are agents in the act of "Knowing"; not knowing can cause cultural instability. African dance must therefore bear the burden of its history. Its traditions are especially battered, given the constant onslaught of bias, racism, and pejorative descriptions that have accompanied the genre since it was simply traditional. Over time, however, personal memory gives way to collective memory as African dance is taught more often to differing people.

Philosopher Jean Paul Ricouer talks about the "vulnerability of memory": "It is the link between imagination and memory" that gives this vulnerability.[53] Social identity comes from memory; thereby, remembered and practiced African dance has contributed to generations of African American identities. Knowing African dance is a link to the continent; "traces" continue that link, at least in terms of heritage, geography, and the performing arts, but also in terms of cultural perspective.

In conclusion, this intervention of African dance terminology, history, and personages has brought forth my personal values regarding African dance; my heartfelt attachments to it have generated much thought and documentation over the years. Here, I call such thinking and its resolutions a "Gospel" because it involves teachings that I have amassed over decades of contact and exchange among African dance experts and teachings that I have given to generations of students over thirty-five years of university teaching. I call it a "Gospel of memory" because memory is the most critical and pivotal element. As my chapter discussion instructs, memory is responsible for the past, the present, and the future. We all participate in a narrative that is gospel at one time or another. That gospel has empowered African descendants when there was so little known about African dance. There is more known today, but not enough; information is out there so that we don't have to own every truth and mistruth. Knowledge and information change, however, and what was true a year ago may not be true today. The Gospel of which I speak projects a finality that fosters security; within that security there is fluidity and flexibility.

As an elder in African dance in the United States, I send forth these understandings, which have guided my generation in its presentation of African performance practices during the last half-century. These perspectives are shared among the committed choreographers and performers I have highlighted, as well as the informed and respectful African dance researchers I have cited. I offer this chapter as a treasured gift to the documented record of UNESCO's decade of the African descendant.

Notes

1. Daniel P. Mannix and Malcom Cowley, *Black Cargoes: A History of the Slave Trade: 1518–1865* (New York: Viking, 1962), 5.

2. Hélène Neveu Kringelbach and Jonathan Skinner, eds., *Dancing Cultures: Globalization, Tourism, and Identity in the Anthropology of Dance* (Oxford: Berghahn, 2012), 2.

3. Ibid., 6.

4. "Historically, part of the debate over the use of the word 'African' began with the landing of the Africans in Jamestown, Virginia. . . . In 1619, when the very first Africans were brought to Jamestown, John Rolfe wrote in his journal that a 'Dutch ship sold us twenty Negars.' This was the first reference made to blacks in North America even though the term African has been used since the thirteenth century to identify black people from Africa" (Joseph E. Holloway, ed., *Africanisms in American Culture* [Bloomington: Indiana University Press, 1990], xix).

5. Theresa Buckland, ed., "Dance Authenticity and Cultural Memory: The Politics of Embodiment," *Yearbook for Traditional Music* (2001), 33:1.

6. Kofi Agawu, *Representing African Music: Postcolonial Notes, Queries, Positions* (New York: Routledge, 2000), 3.

7. Lynne F. Emery, *Black Dance: Dance from 1619 to Today* (Princeton, N.J.: Princeton Book, [1972] 1988), 2–12.

8. Compare with Eric Hobsbwan and Terence Ranger, eds., *The Invention of Tradition* (Cambridge: Cambridge University Press, 1983).

9. Yvonne Daniel, *Rumba: Dance and Social Change in Cuba* (Bloomington: Indiana University Press, 1995), 138.

10. See Eric Charry, *Mande Music: Traditional and Modern Music of the Maninka and Mandinka of Western Africa* (Chicago: University of Chicago Press, 2000), 239.

11. See "The Real Mandiani," n.d.; video of a traditional *mandiani: "Mendiani à Koumana,"* https://www.youtube.com/watch?time_continue=194&v=2EiTQjNJU90.

12. See Karien Sondervan and Sophie Schouwenaar, "Sabar Dancing in Senegal," January 16, 2007, https://www.youtube.com/watch?v=RTDC7hJEqT4.

13. See Sule Greg C. Wilson, "The Story of Fanga," as told to *Rhythmbridge* (n.d.), https://www.rhythmbridge.com/fanga.

14. See Alex Moore, "Cross-cultural Perspectives on the Creation of American Dance," senior thesis, Hofstra University, December 2010.

15. See Katherine Moss, "Adowa: Funeral Dance of Asante as a Vehicle to Express Ethnic Identity," *African Diaspora* (1998), 62, http://digitalcollections.sit.edu/african _diaspora_isp/62.

16. See Sharon Freda Kivenko, "Mobile Bodies: Migration, Performance and Social Belonging in Malian Dance," PhD diss., Harvard University, 2016, 166, 169; also http:// www.youtube.com/watch?v=rEmxN-2hznA.

17. See Willie Anku, "The Contexts and Meaning in Asante Dance Performance: The Case of Kete," master's thesis, University of Ghana, 2015, 8.

18. See Steve Reich and Paul Hillier, "Gahu—A Dance of the Ewe Tribe in Ghana (1971)," in *Writings on Music 1965–2000*, Oxford Scholarship Online, 2004, doi:10.1093/ acprof:oso/9780195151152.003.0009; Cudjoe, E. "Drumming among the Akan and Anlo Ewe of Ghana: An Introduction," *African Music* 8 no. 3 (2009). 38–64.

19. See Debora Kodish, Lois Fernandez, and Karen Buchholz, "The African American Festival of Odunde: Twenty Years on South Street," *Pennsylvania Folklife* 45, no. 3 (1996): 126.

20. See Hosea Jaffe, *The History of Africa* (London: Zed, 2017); Kevin Shillington, *History of Africa* (New York: Palgrave Macmillan, 2012); also, Genvieve Fabre, "The Slave Ship Dance," in *Black Imagination and the Middle Passage*, ed. Maria Diedrich, Henry Louis Gates, and Carl Pedersen (New York: Oxford University Press), 33–46; and Mannix and Cowley, *Black Cargoes*.

21. Esailama G. A. Diouf, "Staging the African: Transcultural Flows of Dance and Identity," PhD diss., Northwestern University, June 2012, 26.

22. See Agawu, *Representing*, 25–26.

23. Ibid., 26.

24. Sally Ann Allen Ness, "Being a Body in a Cultural Way: Understanding the Cultural in the Embodiment of Dance," in *Cultural Bodies: Ethnology and Theory*, ed. Helen Thomas and Jamilah Ahmed (Oxford: Blackwell, 2004), 126.

25. Shillington, *History of Africa*, 405–6.

26. The Berlin Conference began November 15, 1884. For additional details of the historical summary I give in this section, see also John Thornton, *Africa and Africans in the Making of the Atlantic World, 1400–1800* (Cambridge: Cambridge University Press, [1992] 1998); Linda Heywood and John Thornton, *Central Africans, Atlantic*

Creoles, and the Foundation of the Americas 1585–1660 (Cambridge: Cambridge University Press, 2007).

27. See, for example, Welsh-Asante, "The Jerusarema Dance of Zimbabwe," *Journal of Black Studies* 15, no. 4 (June 1985): 381–403.

28. Shillington, *History of Africa*, 118–19.

29. Jaffe, *History of Africa*, 18, 30.

30. St. Clair Drake, *Black Folk Here and There* (Los Angeles: UCLA Press, 1990), 130.

31. Jaffe, *History of Africa*, 20.

32. Ibid., 136.

33. Ibid., 22.

34. Shillington, *History of Africa*, 121, 295, 327.

35. Ibid., 108–11.

36. Drake, *Black Folk Here and There*, 290.

37. Ibid., 240.

38. Shillington, *History of Africa*, 237; Philip Curtin, Steven Feierman, Leonard Thompson, and Jan Vasina, eds., *African History from Earliest Times to Independence* (London: Longman [1978] 1995), 182–212.

39. Shillington, *History of Africa*, 240.

40. Ibid., 271.

41. Ibid., 314.

42. Ibid., 287–89.

43. See examples of Senufu (Poro or Lo, Ivory Coast), Gu (Ivory Coast), Mende (Sierra Leone), Bobo (Burkina Faso), Bete or Nimba (Guinea), and Ikem (Nigeria) sculptural traditions; see also Franco Monti, *African Masks* (New York: Hamlyn, 1969), 16, 20, 42, 57, 71, 91.

44. Marcia Heard and Mansa K. Mussa, "African Dance in New York City," in *Dancing Many Drums*, ed. Thomas F. DeFrantz (Madison: University of Wisconsin Press, 2002), 143.

45. Ibid., 144.

46. Ibid., 147.

47. Ibid., 148.

48. Ibid., 143–44, 149, 151.

49. Ibid., 151.

50. Edward E. Shils, *Tradition* (Chicago: University of Chicago Press, 1981), 240.

51. Maurice Halbwachs, *On Collective Memory*, edited, translated, and with an introduction by Lewis A. Coser (Chicago: University of Chicago Press, 1992), 183.

52. Michael Hertzfeld, *Cultural Intimacy: Social Poetics in the Nation-State* (New York: Routledge, 1997), 12, 82.

53. Ricouer in Kathy Birat, "The Conundrum of Home: The Diasporic Imagination in The Nature of Blood by Caryl Phillips," in *African Diasporas in the New and Old Worlds: Consciousness and Imagination*, ed. Klaus Benesh and Geneviève Fabre (Amsterdam: Rodopi, 1994), 200.

Kankouran West African Dance Company, Washington, D.C.

William Serrano-Franklin

"African dance is not boogie, boogie, boogie. It's a history. It's a musical the-ater," says the co-founder and artistic director of Kankouran West African Dance Company (KWADC or Kankouran), that is, Assane Konte. "Baba Assane," as he is affectionately known, has not only challenged widely dis-seminated misrepresentations of West African dance, but he has also been a pioneering force in reintroducing and reorienting African Americans and other diasporan Africans to the cultural values embodied in the techniques of West African dance.

In this chapter, the term "Diaspora" is used as shorthand to refer to people who descend from those West and Central Africans who were trafficked to the Americas during the transatlantic slave trade. While the world African Diaspora encompasses a much broader group of populations throughout Europe, the Middle East, and Asia, the historical relationship between West Africans and people of African descent living in the Americas is of criti-cal relevance to Assane Konte's work with Kankouran West African Dance Company. Thus, "Diaspora" warrants a narrower usage here; it refers more generally to the journey of West African culture as its values and customs have spread through dance practices across the United States.

African dance is a kinesthetic heritage from which African Americans were brutally separated. Konte teaches students of all backgrounds in the Washington, D.C.–Maryland–Virginia area; he bridges the cultural divide between continental and diasporan Africans. He considers instruction both an academic and a spiritual undertaking. Through his approach to staging the

PHOTO 6.1. KWADC, George Washington University's Lisner Auditorium, Washington, D.C., ca. 1980.

complexities of choreographic presentations for bi-continental audiences and managing the interpersonal dynamics within a vivacious, professional dance company, Konte creates an authentic feeling of immersion into traditional village life.

Born in 1951 in Dakar, Senegal, Assane Konte began learning the traditional dances of his own Mandinka ethnic group as a child. Konte began his professional dance career at age fifteen when he joined the Dakar-based Ballet Africaine de Diebel Guee. He toured several West African countries with this company throughout the 1960s and 1970s: Gambia, Guinea, Mali, Togo, and Cote d'Ivoire, among others. To the extent that one can think of dance as a language, Konte's years with Ballet Africaine de Diebel Guee resulted in the mastering of several dance vocabularies with no apparent "accent" or disproportionate proficiency in any one particular form. As a young man, Konte took up residence in Cote d'Ivoire, where he worked with local dance companies before moving to the United States in 1978. When he first came to the States, Konte performed throughout the Midwest at various theme parks and other performance venues with other immigrant African artists before settling in Washington, D.C.

PHOTO 6.2. Diamano Coura Dance Company (Assane Konte on right), Wild Animal Park, San Diego, California, Easter 1983.

Konte saw the opportunity to immigrate to the United States, particularly to Washington, D.C., as a chance to actively shape the future of West African dance traditions on the world stage. Several African nations were newly independent, and their recently formed national dance companies were sharing knowledge and shattering stereotypes of Africa and Africans. In addition to his deep concern for the future of his artform, Konte was also deeply concerned about the well-being and future of the African American communities from which his students and company members hailed. As a result, he saw and continues to see the cultural and subsequent spiritual reawakening that

PHOTO 6.3. KWADC, Children's class, George Washington University's Lisner Auditorium, Washington, D.C., 1998.

West African dance can initiate as critical to those communities in facing what will come their way—good or bad. Indeed, Konte's work with children and teenagers over the years has been especially influential, mandating that their participation in KWADC programming is contingent on their academic performance. In that way, Konte has imparted, and continues to impart, values that reinforce the messages most of his young students likely receive at home, albeit in his inimitable way. However, his message is also rooted in a cultural context beyond the direct experiences of African Americans. Because KWADC has been in existence since 1983, Konte has been able to see students he first encountered as children matriculate through all levels of instruction and company membership. With his legacy coming to fruition before his eyes, Konte's confidence in the effectiveness of his approach is unimpeachable.

When discussing the series of events that led to his migration to the United States and to the eventual founding of KWADC, Konte speaks with the wisdom of well-earned eldership. He is deeply concerned about passing on all that he has received from the multi-arts performance practices of his West African heritage, as well as his artistic education throughout years of performance. These are multivalent practices enriching the art of West African dance and music but also the very lives of performers.

Initially, Konte moved to St. Louis, and Melvin Deal, founder and director of African Heritage Dancers and Drummers, invited him to come to D.C. to teach some classes and work with his D.C. dance company. When Konte arrived, he discovered that his childhood friend, Abdou Kounta, was living there also. Each time he came to D.C., he and Kounta would discuss the idea of establishing a dance company in the nation's capital. Eventually, he packed his belongings and relocated.

Once in D.C., Konte immediately started teaching classes, and Kounta would drum. Through their classes they began to identify dancers for their new company. They were literally teaching, training, and recruiting at the same time. When they finally formed Kankouran West African Dance Company in 1983, Konte became the artistic director and Kounta became the director of music. Kankouran presented its first full-length concert, "A Visit to Africa," in 1985, and with that performance an institution was born. Over the years, Baba Assane has been invited to move the company to Maryland or Virginia in order to have more state support, better funding, and his own space (outside the university system), but he refuses to move the company from D.C. He feels strongly that as long as D.C. remains the nation's capital, Kankouran will be the nation's dance company.

For his African American students, many of whom have *not* had the opportunity to travel to Africa, direct engagement with West African cultural traditions is a vital preliminary phase of a broader cultural healing process, which serves as a treatment for the sociocultural wounds many African Americans carry from the compounded intergenerational trauma of the Middle Passage, enslavement, and institutionalized oppression; it is initiated through the adoption of various traditional practices that were originally performed by pre-enslavement ancestors. Cultural healing for African Americans thus begins with the deconstruction of indoctrinated beliefs about the innate inferiority of Africa and Africans.

Throughout the history of the United States, Africa—the so-called "dark" continent—and its people—have been consistently depicted as backward and unintelligent at best, or as deranged and violent subhumans at worst. Across many mediums and art forms, African dance was presented to reinforce those tropes. For example, in Tarzan movies of old, dance was presented as orgiastic, uncontrolled mayhem. While it was presented in a more positive but equally unrealistic light in more recent films such as "Coming to America," starring Eddie Murphy and Arsenio Hall, the true artistry and cultural depth of African dance have been largely absent from European

PHOTO 6.4. KWADC, White House Rose Garden, Washington, D.C., 2007.

and American media. Considering the prevalence of these representations, Konte is nothing short of astounding—playing a critical role in conveying not only the performative beauty of West African dance but also in establishing African dance as a serious and rigorous art form within U.S. American institutions. Because of his meaningful contributions, the invitation to bring KWADC to the White House in 2007 was a fitting tribute for his work over twenty-four years. While the presidency of George W. Bush is not without its controversies, extending the prestige of the presidency of the United States of America to KWADC—an institution dedicated to the transmission of West African cultural values to African Americans through dance—was an incontrovertible advancement for West African culture on both the national and international stage, as well as Konte's favorite memory of KWADC.

To really understand the guiding principles of KWADC, its name must be understood. For the Mandinka people of the Senegambia region of West

Africa, the "Kankouran" is a spirit guide, a spirit of leadership, wisdom, and foresight. As Konte leads creatively and pedagogically, he eschews the spotlight. He limits the number of solos in performances to avoid unhealthy competitive dynamics, and he prefers to dance alongside his students and company members, in keeping with the communitarian principles at the core of most West African societies. "I don't want somebody to look at the performance and say, '*She's* good.' I want them to say, '*They're good.*'" By prioritizing community over competition, Konte directly contradicts the common model of dance excellence in the United States and most of Europe. KWADC does not have auditions. Company members matriculate from Konte's dance classes when they are ready for the stage. This, in turn, makes West African dance accessible to people of all ability levels and body types without diminishing the technical rigor or cultural integrity of the art form. Konte thus lives up to the concept of the Kankouran spirit; he embodies the leadership, wisdom, and foresight necessary to advance West African dance for the betterment of African American communities.

In many ways, Konte's work of educating African Americans about the deeper meanings of African dance forms is paralleled by his work to educate dance critics. Konte provides a useful analytical context with which critics can offer valid (and hopefully constructive) criticism beyond a basic reporting of the events on stage. "When they review a ballet performance, they already know the meaning of what they're looking at." Konte ensures that critics know the story that the dance attempts to tell, in addition to the values the body techniques attempt to evoke. In this way, Konte reveals the artistic validity of West African dance to the outside world; he opens himself to well-informed criticism, establishing the tradition as a fully realized peer to other dance traditions that may be more familiar to audiences in the Americas. In addition to critics, Konte also strives to educationally influence other dance companies, imploring them to use their choreography and staging to augment the dance. "You can't just do the dance and then get on the mic to tell the audience that this dance is done for initiation or for the harvest. You have to choreograph the harvest or the initiation from the beginning to the end." While not a griot or traditional Mandinka historian/storyteller per se, Konte, in his approach, is deeply engaged with the practice of danced narratives. His choreographies communicate the full contextual depth of West African dance in an immersive experience for spectators and performers alike.

There is an underlying thread of simulated immersion that unites each component of Konte's pedagogy and approach to performance; this is most apparent in KWADC's well-known annual Unity Conferences. Unity Confer-

PHOTO 6.5. KWADC, Workshop with public school children, Washington, D.C., 2010.

ences allow African dance enthusiasts from across the country and the world to come together on the Howard University campus in Washington, D.C., in celebration and observance of the values Konte strives to transmit. Scores of vendors selling African clothing, art, musical instruments, and foods re-create the atmosphere of an African market, while intensive dance and music workshops provide attendees with a unique opportunity to train under an array of instructors from across the African continent and the Diaspora.

While the Unity Conferences are a culmination of Konte's present philosophy, that philosophy took form over the course of his life and the inception of KWADC. After first performing at amusement parks in several American cities, Konte was attracted by the cosmopolitan diversity of Washington, D.C. He and Abdou Kounta began their outreach at local African American churches, encouraging community members to participate in the heritage they had recently begun consuming. As the popularity of Afro hairstyles and other aesthetic implements of black culture faded in the early 1980s, Konte found that many African Americans would attend African dance performances as spectators, but in many ways they "ran away from themselves" by maintaining a palpable distance, a sort of plausible denial of self. But Konte—and West African dance—prevailed.

Today, Konte and KWADC face new headwinds: the dominance of technology in the "information age" and the broader decline of the arts in U.S. American education. Even among those whose parents and sometimes grandparents have been company members, Konte finds that youth engagement has become increasingly difficult as technology products have become ubiquitous among children and adolescents. Additionally, funding and attendance for youth summer programs have also diminished. In the 1980s and 1990s, KWADC often held six eight-week summer camps in which children were instructed in African dance, costuming, and history. These usually culminated with performances in public parks around Washington, D.C. Yet, in the early years of the twenty-first century, Konte finds himself competing with video games, social media, apps, and smartphones to engage youth in their free time. The proliferation of play-oriented consumer technology, Konte finds, has eroded youth interest in West African dance to a considerable extent. Although Konte and KWADC still successfully reach out to youth, moving forward, Konte would like to have a more decisive triumph over the grip of technology on young people. Perhaps positive representations of Africa and its people, like Ryan Coogler's 2018 blockbuster film "Black Panther," will stoke a new interest in West African dance among youth.

Additionally, one of Konte's most powerful memories is the way KWADC has been received by continental African audiences. Parallel to the histories of suppression in the Americas, African traditions on the continent were severely affected by colonialism and have seen their own decline. Indeed, Konte found fertile grounds for developing and training a new crop of West African dancers in the United States. KWADC's performances with mainly African American performers have often surprised continental African audiences with their level of refinement, sometimes to the point of affectionate disbelief. Konte attributes much of this to the caliber of students he attracts, many of whom have extensive backgrounds in other forms of dance and thus bring technique and critical vocabulary that allow them to excel in multiple fields of performance. Their experience notwithstanding, these students also bring a unique sense of appreciation for the art forms to which Konte has granted them access; they express a degree of reverence in their performances that may well be a manifestation of the experience of Africans in the Diaspora and the healing dynamic Konte engenders through his pedagogy.

PHOTO 6.6. Assane Konte and Medoune Dame Gueye with KWADC, Lisner Auditorium, Washington, D.C., July 30, 2014.

As Konte and KWADC face the current era, with the uncertain future of the arts in the United States, the communitarian values embedded in West African dance and the twin ethos of survival and resistance they engender are apropos to the current domestic zeitgeist. For his part, Konte sees the future of African dance and its meaning for African Americans as still progressing. As African Americans broaden their understanding of African cultures beyond music and dance, there is potential for different kinds of experiences through spirituality, travel, cuisine, fashion, and education. This multifaceted future is still about healing, growth, and renewal at its core, just as it has always been throughout the history of KWADC. As Konte says, "Many people call (African) dance their therapy." There is true power in what Konte has already done and in the seeds he has sown, culturally and socially, in diasporan African communities through KWADC.

Muntu Dance Theatre of Chicago

1972–2018 and Still Thriving

Amaniyea Payne

This is a story about a dance company; it traces the origins and history of Muntu Dance Theatre through the memories and assessments of its present artistic director and documents a U.S. city with tremendous African dance influence—in the Midwest. It shows how artistry, education, and politics intertwine at the core of many West African–based dance companies and how African dancers and musicians have joined African American communities in using dance practices and dance performance not only to confront racism and injustice but also to establish more equitable neighborhood relations involving Chicago's multicultural communities.

■ ■ ■

As artistic director of Muntu Dance Theatre of Chicago for thirty-one years, I now reflect upon the trailblazing journey that has left an indelible mark upon the lives of many. From the inception of UHCC (Unifying Humanity through Cultural Creativity) to Muntu (The Essence of Humanity) (the originating names of the company), the dance/music artists of this organization remain standing as one of the oldest African dance organizations in the United States to have artists on payroll. The executive leadership has always found ways to provide funding stability that has permitted Muntu Dance Theatre to thrive and flourish—even in times of major challenges. With three artistic directors at the helm since its beginning, the organization has contained all necessary ingredients for positive continuity. It is unusual and a bit ironic that the three

PHOTO 7.1. Muntu Founder Alyo Tobert (center) and Muntu original members, ca. 1980.

directors were friends and were able to work together respectfully over time: the late Alyo Tolbert (founding artistic director) was from Chicago and laid the visionary track that established the mission of the company; Papa Abdou-laye Camara from Senegal, West Africa, and the National Dance Company of Senegal, brought folklore, songs, and language, which provided cultural understandings and led to the application of African ballet; and I, Amaniyea Payne, brought stability, diversity, globalization, and additionally carried the vision forward, remaining true to the development and maintenance of this remarkable company. Throughout the years, all three directors have instilled in our artists the assumption of excellence, which cannot be dictated. Thus, we have developed programs that feature particular value systems and cultural upbringing, programs that emphasize cultural validation, cultural equity, and specific management toward creative cultural diversity.

The company is intergenerational and deeply rooted in the concept of family. It is composed of fathers, daughters, sons, nephews, cousins, sisters, and mothers, from sixteen to about fifty-five years old, providing audiences with both young and still-dancing senior dancers/teachers. We are all teach-ers—through our choreographies as well as in technique or studio classes.

Our community attachments and outreach involve African and Diaspora dance classes for hundreds of young children per week, and many of the elders in the company grew up in times of serious social change, when artists were laying foundations and archival platforms for the recognition of a continuum of great works made by our dance icons. This uplifted the entire Chicago dance community and gave distinct purpose to our danced expressions. In the past, we envisioned our development: how we educated ourselves, how we took pride in our existence, and how we recognized African and Diaspora contributions to the history and development of dance. Now we are the keepers of our history and responsible for the development of African-inspired dance performance as we advance our students with the knowledge we have acquired and continuously impart. We are pleased to express our ideas artistically without excuses.

Muntu found it important to bring politics and cultural presence together, for there is an advantage to the conglomeration and consistent networking with our brothers and sisters from the African continent, the Black Caucus, Hispanic Caucus, the Native Caucus, and the association of various Caribbean and Latin American cultures—to name a few. Dance and music are our organic links to Africa. Throughout history, dance and music have been used to combat the isolation that threatens the cultural heritages of individuals from Africa, the Caribbean, or the Americas. The company addresses such potential individual isolation by providing professional training and performance experiences to new artists through our "Workshop Training Component." Upon completion, new and young performers graduate to an "Apprenticeship," which leads to potential open slots as company members. Muntu maintains a full schedule of artistic programming through its "ACE" component (Arts for Community Empowerment), serving more than ten thousand youths in community centers.

Arts education is vital; it is imperative to teach children the value of maintaining cultural arts and the importance of respecting cultural artists. We've had the opportunity to serve as an information resource center for our children, peers, adults, and local educators, projecting and creating an educational curriculum with a new perspective that has given assistance to broadening the public school's view of cultural programming. Working in partnership with Chicago's public schools has helped shift learning and learning enrichment to meaningful ways of self-learning, ways of knowing each child's historical background, and also ways of respecting several, if not many, ancestral heritages—not just her/his/their own. Children, and teens especially, have learned to understand diversity by recognizing and honoring their own culture and then acknowledging similarities and differences within other cultures. Public school teachers and administrators now look to and cooperate with Muntu in its multiple cultural dance programs. For example, we produce two concerts annually (spring and fall) that are presented in arts teaching venues such as DuSable African American Museum and Performing Arts Center, the David and Reva Logan Center for the Performing Arts, the Gary Comer Center, and the Harris Music and Dance Theater. Students are able to visit museums and performance centers and witness and participate in lively dance/music presentations. Also, during the summer season, Muntu Dance Theatre produces "Summer Jamboree" in collaboration with the University of Chicago and the Gary Comer Center; this is a series of performances and "hands-on" workshops for inner-city youths at primary and secondary levels. Thus, Chicago school administration has partnered with Muntu to make relevant, engaging cognitive experiences and also informative body experiences for children, parents, teachers, and administrators.

In many of our presentations, we have learned from the marriage of dance and music and embraced the art of collaboration. On some occasions we mesh other aesthetic interests with our own, such as West African dance and modern concert dance or Afro-Brazilian and U.S. African American. We work with live music from the African Diaspora, dwelling as often as possible in the realm of Black aesthetics—that is, relying on the intimate relationships between instrumental or vocal lines and movement phrases, the "call and response," "the give and take" between dancing bodies and a battery of independent but interwoven drumming patterns. When I say Black aesthetics, I also include emphases on themes relating to the political issues confronting our communities, themes of spiritual concerns that enter and affect our performances, as well as displaying family concerns among our neighboring communities.

Our Black aesthetic preferences guide our dance performances and practices. We are concerned with notions of beauty in a holistic sense; we are confronting historical biases where Africa and anything African was considered backward, strange, superstitious and something to be ashamed of. We are concentrated instead on seeing the beauty, the strength, and the courage exhibited in the beliefs and behaviors of smart, sensitive, and creative African peoples. Our concept of Black aesthetics involves a "whole-ness of beauty" that encourages us, our students, and elder community members to be strong and positive, to let go of shame and confront negativity with a springboard to cultural respect. We hold the principles of Kwanzaa[1] dear, building programs onto its viable expressions; we are healing fragmentation of a people and using dance arts to reveal the beauty we are and to underscore the beauty we produce. As a result, Muntu has collaborated with an array

PHOTO 7.2. *Kosonde (Balante)*, choreographed by Babacar N'Diaye; performed by Muntu dancers and musicians, 2013.

of international, national, and community musical organizations, as well as solo artists and artistic groups from diverse backgrounds. This has made our repertoire culturally and technically diverse.

Two choreographies from our repertoire can add specifics to what our company is known for and why it has gained respect over time. In 2005 I choreographed a new work for Muntu called "Yanga," which was based on research, completed that same year, in Yanga, Mexico. The choreography premiered in 2006 at the Mexican Fine Arts Center in Chicago, before most Mexicans knew of or could acknowledge the African heritage within their homeland. This work told the story of Yanga, an enslaved African in Mexico in the earliest years of the seventeenth century, who became the founder of the first town of freed enslaved peoples in the Americas (January 6, 1609). My company members and I went to Yanga to witness their pyramids and scrutinize their ancient sculptures and masked images. In accordance with

PHOTO 7.3. *Manifest*, choreographed by Christopher Walker; performed by Muntu dancers, 2015.

the rule of that era regarding "black blood"—that is, if you had even a single drop of African blood, you were considered Black, not white—Mexicans had avoided African identity in favor of mixed Native and European blood, or *La Raza*, to define and publicly promote Mexicanness. Muntu researchers were able to show them that that drop of Africanity was a "drop of gold": we educated Mexicans, as well as our Black community audiences in the States, with the performance of "Yanga," replacing old, undocumented notions of origins with researched, documented, and bodily displayed African heritage. Again, our mission involves making excellent art and educating ourselves, our communities, and our diverse audiences regarding the wealth within and significance of African history and its heritage in the Diaspora through dance.

We have also presented honorific choreographies dedicated to renowned artists, such as for Dr. Pearl Primus ("I've Known Rivers," 2009), and in special tribute to Baba Camera of Senegal ("Hard Times Blues," 2010). We have

PHOTO 7.4. *No More Trouble*, choreographed by Stacy Letrice Smith; performed by Muntu dancers, 2015.

also maintained learning dialogues and teaching consultancies with dance specialists in other parts of the Diaspora. Brazilian dancer/choreographer Roseangela Sylvestre, for example, has had an ongoing relationship with our company development ever since our mutual experiences with students at the Bates Dance Festival in the 1990s. Rosangela consulted on the choreography titled "*Guias*," which drew on the spiritual energies she shared with us about the African divinities in Brazil's Candomblé religion.

Here's a short listing of dynamic artists who have shared their creative expression and vision with our organization; we have been honored to perform with them:

Saxophonists: Ernest Dawkins, Mark Durham, Duke Payne
Harpist and saxophonist: Light Henry Huff
Trumpeters: Ameen Muhammed—Sonny Covington, Corey Wilkes

Kora players: Djimo Kouyate, Mousa Souso, Vieux Diop, Mori Keba Kouyate
Drummer/Spiritualist: Baba Chief James Hawthorne Bey
Pianists: Willie Pickens (The Willy Pickens Quintet), Theophilus Reed,
    Buddy Lucus, and Artist activist and lyricist: Oscar Brown Jr.
Blues artist: Billy Branch
Vocalists: Dee Alexander, Maggie Brown, Frances Pace Moody, Jonita Lat-
    timore, Charles Hayes and The Spiritual Warriors
Choreographers and producers: Saladeen Alamin, Gloria Farr, Rosita Rea-
    gun, Kunute Bernard, Skip Burney
DanceAfrica: Baba Chuck Davis (New York, Chicago, Philadelphia, Texas)
Tone Foundation: Reginald Robinson (Ragtime)
Conjunto Folklórico Cutumba (Santiago de Cuba)
Milton Baptists and The Olympia Brass Band (New Orleans)
Educator of Black creative music: Phil Cohran
Guinean consultants and choreographers: Youssouf Koumbassa, Moustapha
    Bangoura
Liberian consultants and choreographers: Nimely Napla, Kai Pai Passawe
Congolese consultant and choreographer: Biza Sompa
Senegalese consultants and choreographers: Abdoulaye Camara (folklorist
    and former Muntu artistic director), Marie Basse, Silimbo Ballet, Babacar
    NDiaye, Mariama Faye, Souleymane Diop, Mame Diarra N'Dong, Idy
    Ciss, Assane Konte, Katbah Cissoko, and Tacko Cissoko
Ghanaian consultants: John Darkay Kwabena, Asante Donkor
Brazilian consultant and choreographer: Roseangela Silvestre
U.S. contemporary and African American choreographers: Cleo Parker Rob-
    inson, Kim Bears, Norma Miller, Frankie Manning, Diedre Dawkins, Ron
    Brown, Asiel Haridon, Jeffrey Page, Kwame Opare, Jawole Zollar, Abdel
    Salaam, Dr. Sherille Johnson, Mickey Davidson, Deeply Rooted, Theodore
    Jamison, Arthur Hall, Reggie Wilson, Obba King of South Africa, Thuli
    Dumaeke, N'diko Xaba, Opah Resurrection Dance Ensemble
Jamaica and the West Indies: L'Antoinette Stines, Third World, Christopher
    Walker, Alfred Baker
Ile Aiye Ballet Folclorico Do Brasil (Bahia)
The Jubilate Children's Choir (performing "Betelehemu," the Nigerian carol
    depicting the joy of going to Bethlehem, originally brought to the U.S. by
    Babatunde Olatunji)
Kalapriya and American India Foundation

As we continue to face the challenges of trying economic times, we are currently taking an opportunity to review and plan for an artistic and organizational viability that is futuristic above all else. The fact that we are a continuously growing institution, constantly presenting new and innovative experiences to our audiences, displays our ongoing complexity. Through teaching and performances, Muntu reflects the parallelisms and the oneness of diasporic art expressions and seeks to maintain its national and international respect. On behalf of Muntu Dance Theatre of Chicago, I publicly thank all of our constituents for their continued support, which has made our existence possible. We have a long history and an ongoing and broad commitment to serving our communities at large.

In keeping with our mission and revered ancestral traditions, we celebrate the legacy, cultures, and artistic expressions of the African Diaspora, knowing there is no perfection without practice and no ovation without passion. With this knowledge, we artists, with our combined talents and ancestral guidance, always take a close look at ourselves and our intentions for the continued momentum of the work we've already undertaken. For all people of good will, humanity, and understanding, we, Muntu Dance Theatre, send our message of peace, love, strength, and hope to our world community neighbors. We must continue to remember and respect the legacies that were left by never saying goodbye to yesterday and by understanding the importance of "Build, Build, Build!" For we still stand on the shoulders of yesterday, which have made our present possible. In the words of George Washington Carver:

> How far you go in life depends on your being tender with the young, compassionate with the aged, sympathetic with the striving and tolerant of the weak and of the strong . . . because some day in life you will have been all of these.

Muntu Dance Theatre of Chicago celebrates forty-six years of being steadfast in perpetuating an awareness, appreciation, and understanding of the invigorating spirit of African cultures through the idiom of dance/music. With an intense commitment to its artistic vision and the identification of young artists, Muntu provides aesthetic joy, artistic history, and culture, as well as significant employment opportunities to numerous artists, choreographers, and instructors who are in studious pursuit of African and Diaspora histories and cultures.

Note

1. Kwanzaa is an African American ritual, created by Dr. Ron Karenga, a Black university professor, who during the heightened battles of the Black Power Movement in the United States of 1966 constructed a seven-day period of remembrance and dedication. At the end of the calendar year through the first day of the new year, African descendants today rededicate themselves to lost Pan-African histories and honorific principles of life shared by many African ancestors.

Kumbuka African Drum and Dance Collective

In the City and a Prison of New Orleans

Ausettua Amor Amenkum

At the founding of New Orleans around 1805, when the French and Spanish were removed by the new United States American government,[1] three dynamics prevailed: the institution of African enslavement, the destruction of the Native population, and the colonial robbery of natural resources and land. For survival, and to insure prosperity for its future elite, the early leaders of New Orleans had to oppress part of its population in their pursuit of this objective, and this effort continues today post–Hurricane Katrina. In spite of the small economic gains and political prestige that African Americans have achieved, people across the country do not sense the tremendous value that the African people of New Orleans possess; our New Orleanian heritage and continued presence are worth more than money. The essence of who we are gives wealth that the world cannot measure, and the undeniable fact is that New Orleans is what she is because of this African presence.

This chapter documents the founding and extensive work of Kumbuka African Dance Collective in New Orleans. Its name, Kumbuku, means "to remember" in the Swahili language of Kenya; however, most important, this chapter is a story about how Kumbuka has been able to use the teaching and practice of African dance and music cultures to touch and change not only the lives of the members of Kumbuka but also the lives of hundreds of youth, adults, and, particularly, incarcerated women.

Physically, the city of New Orleans is below sea level, which means it sits in a bowl—the bottom of the bowl to be exact. It is surrounded by water, and its citizens bury their dead above ground. New Orleans is also regularly battered by hurricanes, floods, mosquitos, and even flying cockroaches, yet we, New Orleanians, somehow find a way to peacefully coexist with nature. This positioning causes Spirit to hover auspiciously over the city, like a celestial vapor that allows most inhabitants, as well as some visitors, to experience an inexplicable euphoria; that feeling solidifies a vow to never leave this city, in spite of the many challenges and obstacles that can make it difficult to maintain a sustainable life in "the Big Easy" (the city's nickname).

Spirit from drumming and dancing oozes from the cracks in our raggedy streets; Spirit permeates the humidity and rests on the brows of masking Black Indians (commonly called Mardi Gras Indians), on the shoulders of brass bands members and their "second liners," on high school marching band members and dance teams. Spirit shows up in that beat commonly referred to as "New Orleans bounce music." In New Orleans, the beat of the drum has always been, and continues to be, the core, the essence, the epicenter of everything. New Orleans has often been nicknamed "America's most African city," which is evident in nearly every aspect of local culture: in the food, traditional housing, burial rituals, and the inclusion of music and dance in almost every life event.

All Roads Lead to Congo Square

Manifesting Spirit and public playing of African drums were significant occurrences in New Orleans's history, especially in sacred spaces such as Congo Square. In spite of the Euro-American slave masters' attempts to separate Africans from their essence—their languages, names, family lineages, ways of life, or any associations to Africa whatsoever—they permitted drums and dancing on Sunday evenings after regular church prayer and on some holidays.[2] Although there were periods when the drums were banned for fears of inciting rebellions,[3] slave masters failed to understand the significance of African drums: their connection to most African cosmological perspectives. The slave masters' way of processing prevented them from comprehending the power that the drums had for the African. They did not understand African cultures and had very little knowledge regarding the holistic approach to life that Africans possessed, particularly their commonly held beliefs about human life existing simultaneously on several realms and that these realms could be reached with sacred rhythms played on the drum.

As African descendants, we believe we are Spirit and our family consists of those spirits who are present, those spirits waiting to be born, and those spirits who have transitioned from the earth plane. The drums are a portal of spiritual power between Africans and their ancestors. They have been the catalysts for calling the African "nations"[4] to come to a specific place—in the case of New Orleans, to Congo Square, where we could and still can be free for a brief moment in time. The use of the drums in African culture is a perfect example of how Indigenous people across the world manifest a reverence for communing with the higher Spirit and the spirit world (of deities, *loas*, *neteru*, angels, and the like) through nonverbal communication called dance. Viewed in this manner, drumming and dancing are the foundations of African culture. Drumming and dancing animated African bodies, causing their ancestral DNA to vibrate and resonate, which allowed them to cope with the inhumane conditions of enslavement. Devotion to the rhythms of dancing bodies and playing drums, which shaped the atmosphere of Congo Square, resurrected age-old movements that continue in New Orleans today.

All roads continue to lead to Congo Square, which is located in the heart of the city. Today, that spiritual gateway to the foundational culture on which New Orleans rests is reduced to fragments of its original glory. It sits inside of Louis Armstrong Park, behind locked gates, and concrete has been laid over the sacred soil. If only the majestic oak trees that still stand there could tell what they have witnessed. Instead, we are at the mercy of those few observers who wrote down what they think they saw, corrupted by their personal biases and interpretations. Those accounts often describe the activities as lewd, savage, and without form or direction. It is safe to assume that colonial observers viewed bodily movement and heard rhythms for which they had no frame of reference; African music and dancing were totally foreign to them. We cannot be certain of what they saw, but the specific dances that they wrote about have roots and related branches in West Africa, Haiti, and Cuba. We know that African dance has existed in this place since the origins of New Orleans, and it continues to this day.

We have a unique New Orleans culture and we wear it proudly. While the rest of the world has *breakdance*, *krumping*, *step*, and various other forms of *hip-hop* dance, we, in New Orleans, have *second line*.[5] Simply put, *second line* is a New Orleans street parade for a funeral, a wedding, or another occasion worthy of celebration. The group leading the parade and the brass band that accompanies it are considered the parade's "Main Line"; the large group of family, friends, and onlookers who follow along behind, enjoying the music and the social scene, are the "Second Line." Traditionally, *sec-*

ond lines formed organically and without planning whenever a procession took place. Nowadays, the routes and bands are generally announced to neighborhoods in advance so that people can plan to participate or not. We represent our municipal district voting wards, as if they were independent nations within the city, by *second line* dancing. Each second liner has her/his/their own style, called *bucking*; it is unique movement gestured in mock competition, improvisation, and self-expression, bordering on a trance or trance-possession state. Make no mistake; *second line* dancing, in all of its elements, IS African dance. Even the idea of people parading in the streets for hours in a day is a concept and practice that is deeply connected to African cultural practices that still exist in Africa and among African descendants around the world.

THE SECOND LINE

Like ants blindly
Proceeding in a line
Going nowhere in time,
Black bodies draped in
Vibrant colors and gold-filled grins;
Pound blocks of gray concrete
That reveal
The sacred point
Where the reality
Meets the eternity
Of our survival.
We proceed in syncopation and bliss
Because in those short moments
We do not miss
The troubles of this world.
So, we second line.
Ah-huh, we second line.
We do what we wanna;
We stand on the corner. . . . .
We second line, till we become
Oblivious
To the reality
we exist in. . . .
So, we transcend
And we give in
To the hypnotic beat of the drum
And the call of the horn.
We second line so hard till

Our pants come down.
We sweat back our hair.
Our legs start to burn
But we really don't care . . .
ANYTHING to numb the pain
Of it all,
Of a life where we realize
That we still don't matter!
Yes, we second line.
We born in this, ya heard me?
We bout that second line;
Because we are the Second line. . . .
Second line for food, housing,
healthcare and education.
And lack of access to these
Directly leads to incarceration,
Where we ARE the first line.
So, the next time when you
buckjump behind the hearse,
ask yourself, when will second
become first.

"Kumbuka": A Swahili Word That Means "To Remember"

New Orleans has historically had a unique culture, with music and dance woven throughout. Everyone dances, from the youngest to the oldest, and dancing has always been encouraged. It is common to dance at all family gatherings, funerals, and other celebrations. Whenever someone dies, New Orleanians "break out" into celebratory dance and music to memorialize the life of the deceased. Dancing has been and is our way of mourning, eulogizing, and rejoicing simultaneously; the body speaks for the emotions, what words cannot do adequately. Thus, Black people of New Orleans have been so committed to their particular New Orleans culture that they (we) really did not view themselves (ourselves) as being African; we were New Orleanians. We had experienced being "Negroes," "Coloreds," "Blacks," and now we are supposed to be "African Americans"?!

New Orleans, like many other American cities with significant Black populations, has lacked a global view; we, and everyone else, were subject to the worldwide indoctrination that Africa and Africans were "backward" and "corrupt." Thus, for a time, Black people—especially in New Orleans—did not want to have any connection to Africa. It is a curious conundrum, that whenever a reference was made to some component of life in New Orleans as being "African," New Orleanians usually stated rather proudly, "It ain't got nothing to do with Africa" or "I ain't no African." This was the cultural climate in which I and other founding members of Kumbuka, our African Drum and Dance Collective, grew up and experienced firsthand in the 1960s, 1970s, and 1980s.

The first time I was introduced to a drum was in the early 1980s through a locally well-known New Orleans conga drummer and percussionist, Alfred "Uganda" Roberts. I had seen bass drummers in *second line* and marching bands and seen trap drummers in R&B bands and at church, but I had never seen someone playing the drum with their hands. (I don't count how I used to beat on my mama's table with my hands.) I remember Uganda teaching me my first drum lessons on the congas, and I must say I was good! He would take me with him to private parties where he accompanied an iconic man who sang in a strange voice and played the piano with a fierceness. I later learned that man was Henry Roeland "Roy" Byrd, better known as "Professor Longhair," New Orleans' most renowned pianist and blues singer. I was in the midst of royalty and knew nothing of it.

The first time that I danced to live drums was at the Tremé Community Center, located in the oldest Black neighborhood in the United States. Tremé is in Congo Square; its land was an essential part of the original Congo Square, outside the city proper beyond the French Quarter, bounded by Rampart Street. The square was not only the contemporary small space that is indicated by the historical marker; it extended farther back, away from the city. Some accounts have the square going all the way to Claiborne Avenue or Broad Street, which, at the time, was marshy, undeveloped swampland, deemed uninhabitable. It was, however, the perfect location for enslaved Africans to be "free," to be their true selves, to commune with ancestral spirits, plan escapes, dance, sell wares, or whatever they fancied.

In 1980 a sister named Safiyah Harrison, who was a "transplant" from Atlanta, was teaching an exercise class with drums at the Tremé Community Center. I was invited to the class by Zohar Israel, whom I knew from my Dillard University days when he, another drummer named Kamau, and a brother named Shabaka used to canvass the campus recruiting students for the All African People's Revolutionary Party—a political advocacy group led by Sekou Touré (Stokley Carmichael). I joined the class at Tremé, and to my surprise, I found a large gathering of dreaded, braided, "afro-ed up," patchouli[6]-smelling, tie-dye-wearing, veggie-eating, educated brothers and sisters from all parts of the United States. This eclectic group was probably my first encounter with Black hippies. They had a musical group called "Peaceful

Vibrations" and had decided that New Orleans was their "new" Africa. There were drummers playing all kinds of drums—congas, trap drums, bongos, and even timbales. Additionally, they had violins, saxophones, flutes, upright basses, and trumpets.

The energy was inexplicably intoxicating. Safiya would lead the exercises and interpretive movement and we would imitate her; yet something exciting started to happen: our ancestors began to speak through our bodies. That was the beauty of African dance; several people could perform the same movements, but the different spirit of each individual could still be seen. It was the perfect example of unity within diversity. The atmosphere was supportive and everyone was encouraged to allow the rhythm to live in her/his/their bodies. Inspired by the 1970s Black Power Movement, Black Arts Movement, and national dance companies that were touring the United States from countries like Mali, Senegal, Guinea, and Ghana, we felt a deep connection to African music and dance and saw ourselves wanting that music and dance to be a part of our everyday lives. We saw the immediate connections between the polyrhythms of the *djembe* drums from Mali and Senegal to the footwork in *second line* dancing. We recognized how these African national dance companies used call and response, and we immediately saw how continental dance and music connected to our own Mardi Gras Indian culture. We saw Africa in the United States and the United States in Africa—and knew Kumbuka was our way of "remembering" Africa and ourselves.

Every Friday, we would come to class, and the crowds got larger and larger as word traveled. Pretty soon, folks were lined up along the center's side walls on the second floor. The floor was concrete—cold, hard, and brown—but we were young and had no idea of the damage that we were doing to our bodies by dancing hard on cement. All we knew was that coming to that class was like going to church. We danced and sang until we called Spirit down and changed the atmosphere. We offered our bodies as living sacrifices to be used by Spirit.

Mamas danced as nursing babies bounced on their backs or crawled on the floor behind them. Pregnant sisters danced, creating dancers and drummers in the womb. The exchange between drummers and dancers in class was indicative of how we needed to work together as Black people in the wider community. We danced long and hard, and it became obvious eventually that something else was being created. Spirit was moving ultimately toward a lifetime of relationships, the development of cultural programming, benchmarks used in school curricula, and a cultural revolution in New Orleans.

Although the musical group accompanying our dance classes and performing around New Orleans was formally called "Positive Vibrations," it was decided—after coming together and sharing energy for more than a year—that we needed another name to formalize a new "dance company." Dancers and musicians from the class met at my house in January 1981, and our new dance company, Kimbuka, was born. Zakiyah Neely, from Chicago, offered the name "Kimbuka" and said its meaning was "to remember." It was unanimously accepted, and, for a short while, that was our company's name; however, after further research by Sister Zakiyah, we discovered that "K-u-m-b-u-k-a" was the correct spelling in Swahili, and we corrected ourselves and elected Safiya Harrison as our first director.

We also deliberated the order of the name. Was it going to be "Kumbuka African Drum and Dance Collective" or "Kumbuka African Dance and Drum Collective"? As anyone can imagine, dancers and drummers disagreed along predictable lines about what the order should be. The debate was a direct result of the philosophical discussion of what came first: the rhythm or the movement. The first dance that we learned was *funga*, a traditional African American dance of welcome, created by Pearl Primus and taught by Sister Safiya, and our logo was created by the late Douglas Redd. The group consisted of lawyers, nurses, teachers, jewelers, 911 dispatchers, and audio-visual technicians. Kumbuka hosted the first Congo Square Festival and Conference in 1981 and continued until 1986.

Sister Zakiyah had direct connections to Chicago's African dance company, Muntu, and, as a result, Alyo Tolbert taught our first "authentic" traditional African dance class and Brother Atiba Walker taught the drum rhythms. New Orleanian Baba Kenyatta Simon already had a djembe drum but lacked the drumming technique to make the drums "talk." When Atiba introduced the djembe, Baba Kenyatta was the first in our group to learn the roping system and master the tones of the drum. The first traditional dances we learned were *mandiani* from Senegal and *basket dance* from the Congo.

We were on our way. We were bursting with pride and yielding to Spirit, which ultimately transformed our lives. We were not just a dance company, we were family. We ALL danced together as a family regardless of skill level because, to us, that is what family was; that was "African" for us, as we came into understanding; and that was our New Orleans culture. We ate together, studied together, and raised our children together. Many members even lived together or very near each other. After spending hours dancing and rehearsing, we would spend additional hours socializing—just talking and philosophizing. We could not get enough of each other. We came to understand the power of community and what that means in raising our children. The extended community we had created resulted from a spiritual bond, and we learned that our coming together was not an accident. Somewhere on the spiritual plane, our ancestors determined that we were to be. The company was incorporated in 1983 with more than thirty members; we were Louisiana's premiere *traditional* African dance company—the first to use traditional drums, rhythms, and movement. We performed in schools, festivals, weddings, and concerts. The original founding members from New Orleans were: Gaidi Alafia, Ausettua Amor Amenkum, Zohar Israel, Efuru Johnson, Kufaru Mouton, Jamillah Peters-Muhammad, Kenyatta Simon, and Majeeda Snead. Additional founding members included: Zakiyah Neely (Chicago), Teja Carey (Baltimore), Safiya Harrison (Atlanta), Sister Rukiyah (Augusta), Gary Jamil Owens (Seattle), and Tyra Young, Sister Rashida, and Amon Sheriff (California).[7]

How We Moved

Our concept of a dance company had a very simple goal: community engagement—that is, to bring the dance/music experience to the people where they lived. Kumbuka offered African dance classes at no cost to the community in exchange for rehearsal space—it was a win-win situation for New Orleans. The collective's classes started at Tremé Community and moved throughout the city, utilizing New Orleans Recreation Department (NORD) facilities: Stallings Center, St. Bernard Center, Gernon Brown Center, St. Mark's Community Center, and the New Orleans School of the Arts. Powerful sisters and brothers would converge in local neighborhoods, creating a slight spectacle but also arousing the curiosity of the community, especially the children. Everyone wanted to know who those "Africans" were—dressed in traditional garb, dancing and drumming, and giving tidbits of wisdom and encouragement. And who had "Mama" or "Baba" in front of their names, and why?

It is difficult to estimate the number of people that Kumbuka has impacted, but we continue to meet adults whom we taught when they were very young; they repeatedly report that they have never forgotten the moment when they were first told that they were of African descent. It was at moments like these that we realized we were making a difference in the lives of all those we encountered. We were a wave of cultural revolution in New Orleans.

In 1984, Kumbuka was housed in the New Orleans School of the Arts, which was founded by pioneering modern dancers Greer Goff and Lula Elzy. Mariama Curry and Baderinwa Rolland joined the company, followed shortly by Amauunet Ashe, Menhati Singleton, Luther Gray, and Curtis Pierre. At the same time, New Orleans was host city to the World's Fair, and the African Pavilion sponsored several continental African dance companies that were on tour.

As I look back, maybe the ancestors determined that this was the time to expand our repertoire. Senegalese master dancer Marie Basse and her husband, the late Olukose Wiles, taught *lamban*, a sixteenth-century Malian dance of healing and celebration, and it was an amazing experience. Her humility and grace demonstrated that African dance was not always rapid footwork and high energy. She showed how African dance could also be graceful and flowing. It was a new chapter for Kumbuka and for our perceptions of African dance. We were quickly learning that African dance had technique, as demanding and developed as that of ballet and modern dance, and students needed to study and perfect it.

It was as if the portal had been opened and we were privileged to sit at the feet of some of the greatest teachers of African folklore. Kumbuka was blessed with many pioneers of African dance and folklore who unselfishly passed on the traditions and to whom we are forever grateful. That list includes: Alyo Tolbert (Chicago), Atiba Walker (Chicago), C. K. Ganyo (Ghana), Baba Ishangi (New York), Sundiata Keita (Detroit), Abdoulaye "Papa" Camara (Senegal), Siquan and Souleymane Diop (Senegal), Meschah and Nahgeree Silas (Chicago), Babatunde Olatunji (Nigeria), Chuck Davis (New York), JaJa Uthman (Kentucky), Missa Thurop of Ballet De Sengarmoore (Senegal), Sister Tourkwase, Sister Rehema Namsa (California), Serigne Babacar Mboup (Senegal), Kimati Dinizulu, Kwame Ross, Richard Gonzales (New York), and Jean-León Destiné (Haiti).

Our quests for information led many of Kumbuka's members to travel to every known African dance conference, including DanceAfrica and Kankouran, to master more techniques. We quickly learned that while conferences offer opportunities for networking and exchanging energy with dancers and musicians from all over the world, the best way to learn the dance was to bring the teacher for a New Orleans residency. While we acknowledged the unselfishness of the Africans from the continent, we have to also acknowledge our naïveté in our infant years.

Once some Africans who were born on the continent yet living in the United States understood that Black Americans wanted to learn dances from West Africa, we fell victim to hustlers and deceivers of the culture; we were tricked, bamboozled, and hoodwinked. We soon discovered that many Africans who professed to be dancers were not artists and were unqualified to teach some materials because they were not from the region of the dance's origin, or they were not legitimately trained as dancers, drummers, or choreographers. In addition, they required payment for classes and said that the dances we had learned before they came were incorrect. We were blinded by the fact that they were Africans from the continent, thinking they must be "the real deal." As a result, we went through a period of constant change in movements, rhythms, and repertoire, because we wanted to be the best authentic African dance company that we could.

We give thanks that we were introduced to elders like Baba Ishangi, Baba Olatunji, Nana C. K. Ganyo, and Papa Camara, who directed the appropriate ways to navigate through the cultural highways of traditional dance. By the 1990s, we had all traveled to Senegal, Ghana, Mali, and Nigeria and realized that Kumbuka's repertoire consisted of traditional and contemporary African dance. Yes, we saw *lamban, kakilambe, mandiani,* and *sabar* performed on the continent, and we recognized the steps; however, in African villages, those dances were not so grand or as developed as we had believed. Dances performed on the continent, *not on stage,* consisted only of about two or three steps.

In retrospect, Kumbuka also served as an incubator for the creation of many contemporary companies in New Orleans. We believe that Kumbuka members are family members for life. With this understanding, a time comes when the maturing young leave the family, but they are forever a part of the village. Several Kumbuka members left to found their own companies: Mariama Curry founded Culu and N'Kafu Traditional African Dance; Curtis Pierre founded Casa Samba; Kenyatta Simon founded Percussion Inc.; Luther Gray and Jamillah Muhammad founded Bamboula 2000; Efuru Johnson founded Salongo Productions; Zohar Israel founded Free Spirit Network; Baderinwa Rolland founded Chakra Dance Theater; and Shaka Zulu founded Zulu Connection. Even though all these individual dancers and musicians have their own companies, we continue to collaborate and perform together. These organizations comprise the cultural makeup of New Orleans; they continue the legacy of providing the community with examples of outstanding women and men who represent African principles and who untiringly give of themselves for the uplift of our people.

Historically, Kumbuka has never held auditions. We have felt that any person who expressed a desire to learn African Dance deserved to be taught. We recognized that the dances we learned did not belong to us; they belonged to the people. Also, many artists had shared dance sequences and full choreographies for little or no compensation; we were obliged to return that service to the community. As a result, many phenomenal artists have been members of the company: Oshun Taye Brown, Erica "Famata" Larkins, Stephanie "Qena Tchass" Mckee, Kelly White-Burrell, Michelle Gibson, Kai Knight, Naimah Zulu, Sannyu Brown, Michal Israel, Gaynell Anaya Sorina , and Giselle Nakid.

PHOTO 8.1. Kumbuka African Drum and Dance Collective Founding Members: (left to right, first row) Kenyatta Simon, Ausettua Amoramenkum, Efuru McAlpine, Jamilah Muhammad, Majeeda Snead, Mariama Curry, Zohar Israel; (left to right, second row): Amauunet Ashe, Sis Pat, Charmaine Johnson, Baderinwa Ain (1981).

The Present

In an effort to document the dances and culture of Africans born in New Orleans and the significance that their presence has had on the music and culture of New Orleans, Congo Square became the next focus of our collective. That focus led to a partnership with the Contemporary Arts Center, the Rockefeller Foundation, and the late Jean-León Destiné, regarded as the father of Haitian dance.

I was in New York taking classes at Djoniba's Studio when Spirit led me away from the West African class for which I was originally scheduled. I decided to take a Haitian class with Jean-León Destiné, with whom I was unfamiliar at that time. While in the class, he announced that he was going to do a different dance that day—*calinda*. My heart jumped. How could he have known that I was researching that dance? He went on to explain how this dance was performed in Congo Square and how he had always wanted to go to New Orleans. He shared with the class that he had no idea why he wanted to teach *calinda*, a dance he rarely taught, or why he wanted to teach it on that day: Spirit.

Spirit moved again when I met with him afterward and explained that I was from New Orleans and would work to make his trip possible. I returned home and shared my news with Elena Ronquillo—at the time an administrator within the Contemporary Arts Center. A few months later, she notified me that she had secured a grant from the Rockefeller Foundation to bring Mr. Destiné to set the dance *calinda* on the company. Spirit moved again when *calinda*, a dance that was performed in Congo Square in the 1800s and which originated in Haiti, was resurrected in New Orleans. Since 1992, Kumbuka performs this dance regularly, and it has become its signature piece. We had the opportunity to perform "*Calinda*" in front of the late, great Katherine Dunham and got the "thumbs up!" approval. Other Haitian dances that are now included in Kumbuka's repertoire are: *juba*, *Mayi*, *yenvalou*, *banda*, and *Nago*, taught by Kwame Ross and Richard Gonzales (both from New York). Additionally, Kumbuka's repertoire has extended to include three *Orisha* dances: *Oshun*, *Yemaya*, and *Oya*.

As a natural extension of presenting African dance/music traditions, many members of Kumbuka participate in the African American Black Indian masking tradition. The elders of that tradition prefer the term "Carnival Indians" because historically, Black folks could not celebrate Mardi Gras, which was reserved for the Europeans and white folks on Canal Street, St. Charles Street, and sites uptown. Black folks traditionally congregated for Carnival downtown on Claiborne and Orleans Streets, and this is where all the Black Indians would meet. Black Feather, Yellow Pocahontas, and Washitaw Nation are the tribes that are represented in some of Kumbuka's repertoire.

Other members of Kumbuka participate in the Skull and Bone Gangs, groups of men who dress as skeletons, carry bones, and parade on Mardi Gras to remind everyone about the significance of life. The Skull and Bones tradition dates back to the early days of the Tremé Center in the 1800s. Its purpose is to emphasize the thin line between life and death; death is always lurking, and sooner or later, it will come knocking at each front door. The Skull and Bone Gangs come to wake up the spirits in the cemetery and set them loose in the streets on Carnival morning.[8]

We found through this example and others that we had traveled all around the world only to discover that Africa was already in New Orleans. For example, Zohar Israel, founder of Free Spirit, was instrumental in bringing the art of stilt walking to Kumbuka's performances, which exposed audiences to another component of African masquerade and dance.

The company is a mere shadow of the numbers we had when we first organized almost forty years ago, but Kumbuka is now like a fully-grown woman: clear in focus and confident in knowing how to manifest African principles in the community. Our original mission declared that the collective is dedicated to the preservation, presentation, documentation, and research of traditional African and African American culture, as expressed through the medium of the drum, dance, and song. We are still committed to that mission, but we realize that African dance is not the totality of culture. We must continue to find ways to translate the principles African dance teaches into tangible, measurable forms that impact the self-esteem, self-discipline, and self-love of our people. The goal now is to go beyond just teaching dance but to teach how to tap into divinity within, so that everyone can fulfill her/his/their destiny. This is what will make our families, communities, and, ultimately, the world a better place.

Consequently, Kumbuka member Baderinwa and I have begun a mentoring relationship with the newest dance company in New Orleans, Nkiruka Dance Company. In accepting our roles as elders, we believe that we should assist young artists and new companies in whatever ways we can so that this dance and spirit culture can continue. Additionally, I teach African dance at the Louisiana Correctional Institution for Women, as a vehicle for the self-discovery and self-analysis of incarcerated women. Kumbuka and the Mardi Gras Indians have performed inside the prison in an attempt to connect to our incarcerated family members who may be locked up but are still a part of our community. Teaching at Tulane University for the past twenty-two years has also positioned me to influence the lives of young people and their understanding of African dance and its relationship to other dance forms and cultures. In the past two years, we have performed a dance, *ajaja*, that was taught to Kumbuka by the late Baba Olatunji. It is a dance originally performed by some Yoruba peoples en route to their ancestor shrine. We have performed it for several of our community members' funerals to help grieving families. The dance has generated a rite that is becoming a burial tradition in New Orleans.

The life of an African dancer is fulfilling, but it can take a toll on the body. There is a constant need to recruit younger company members. I am grateful that the children of the pioneers are taking on leadership roles and preserving the tradition of their parents. Jawara Simon (Kenyatta Simon), Judah and Solomon Mason and Shaka Zulu (Zohar Israel), Bomani Pierre (Curtis Pierre), Namdi Neville (Mariama Curry), Bakari and Chemwapuwa Blackman (Baderinwa Rolland), Rashidi and Kito Johnson and Shangobumi McAlpine (Efuru McAlpine), and Nailah Smith (Ausettua Amor Amenkum) are premiere dancers and drummers in New Orleans. They are our future; and our future looks bright.

Kumbuka continues to perform, offering dancing and music-making bodies as a living sacrifice, holy and pleasing to God. We continue to honor our ancestors and lift them in love and light. We remain true to the liberation struggles for African peoples everywhere, from young people in the educational system to those in the prison system. Kumbuka's work is exemplified through public classes to community members, arts in education programs, and performances. Yet I have come to believe that Kumbuka's legacy will be its work within the correctional system, where we are able to use African cultural arts to remind our incarnated brothers and sisters of who they truly are and where they truly come from—Africa. And our experiences with them tells them that we, the Black community, will continue to love them and support them in spite of their mistakes and regardless of how the justice system has debased them. Kumbuka works to reclaim the dignity of inmates and reminds them that they can teach and lead, by living the ways of our ancestors, by continuing to praise with our bodies, our voices, and our dance.

Dancing in the Prisons

I would like to do one of our African dances that we have done throughout the years; and yes, we need to wear the traditional attire.
—Candace, a lifer at LCIW Drama Club

I add an outgrowth of Kumbuka as an ending to this story of New Orleans, Congo Square, and African dance. I discuss more fully the prison project I mentioned above; however, I stay in the frame of Spirit—Spirit that comes through dance and produces unique culture and character. As readers must have noticed already, my life has been affected immensely with the entrance and abiding closeness of Spirit, and it is Spirit that has directed me to the plight of women and Spirit that has radiated back at me in the dance and poetic productions of local New Orleanian women prisoners.

The growing rate of women's incarceration demands a critical evaluation of the impact punitive techniques have at the exclusion of holistic approaches to rehabilitation and reentry in the U.S. penal system. August 27, 2016, marked the twentieth anniversary of the Drama Club within the Louisiana Correctional Institute for Women (LCIW) at St. Gabriel, Louisiana. Kumbuka African Drum and Dance Collective, with ArtSpot Productions, has been an active sponsor of the Drama Club for seventeen years and has produced performances of several traditional African dances, the playing of African instruments, and singing of African songs. Incarcerated women of African descent have worn traditional African clothing, and, for the first time for many of them, they have realized that they knew little of African culture before exposure and study with Kumbuka. Kumbuka was also a regular performing group in the late 1980s and early 1990s at the Louisiana State Penitentiary (also known as "Angola") for men via the Drama Club, headed at that time by formerly incarcerated performer Gary Tyler. Tyler and Kumbuka were the first to bring African traditional drumming and dance to the Louisiana prison system.

African dance, song, and folklore have been vital forces in the development of artistic performances that have been presented for the prison population and a few invited outside guests. Concepts within African culture have laid the primary foundation and development of Drama Club events, the first principle of which is acknowledgement of God, ancestors, and community. Through African dance and culture, many incarcerated women have been introduced to a holistic way to embrace the attributes of spirituality, womanhood, and perseverance. Some performances have focused on race, religion, and concepts of beauty and integrity, and, often for the first time, many women have been introduced to African deities from Ifa, Akan, and Kemetic cosmologies. The concept of female deities—Yemaya, Osun, Oya, Sekhert, Auset, and Het Heru—has given the women a view to a parallel realm of existence in which the power of God is manifested through all living things. It is also a view of the diverse ways in which women function. Participating women readily embrace such concepts when they discover that African cultural principles are not in conflict with their Christian belief system.

The Process

The Drama Club meets for two hours on Saturdays, excluding days when the institution prohibits volunteer services due to a religious event or an institutional cancellation—Children's Day or Ladies' Day for example. Sessions begin with each member "checking in," sharing what she is personally experiencing at that moment or has experienced during that week. At times, this can be lengthy, but it is necessary to allow members to process emotions, reactions, and reasoning. We then warm up physically, performing movement routines with singing and throat exercises, and we add the creation of original songs. After we are all physically conditioned and mentally and creatively relaxed, we decide which issues need to be addressed in the lives of the women on the prison compound. We provide the women with journals, but they are not always willing to write down their feelings or experiences. So, in keeping with African traditions, we honor the oral tradition of storytelling.

The women are encouraged to share their personal stories, and all Drama Club members honor the code that these stories cannot be repeated outside of Drama Club meetings. From the stories we create poems, dances and movements, skits, and monologues. The process can be tedious because the focus is not on the result but on the process that leads to an end. We recognize it is most important for the women to dissect their understanding about a particular topic and then to determine if that understanding has benefited or worked against them. Going through the process can be difficult, but the women have discovered that there is something magical that happens when they express emotions or deep feelings through a poem or dance. We have discovered that some have difficulty expressing emotions to a social worker or psychologist. The women are extremely talented, and when they come together to perform, their energy is so powerful that they cause changes in the atmosphere.

The structure of the Drama Club is designed to communicate to each member that the whole is greater than its parts, but also that the parts are integral to the whole. Through African folklore, we learn that God exists in all living things and thus all living things demand respect and care. This directly translates to how the women relate to one another, especially when Drama Club sponsors are *not* around. This has led to the development of a sacred space where trust exists and where the women can breathe and relax outside their prison confinement. In this sacred space, the masks, which many of them wear in order to survive or function in the prison environment, are removed. The women learn the art of listening to one another, and they learn to observe others in their surroundings. They learn that through sharing and creating stories, they and others can learn from their experiences.

In their story circles, we all learn that our destinies are interconnected. This allows the bond of sisterhood to prevail and a sense of community to develop. The community that exists in the Drama Club affords the elders time and space to determine the ways the club can function, to resolve conflicts, and to take the lead in encouraging all members to participate in the process. The existence of this process and its practice is very important, especially in cases of a life sentence. Adult humans have a need to contribute, create, and control their environments, and this is especially difficult in prison, where everything is controlled for inmates.

"Won't Bow Down"

The good news is that when the women do leave prison and return to their communities, they want to continue telling their stories. Additionally, Kumbuka and ArtSpot have more flexibility and creative license to work with released women, since all inmate performances must be approved by the prison administration. This has led to the creation of a new group called "The Graduates," consisting of formerly incarcerated women. Sherral Kahey, a founding member of the LCIW Drama Club, created that name because she felt that when a person goes to prison, it is the school of hard knocks, and if that person is fortunate to get out, he or she has "graduated" to the free world.

The Graduates have been performing for five years and have successfully created a public "buzz" about the factors contributing to and the effects of women's incarceration in Louisiana. Seven powerful women have acted as sacrificial lambs and have publicly told their stories and the stories of their sisters (without individual identities) who are still behind prison walls. The women's stories are poetic statements, danced dramas, and choreopoems, powerful testaments in spite of the realities and inadequacies of the criminal justice system. These women are survivors; they have something to say; and they demand to be heard.

In order to tell these stories, Kumbuka and ArtSpot have received funding for The Drama Club and The Graduates from: The Emerging Philanthropists of New Orleans, Louisiana Divisions of the Arts, Alternate Roots, Surdna Foundation, and the Open Society Foundation. The Graduates' powerful voices have an even larger platform through their recently awarded Artist as Activist Fellowship from the Robert Rauschenberg Foundation, which addresses racial justice through the lens of mass incarceration. Their project, "Won't Bow Down," allows performances throughout the state and the shared stories of the women's personal experiences within the criminal justice system. They are working to raise awareness about the factors that cause mass incarceration of women and to stimulate and participate in needed reform to the criminal justice system. The project culminates in a national gathering in New Orleans in spring 2018.

Having the stories made public of those who are primarily affected helps to keep incarcerated women included in community and society. They are no longer the forgotten segments of our families whom society deems unworthy or unable to be rehabilitated. Incarcerated women, on the contrary, want to be relevant and are capable of contributing to society. Given the opportunity, prison inmates and the formerly incarcerated will step forward as active participants and make significant changes in society.

Conclusion

With recognition of the principles within African dance and music culture, Kumbuka members and associates have reaped the joys and wisdom of motivated lives and stimulating projects. From learning the dances of Africa and its Diaspora and accumulating a representative repertory for a major regional dance company to re-signifying the African purposes of Congo Square and affecting change in the lives of local community members who are in need, Spirit has obviously guided Kumbuka's efforts. Kumbuka members know that everyone has a unique destiny to fulfill when he or she comes to this earth. Some get the support and guidance needed to fulfill that purpose; others encounter detours along the way. Still, everyone should have the opportunity to direct OR re-direct his or her efforts and live to fulfill his or her destiny. Participation in the Drama Club or The Graduates of LCIW has allowed the creative process to shape how that destiny looks to incarcerated or formerly incarcerated women and has confirmed to them and others that their lives matter.

To date, this and other projects, described throughout this chapter, are what Kumbuka has created and developed over its thirty-nine-year existence. It is a formidable example of what African dance and music have accomplished in and for New Orleans.

LIFE IS

Life is
What you make it.
Life is
Happiness.
Life is
Where you going.
Life is
Where you been.
(Song by the Women of LCIW Drama Club).

Notes

1. Lynne F. Emery, *Black Dance from 1619 to 1970* (Palo Alto, Calif.: National Press), 156; Katrina Hazzard-Gordon, *Jookin': The Rise of Dance Formations in African American Culture* (Philadelphia: Temple University Press), 38.

2. Emery, *Black Dance*, 18, 80, 156–66.

3. Hazzard-Gordon, *Jookin'*, 33–35.

4. These are not "nation-states" but rather the reference that Africans used repeat-

edly across the Diaspora to identify which of the many hundreds/thousands of ethnic groups they claimed as their ancestral heritage.

5. See especially the writings of Kalamu ya Salaam, including "Second Line: Cutting the Body Loose," *Wavelengths* 21 (1982): 26–30. Kim Marie Vaz also writes about *second line* dancing in the context of women's role in *jazz dance* history of New Orleans; see her book, *Baby Dolls: Breaking the Race and Gender Barriers of the New Orleans Mardi Gras Tradition* (Baton Rouge: Louisiana State University Press, 2013). Also see Rachel Carrico and Esailama Artry-Diouf, "Flying High: Function and Form in New Orleans Second Line Dancing," in *Freedom's Dance: Social Aid and Pleasure Clubs in New Orleans*, ed. Karen Celestan and Eric Waters (Baton Rouge: Louisiana State University Press, 2018).

6. Patchouli is a favored perfume oil (made from leaves of an Asiatic tree, of genus *Pogostemon*, especially *Patchouly*, which is a species of plant in the mint family) and often used in oil extractions to create body oil or incense manufactured products.

7. Two dance troupes came before Kumbuka: Nongowa African Dance and Drum Troupe and Laini Kuumba Ngoma Dance Troupe, but they did not have traditional rhythms or drums.

8. These gangs share concepts and dances that are associated with the *Lwa* (spirit/divinity) named Gede, who is found in Haiti and Haitian enclaves in the Diaspora.

"The Fierce Freedom of Their Souls"

Activism of African Dance in the Oakland Bay Area

Halifu Osumare

The Oakland–San Francisco Bay Area has long been a center of African dance, from a fledging search for roots in the revolutionary 1960s of the Black Arts Movement to the current prolific twenty-first-century West and Central African dance companies run by continental African dance and drum masters. In this chapter, I illuminate this regional African cultural trajectory, exploring the artists, dance companies, arts organizations, and community influences that established the Bay Area, and Oakland in particular, as a center for African dance and culture.

Pearl Primus opens her famous essay "African Dance" with a compelling poetic argument for what African dance does to the individual, as well as the community:

> Very early in her research the investigator learned that people who truly dance are those who have never bartered the fierce freedom of their souls, never strangled their hunger for rhythmic movement, nor frustrated their joyous physical response to music and song. . . . When these people truly dance, there can be no observers, for those who seek to watch soon join one of two groups.[1]

Primus described one of those groups as those fearful ones who "remove themselves back to their comfortable living rooms and shut out the scene." But the ones who stay "are snatched, plucked up by an invisible force and hurled into the ring of the dance."[2] This is exactly what happened to the Oakland Bay Area as traditional African dance from the continent, with its "fierce freedom of the soul," began to infuse the community that had already been "raised" on African Diaspora dance.

Through Afro-Haitian dance classes and the Katherine Dunham Technique, the late Ruth Beckford (1925-2019), a former member of the famous Katherine Dunham Dance Company, exposed several generations in the 1950s, 1960s, and 1970s to Afro-Haitian dance that prepared us physically, psychologically, and intellectually for the community-galvanizing dances from Africa. Instead of the typical infusion of tap, ballet, "interpretive," and acrobatic classes taught to young black girls in most black communities across the country, the Bay Area had Afro-Haitian dance that permeated the Oakland Parks and Recreation centers, with Ruth Beckford as its first director of dance. Live drumming was used in most of her dance classes, and her overall mission was not only producing good dancers but socializing her mostly female dance students into proud, respectable young women of the community.[3]

Beckford's approach was very traditional, in the sense that dance in African societies is first and foremost a community expression that inculcates the values of the society in each generation. Beckford has often publicly stated that the use of dance as a socialization tool was her mission. Hence, African dance and drum masters defecting from their national dance companies from countries like Senegal, Congo, and Ghana and migrating to the Oakland Bay Area found a receptive dance community that had been trained to receive traditional African dance and, indeed, Africa itself. In fact, Bay Area black dance students were eager to receive "authentic" African dance and drumming from the first African artists arriving in the Bay Area in the 1970s, such as C. K. Ladzekpo from Ghana, Malonga Casquelourd from Congo-Brazzaville, and Zak Diouf from Senegal.

Katherine Dunham's Legacy in the Bay Area

Before exploring traditional African dance in the Oakland Bay Area with these African dance and drum masters, it is crucial to further examine the legacy of Katherine Dunham for which Ruth Beckford was the regional transmitter. Not only was Dunham the first to research the legacy of African dance retentions in the Diaspora and put them on stage, but she intellectually conceived of the cultural relationship among Africa, the Caribbean, and the United States—the Black Atlantic—as early as the late 1930s. I have discussed her conception elsewhere:

Dunham clearly envisioned the African diaspora—the Black Atlantic—long before that nomenclature was ever used. Although Paul Gilroy conceptualized the Black Atlantic as an "intercultural and transnational formation" in the 1990s,[4] Dunham implicitly understood and utilized this formation as both geographical and cultural in the 1930s, sixty years earlier. Her intellectual prescience illuminated crucial links between movement styles of African descendent peoples in the Americas and their overarching societies, revealing a legacy of creolized African culture in the Caribbean, the expressive dances and rhythms of which she wanted to dignify as important contributions to world culture.[5]

Katherine Dunham's emphasis on dignifying African Diaspora dance on European and Euro-American stages was key to the Dunham legacy. African dance heritage permeated Beckford's and her protégés' Afro-Haitian dance classes in Oakland and San Francisco for three decades.

Utilizing the late Caribbeanist scholar VèVè A. Clark's development of French historian Pierre Nora's concepts concerning memory and history,[6] the Bay Area became a *lieu de mémoire* (site of memory) where an Africanist cultural memory was conjured. As we performed the five levels of *yanvalou* to 6/8 rhythms in Beckford's classes at Good Hope Temple on 55th Street and Shattuck Avenue in Oakland or Peters Wright Studio on Fillmore Street in San Francisco, we delved into African-derived movements that had been repeated over centuries and generations. Indeed, Clark first analyzed Dunham's methodology in her 1994 "Performing the Memory of Difference in Afro-Caribbean Dance: Katherine Dunham's Choreography, 1938–87," which applied to Dunham's foundational dance technique as well as her creative stage choreography. In this seminal essay, Clark reminds us, "When the dance steps, music, and other cultural forms were transformed for stage representations, they became *lieux de mémoire*, reworkings and restatements of historical danced events whose memory Dunham had also preserved in writing and on film."[7] In Beckford's Bay Area dance classes, after the strenuous Dunham barre, and center floor isolations, Haitian dances, reenacted in progressions across the floor, were the moments of *lieux de mémoire*, where our spirits would be awakened to a cultural memory to which we had been unaware; but if we were lucky, it surfaced in our sweat and behind our eyes. We would "remember" our African heritage through our bodies and the rhythmic movement in Afro-Haitian dance and Dunham Technique.

Dunham had chosen anthropological fieldwork in the Caribbean during the 1930s for her master's thesis at the University of Chicago. The Caribbean became a *milieu de mémoire* (environment of memory), where our West Indian cousins had retained more of the direct African heritage in drum patterns and dances, particularly Haiti and Cuba. The Caribbean became crucial to Dunham's conscious motivation to find and articulate the fundamental nature of African-derived dances. She chose Trinidad, Martinique, Jamaica, and Haiti to examine African dances remaining in the Americas. After her sixteen months of fieldwork between 1935 and 1936, she started her dance company, which would become one of the most famous internationally touring dance companies from the United States.

Dunham replenished her company at every port of call with auditions for new dancers, making the Katherine Dunham Dance Company into a little cultural United Nations. Ruth Beckford had auditioned for Katherine Dunham when the company appeared at the Curran Theater in 1940 in *Cabin in the Sky*, starring Ethel Waters. The young Beckford was a teenager still in high school, but she passed the audition and became "the youngest and newest member of the company, [and] . . . was graciously given help by everyone." Beckford remembered, "Miss D herself was always patient, giving instructions and corrections in a calm, encouraging manner. I definitely wanted to please her. I was determined to be good."[8] After several weeks of intense rehearsals, Miss B went on tour with the company from San Francisco to Canada, with her mother accompanying her—and becoming the "mother of the Dunham company," during Beckford's tour. After the tour, Beckford's mother allowed her to make the decision between signing a seven-year contract with Dunham or going back home to finish high school and attend the University of California, Berkeley (UCB). Fortunately for the Bay Area she chose the latter, and the Dunham dance legacy became entrenched in our region. Three generations of Dunham dancers and teachers have served the Oakland Bay Area, including professional dance companies like the Naima (Gwen) Lewis Dance Experience (1968–1978) and Deborah Vaughan's Dimension Dance Theater (1972–present). This Dunham legacy, through Beckford, was what nurtured and ripened the Bay Area black dance scene for the African dance masters that were to come.

The African Dance Triadic Foundation in the Oakland Bay Area

The African dance scene in the Bay Area is founded on three major master drummer-dancers: Zakarya "Zak" Diouf of Senegal, C. K. Ladzekpo from Ghana, and Malonga Casquelourd from Congo-Brazzaville. All three came to the Bay Area and worked primarily in the East Bay. During the 1970s, the city of Oakland, with a population of about 360,000, was approximately 47 percent African American and 62 percent people of color. Oakland was viewed as the "colored" East Bay city; Berkeley was the intellectual counterculture small town with the University of California; and San Francisco was considered the cosmopolitan city. African immigrants arriving in the Bay area would have more immediate access to a black community in the East Bay, consisting of not only Oakland and Berkeley, but also Alameda and Richmond. Although all three African masters settled in the East Bay, as their dance companies grew they also taught and performed in San Francisco's major venues, like the annual Ethnic Dance Festival. All three became integrally involved with the African American community, training and educating young dancers and drummers to build their public classes and eventually their dance companies, which have become Bay Area institutions.

Zak Diouf and Diamano Coura West African Dance Company

I begin with Zak Diouf, the one with a direct connection to Katherine Dunham before coming to the Bay Area. He arrived in Oakland in 1973 and began studies in ethnomusicology at UCB. Somewhat of an anomaly, Diouf had already received a PhD in biochemistry from the University of Chicago (1971). He had completed all requirements while working with Katherine Dunham at her Performing Arts Training Center (PATC) in East St. Louis, Illinois. Dunham was responsible for bringing two Senegalese master musicians to the United States: Zak Diouf and master drummer Mor Thiam, having met them both in Dakar with the National Ballet of Senegal during the First World Festival of Negro Arts in 1966. Dunham had just disbanded the Katherine Dunham Dance Company, and working in Senegal was an interim period between her world tours and her settling in East St. Louis with a new position as artist-in-residence at Southern Illinois University.

Dunham was impressed with both Diouf and Thiam as master artists and convinced them to come to East St. Louis to help her establish her PATC community arts project as an experiment in the arts to uplift the city's residents out of the downward spiral of poverty and gangs. In an interview Diouf stated:

> Dunham was a smart cookie. She always got the best drummers; she had modern dancing and Haitian dancing, but she didn't have African dancing. So in 1967, I came to work with her in East St. Louis, and she pushed the University of Chicago to give me a scholarship for ten years. Every Monday and Wednesday, I made that five-hour drive to Chicago to attend classes and returned to work with Miss Dunham in East St. Louis.[9]

In this way Zak Diouf helped Dunham build her community arts school after a long choreographic and cinematic career, and at the same time he earned his first academic diploma in the United States. Eventually he moved to California, where he earned his second.

Indeed, Dunham usually chose the best, because Diouf had already been the artistic director of Ballet Mali, as well as having acquired a master's degree in African history, studying with the renowned historian Cheikh Anta Diop (1923–1986). Culture became an important tool in the struggle to develop unified polities out of the newly independent African countries during the immediate postcolonial era. The result was the birth of several national African dance companies that utilized their country's greatly varied ethnic festivals, rituals, and rites as source material for staged productions.[10] Diouf revealed that after the independence of the Francophone countries of Senegal, Guinea, and Mali, they formed *one* dance company, and Diouf was the artistic director of the conglomerate company, called the "Mali Dance Ensemble." Unfortunately, nationalism prevailed in the end and the tri-national dance company was short-lived, splitting into separate national dance companies. Dunham saw Mor Thiam and Zak Diouf in the resulting National Ballet of Senegal.

Diouf originally came to the Bay Area to accept a job offer in biochemistry; however, always the student, he deepened his music and dance expertise with doctoral studies in ethnomusicology at UCB. "I got tired of Chicago and St. Louis, and came here, after Suzette Johnson of Dimensions Dance Theater came to take classes with Dunham, and invited me to come to the Bay Area because she was working with Elendar Barnes and Deborah Vaughan."[11] This statement establishes one of Diouf's motivating reasons for choosing the Bay Area. By coming to work with Dimensions Dance Theater, one of Oakland's first black dance companies (and now, certainly the most enduring black dance institution), he came in direct contact with the dance populations that Ruth Beckford had readied.

During the intervening four years of ethnomusicology, Diouf established himself in the Bay Area's black dance and music scene. The Wajumbe Dance Ensemble, founded by Nontsizi Cayou at San Francisco State University, was one of the first black dance companies to hire Diouf to teach traditional rhythms to its drummers, to prepare them for their first trip to Africa and for representing San Francisco at FESTAC, the second World Black Arts Festival in Lagos, Nigeria, in January 1977. "I came with the *djembe* and trained their drummers," he remembered, "like Michael Bass, Cedric Wilson, and others. I'm teaching my fifth generation of students now [in Oakland]."[12] With the help of Zak Diouf, the black dance community was learning traditional dances and the *sabar*, djembe, and *kutiro* rhythms of West Africa, pushing beyond cultural memory to specific rhythms and dances that would become its regional trademark.

Diouf founded Diamano Coura West African Dance Company in 1975 and with his wife, Naomi Diouf (from Liberia), developed the company as one of the earliest African dance companies in the Bay Area. Today they are the dynamic duo behind Diamano Coura, which means "those who bring the message" in the Senegalese Wolof language. As artistic director, Naomi Diouf teaches the majority of the company's community dance classes and teaches West African dance at Berkeley High School to more than four hundred students per semester. Four of Naomi and Zak's children, Esailama Artry-Diouf, Madiou Diouf, Ibrahima O. Diouf, and Kine Diouf, dance and drum with the company, making it an Oakland family dynasty. Yet the company is also populated with several African Americans who have studied for years with the Dioufs. Additionally, the professional choreographer and former director of the Liberian National Cultural Troupe, Nimely V. Napla, has also been a member of the company, simultaneously having his own company, the Nimely Pan-African Dance Company in Minnesota and California.

Although Zak and Naomi represent two West African heritages—Senegal and Liberia—the senior dancers-drummers of Diamano Coura, over the years, have also encompassed the dance cultures of Mali, Guinea, Cote d'Ivoire, and the Gambia. This has made their performance repertoire rich and eclectic. Besides the usual traditional dances that have become staples in West African dance across the United States, such as *sabar* of the Wolof, the national dance of Senegal; *mandiani* of the Malinke or Maninka of Guinea and Mali; and *lenjengo* of the Mandingo people of Senegal, they have also featured dances of the Kpellé, Kru, Vai, Gio, Loma and Grebo ethnic groups as well.

In an interview for a 2014 memorial celebration for Nelson Mandela in San Francisco, Naomi expressed her image of the Bay Area African dance dynamics over the decades:

> It operated [in earlier days] on a smaller scale, but there was a passion and a desire among people to make this thing bigger—a desire to get back to their roots. People came from all over to be part of the African dance community in the Bay Area. There was this unity in the community that was fantastic. It's not that it doesn't still exist, but it was on a different scale—it was much more intimate.[13]

Naomi's assessment of the Bay Area African dance community in the 1980s and 1990s reinforces my perspective of an enthusiastic roots community that was thirsty for a sense of "authenticity" that she and Zak installed. As Zak told me, "This is the center for African and African-derived dance. Oakland

and the [larger] Bay Area have a gift. The people here are so conscious about blackness and dance. That is what saved them."[14] The San Francisco–Oakland Bay Area—as the political home of the Black Panthers, the cultural home of the Black Arts Movement–West, as well as the initiator of Black Studies in higher education—was ripe to become one of the main centers for African dance in the United States.

Diamano Coura's biggest event is their annual Collage des Culture Africaines, usually held in early March. The event is a four-day dance and drum conference, including panel discussions, dance and drum classes, and performances. The 2014 conference, titled "Reflections—Looking at Where We Have Been," was their twentieth anniversary of the Collage and featured sixteen master classes taught by African and Diaspora artists from ten major cities in the United States. Master classes were taught by Oumou Faye of Senegal, Mabiba Baegne of the Congo-Brazzaville, Assane Konte of Washington D.C.'s Kankouran West African Dance Company, Senegalese Idy Ciss (based in Chicago), Guinean dance master Youssouf Koumbassa, Senegalese Mareme Faye (based in Los Angeles), and Malian Djeneba Sako (based in Denver). Headliners of the performances included Julia Tsitsi Chigamba and Chinyakare from Zimbabwe, C. K. Ladzekpo's African Music and Dance Ensemble, their own Diamano Coura West African Dance Company, and Bay Area Diaspora dance companies: Dimensions Dance Theater, the premiere Bay Area Brazilian dance company Fogo Na Roupa, and Mahea Uchiyama, an African American Hawaiian hula and Polynesian dance master with her company.

In their press release, Naomi put their twentieth-anniversary conference in context: "Our culture is strong and alive and it's what binds the community. We come from all walks of life to display our journey from Africa to the West Indies, North America, and South America; we come to celebrate!" The activities were held in two important community locations: the Malonga Casquelourd Center for the Arts, the cultural center for African dance in Oakland (discussed below), and the Farnsworth Theater at Skyline High in the Oakland hills. The 2014 Collage des Culture Africaines was, in fact, a culmination of the decades of the unique African and Diaspora focus of the Oakland Bay Area, where African dance masters recognize the Diaspora, and vice versa, promoting a Pan-African consciousness that is unique to this area. Diamano Coura has also grown over the decades as a stable nonprofit organization that has received funding from major funders. The twentieth anniversary African Culture Conference was funded by the City of Oakland, Alliance for California Traditional Arts, the William and Flora Hewlett Foundation, and the Zellerbach Family Foundation.

In looking to the future, Diamano Coura has established a junior company of fifteen members; they are a part of the company's Youth and Arts-in-Education Program that performs and offers classes not only in the Bay Area but also in San Diego and Los Angeles areas as well. As Zak has focused his artistic work across the state of California, he continues to affect youth statewide. The emphasis on a youth program means that the company will continue to replicate itself, extending a socialization through the arts process, which is a primary function of dance and music in traditional African societies.

During my interview with Zak, he discussed African dance in relation to contemporary modern dance and ballet in the United States. When I asked him what he perceived had changed over the decades in the Oakland African dance community, he reflected and said:

> Modern dance used to be much more popular. The old-timers knew it all, which made them much easier to work with, because [of] their knowledge of other dance forms along with their craving for African dance. Now, today, they are coming only from a social dance background.[15]

Zak remembers when he worked with Dimensions Dance Theater in Oakland and Wajumbe Cultural Institution in San Francisco in the 1970s. Their artistic directors had trained in Dunham Technique, modern dance, and ballet, which gave them a body and stage awareness from which he could build his African repertoire. Many of today's African dance students have eschewed that kind of formal dance training. Zak perceives that omission as an artistic deficit, which he bemoans today.

In fact, Zak and Naomi appreciate other cultural dance forms and have worked with the San Francisco, New York City, Tulsa, Singapore, and South African ballet companies. For example, in 1993 Zak collaborated with San Francisco Ballet's choreographer Val Caniparoli on the ballet "*Lambarena*" that blended West African dance and European classical ballet to the music of Johann Sebastian Bach and traditional music of Gabon.[16] This unlikely dance collaboration is happening more and more in the United States, as African dance becomes entrenched in the American fabric. Companies like Diamano Coura understand the history of dance in their chosen home of the Bay Area and are willing and eager to bring local communities together through their humanistic approach to African dance and music.

C. K. Ladzekpo and African Music
and Dance Ensemble

C. K. Ladzekpo of the Anlo-Ewe ethnic group of southeastern Ghana also arrived in the Bay Area in 1973. As Zak Diouf had been in UCB's Music Department, it was acclimated to some extent to African Music, and C. K. was able to assume an adjunct faculty position almost immediately. Whereas Diouf was focused on academic studies and was only occasionally teaching a music class, C. K. established a strong public persona at the premiere academic institution of the Bay Area. Since he came with impeccable credentials, he quickly formed a company, the African Music and Dance Ensemble, and became artistic director, choreographer, and lead drummer. He had come originally from one of the most famous musical families among the Ewe of Ghana; he had been a lead drummer and instructor with the Ghana Dance Ensemble, the University of Ghana's Institute of African Studies, and the Arts Council of Ghana; and, like Zak Diouf, he had performed at the highest levels of dance and music in his native country before coming to the United States. Thus, upon arriving at UCB, he was immediately able to introduce the Bay Area to traditional Ghanaian music and dance.

His classes were taught primarily for enrolled music students at UCB; but they became hugely popular in the 1970s, and community people flooded his courses also, including myself. He had actually been recruited by noted African American composer and musicologist Olly Wilson and was to come initially for only one year, while on hiatus from the University of Ghana, Legon (UG-Legon). He developed the African Music Ensemble within the Department of Music and, later, a corresponding dance course through the African American Studies Department. C. K.'s popularity grew further, particularly through Richmond's East Bay Center for the Performing Arts. He ended up staying in the United States and becoming an important fixture in Bay Area African music and dance.

Not only did C. K. become an established figure, but his brother Kobla Ladzekpo came to the United States and joined the Department of Ethnomusicology at University of California, Los Angeles (UCLA). Kobla started his own performing ensemble, the Zadonu African Dance Company, and today is an emeritus adjunct assistant professor. Together, C. K. and Kobla became the performing Ladzekpo Brothers throughout California. When asked why he chose to remain in the United States,

C. K. responds that he enjoys the new challenges of representing West African music to American students and audiences. Deeply interested in developing teaching methods to effectively communicate his music to foreign students, he has mapped out a process that involves lots of transcriptions of traditional repertoire from which new pieces for presentation can be created.[17]

To C. K., teaching, therefore, is equally important as his performing.

The model developed at the School of Music, Dance, and Drama (SMDD) at UG-Legon, with which C. K. had honed his skills, represents the dances and music of the primary ethnic groups of Ghana. Similarly, C. K. built his classes and the repertoire of his own African Music and Dance Ensemble on several Ghanaian cultures. The UG-Legon curriculum consisted of various traditional dance and music techniques of the Ashanti, Fanti, Ewe, Dagomba, Lobi, Dagari, and others. Coming from the Ewe Volta Region of Ghana, he was the department's expert in Ewe drumming and dance; but the format of the SMDD was to learn the music and dance of the other ethnic groups as well. C. K.'s UCB classes included not only the music and dances of the Ewe—*agbadza*, *gahu*, and the dynamic *atsiagbekor* war dance[18]—but the Ashanti *adowa*, Ga *kpanlogo*, and the Dagomba *damba* and *takai*.[19] In this way C. K. built his student clientele, as well as his own performing ensemble that drew from his consistent university students. Among these students, he found his African American wife, Betty Ladzekpo, who has been a principal dancer with the company since 1974, as well as Val Kai, another long-term member of the ensemble.

The multiethnic model of African dance companies grew from the national dance companies in the African postcolonial era, in which various ethnic groups configured under new African countries established by their colonial masters. The challenge for the master drummers and dancers, chosen under this multiethnic model to represent the newly independent nations, was to learn the many dances of each group and play all the various drums styles of groups beyond their own. For example, C. K. was already an expert at the Ewe master drum, the *atsimevu*, which instructs and leads the Ewe drum battery—*sogo*, *kidi*, and *kaga*—along with the *axatse* rattle and the *gankogui* bell. He had to also master the *atumpans* of the Ashanti and the *brekete* and *dondon* drums of the Dagomba in Northern Ghana. When he taught his classes and his company performed these varied cultural dances, he was introducing the immense diversity of West Africa. His instruction at UCB prepared me well for my 1976 trip to Ghana to study at UG-Legon, as well as for my travels throughout several regions to directly learn the dances and rhythms. I had a chance to study *adowa* with Auntie Grace Nuamah from the Ashanti region, and Ewe drumming from Kwashi Amevuvor, who eventually came to the United States also to teach at UCLA. Indeed, C. K. Ladzekpo became an important African drum and dance master in the Bay Area for generations of Americans interested in Ghanaian dance and music.

An important aspect of African dance and music is its functionality and the many roles it plays in its social and cultural contexts. For example, even the rhythmic *structure* of the music serves significant purposes on various levels. As C. K. states:

> Africans learned a long time ago that music is functional. . . . We may have several beat schemes going simultaneously, [and] when those beats agree, you have peace; when they don't, you have tension. These simulated stress phenomena or cross rhythmic figures are embodied in the art of dance-drumming as a mind nurturing exercise.[20]

Because this understanding is cultural and particular to traditional African settings, some of his students did not understand why they were attracted to the complex yet compelling African rhythms when C. K. brought these same rhythms to the United States. He reflected in the early '90s about the historic racial and cultural dimensions of the rhythmic transference across the Atlantic: "There are white kids who may be confused because they like this black art form. . . . We let them know that there's nothing wrong and that these rhythms and movements have been a part of their culture [part of the Americas] for a long time."[21]

There have been key moments of recognition of African dance in the United States by the concert dance world, and *African Dance and Music at Jacob's Pillow* in Lee, Massachusetts, in 1987 was one. The performances at "The Pillow" were the brainchild of Liz Thompson, who joined the staff in 1980, and according to The Pillow's website, Thompson "initiated an artistic resurgence by welcoming new artists and audiences."[22] African dance performance was one of those new initiatives for Jacob's Pillow in the late '80s. The film documentary was written and produced by Nancy R. Savin for Connecticut Public Television and featured a who's who in African dance and music, including Pearl Primus, Gambian griot Foday Musa Suso, Swazi Women Singers and Dancers from Swaziland, and, from the Bay Area, Malonga Casquelourd's Fua Dia Congo and C. K. Ladzekpo and his ensemble with his brother Kwaku Ladzekpo. It is noteworthy that the primary dance companies were from California—Fua Dia Congo and the African Music and Dance Ensemble—while the many fine New York African dance companies, which were closer to Massachusetts, were not included. *New York Times* dance critic Anna Kisselgoff was thoroughly impressed: "It is one of the most thoughtful and engrossing programs of African dancing, singing, and instrumental virtuosity to be seen in this country in many years."[23] This important event in the dance world was a chance to showcase Bay Area African dance and music within a larger context of the national dance scene.

For its presentation at "The Pillow," the African Music and Dance Ensemble featured the *atsiagbeko* traditional war dance drumming suite, which prominently demonstrates C. K. Ladzekpo's virtuosic mastery. It obviously impressed the audience and Kisselgoff alike. She wrote:

> In contrast to the graceful if exuberant [Swazi] women's group, the dancers and musicians of the Ladzekpo Brothers and the African Music and Dance Ensemble were energy personified. In their dances of the Ewe people of Dahomey, six women and two men, holding whisks, spurted into staccato bursts of movement. Yet these were collage-like phrases, performed in place: gestures, steps and torso contractions erupted and ended suddenly like the torrent of drums accompanying them. The dancers held themselves in flattened, angular shapes—those that had inspired Picasso's Cubism, perhaps. The group, directed by C. K. Ladzekpo, includes faculty members at various universities in California.[24]

Kisselgoff's recognition of the aesthetic of the Ewe *atsiagbeko* dance coincides with analysis by Africanist performance scholars, like Roger Abrahams, who have brought attention to the short, text-like tendency of black performance in general:

> [There is a] circular, vertiginous organization of performing groups; heavy emphasis on involvement through repetition of sound and movement; retreat from closure in favor of the ongoing and open-ended; *tendency to break up performance into short units or episodes, each of which is a whole, related to the other units because of intensity of contrast.*[25]

Indeed, the rhythmic virtuosic *atsiagbeko* dance is a perfect example of the rhythmic danced *text* of traditional African dance, with drum breaks that insure episodic spurts of movement verbosity. And, as dance journalist Shimon-Craig Van Collie says, "African dance and music grew out of the need to communicate and to find ways to cope with life's passages and stresses."[26]

Mandeleo Institute and "The Africans Are Coming"

The Ladzekpo Brothers—C. K., Kwaku, and their brother in Southern California, Kobla—are not only consummate artists, they are also effective organizers and administrators. Kwaku and C. K. started the Mandeleo Institute as a nonprofit African Heritage coalition dedicated to conserving African folklife in the United States. As their stated history says, "It was developed from a group of Bay Area African teachers, master artists, and ethnomusicologists who began offering African cultural arts workshops and classes in 1974." In 1979 the group produced its premiere season of the critically acclaimed annual African Cultural Festival, popularly known as the "Africans Are Coming!"[27] Kwaku, as executive director, continued to develop this festival until the mid-1990s.

The Ladzekpo brothers produced the festival in union venues, the Henry J. Kaiser Center in Oakland, while in San Francisco it was the Cowell Theater at Fort Mason Center. It became a central and reliable production where many of the increasing numbers of African dancer-drummers coming to the Bay Area could perform to a large audience. "Africans Are Coming!" became a much-anticipated African cultural event, drawing about one thousand people annually and becoming the precursor to Zak and Naomi's current Collage des Culture Africaines.

The Ladzekpo brothers conceived of their nonprofit umbrella organization to develop African culture in relation to the growth of Oakland: "Mandeleo maintains four professional African repertory dance companies in-residence and is credited for the emergence of the city of Oakland as the major center for African music and dance activities in the United States," stated their 1991 concert program. It was the quality of the dance companies like their own African Music and Dance Ensemble, Diamano Coura, and Fua Dia Congo, as well as their administrative expertise that increased the visibility of African dance and music in Oakland and corresponded to the city's history of black consciousness and activism.

In fact, it was this Bay Area black cultural history, along with the African triad of Zak, C. K., and Malonga Casquelourd (see below) that attracted other African dance and drum masters to the area. Master Senegalese dancer Alassane Kane and master drummer Abdoulaye Diakite arrived in the early 1990s and founded Ceedo Senegalese Dance Company in Oakland. Also, the Zulu Dance Theatre of South Africa, consisting of defectors from the South African musical *Ipi Tombi* that toured the United States in the early 1980s, found their way to Oakland. Together with Bay Area long-term dance company Dimensions Dance Theater (directed by Ruth Beckford protégé Deborah Vaughan), Chicago-born drummer Mosheh Milon Sr. (who moved to the Bay Area in the early 1980s and formed Bantaba Dance Ensemble), as well as Brazilian-born Jose Lorenzo's Batucaje Dance Company (prominent in the late 1970s), the African and African Diaspora dance community flourished and was highly organized in Oakland during the 1990s.

Malonga Casquelourd and Fua Dia Congo

Congo-Brazzaville's Malonga Casquelourd was the third African pillar of the early Bay Area African dance community. He first lived and worked in East Palo Alto and arrived in Oakland in about 1975. Malonga and I crossed paths from the beginning, with our dance careers bringing us together in many artistic projects while developing a life-long friendship. I first met Malonga as a fellow teacher at the original Every Body's Dance Studio in Oakland at Fifty-First Street and Broadway in 1975.[28] After a year studying dance and music in Ghana, I returned to buy the dance studio, turning it into a nonprofit organization called Everybody's Creative Arts Center in 1977. Malonga was already an established teacher of Congolese dance who simply came with the sale of the dance studio, cementing our decades-long relationship.

Malonga was born Auguste Leonard Malonga Casquelourd in Douala, Cameroon, while his Congolese father, Malonga Fidel, was stationed as an officer in the French army in Cameroon. Malonga's daughter, Muisi-Kongo Malonga, paints a picture of her father (the fifth child of ten) as a youth leader in Congo-Brazzaville who "became an influential organizer and major force within a network of youth-led militias whose purpose was to create a climate that would lead to the Congo's independence."[29] Malonga and I had many conversations about African politics that would leave me in disbelief at his command of African history and politics, belied by his usual casual, playful, and humorous demeanor.

In the Congo he had become a principal dancer with the national Congolese Dance Company in his teens, subsequently leaving for Paris where he joined Le Ballet Diaboua in his early twenties. He then moved to New York and, along with fellow Congolese dancer Titos Sompa, founded the first Central African dance company in the United States, Tanawa. Yet he would make his greatest artistic and cultural impact in Oakland, California. Muisi-Kongo muses, "And it was here in Oakland that he found a home. A home that was full of people with familiar faces and eyes that longed for him to share his culture and history with them, a longing that he was happy to oblige."[30] It was Oakland's black dance legacy that became the fertile ground on which Malonga's legacy could be formed.

Today, Oakland's major center for African dance now bears Malonga's name. The dance center that I founded in 1977, Everybody's Creative Arts Center (ECAC), eventually became one of the anchor tenants in the city-owned Alice Arts Center on Alice Street at Fourteenth Street in 1986. When Malonga was killed in a tragic car accident in 2003, there was an overwhelming effort by the African and African Diaspora dance community to name the entire center after him. ECAC had become CitiCentre Dance Theater (CDT) in 1987 and finally became defunct in 2005, but the Alice Art Center itself became the *Malonga Casquelourd Center for the Arts*, and in 2005 the building was designated Oakland Landmark #138.

However, this honor and recognition of the African dance community was hard-won. The vital African dance program at the Alice Arts Center in the early 2000s, during the mayoral administration of Jerry Brown (34th and 39th governor of California, 1975–1983 and 2011–2019), was put in jeopardy, prompting Oakland's historic black activism to be reactivated. When the primary black arts organizations, including CitiCentre Dance Theatre, were first established in the Alice Arts Center in 1986, Judge Lionel Wilson was in office as the first black mayor of Oakland. The arts organizations had gone through several business arrangements of occupancy, from paying full downtown rental rates to becoming rent-free by the time Jerry Brown was elected in the early 2000s.

Denise Pate, former dancer with Dimensions Dance Theater and now the cultural funding program coordinator for Oakland, elucidated the central issue around the fight for the Alice Arts Center and its renaming. Jerry Brown was elected with a "10K Housing Plan" that included an Oakland School of the Arts. His projected plan was to bring in ten thousand new residents to live in downtown Oakland; a school of the arts was to be part of the attraction. As the Alice Arts Center already had a vital dance community with many weekly community students, there was ostensibly a school of the arts already. If Brown had recognized this, his plan would have been a boost to the African dance community. However, Mayor Brown saw his Oakland School of the Arts as an actual full-time charter school, with the dance curriculum based in ballet and modern dance. Hence, there was a lack of comprehension of Oakland as an established center of African dance, at the heart of the city's identity.

There was also a severe lack of communication with the already existing anchor tenants of the arts facility. There was a concerted attempt to remove these arts organizations and put them in another, inadequate location.[31] Artists like Zak and Naomi Diouf, Deborah Vaughan and Malonga, along with Judith Smith of Axis Dance Company, Edsel Matthews of Koncepts Cultural Gallery, and Carla Service of Dance a Vision Entertainment, began to realize the need for arts activism in order to save their flourishing community in the Alice Arts Center. Journalist Chiori Santiago wrote for *Dance Magazine* about the competing political interests that become a performing arts crisis in Oakland:

Oakland's latest charter school could be a model for other public arts schools interested in sharing space with dance centers. But there is a cautionary tale here. The road to OSA [Oakland School of the Arts] may have been paved with good intentions, but an explosive mix of art and city politics quickly dropped the project into a sinkhole filled with facility issues and misunderstanding, delaying the school's opening for a full year and alienating a part of the arts community. The Alice Arts Center has a national reputation as a center for music and performance, particularly those forms derived from African traditions. City-subsidized rent and a downtown location have made it a haven for then nonprofit enterprises, including AXIS Dance Company, Diamano Coura West African Dance Company, Dimensions Dance Theater, and Oakland Ballet.[32]

The confrontation between the anchor Alice Arts Center organizations and city officials grew to a crescendo in 2003. Representatives of the Alice Arts Center testified at two City Council meetings about the need to preserve and support the current arts organizations in the Alice Arts Center. Following that, according to Denise Pate, cultural funding program coordinator of the Cultural Affairs Commission of Oakland, the commission members attended a meeting convened at the Alice Arts Center to continue negotiating the artists' concerns. In spring 2003, a huge representative group from the Alice Arts Center community marched to City Hall and held a rally in Frank Ogawa Plaza during the meeting of the Oakland City Council, complete with African drumming and dancing, and with signs saying, "Save the Alice!" and "The School of the Arts Must Go!"

Soon after the protest demonstration, Malonga Casquelourd himself insisted on a meeting with Mayor Jerry Brown, according to Denise Pate, "to discuss his concerns about displacement [of the Alice organizations and the African dance community]." Tragically, in June 2003 Malonga was killed in the car accident, and Jerry Brown ended up speaking at his funeral. The mayor said, "Malonga told me not to touch the Alice!" And from that point onward the intention of moving the anchor arts organizations out of the Alice Arts Center was never mentioned again.

Malonga had taken an activist stance: he met with Mayor Brown to represent the arts community that had built Oakland as a center for African dance for decades, about which the (white) mayor had no real understanding. Malonga's articulate stance, coupled with his untimely death, had convinced Jerry Brown that the character of Oakland's dance scene was already established, and he backed off from his plan for a school of the arts, realizing that it already existed in a *black* form. African dance is central to the identity of

Oakland, California, because of the long-term teaching, performing, and community activism of Malonga Casquelourd and the other African dance and drum masters since the 1970s.

One of Malonga's primary vehicles for promoting Central African culture was (and is) his professional dance company, Fua Dia Congo, which he started in 1977. The company's name means "Congolese Heritage," which is what Malonga was all about. Denise Pate has written about the company, illuminating Fua Dia Congo's purpose:

> The stellar dance and music ensemble draws its repertoire from the religious, social and military traditions of the Kongo Kingdom, which includes the modern day Republic of Congo, Democratic Republic of Congo, Angola, Gabon and the Central African Republic.[33]

The company is also known for its colorful and authentic costuming. Many of the dances call for braided raffia, painted red from a rare Congolese plant called *mpussu*, to signify spiritual power. The dancers and drummers alike wear *dibu* ankle rattles, adding extra rhythms to their feet movements, accenting the drumming. Congolese rhythms and movements, in particular, are an important foundational cultural aesthetic underlying many African Diaspora forms, such as Brazilian *samba*, Cuban *rumba*, and U.S. American *funk*.

Malonga was an equally strong dancer and drummer, often strapping his *ngoma bakongo* master drum around his waist and dancing *zebola*, his signature Congolese dance. He would dance around the stage with his punctuating hip-swiveling movements and infectious smile, never missing a beat. After Malonga's untimely death, his four children, the long-term members of Fua Dia Congo, and the Congolese community in Oakland unified to continue the dance company and the community dance and drum classes. His elder daughter, Muisi-Kongo, the daughter of the late linguistic scholar Dr. Faye Knox, became the artistic director of Fua Dia Congo, while his younger daughter, Lungusu, helps teach many of the community dance classes. The elder son, Kiazi, became the company's music director, drumming for and also teaching many of the classes, calling down the spirit of the Congo as his father did in the past. The younger son, Boueta, has become a noted drummer and performs with the company as well. The elder members of Fua Dia Congo, such as Congo-born Regine N'dounda, Sandor Diabankouezi, and Matingou Rafael, along with the long-term African American members, Regina Calloway, Erica Simpson, and Janeen Johnson, continue bringing their years of experience to the performances.

The power of Malonga's cultural and artistic contributions to the Bay Area continue through his children and the many dancers and drummers he taught. Kiazi Malonga embodies so much of what his father taught him when he illuminates Congolese culture:

> Drumming and dancing are codependent. There can't be drumming without dancing, but if the music is good, you want to move. I think that they feed off of each other. The drummer provides the music and support for the dancing, and the dancing in turn inspires the drummers. If the drumming is sweet, the dancing level rises.[34]

Indeed, this scenario can be witnessed during the Saturday midday Congolese dance class first established by Malonga back in 1975, which continues today with his children, as he smiles as honored ancestor. Malonga Casquelourd's legacy also continues in his namesake building, the Malonga Casquelourd Center for the Arts, the hub of African dance in Oakland.

Conclusion

Oakland and the Bay Area have had a long history of black cultural and political activism. As the African dance community grew, it took on this proactive sociopolitical stance by establishing its prominence as a dance genre. Oakland has become a center for African dance and music because of the cultural and personal expertise of the continental Africans who migrated to the city. Black consciousness at the historical foundation of this region of California provided a ripe environment for these particular African cultural forms to thrive among enthusiastic performers, as well as among huge audiences of committed fans. From the Ladzekpo brothers and their Mandeleo Institute's annual production "The Africans Are Coming!" in the 1990s to Zak and Naomi Diouf's annual four-day conference with its performances, workshops, and panels within Collage des Culture Africaines today, the African dance and drum masters who chose the Oakland Bay area have consistently provided comprehensive, proactive African cultural programs and organizational institutions that can compete anywhere in the world.

Moreover, the Oakland Bay Area region had an early latent propensity for African dance and music of the highest order with the Dunham dance and cultural legacy through Ruth Beckford and her protégés. Deborah Vaughan's Dimensions Dance Theater has fostered this legacy for over forty years through her African, Diaspora, and modern dance aesthetic. Deborah has taken the Dunham legacy to a twenty-first-century level with projects that have not only illuminated the political legacy of the region, such as her "Project Panther" about the Black Panther Party for Self-Defense that premiered in 1996 and was revived in 2016 for the Panther's fiftieth anniversary, but have also developed strong African and Diaspora dance collaborations. In the early 2000s Dimensions premiered "From Africa to America," an international collaboration between the company and Cuban choreographer Isiais Rojas and Zimbabwean *mbira* player Stella Chiweshe. These African Diaspora productions have earned Deborah Vaughan respect from the African dance and drum masters.

The black cultural activist tradition of the Oakland Bay Area, which has usually included a Pan-African consciousness, has produced both a receptive black community and a large multiracial regional community for African-based dance and music as well. Such a distinctive regional community has provided willing and knowledgeable students and company members for the triad of African dance and drum masters I have explored in this chapter. Additionally, the audience base remains strong nearing the third decade of the twenty-first century. When the 2003 Alice Arts Center crisis occurred, threatening the physical center for African dance, support from this regional African dance and music constituency rose up in protest in front of Oakland's City Hall. The legacy of cultural passion and commitment to the great African legacy that underpins the cultural development of the United States is alive and well in the Oakland Bay Area. Dedication to this legacy, as a counternarrative to one in which African dance and music are somehow inferior to European classics, which was suggested by the Oakland School of the Arts proposal in the early 2000s, only made the community more cohesive and articulate in promoting its counternarrative. Now the center for African dance in the Bay Area is forever etched in Oakland with the name of one of the culture's main proponents, Malonga Casquelourd.

The observations of Mama Pearl Primus in the 1950s about the power of African dance can be observed in the twenty-first century within the African dance community in Oakland: "People who truly dance are those who have never bartered the fierce freedom of their souls, never strangled their hunger for rhythmic movement, nor frustrated their joyous physical response to music and song." African dance and music have bolstered "the fierce freedom of their souls," from the training and performance of the triad of Oakland African masters—Zak Diouf, C. K. Ladzekpo, and Malonga Casquelourd—to the next generation of African-based artists in the Oakland Bay Area, including other dance and drum masters of Bay Area African dance companies, as well as the children of these masters like Muisi-Kongo, Kiazi, and Esailama. The African dance and music community in Oakland has never retreated to a safe ground, but instead, as Mama Pearl reveals, it has been "snatched, plucked up by an invisible force and hurled into the ring of the dance."[35]

Notes

1. Pearl Primus, "African Dance," in *African Dance: An Artistic Historical and Philosophical Inquiry*, ed. Kariamu Welsh Asante (Trenton, N.J.: Africa World, 1996), 3. (Reprinted with permission by the author from her dissertation, "Masks in the Enculturation of Mano Children," New York University School of Education, Nursing and Arts Profession.)

2. Ibid., 3.

3. Ruth Beckford, speech to the audience, "Celebrating the Dunham Legacy," Katherine Dunham Legacy Northern California Memorial, Laney College Theater, Oakland, June 8, 2006.

4. Paul Gilroy, *The Black Atlantic: Modernity and Double Consciousness* (Cambridge, Mass.: Harvard University Press, 1993), ix.

5. Halifu Osumare, "Dancing the Black Atlantic: Katherine Dunham's Research to Performance Method." *AmeriQuest*, Special Issue: "Migration of Movement: Dance across Americas," September 19, 2010, http://www.ameriquests.org/index.php/ameriquests /article/view/165.

6. Pierre Nora, *Les Lieux de Mémoire* (Paris: Gallimard, 1984).

7. VèVè A. Clark, "Performing the Memory of Difference in Afro-Caribbean Dance: Katherine Dunham's Choreography, 1938–87," in *History and Memory in African-American Culture*, ed. Geneviève Fabre and Robert O'Meally (New York: Oxford University Press, 1994), 190.

8. Ruth Beckford, *Katherine Dunham, A Biography* (New York: Dekker, 1979), 2–3.

9. Zak Diouf, personal interview at Malonga Casquelourd Center for the Arts, Oakland, Calif., April 23, 2015.

10. For a study of the role of African dance companies in nation building during the postcolonial era in Africa see John A. A. Ayoade, "The Culture Debate in Africa," *The Black Scholar*, (Summer/Fall 1989), 1–10.

11. Zak Diouf interview.

12. Ibid.

13. Rob Taylor, "Bringing the Message: Naomi Diouf and Diamano Coura West African Dance Company." *Dancers Group: Promoting the Visibility and Viability of Dance*, July 2014. http://dancersgroup.org/2014/07/bringing-message-naomi-diouf -diamano-coura-west-african-dance-company.

14. Zak Diouf interview.

15. Ibid.

16. See "Fusion: *Lambarena* by Val Caniparoli" for a rehearsal of the piece and a commentary about the collaborative dance process, https://www.youtube.com /watch?v=ohV2zVhq8bI.

17. African Music Ensemble Description/History, Department of Music, Univer-

sity of California, Berkeley, http://music.berkeley.edu/performance-opportunities /african-music-ensemble.

18. These first three Ewe dances are the staple dances of Ewe people in Ghana and Togo. *Agbadza* is their signature dance that today is performed on social occasions, belying its war-dance origins. This fun dance is often called "the chicken dance," because both male and female dancers use the arms and elbows to the side of body in an up and down motion like a chicken. *Gahu* is a group dance performed in a circle with an emphasis on swiveling hips. Each dancer holds the hips of the person in front of him/her and helps the dancer move the hips more vigorously. *Atsiagbekor* is originally a war dance performed after battle when warriors returned from war. Now it portrays historic battle sequences and strategies at social occasions. An important feature is the interaction between the master drummer and the dancers.

19. These latter named dances are staples in the repertoire of the Ghana Dance Ensemble at the University of Ghana, Legon, representing its commitment to ethnic diversity within the repertoire. *Adowa* is the signature dance of the Ashanti people and is performed as a solo dance, particularly at funerals. The skilled *adowa* dancer can express many Ashanti proverbs through intricate hand gestures. *Kpanlogo* is a well-known dance of the Ga people of Greater Accra and has the distinction of being a relatively new dance. It was an innovative dance of the 1960s by Ga youth that was influenced by American pop music; however, it is accompanied by old Ga drumming traditions. *Takai* is one of the oldest rhythms and dances of the Dagomba people of Northern Ghana and tells how the Dagomba became close to the Mossi people of that region and Burkina Faso. Male dancers, wearing large woven smocks, form a large circle and hold rods in the right hand and strike the rod of another dancer, forming another percussive rhythm with the drumming.

20. Shimon-Craig Van Collie, "What Is African Dance in America?" *Dance Teacher Now* (July/August 1992): 63.

21. Ibid., 64.

22. "The Jacob's Pillow Story," https://www.jacobspillow.org/about/pillow-history /jacobs-pillow-story/

23. Anna Kisselgoff, "Dance: 'Dance and Music of Africa' at Jacob's Pillow." *New York Times*, July 22, 1987.

24. Kisselgoff, "Dance."

25. Roger Abrahams, "Concerning African Performance Patterns," in *Neo-African Literature and Culture: Essays in Memory of Janehinz Jahn*, ed. Bernth Lindforsand and Ulla Schlid (Wiesbaden, Ger.: Heymann, 1976), 40. Emphasis added.

26. Van Collie, "What is African Dance?," 63.

27. Kwaku Ladzekpo, "Organizational History and Purpose," 2nd Annual African Dance Season at San Francisco (program), Cowell Theater, Fort Mason Center, February 8–9, 1991.

28. Every Body's was a dance cooperative started by Michelle Berne, Ferolyn Angell, and Sharon Arslanian, seven years before the start of the nonprofit organization Everybody's Creative Center, which I created in 1977 (after buying the business from

Angell and Arslanian). There, local dance teachers successfully planted the seed of a center for dance instruction beyond ballet or modern dance—in other words, emphasizing and sharing ethnic and folkloric dance forms that were taught by local and transnational teachers (personal communication from Yvonne Daniel, as corroborated by Sharon Arslanian, June 13, 2017).

29. Muisi-Kongo Malonga, "Malonga: The Spirit of a Master Teacher," *Movement Stories: I've Known Rivers: The MoAD Stories Project*, Museum of African Diaspora, San Francisco, January 2006. http://www.iveknownrivers.org/read-2.0.php?id=56.

30. Ibid.

31. Denise Pate, email correspondence, July 10, 2015.

32. Chiori Santiago, "Lessons Learned at Alice Arts Center: Art and Politics Don't Mix at New Arts-Based Charter School," *Dance Magazine*, February 1, 2003, https://www.thefreelibrary.com/Lessons+learned+at+Alice+Arts+Center%3A+art+and+politics+don%27t+mix+at . . . -a097174133.

33. Denise Pate, "Fua Dia Congo: Dancing Malonga Casquelourd's Legacy," Dancers' Group, December 2007, http://dancersgroup.org/2007/12/fua-dia-congo-dancing-malonga-casquelourds-legacy.

34. "Fua Dia Congo—Oakland Based Drum and Dance Group—Interview Excerpts with Kiazi Malonga," *Music Ethnography of the Bay Area*, https://musicethnographybayarea.wordpress.com/bay-area-musics/fua-dia-congo-oakland-based-congolese-drum-dance-group.

35. Primus, "African Dance."

The African Choreographer's Envisioning

Naomi Gedo Johnson Diouf

The experience and training of an African dancer in the United States is different from that of an African dancer on the African continent. Unlike her/his/their African counterparts, the African dancer in the United States has to understand that he/she/they are executing historical and communicative movements as opposed to a series of separated physical steps or bodily movements. What's being executed is a sequence of African dance movements, but in reality, it is a narration, a story of an event or an emotional moment within the daily life or extraordinary circumstances of the community. Yet the advantage of the African dancer in the United States has is access to a larger dance vocabulary than many dancers on the continent. This is mainly due to the various movement techniques and dance repertoires that are learned from a variety of African dance teachers who have migrated to the United States. Typically, that migration route includes major cosmopolitan cities, such as New York, Washington, D.C., Chicago, Atlanta, Los Angeles, Oakland, or Minneapolis and other urban centers where there are many African migrant artists.

In addition to the kaleidoscope of African dance styles and techniques, students of African-based dance in the United States are able to study the cultural relevance of drumming and extremely varied drumming techniques, to which many continental dancers do not always have access. By taking drum classes, learning dance from drummers, and studying how the music is applied to the dance, students of African-based dances are able to enter a deep appreciation and understanding of how the music informs and grounds various body positions.

Another important difference is revealed when we consider how African dances are understood among African communities and how the non-African media, and critics especially, report and instruct audiences about African dance. Africans from all fifty-four continental countries primarily associate dance with ideals and philosophies of agreed-upon cultural principles and social behaviors. In the dance performance, the morals of African societies are made visible; values for nature itself, human, animal and plant life, and cooperative social relations are played out in dance dramas; and life-giving parts of the body are featured and revered. In contrast, and especially until recent decades, critics have challenged African dance practices with descriptions and analyses that often viewed lively body-part isolations and exaggerated body positions as "sexual," rather than instruct nonnative, diverse audiences regarding African aesthetics that not only emphasize the torso as the container of life-giving organs (the heart, the sex organs, the womb) but also augment notions of vitality in dances that accentuate the life-giving pelvis. Until recently, observers of African choreographies looked at the pelvic squat, the lowered upper torso, or the shimming of the shoulders and breasts as indecent, impolite, inappropriate, or "vulgar" movements. On the contrary, these positions, poses, and so-called sexual movements most often reinforce African philosophies and spiritualty with life-giving at their centers, provide African dancers with a firm and steady base, and, additionally, lead to exquisite execution.

There are also similarities, of course. For both continental African dancers and dancers in the Diaspora, correct placement of movements within the timing of a dance sequence is crucial. No matter the tempo or speed of the rhythm, the dancer must acclimate to the meters and patterns within the rhythm of a choreography in order to execute precise, effortless movements. And, in both sites, dance and music can be used simultaneously to tell the stories of a people, to relax and have fun, as well as to provide economic survival. It is important to note that the weaving of music and dance opens up a spiritual space in African dance performance that most performers and spectators find pleasing and, sometimes, healing. With these African dance understandings in place, I offer lessons learned as an African artist, performing and teaching African dance to mainly United States students and adult members of the Oakland Bay Area in California. I ultimately fathom possibilities for African dance and African dance artists in the future.

African Dance Styles—Forest, Earth, Savannah, and Ocean

In traditional African dances, the metaphysical and the spiritual are routinely invoked. Since there is always a connection between the physical and spiritual worlds in African cultures, most believe that connection is the foundation of who we are. In many African cultures, the indoctrination into the ways of the spiritual world occurs in the forest (called forest, "bush," or bush forest); this is the environment where many rites-of-passage initiations and traditional trainings occur.

As an African choreographer living in the United States and working mostly with American-born adults and youth, I have utilized specific words in my teachings to reference the various styles that are prominent in the western region of Africa specifically. "Forest" or "Earth" style refers to movements that are performed close to the earth. "Savannah" or "Air" style refers to upright movements. "Ocean" or "water" style refers to movements that are fluid and imitative of waves, the ocean, river, or ripples of water.

Earth dances, representing everyday tasks such as planting, farming, food preparation in squatting positions, sweeping, et cetera, can occur in the forest or wherever movements are executed close to the ground. Forest and earth dances are usually very difficult for dancers in the United States because dancers must utilize all of the largest muscles in the body (the glutes, quads, obliques, back muscles, and abdominal muscles) to execute the distinctive semi-squat position, which is foreign to or out of usual range within daily American activities. In these positions, dancers have to engage the hip flexors to have the stomach and chest almost touching, as in the *klakan* water or *krahn* monkey dances of Liberia or the *achebekor* war dance of Ghana. Dancers in the United States usually have to commit to extra body and leg conditioning to achieve ease and flow within forest and earth movements. Conversely, in African villages, this conditioning is an inclusive aspect of daily tasks and activities from childhood to adulthood.

On the other hand, people living in the savannahs or open spaces with tall grasses tend to perform dances that require upright torsos in which elevation and elongation are emphasized. The functional objective is to elevate the body in an aerial fashion to see above the tall grasses. Savannah dances often seem to defy gravity; for example, the Maasai of East Africa can leap up to seven feet, while keeping a statuesque position. Also in this category are the acrobatic dances of the Fulani and Gola ethnic groups, who engage in effortless backward and forward aerial flips; or the Malinke dancers, who suspend their bodies in the air with continuous barrel turns or perfect straddle jumps.

All people rely on the element of water for their survival and existence. Many African water dances imitate the waves of the ocean and ripples of the river, as in the *klakan* rites-of-passage dance of the Kru people of Liberia. In dances where water inspires the movement, dance performers enter the world of fluidity, flow, shape-shifting, and surrendering of attachment to form. Water, in many dances, can represent purification and cleansing, both in everyday tasks and also within sacred spiritual practices, such as within the *Yemoja* dances originating in Nigeria and the *ndep* practices in Senegal.[1] African dances that carry oral narratives of water deities or spirits, such as Yemoja and Mami Wata, are also prominent within many ethnic groups and often become a popular part of many national dance companies' touring repertoires.

As stated, African dances are influenced and motivated by the contrasting geographic regions that various ethnic groups inhabit. On the continent, as the dancer goes through daily life—squatting, cooking, washing clothes, giving birth—he or she becomes quite comfortable using these postures and positions in choreography. In the United States, however, students of African dance are accustomed to chairs, cars, washing machines, or lying on hospital tables or beds for birthing. Consequently, as dancers, they are required to make up the difference between their ordinary lifestyles and the extraordinary expressive movements required in more traditional African dances.

Diamano Coura West African Dance Company

Diamano Coura, which means "Those Who Bring the Message" in the Wolof language of Senegal, is a West African dance company that prides itself on including as many West African dance styles in its repertoire as possible. My husband, Zakarya Diouf of Senegal, and I created and developed the company to perform the many varieties of forest, earth, savannah, and ocean dance styles that are found in West Africa—mainly Guinea, Mali, Sierra Leone, Liberia, Ivory Coast, and Senegal. Diamano Coura presents artistic productions that are multidisciplinary, utilizing rhythmic movement, visual art, poetry, spoken word, song, percussion, and digital media. In this way, the company keeps alive the art of African oral tradition and multiple dance styles while keeping the subject matter and presentation relevant for contemporary audiences.

For example, let's look at one of Diamano Coura's original pieces, a two-part dance drama titled *Jusat* which premiered in 2007 at the San Francisco Ethnic Dance Festival.[2] The first part of *Jusat* blends traditional West African dance movements with traditional and pop music from Senegal and Mali to depict excerpts from the lives of first-generation Africans born in the United States. The second scene, subtitled "The Birth," is based on an old creation myth. Mawa, the Supreme God, in a thunderous conversation with his demigods, sends his strongest, most beautiful goddesses down to earth to give birth to the children and nations of Africa. The third scene, "The Initiation," speaks to the secret-society process of rites of passage young boys and girls undergo and the joy and pride parents experience when their children return from the secret society transformed into young men or women. Their esteem is both for their children's coming of age and also for the veneration of the family's ancestral divinities and their connection to nature. In the closing scene (of Part One), "The Harvest" depicts the celebration of the rites of passage and a time when the community harvests its best crops in preparation of a grand feast.

Jusat was a production created in response to documented research literature and media news about the discovery of one of the oldest archeological remains found in Ethiopia, East Africa.[3] The historic find was one of the most complete African female fossils; it occurred at the same time that I was thinking about the chaotic effects that the Liberian war was having on women and children. As the choreographer, I wanted the audience to see this woman—the first human being—come to life. I wanted her to become larger than life for the audience. I wanted them to imagine her giving birth to the diverse people of the world!

Creating such powerful imagery on a very limited budget was challenging, especially due to the limitations of the theater and production equipment available. Meager budgets and limited access to technically advanced theater spaces are common constraints that African productions face—and yet we somehow manage to overcome.

The vision of the piece was multidimensional and multidisciplinary. For instance, the aim was to project a digital image of the archeological find on the cyclorama screen upstage. I envisioned a woman, dressed in a super-wide, long white dress, ascending to the stage from the orchestra pit and standing atop a stair platform—all to convey her omnipotent and overarching power. As *Jusat* unfolded, it expressed past and current events and also served as inspiration for upcoming choreographers to discuss the future and expansion of African dance in the twenty-first century and beyond.

In light of all the recent natural disasters and social-justice tragedies, including various health and political challenges within our society, in creating *Jusat* I felt that the local community needed to use its inherent powers to heal and guide young people—in these times. I believed that an effective

PHOTO 9.1. *Jusat*, choreographed by Naomi Diouf. Dancers (left to right): Latashia Bell, LaDonna Higgins, Naomi Diouf, Jacqueline Burgess, Ibrahima Diouf, Antoinette Holland. R. J. Muna, photographer (2007).

guide for accomplishing this objective could be found within ancient African oral traditions, folktales, philosophy, and belief systems. An important entity in my experience of traditional African village life has been the strong presence of a council of elders and various ceremonial masks, which serve as mediums between what is seen and what is unseen while, at the same time, giving direction to the community.

In *Jusat*, masks and masked dancers were used as a way of representing the dynamic relationship between the natural and spiritual worlds. In many African cultures, masks dance and do not speak, passing messages through elder priests and other designated persons. In creating *Jusat*, we used the function of the mask and the community of elders within West African traditional society to shape our choreography while applying these to the contemporary issues being faced by young people in contemporary society. As a high school teacher for more than twenty-seven years, I have come to realize that in American society we have long witnessed and been sensitive to our youth with their often-nonchalant attitudes, rebellious nature, and the absence in their lives of a sense of deep belonging. As adults, we are uncomfortably aware of our inability to communicate with them thus far, but we want to respond to their obvious cries for help. The following performance sketch provides a viable answer through the artistry and foundational structures of West African dance drama, which teach and heal, as well as entertain.

The Performance—*Jusat*

Prologue

Before the existing maladies of modern, "civil-lies-zation," there was the original civilization. This civilization was an advanced state of human organization, culture, and technology, based on the philosophical truths of communalism, harmony with nature, common good for all, with spiritual growth and integrity as the highest rewards.

The ancient African civilization of Egypt, steeped in truisms, educated the Greeks, Persians, Turks, and other invaders. The Egyptians implanted writing, reading, math, science, true Democracy and politics, advanced science, medicine, spiritual insights, and rules still not honestly understood—even by modern society's most brilliant minds. These principles of life are incorporated in the reality, mysticism, and truthful traditions of all African cultures.

As Diamano Coura—"Those who bring the message"—we present you, our audience, with this moment of "Jusat." To see, feel, understand, and know truth is to really be civilized. To know the truth of the past is to bring forth the future.

Program Notes

The importance of rituals in African societies, as in others, can be seen through life-cycle developments. Rituals announce changes in the individual and the community and are also invoked to foster social unity. In order for the outside world—in this case, dance students and audiences in the United States—to properly assist Africa in the adaptation of foreign systems, audiences in the United States must first open themselves to learn and respect Africa's life-cycle rituals. Audiences must also participate by providing assistance within the context of the African theatrical environment and focus on whichever aspect is at the center of activities—perhaps a ritual dance or a religious ceremony, a birth, an initiation, a rite of passage, or a marriage. Another important African cultural event is the honoring and ritual support of the complete mourning process. Healing, associated with the mourning process—also an important part of the life cycle—is a process mostly ignored in the United States.

Part One

Scene I, "The Birth"

Mawa, the supreme God, speaks to his demi-gods in thunderous sounds and sends one of his most beautiful and strongest goddesses down to earth. She gives birth to the children and nations of Africa. The demi-gods assist by giving the goddess supportive powers to accomplish this important task.

A dance example: This section alternates between the solo section of the goddess descending to earth and the group section featuring the collective powers of other demi-gods. The movements start with uplifted arms followed by light running movements across the stage. In the end, the movement is in unison, bold and stately, with the goddess at the center expressing agony and pain. Everything slows down as the lights fade slowly to black and, with a piercing scream, the goddess brings forth the nations.

Scene II, "Civilization"

Each great nation and empire that rose thereafter was led by a great and powerful King or Queen who built and strengthened his/her nation and contributed abundantly to Africa. These leaders were adored and respected by their people, and also by people living afar. The empires the leaders built were: Mali, Zululand, Egypt, Angola Congo, and Ethiopia, to name a few. These were some of the wealthiest, most learned and organized nations in the world.

In this scene, individual actors perform short monologues about the great empires of Axum, Ethiopia, Ghana, Mali, Songhai, Benin, Congo, and Angola. The scene transitions into the *lamba* rhythm of Mali as dancers in large tie-dye gowns perform figure-eight patterns across the stage around each standing actor.

Scene III, "The Initiation"

Mawa provided an educational system by which his people became supportive, cooperative, and functioning members of society. A traditional sequence of ceremonial rites marked the transitions from childhood to womanhood or manhood; large celebrations were organized to welcome those individual and community changes that took place, as well as changes that took place routinely in the environment—like the rainy and dry seasons, times to hunt and gather, times to pay attention to the living, and times to attend to the ancestors. The most prominent ceremonies involved initiation of girls and boys.

Boys and girls are initiated separately in a secret school located in the bush forest, where all training takes place. Information given to the uninitiated youngsters refers to the rules and boundaries within the socialization of men and women, but there is a definite accommodation to age. Mental development occurs at various stages; therefore, secret-society groupings are in age sets that combine children with similar readiness—in other words, they match physical strengths, mental abilities, and maturity for each group. Family and village members take a girl or boy into the forest at dawn in order to "feed" her/him to the forest spirit. At a later date, when the initiation process is complete, the former child is considered re-born as a new adult member of the society, and it is time to return home.

Some societies perform female circumcision in similar ritual practices, and there is resistance to this practice from all over the world, including African mothers who disagree with its continuance. However, African governments cannot compel people to abandon age-old traditions, nor can outside governments. These wishes need to accompany educational programs for indigenous people in conjunction with improved health practices. Traditional families need sanitized equipment at the least, but also education that points out the physical pain and mental scars that are damaging and that this cultural practice encourages. Adults, but especially women, need to be convinced that such practices are unnecessary for young girls.

While female circumcision is one controversial part of some rites-of-passage ceremonies, most African rituals bring forth the joy and pride of parents and other community members, as they see their children have grown up in the secret society of traditional school. Their children, after sometimes two to four years of rites-of-passage schooling, now new community members, return as respectable and resourceful young women and men. The whole community is assured that the next generation is prepared with survival knowledge in nature, but also with some understanding of the ancestral divinities as well.

This section is narrated by a storyteller while, simultaneously on stage, dancers dramatize various moments of young girls learning to wash clothes, cook, and farm, young boys learning to fish, hunt, fight, and build. Within each of these dramatic scenes there are musical moments wherein the boys and girls also learn movements from dances, such as the *ching* and *nyaka* rites-of-passage dances, for males and females respectively, of the Manding people from Casamance in southern Senegal.

Scene IV, "The Harvest" and Celebration

To give back to the newly initiated young people—for being so courageous—the community harvests its best crops, prepares small animals for cooking, and organizes a special celebration that lasts for days. African people believe in living harmoniously with nature, so they harvest just enough crops and prepare just enough animals to satisfy all. Africans use every part of what is destroyed in their eating and celebrating: but beforehand, they say prayers to bless what they have taken from nature and to ask for forgiveness for the taking.

In this scene the dramatic celebration is accompanied with rhythms and dances, such as *mendiani* from the Malinke people of Guinea and *wango* from the Toucouleur people in southern Mauritania and northern Senegal. These dances involve high kicks, jumps, and fast spins and are usually performed by the young people to show their skills and style within this celebratory social setting.

Scene V: "The Division"

Amid the celebration, an argument erupts between two young men from two different ethnic groups over a young woman. To resolve the situation, the council of elders from both ethnic groups are called upon to meet with the young people involved. It is also revealed in this scene that historic ethnic strife has fueled the young men's rivalry with each other. In many African cultures, disagreements are settled by a council of elders, paramount chiefs, and kings, or through spiritual guidance. Africans historically fought each other, and the victors left with the possessions of those who were conquered and sometimes with "slaves." These were not the enslaved Africans of the transatlantic crossings; these were "captives" that were respected as human beings who could earn their freedom, acquire property, and, in some cases, marry within the family and eventually rise high in the village leadership system.

The African system of slavery, before the colonial era, was misunderstood by Europeans. Europeans viewed enslavement as an opportunity to acquire human laborers and take valuable land and resources. They were able to feed on the dissatisfaction and greed of a few Africans, which is exhibited in major literary and historical documentation.[4] Most Africans could never have envisioned the impact of European slavery and colonialism on their people.

Intermission

Part Two

Scene I: "Division and Grief"

Even when enslaved people of African descent were freed, the minds of many remained enslaved, and that period lasted over generations for at least three hundred years. Africans adopted the European system of living with a worldview that differed dramatically and often came into conflict with their own. Coveting European products and worldviews has aided African divisions, not just along political borders but also in social, economic, and cultural contexts. In addition, the exodus of continental Africans, leaving Africa due to war or for "a better life," has created a brain drain within the continent, allowed African resources to be significantly diminished, and sometimes caused cultural traditions to go extinct. In the end, the African masses, supported by foreign aid, have released their frustrations with increased civil wars, which have left behind records of atrocious behaviors, like mass murders and mass displacements.

Globally, wars have caused much heartbreak as atrocities have prevailed. Sometimes, parents have been executed at gunpoint by their young children, who were trying to prove their loyalty after brain washings, forced drug use, and/or sexual abuse. Fetuses have been found dislodged from pregnant women while the mothers were alive. Families have been annihilated solely because they belong to a particular ethnic group or tribe.

Within the theatrical scene, the audience sees Mother Awoya, who has lost her two sons to the Liberian civil war. Within her grief, she performs a monologue and a song that asks "Why?" and pleads for Africans to make peace and to return to some of the old ways, also encouraging governments to work closely with the people.

Scene II: "Unity and Final Strength"

We return to an egalitarian society with mutual respect between males and females and where love is pure, simple, and joyous. The body is the temple of godliness and the mind is the splendid machine that works wonders. Children, our pride and joy, are cared for and respected as the leaders and innovators of the future. We bask in their energy, which is only an evolution of our own; our hope is in their eyes. All have come together, and we are free to build great empires and solve mysteries of the universe once again. The people have understood why Mawa created them. They say "Ahhh, Mawa is good," and they organize a big celebration in his honor.

Rhythms in this section transition from the more melancholic song of Mother Awoya to the collective voices of children, blended with the melodies of the *kora* (a string instrument). They sing happily about a new future, a brighter future. Just before the sun sets, along with the song of the children, the adults also begin to celebrate with a suite of intra-African dances: the *Vai* and *Gio* dances from Liberia, the *koukou* dance from Guinea, and *sabar* from Senegal, dancing into the night.

The End

Conclusion

While the dance drama sketch I have presented informs the audience as it entertains, the process of mounting such a choreography is filled with artistic, historical, philosophical, and moral lessons—for both younger and older performers. In choreographing African dance, we have to ask ourselves, first and foremost, what it means to take a folk narrative and bring it to the stage. As a choreographer, how do I transfer and translate what is in my imagination, my dreams, onto the bodies of dancers who may or may not be from the culture from which these imaginative dances and dream-filled stories have originated? What is at stake in bringing this "old tale" to new foreign audiences? The performance itself opens up a world in which the artist can assume a transformative role and engage the audience. The performance becomes the vehicle whereby information accumulates and societal lessons are palatable.

For me, as an African choreographer in the United Sates, I have been provided with the dancers, musicians, and production resources that have allowed me to dream big. If I wanted a forest on stage, I could put one there. If I wanted the costumes to be inspired by both indigenous folk culture and technology, I could make them so. Choreographing in the United States has allowed, supported, and challenged my imagination. In the United States, there is a large contingency of African dancers and companies that are using African cultural arts to build healthy communities, just as I am. For example, just as Diamano Coura does, several African dance companies are restoring cooperative, caring communities, assisting education in prisons and in anti-re-incarceration programs, and we all champion compassionate senior-center activities. We work with hospital rehabilitation centers, and we support public-school and university educational systems by incorporating the visual and performing arts into Science, Technology, Engineering, and Math, or STEM-based curricula. These artists and companies, like me, are fortunate, and we are using our fortunes and privileges in African traditional ways of cooperation and survival together.

My hope is that the next generation of choreographers can look at what I have done with limited resources and review and evaluate larger productions, like the "Lion King"—combining African narratives and aesthetics with modern technology and stagecraft—and see how far the staging of African narratives and choreographies can soar. I want the next generation of African choreographers to always remember that African dance is multilayered—encompassing music, storytelling, visual art, costuming, history, politics, dance, and theater. Keeping what is basic to and engrained within African cultural arts—the educating narrative—is what makes African dance distinct from other contemporary forms of dance performance.

In addition, as I refer to the importance of African cultural arts, I must raise my voice again to emphasize and underscore that African dance is a technique that makes significant impact within our local and neighboring communities. Through African dance training and performance, both males and females, youngsters AND elders, can have a viable career or life path. More than just a form of entertainment, although relaxation and recreation are important to human behavior also, dance training and performance are integral to humane human life. This is the real work of African dance in the future I envision for African artists in the Diaspora.

Notes

1. *Yemoja* dances are found within varied ethnic groups that make up the Yoruba peoples. *N'dep*, also spelled *ndepp* or *ndëp*, is a collective healing ceremony among the Lebu people of Senegal that involves drumming, singing, and dancing. The ceremony may be conducted to appease the *rab* (spirit) and/or break the link between the rab and the human.

2. To my knowledge "Jusat" has no meaning outside of this dance drama; the name and concept came to me in a dream.

3. Donald C. Johanson and Maitland A. Edey, *Lucy: The Beginnings of Humankind* (New York: Simon and Schuster, reissue edition, 1981; see also https://www.berkeley .edu/news/berkeleyan/1994/0921/fossils.html; https://nypost.com/2009/10/01/oldest -human-remains-found-in-ethiopia.

4. For example, see Chinua Achebe, *Things Fall Apart* (New York: Knopf, 1994 [1958]) and Cheikh Anta Diop's *The African Origin of Civilization: Myth or Reality*, edited and translated by Mercer Cook (Chicago: Chicago Review, 1989 [1955]).

Mentoring Notes on African Diaspora Dance Styles and Continuity

Yvonne Daniel

Introduction

This chapter focuses on the Caribbean and parts of Latin America as pivotal and related sites that inform definitions of "African Dance" and discussions regarding diaspora dance communities. I deeply believe that my research in geographically and historically isolated African communities has a contribution to make concerning the continuity of African dance practices in the United States, the Caribbean, and the Afro-Latin cultural sites of Canada, Mexico, and Central and South America. In looking carefully where African practices, including dancing and music-making, have continued over centuries due to both the preponderance of African heritage populations and the distinctly different colonial histories of many small islands, the data accumulate to show decided continuity as well as creative development of African dancing and music-making despite marginalization of denigrated peoples and inattention to ongoing cultural behaviors.

Today, African dances have stimulated respectful attention as entertainment and cultural history throughout the Americas; however, in the public arena, within social media, and especially among some arts funding organizations, African dance distinctions and histories are often blurred into one or two African dance stereotypes. Thereby, naming dances "African" becomes important. In local studios, university course listings, dance competitions, and funding sources, dance names publicly state convictions about dance, position dances and dancers with regard to other dances and dancers, and augment or limit development possibilities for productions and research. Performers, researchers, and funding sources need to embrace the name that provides the most concern for African dance—in other words, "African," "Black," "Diaspora," "Neo-African," "Africanist," "African-Creole," or "African Performing Arts"—but names can and should be based in history or cultural legacies as accurately as possible.

The Caribbean and Afro-Latin sites I have worked in have a wealth of distinct sacred dances (for example, Vodou, Orisha, and Palo Monte dances) and several African-related popular dances (*zouk, reggae, salsa, merengue, soca, konpa,* and the like). Some dances came from colonial legacies and others have come since the mid-twentieth century, when Africans migrated from the continent after nation-state independence. Distinct Central and West African dance heritages have histories well before the twentieth century and have general but identifiable characteristics across the Americas, permitting new styles and forms to be noticed easily and allowing research, marketing, and production to be precise, publicly visible, and politically viable. Unfortunately, African dances are still considered inconsequential, even "indecent," in some Diaspora sites.

Of all Caribbean and Latin American documented dance research, Cuban organization of African dance heritage is the largest and most thorough African Diaspora dance categorization. In this chapter, I start with Cuba's dance distinctions to determine what is "African dance" within Caribbean and Afro-Latin sites. I document the extent of African dance continuity in the Caribbean and Afro-Latin America and confront claims of African dance and African heritage. I conclude with recommendations for African dance performance and research, proposing a multifaceted, practical mentoring guide.

Stylistic Distinctions

While there is tremendous dance variation within most locales—and variation galore on the continent—there is also distinct, characteristic African dance movement in the Caribbean and Afro-Latin America. Throughout the World African Diaspora, African dances have been handed down for generations. Anthropologists, like me, examine World, European, Asian, Indian Ocean, "Original," American and "Internal" (especially in the United States) African Diasporas and when they investigate dance, they look for and first examine certain generalized body movement characteristics.

In the American African Diaspora, African dances involve full-bodied movement, mainly percussion and vocal music, and women and men often dancing separately. African dances are mostly drum/dances, sacred performances that connect to honored ancestors and spiritual practices; they also include social performances that delight and piece together remembrances of differing African ethnic groups. Drum/dances exhibit call-and-response form, polyrhythmic body-part isolation, divided-torso and torso-generated movement, and exuberant projection or hypnotic implosion, compelling group excitation, participation, and transcendence—that heightened state of unusual transformation. African dance—encompassing bodily movement, music, storytelling, history, play combat, poetic speech, spirituality, and the visual arts of representation, abstraction, and adornment—has historically lifted the burden of exploited African descendants. Such drum/dances have signaled "home," "family," "Guinea," Africa, and they still do.

The following section of this chapter closely examines dance styles that have developed among the amalgams of African ethnic groups brought involuntarily to the Caribbean and mainland American territories; it looks at African dances in contemporary times.

Cuba's Dance Organization and Diaspora Matches

Cuban researchers identify four African heritages through differing dance/music traditions, resulting in distinct styles: one Central African heritage or Congo/Bantu style (as they say[1]) and three West African heritages: Arará, Yoruba, and Abakuá. Cuba's dance organization includes both fiercely aggressive and festive flirtatious dance types within each style of African dance heritage, and dances are often discussed in terms of "nation" or "family," indicating the dearly held linkages to historical African ethnicity or remembered and believed genealogical heritage.

Cuba's Congo dance/music refers to an expansive region with hundreds of ethnic groups—the Congo/Angola region of Central or West Central Africa (Gabon, the two Congos and Angola). The region is known for the sociopolitical influence of the Kongo Kingdom and the establishment of Catholicism as the state religion early in sixteenth-century Angola. Congo/Angola peoples were the majority who landed in the Americas between the sixteenth and eighteenth centuries, and they continued to enter through much of the nineteenth century, but in smaller numbers destined to fewer sites. This movement of peoples resulted in four centuries of pervasive Congo/Angola culture throughout the Americas, much of which was exuberant parading and playful social dancing.[2]

Both flirtatious and aggressive dance types are known as "Congo nation" or "Congo/Angola family" in Cuba; these are related to dances called *congo* in Haiti; Angola and sometimes *congada* in Brazil; *kumina* and Myal/

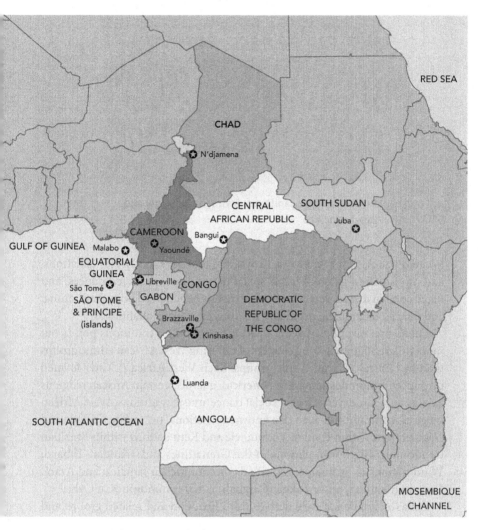

MAP 11.1. Map of West Central Africa

Rivivalist Zion/Poco in Jamaica; and *kongo* in the Grenadines (Carriacou) and Trinidad-Tobago. These Congo/Angola dance/music heritages across the Caribbean and Afro-Latin America have references to nature, relatively unadorned material items, and reliance on a spiritual world that mirrors the earthly world and requires dance and music to invoke well-being and spiritual protection. Congolese-derived sacred dance is called Palo or Palo Monte in Cuba, Congo or Petwo within Haitian Vodou, and Angola within Brazilian Candomblé (see chart 11.1).[3] Congo/Angola dances generally feature

African Dance Styles in
Caribbean and Afro-Latin Sites:
1. Congo/Angola-a
2. Congo/Angola-b
3. Ewe/Fon
4. Yoruba/Anago
5. Carabalí/Abakuá
6. Akan/Asante

CHART 11.1. African Dance Styles in Caribbean and
Afro-Latin Sites

lowered backs, flexed knees, fast rhythmic footwork, body part isolations, and hip isolation galore. Playful social dances, serious sacred dances, and fierce combat dances retain or emphasize this generalized body positioning, and dances accumulate decidedly rigorous expressive qualities.[4]

Cuba's organization of West African dance/music traditions points out more differentiation among clusters of differing West African ethnic groups than in Central African ethnic groups. Each West African cluster formed distinct communities across the Americas, guarded certain African religious beliefs, and conserved African social dance/music traditions. West African religious communities were also known as "nations" or "families": Rada and Nago nations within Haitian Vodou; Jeje and Ketu nations within Brazilian Candomblé; Big Drum nations in the Grenadines and Trinidad-Tobago; Winti nations in Suriname; Etu ritual communities in Jamaica; and Arará, Lukumí (Santería) and Abakuá (Carabalí) ritual communities in Cuba.[5]

Cuba's Arará dance style derives from Ewe/Fon and related groups and shares similar heritage with Rada dance/music in Haiti and Jeje dance/music in Brazil. Cubans distinguish Arará's repertoire generally by very low, forward tilting backs, flexed knees, polyrhythmic body part isolation, and hand gesturing, but mostly by persistent percussive shoulder movement.

Cuba's Yoruba dance style derives from related ethnic groups in West Africa—namely, Ijebus, Iyesas, Anagos, Oyos, and the like—and shares characteristics with Nago dance/music in Haiti, Ketu/Nago dance/music in Brazil, Etu dance/music in Jamaica, and Shango dance/music in Trinidad-Tobago. Cubans characterize Yoruba style generally with slightly tilted backs and gently flexed knees, exceedingly codified gestures for hands, arms, and feet, all influenced by underlying vertical undulation of the spine.

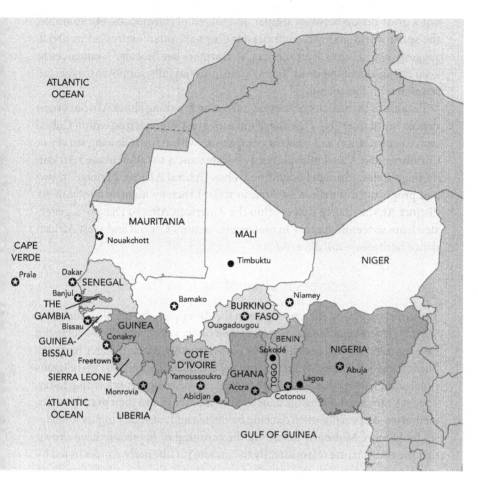

MAP 11.2. Map of West Africa

Cuba's Abakuá style is unique—the only masked dance tradition in Cuba—and originates among Ngbe, Ekbe, Ibibio, and Ejagham secret societies in the Cross River or Calabar region of Nigeria and Cameroon today. It is represented outside of Africa only in Cuba thus far and generally is characterized by upright postures, multiple lunges, and interspersed vibratory movement.[6]

Diaspora Commonalities

All American African Diaspora dances are positioned tenuously between social and sacred categories because, in African-derived contexts, there is not a great divide between secular and sacred performances. For example, the spirit world and sacred understandings are often expressed in jovial, suggestive, or risqué drum/dances. Performers use "secular" sequences to keep the spirits of the dead "happy" and/or to joyfully support an expected reunion with the ancestors.[7]

Because of the scarcity of continental research writing about African origin dances (until recently), I use the distinctions just summarized within Cuban dance organization as a base for comparison within the following survey of Caribbean and Afro-Latin dances. I allocate dances to differentiated African heritage styles, ultimately dividing Cuba's Central African heritage in two and proposing a fourth West African style. I thereby identify a total of six distinct African dance styles within the American African Diaspora, generated from sixteenth-century to nineteenth-century Central and West African dance heritages—*still alive today*.[8]

Caribbean Sites of African Dance

The earliest reported African dances in the Americas—*bamboula* (*bambula*), *calenda* (*kalenda, calinga, caringa*), *djouba* (*juba, yuba*), and *chica*—form the base for maintaining, recovering, or reconstructing African dance heritage. These referenced dances from the colonial era, in addition to African religious ritual and a few combat dances, are what elders insist upon performing today. They say they are dancing the dances of their parents' and their grandparents' memories—especially when dancing *bamboula* and *calenda*. Linguistic analyses by Honoré Mobonda regarding the meaning of *bamboula* have shown that the dance name refers directly to "memory."[9] The early dances noted by missionaries, colonists, and travelers' accounts are replete with references to *bambulas*; they become the precursors to Cuban *rumba* (*yambú del tiempo de España*), Brazilian *samba da roda*, and other Creole creations—fierce and sensual dancing, causing elite outrage but also yielding a plethora of African-Creole and European-Creole dances (see chart 11.2).[10] There are not many Native-African dances, and even fewer Native-European-influenced dances, as Native populations were decimated within the first fifty years on most Caribbean islands; however, one Native-African dance is discussed later (Peruvian *atajo*).

On the French/Kreyol-speaking, Spanish-speaking, and English/Creole/Patois-speaking islands, *bamboula, calenda, djouba*, and *chica* have dominated discussions about dance because missionaries and colonists were preoccupied with dances that featured male and female partnering, holding handkerchiefs or edges of skirts while circling sensuously, and especially with

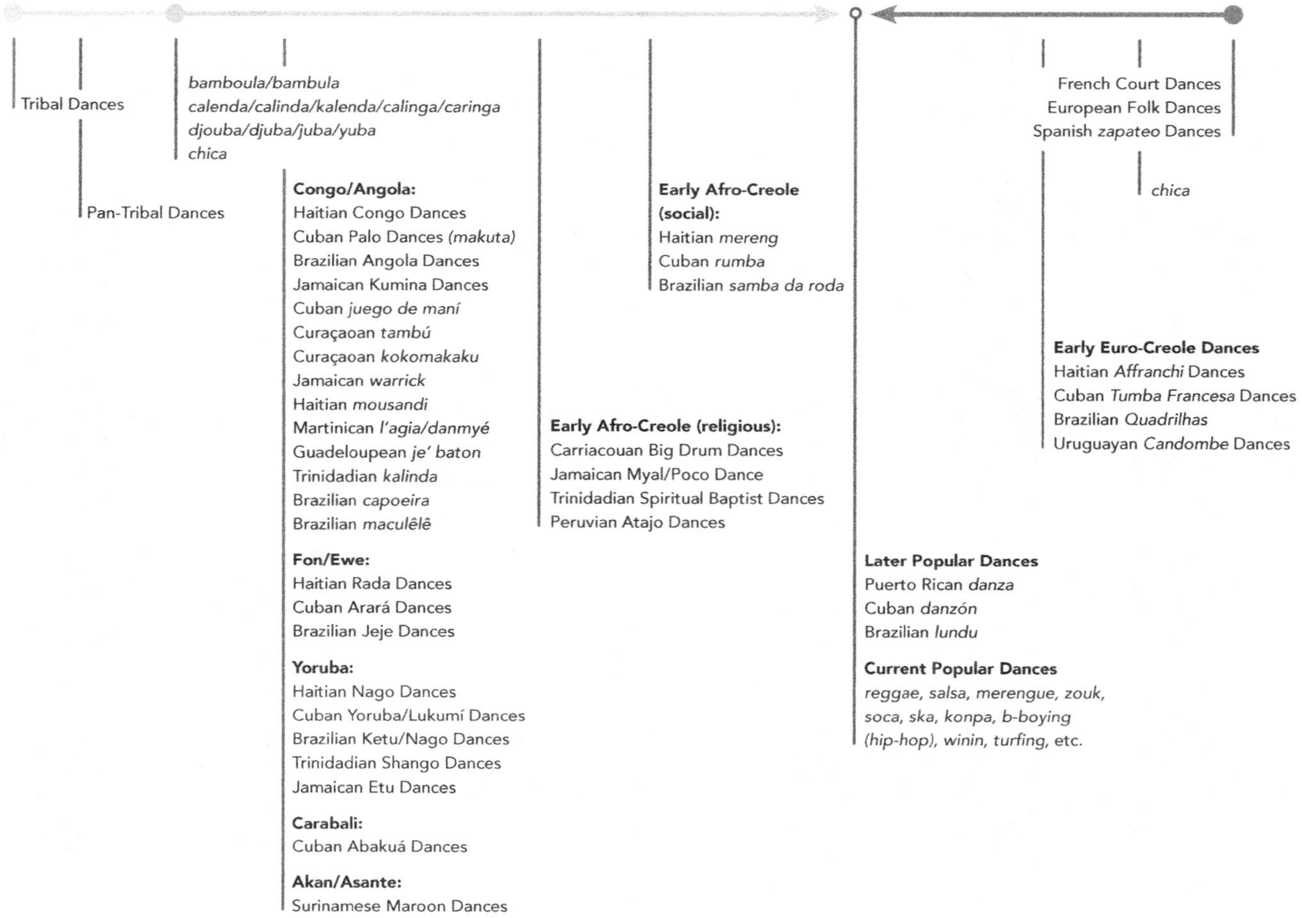

CHART 11.2. Caribbean and Afro-Latin Dance Continuum

Tribal Dances

bamboula/bambula
calenda/calinda/kalenda/calinga/caringa
djouba/djuba/juba/yuba
chica

Pan-Tribal Dances

Congo/Angola:
Haitian Congo Dances
Cuban Palo Dances (makuta)
Brazilian Angola Dances
Jamaican Kumina Dances
Cuban juego de maní
Curaçaoan tambú
Curaçaoan kokomakaku
Jamaican warrick
Haitian mousandi
Martinican l'agia/danmyé
Guadeloupean je' baton
Trinidadian kalinda
Brazilian capoeira
Brazilian maculélé

Fon/Ewe:
Haitian Rada Dances
Cuban Arará Dances
Brazilian Jeje Dances

Yoruba:
Haitian Nago Dances
Cuban Yoruba/Lukumí Dances
Brazilian Ketu/Nago Dances
Trinidadian Shango Dances
Jamaican Etu Dances

Carabali:
Cuban Abakuá Dances

Akan/Asante:
Surinamese Maroon Dances

Early Afro-Creole (social):
Haitian mereng
Cuban rumba
Brazilian samba da roda

Early Afro-Creole (religious):
Carriacouan Big Drum Dances
Jamaican Myal/Poco Dance
Trinidadian Spiritual Baptist Dances
Peruvian Atajo Dances

French Court Dances
European Folk Dances
Spanish zapateo Dances

chica

Early Euro-Creole Dances
Haitian Affranchi Dances
Cuban Tumba Francesa Dances
Brazilian Quadrilhas
Uruguayan Candombe Dances

Later Popular Dances
Puerto Rican danza
Cuban danzón
Brazilian lundu

Current Popular Dances
reggae, salsa, merengue, zouk,
soca, ska, konpa, b-boying
(hip-hop), winin, turfing, etc.

periodic bumping of navels or thighs. Despite official condemnation, such dancing was shared beyond African descendants, permitting the blending of dance elements (Creolization or *transculturación*[11]). According to ethnomusicologist Julian Gerstin's comparative report, *chica* differed in tone and was especially risqué, wherein the man pursued his woman partner less subtly than in other dances, and firsthand reports stated that nuns and "white" females also danced *chica*.[12]

Dancer/researcher Lavinia Williams Yarborough described *djouba* in Haiti around 1958 as "one of the most ancient dances in Haiti: a very sophisticated dance of flirtation. It shows the elegance of the peasant man and the whims of the peasant woman."[13] Interestingly, she adds a religious reference to her social dance description: "This dance is in honor of 'Zacca'" (the Vodou divinity of agriculture).[14] Her quote displays the interchange of African social and sacred performance noted above; more important here, it underscores the continuity of early African dances over centuries.

Makuta and *yuka* are early Congo/Angola dances that continue in Cuba today within sacred contexts and as representative cultural history in tourist settings.[15] *Makuta* inspires spiritual communication and displays collective formations that build group solidarity through fierce, percussive, unison movement. *Yuka* displays playful, festive couple dancing in circle and line formations, with prominent pelvic thrusts.[16]

The Dutch-speaking islands have experienced less scrutiny with dance in mind, but their colonial references include *tambú*, one drum/dance that represents several early Central African combat traditions that Africans danced across the Americas. Most were ferocious fighting dance/games played for self-defense and community protection, but they drew blood within performance and were outlawed eventually because of their lethal consequences. These combat dance/games also threatened colonial hegemony by maintaining martial conditioning in African male and female bodies. Some stick-fight/dancing and unarmed fight/dancing continues today in, for example, Trinidad-Tobago (*kalinda*), Guadeloupe (*je' baton*), Brazil (*maculêlê, capoeira*), and Martinique (*l'agia/danmyé*).[17]

On several English/Creole/Patois-speaking islands, African dance heritages confronted Protestant domination, and by the nineteenth century, African dance body orientation shifted noticeably. African dance characteristics were scarce, if not eliminated, in some Big Drum dances of Carriacou and Trinidad-Tobago, in Spiritual Baptist dances of Trinidad, and in Myal/Revival Zionist dances of Jamaica. Generally, these dances feature upright positioning or rocking backs (down and up), parallel feet, small-step walking/shuffling/chugging[18] in counterclockwise circles, from side to side, or essentially in place;

lower arms swing up and down. Minimal torso movement and minimized expression are characteristic in the English/Creole/Patois-speaking islands except during Carnival, when the body was/is freed from all restrictions.[19]

Upright body positioning and moving *without* body-part isolation, poly-rhythm, or torso division, in addition to traveling minimally in space, were/are contradictory elements (generally) to African dance values, and Cuba had no such dancing to include in its dance organization. Thus, in my con-temporary comparisons, dynamic polyrhythmic and multidimensional body expressions prevail within African dances on historically Catholic islands, while Protestant islands display both a dynamic style and an additional, strik-ingly limited style. The latter drum/dances indicate a new or second dance style (Congo/Angola-b) because the Cuban designated style (Congo/An-gola-a) is also present in the English/Creole/Patois-speaking Caribbean (for example, in Carnival *winin'* dances and other popular social dance forms). The Protestant-influenced style emphasizes inner body dynamics, although with obvious Congo/Angola connections deriving from earlier Kongo and Kumina rituals. The curtailed dance vocabulary suggests Protestant notions of "the evils of the flesh and dancing," but simultaneously, such vocabulary still has references that suggest efforts to carry on African traditions amid conflicting values. For example, these limited-movement dances are still "African" in important ways; they are essentially drum/dances.[20]

Questions arise: Do Protestant-influenced drum/dances really generate an-other style, or did such a style exist in Central or West Africa during colonial times? Is African dance "African" because of its performers and drum/dance heritage or because of its movement analysis? I briefly postpone conclusions and continue my survey.

Latin American Sites of African Dance

Some Afro-Latin communities are located where there has been historical erasure of African peoples—until recently (for example, Chile, Uruguay, and Bolivia). Others are where African identity has been acknowledged for centu-ries but, simultaneously, where African descendants have been marginalized and their cultural practices evaluated as *baja cultura*, or "low culture" (places like Venezuela, Colombia, and Peru). My limited Latin American fieldwork suggests that many dances have been analyzed without African heritage in mind (Argentina's *tango*, Bolivia's *saya*, Chile's *cueca*, and the like).[21] Many Latin Americans believe there is little evidence of African legacies left in Latin America; however, more titles such as "They Deny Me, but I Exist" are surfacing.[22] Anthropologist Sheila Walker and her Afro-Latin colleagues have findings that show African dances are almost everywhere across South and Central America, but they are publicly unrecognized. *Afrosuramericanos* use dance today as an identity marker when they try to secure rights and become more politically visible. "They take their drums and marimbas to constitutional congresses, for example in Bolivia, Ecuador."[23]

African drum/dances are obvious within the Ndjuka, Saramaka, Aluku, Paramaka, Matawai, and Kwinti Maroon nations of Suriname (South America), and each has a sacred repertoire. Additionally, Surinamese Creole Africans have a religious drum/dance repertoire, called Winti, and both Maroon nations and Creole Africans share social drum/dances.[24] These dances relate to Akan/Asante heritages from Ivory Coast, Ghana, Togo, and Benin today. They share some of the three West African dance characteristics inside Cuba and they highlight similar hand gestures to those in Cuba's Arará style.[25]

The significant difference is found in the Akan preponderance of squatting-level dances; performers dance while squatting on the tip of their toes, with straight backs and elaborate finger and hand gesturing. Although Surinamese Maroon dancing looks similar to Cuba's Arará style (without its persistent shoulder isolation), it became a distinct sixth style as I completed contemporary Diaspora comparisons. Akan/Asante dances seemed to be a logical consequence of isolated African ethnic clusters with few influences from European or other African dance/music traditions.

Afro-Uruguayan dance ethnographer, Tomás Olivera Chirimini, completed archival research and re-created in folkloric and tourist form a historical dance/music tradition called *candombe* (*ka*= things of, *ndombe*= black or "things African" in Kimbundu language). *Candombe* also functioned historically as *cofradías* or Catholic mutual-aid associations in which African descendants were responsible for the care of "black" patron-saint statues—like Saint Benedict or Saint Balthazar—and paraded within African versions of European *contredanses* and *quadrilles*.[26]

Recently, *candombe* dancing has been revived and promoted as a Uruguayan national dance.[27] Huge drum batteries (*llamadas*) have historically paraded with from five to five hundred mainly "white," often black-faced drummers, bringing Uruguayans out of their houses into the streets from Christmas to January 6, the Catholic *Día de los reyes*—"Three Kings Day." The elegantly dressed "courtiers" for *candombe de los reyes* have disappeared from community parading, but black-faced musicians and African descendent stock characters remain. A *bastonero* or *el escobero* acts as master of ceremonies or standard-bearer and leads parading performers. He resembles the trickster guardian of all entryways according to many African-derived spiritual practices and folklore. The *gramillero*, or herbal doctor, and *la mama vieja*, the mammy, represent African descendent roles during the enslavement period and, additionally, African divinities.[28]

Contredanses and Catholic parading reference Europe, and their Christian references could be both European and African elements, since many Afro-Uruguayans were historically from Catholic-influenced Congo/Angola. However, the character dances seem to be symbolic remembrances of African religiosity or researched reconstructions that are now claimed in the Rio de la Plata region, despite the fact that an African religion is absent today. For these Uruguayans, proof of their African heritage—beyond some who are dark skinned—is *candombe*, their African imitations of European dancing with "break-out" African improvisation.

Additionally, a strongly perceived African dance comes from the Pacific Coast where Afro-Peruvian dances called *atajos* or *hatajos de negritos* function within cofradías and are performed by men and women in front of a church, a nativity scene inside neighborhood homes, or in procession from one church to another from Christmas Eve to *Día de los reyes*.[29] *Atajo* dancing consists of parading and quick, rhythmic stamps, hops, and kicks (earth-focused and *zapateo* patterns), combined with a narrow range of arm movements and little torso division. Dancers are strictly organized in columns, circles, squares, and zigzagging and processional lines. Thus, Afro-Peruvians have combined dance configurations from Indigenous ancestry (geometric spatial and locomotor patterns, rigid torsos, and drum/dance form), from Spanish/European ancestry (violin playing, *zapateo* steps, and Christian processions), and from African ancestry (drum/dancing form, Christian processions, and pronounced Afro-Peruvian identity).

Afro-Peruvian dances "say," in effect, "Performers are Catholic African descendants in Peru," but their rigid backs, geometric configurations, and reliance on violins, for example, bear witness to strong Indigenous and European cultural influences. While Afro-Peruvians consider this dance a symbol of their African heritage, contemporary identity, and faith, researchers speculate that *atajos* were/are Native/African/European dance/music associations, the result of sixteenth-century cofradías transported from Spain to the Americas, of overwhelming numbers of enslaved Africans in Peru by mid-seventeenth century, of nearby influence of Native populations, and of Catholic Church dominance over centuries.

These last dances produce familiar questions: Is a dance "African" because of its cultural or movement analyses? Can African dance be determined by claimed cultural identity?

Deliberating on Difficult Questions

When I examine African dances in the American African Diaspora, I posit a Native/African/Creole/European continuum and categorize dances fruitfully as "closer to" or "farther from" a Creole center, depending on generalized characteristics. In this chapter, most named dances are African-Creole to some degree; few are placed directly under "A" in "African" on my charts. For example, Surinamese Maroon dances are placed "closer to" the beginning of the African section; conversely, Big Drum dances and Peruvian *atajo* dances are placed "farther from" the African section, going toward the Creole targeted center in chart 11.2.

Yet the term "African dance" takes on unbelievable importance to those who identify as African descendants. That term generates emphatic bodily pronouncements of self- and community-identification, which cannot be challenged easily. For example, *candombe* performers, including many "whites" today, believe they are reproducing their historical African legacies; *atajo* dancers staunchly believe they are African descendants dancing African dance; and similarly, in Jamaica, the Grenadines, Trinidad-Tobago, where most performers are undeniably African descendants, their dance movements do not fit the term "African dance" unquestionably, automatically, or comfortably.

The meaning of all dance genres involves a sense of social identity, "danced belonging," or "danced attachment" to a group—ultimately, an embodied sense of cultural citizenship.[30] This nonpolitical but thoroughly encompassing feeling of citizenship is intense in a dancing community by means of bodily involvement and engaged community commitment as a result of dancing together—especially repeatedly over time. Cultural identities of performers, as opposed to dance categorization, are fiercely held; Caribbeans and Afro-Latin Americans have rights as members of African descendent communities to claim their own dances. However, dance classification must take into account actual dance movements and changes that may have taken place over time. Even as African descendants have tried to conserve and reproduce African dances of origin, their dances are part of a complex, new environment—the American African Diaspora. This does not negate African continuity. Dance analysis can consciously track African continuity and change. But, naming dances is different and important.

I conclude that the drum/dances discussed in the last two Catholic-dominated sites (*candombe* and *atajo*) are not truly "African dances," although they are compelling Creole cases. Performers have not continued to embody the most basic African dance characteristics; their dances are not predominantly based in polyrhythmic body-part isolations or pronounced torso division. Dance patterns and sequences have emphasized the influence of outside cultural contacts, European/African elements in *candombe* and Native/African (plus European) elements in *atajo*. Similarly, in Protestant-influenced Jamaica, Carriacou, and Trinidad-Tobago, drum/dances do not always display unquestionable African dance either; they force acknowledgement of change, particularly within Congo/Angola dance in the Americas, and they account for a second, more European-Creole style. The dance data at hand do not answer the question of whether this second style exists on the continent or not; for instance, could these dances of upright, straight backs and little torso movement hark back to northern, southern, or eastern African dance patterns? According to known data and verified information today, however, Congo/Angola-b dance style appears as a change that took hold in the mid- to late nineteenth century on mainly Protestant-influenced islands and in the United States.

While I vehemently support consistent efforts to retain African heritage, especially in situations of tremendous marginalization, outright intentional destruction of African cultural practices, and conflicting values about the dancing body, I encourage careful dance description and analysis. To name a dance "African dance," there should be a concerted effort to make direct connections to one or more distinct African cultural legacies and their movement characteristics.

The reach toward distinct cultural and ethnic histories of dance movement is an important contribution from the Caribbean and Afro-Latin America; the United States has a different history, and its main reach today, in search of African dance origins, is found within urban centers with African dance teachers from mainly West and some Central African countries. The now-documented case histories of this volume demonstrate the strength and vibrancy of this history. They impressively point to twentieth-century models of continental performance and twentieth-century interethnic sharing of many African "national" dances that now have found a second home in the United States. These roots and exchanges need to be articulated more than they have been in the past. A dance genealogy and/or historical and cultural line of descent should accompany African dance in public performance but, more important, instructional lines of history and ethnic culture should be taught in community African dance classes. African dance history in the United States is being documented for the nineteenth through the twenty-first centuries;[31] however, there is sparse attention to documentation for the sixteenth through eighteenth centuries within United States territories.[32] The Caribbean and Afro-Latin dance research that has been documented for the sixteenth through the eighteenth centuries needs comparison and integration with Gullah, New Orleans, and other southern United States dancing, in particular, to support the understanding of African dance beginnings or continuity within the United States.

Mentoring for Continuity

With clarity about the several styles among African dance heritages that continue in the Caribbean and Afro-Latin America, performers and researchers can analyze African dance forms of interest and use generalized Diaspora stylistic distinctions to name and recruit support for their productions and projects. I turn now to the practical considerations I use for mentoring toward African dance continuity.

1) We Must Celebrate.

Celebration keeps African heritage alive and human communities joyously united. Through celebration, the present is connected organically to the past. Celebratory performance has worked in the face of latent, overt, and ongoing discrimination; it has been the danced and camouflaged agency of our foremothers/fathers and is the source of effective resilience. Without celebration through African performing arts, each individual or community has slower progress toward a gratifying life. Celebratory African dance should be regular, routinely involving all community segments and including a research component within each event.

2) We Must Organize.

Organization is another requisite for African dance continuity. Dance and the performing arts have become exclusive from the public majority and expensive. We must articulate goals and then make and follow a plan for supporting African dance/music. As Ghanaian professor C. K. Ladzekpo said at an Oakland, California, community meeting: "Organization, organization, organization"; however, there are several levels of organization.[33]

A) Organization for youth

We have to find ways to involve younger generations in performance and research. This is a huge challenge because the technology and commercial industries have engaged young people so entirely that many do not participate or support acoustic, live, African dance/music. Certainly, many have lost interest in attending classes that pass on expertise and history to succeeding generations. For example, in Northern California many trained drummers are not culturally

African descendants—that is, from African or African American communities. This can be viewed as the non-African community's contribution to African dance/music, since non-African dancers/drummers have played a role in particular decades that conserved African dance/music, like "white" tap dancers did between the late 1950s and 1980s.[34] Or this can be viewed as a significant shift in control of African expressions and the appropriation of an African descendent male role in many, although not all, African artistic communities.[35]

We need contact with junior and senior youths and community college and university students so that the arts can continue to teach history and culture, as they do in animated television shows or successful Broadway plays, like "Hamilton" (which artistically recounts the contributions of the first secretary of the U.S. Treasury and major advisor to President George Washington in hip-hop style). We must invest time and energy and assist African dance/music programs, if we expect others to do so.

B) Organization of technology

Partnering with current production technologies and advancing music-making expertise provides documented performances for historical and research archives, grant applications, publicity, and fundraising, but also for technological expertise inside the creative process of performing and research. For example, new compositions and arranging skills by young and established musicians enhance both dance and music productions; also, dance researchers can assist choreographic development. African traditional performance can be in sync with contemporary practices, and researchers can use technology to analyze the effects of technology on African dance communities.

C) Organization of leadership

Effective leadership requires delegating responsibilities and modeling principled cooperation. We need to nurture leadership and identify those who are eligible for apprenticeships. One assistant is not enough and African and Diaspora dance is too huge a research area for independent fieldwork. Team collaboration in collective leadership roles has recently given unexpected success to struggling, independent dance artists.

D) Organization of finances

There are many ways to support African dance/music, but we can start with community members who have enjoyed financial success and ask them to contemplate sustaining support of African dance/music collectives to establish, for example, a yearly scholarship or grant competition, or adopt a local dance company. We can simultaneously ask less-fortunate members to save from forgoing a family hamburger or pizza night, buying a pair of sneakers or a new pocketbook, and give that sum as a monthly or quarterly donation to African Performing Arts programming.

The African dance community needs regular, sacrificial savings deposited in accounts for dance companies and training programs. It needs to connect to neighborhood businesses and local corporations so that financial support in grants to artists and researchers is developed, but also for employment of student performers and research specialists. Once bodies are in service to the arts and basic financial maintenance is in place, then solicitation of funding from willing and able others can be more effective.

E) Educational and political organizing

All dance needs activist politics; in other words, the performing arts community needs to know what is going on in local, regional, and national agencies and, additionally, in private funding groups so as to maximize possibilities of creative, financial, and research growth. This type of political activism ensures supportive public policies and continuing leadership development.

In the past, African dance/music has routinely included musical and bodily commentary on the events and politics of the community; local and world news, leadership policies, and the expressive responses to these people and events have been a part of African dance/music across the continent and the Diaspora. However, the consistency and efficacy of such Diaspora performance practices have been uneven or have declined in the past few decades.

An organizational position (or agenda item) that is routinely responsible for scouring local and national politics and reporting back to the dance/music community could resolve this educational/political concern. Perhaps local dance companies and community education programs could share a position and benefit jointly from collaborative planning. Perhaps a researcher could track policies, responses, and outcomes and, conversely, the community's issues could spark topics for dance/music researchers. It would be most effective to have at least one official dance/music representative at the municipal, state, and national levels each, who has a performing background and arts management specialization—to improve the efficiency of African dance/music organizations.[36]

3) We must share knowledge and experience.

The life cycle must be considered seriously for careers in performance or research; artists and scholars must acknowledge training and performance years, childbearing years, adolescent and aging-parent years, as well as tragic interruptions, but they should not give up. We—the individuals who perform, study, and promote African dance/music—have to have clarity about the hurdles that come with living this artistic/scholarly life in contemporary society and reach out for mentoring support in advance of actual crises that will assuredly come.

I cherish my time visiting Katherine Dunham and talking with her for hours about the pros and cons of dance anthropology and, later, seeing her proud eyes as I interviewed her publicly at the Smithsonian, after completing the doctorate in anthropology. I treasure the encouragement I received from Norwegian professor Fredrik Barth, who wrote the thoughtful words that fortified me for a Cuban fieldwork year of no communication with the United States or my family. However, I have relied most on steady friendships with women in the arts and arts research whom I admire greatly.

We have developed "summit meetings" to support one another over the years. We have talked honestly about everything and searched jointly for possibilities and options. We have raised children together, ended and started careers together, and shared the revelations and devastations of graduate training, love relationships, performance openings and closings, and frustrating institutional biases and departmental clashes. The sustaining grace was that we checked on one another and kept our confidence/courage intact. These supportive relationships steadied me, such that I have openly developed mentoring among younger scholar/artists.

I encourage review of my/our bibliographies so that new generations can fathom the American African Diaspora "on the shoulders of what has come before" and also because we all need to study more. I encourage the public presence of "community scholars" and retirees, who can/should share their vast experiences of performance and stimulate curiosity and fascination about dance/music investigation. It is a shame that masters in African dance/music are rarely included as dance/music faculty on university campuses. When they are, they are often marginalized and, on occasion, harshly abused (sometimes deliberately). These are mostly wise women and men who want to share accumulated knowledge as long as possible. I can imagine seminars on "Dancing Matters" or "Conversations with Dance Masters" that could inform the public but also generate respect and potential collaborations among African dance communities. It would be fascinating also to have roundtable discussions between African and other cultural dance masters and have public as well as student participation.

A Coda

Without African dance/music, we are individually imbalanced and collectively threatened. All dance can engage audiences or witnessing strangers, but the manner that African dance embraces the self and others is generally contagious; without any instruction or prompting, observers are converted most often into dancing and music-making participants. Joy registers and mushrooms to overflowing. Our humanity is stimulated and seldom tempted or threatened by self-interest.

My research over forty years indicates that African Diaspora dances are ultimately expressions of healthy and joyous survival. Elsewhere I have called them "Forms of Power" because as ongoing forces, they create and sustain human communities. Dance "Forms of Power" and the dance leadership—dance artists and dance scholars, or the "Voices of Power"—have given ample models for a sane future.[37]

So, manage the present positively. Know that things change and only continuity makes continuity. Most important, make a contribution to your African dance passion and be grateful for all the blessings we have in the consolidated wisdom of our African dance ancestors, here passed on to the next generation.

Notes

1. Bantu is a language or language group and not an ethnic category of people despite the often colloquial (mis)use of the word.

2. For Central African history, see Linda Heywood and John Thornton, *Central Africans, Atlantic Creoles, and the Foundation of the Americas, 1585–1660* (Cambridge: Cambridge University Press, 2007); Linda Heywood, ed., *Central Africans and Cultural Transformations in the American Diaspora* (Cambridge: Cambridge University Press, 2002). For comprehensive West and Central African history, see John Thornton, *Africa and Africans in the Making of the Atlantic World, 1400–1800* (Cambridge: Cambridge University Press, (1998 [1992]).

3. I explain a second Congo/Angola style shortly. For Congo/Angola religion in the Diaspora, see Kenneth Bilby and Bunseki Fu-Kiau, *Kumina: A Kongo-Based Tradition in the New World* (Brussels: Centre d'Études et de Documentation Africaines, 1983); James Hoke Sweet, *Recreating Africa: Culture, Kinship, and Religion in the African-Portuguese World, 1441–1770* (Chapel Hill: University of North Carolina Press, 2003). For African origins, see Wyatt MacGaffey, Religion and Society in Central Africa (Chicago: University of Chicago Press, 1986); Robert Farris Thompson and Joseph

Cornet, *Four Moments of the Sun: Kongo Art in Two Worlds* (Washington, D.C.: National Gallery of Art, 1974).

4. For Congo/Angola dance repertoires, see Graciela Chao Carbonero and Sara Lamerán, *Folklore Cubano I, II, III, IV* (Havana: Editorial Pueblo y Educación, 1982), 89–94; Lorna McDaniel, *The Big Drum Ritual of Carriacou: Praisesongs in Rememory of Flight* (Gainesville: University Press of Florida, 1998), 18–28; Martha Ellen Davis, *Afro-Dominican Religious Brotherhoods: Structure, Ritual and Music* (PhD diss., University of Illinois, Urbana; Ann Arbor: Microfilms, 1976); Yvonne Daniel, *Dancing Wisdom: Embodied Knowledge in Haitian Vodou, Cuban Yoruba, and Bahian Candomblé* (Urbana: University of Illinois Press, 2005), 129–32; *Caribbean and Atlantic Diaspora Dance: Igniting Citizenship* (Urbana: University of Illinois Press, 2011), 135–36, 141–42, 145–46.

5. For a dance anthropology perspective on African Diaspora religions, see Daniel, *Dancing Wisdom*; for an ethnomusicological perspective, see McDaniel, *Big Drum*; for a theological perspective, see Dianne Stewart, *Three Eyes for the Journey: African Dimensions of the Jamaican Religious Experience* (London: Oxford University Press, 2005).

6. Lydia Cabrera, *La Sociedad secreta Abakuá* (Miami: Cabrera y Rojas, 1970 [1958]); Ivor Miller, *Voice of the Leopard: African Secret Societies and Cuba* (Jackson: University of Mississippi Press, 2009).

7. See two examples: Molly Ahye, *Golden Heritage: The Dances of Trinidad and Tobago* (Petit Valley, Trinidad: Heritage Cultures, 1978), 93–84, 99; McDaniel, *Big Drum*, 20, 21–24, 128.

8. The following discussion summarizes dance descriptions for chart 11.2; elsewhere I have described Diaspora dances in more detail: Daniel, *Dancing Wisdom*, 104–63, and *Caribbean and Atlantic*, 41–189.

9. A conference, tentatively titled "Bamboula," was being organized for "understudied dances," Chicago, 2016, but to my knowledge did not develop—unfortunately. Thanks, however, go to Professor Sheila Walker for sharing Honoré Mobunda's exceedingly important research, which is pivotal in Dance Studies and Diaspora Studies, "Les Joutes Musicales Dominicales de Congo Square ou Devoir Délibéré de Mémoire," in *Héritage de la musique africaine dans les Amériques de les Caraïbes*, ed. Alpha Noël Malonga and Mukala Kadima-Nzuli (Brazzaville, Congo: Festival Pan-Africain de la Musique [FESPAM] and Paris: l'Harmattan, 2007), 117–24.

10. For several forms of *rumba*, see Yvonne Daniel, *Rumba: Dance and Social Change in Contemporary Cuba* (Bloomington: Indiana University Press, 1995), 64, 67–71, 79; for *samba da roda*, see the following chapters in *Dancing Bahia: Essays on Dance, Education, Memory and Race*, edited by Lucía Suárez, Amélia Conrado, and Yvonne Daniel (Bristol, U.K.: Intellect / Chicago: University of Chicago Press, 2018): Danielle Robinson and Jeff Packman, "After-School *Samba*: Cultural Memory and Ownership in the Wake of UNESCO Recognition as Intangible Heritage of Humanity," 117–36; Amélia Conrado, "Afro-Brazilian Dance as Black Activism," 17–38; and Yvonne Daniel, "Dance Artistry and Bahian Forms of Citizenship: Isaura Oliveira

and *Malinké*," 39–69. See also Emilia Biancardi, *Raízes Musicais da Bahia: The Musical Roots of Bahia* (Bahia: Oficina das Artes, Governo da Bahia, 2006), 272–82. For later development of *yuka* to *rumba* to *danza* and *danzón*, see Daniel, *Caribbean and Atlantic*, 80, 88–89; for *samba da roda* to *lundu*, see John C. Chasteen, *National Rhythms, African Roots: The Deep History of Latin American Popular Dance* (Albuquerque: University of New Mexico Press, 2004), 141–44.

11. See Richard D. E. Burton, *Afro-Creole: Power, Opposition, and Play in the Caribbean* (New York: Cornell University Press, 1997), 1–12; Fernando Ortiz, *Contrapunteo cubano del tabaco y el azúcar* (Havana: Consejo nacional de Cultura, 1963[1940]), 98–104.

12. For early African dance descriptions and comparisons in the Americas, see Julian Gerstin, "Tangled Roots: Kalenda and Other Neo-African Dances in the Circum-Caribbean" in *Making Caribbean Dance*, ed. S. Sloat (Gainesville: University of Florida Press, 2010), 16–17. For firsthand accounts of African dancing in colonial times, see Médéric Louis Elie Moreau de Saint-Méry, *de la Danse* (Parma: Bodoni, 1803 [1789], 50–55; Père Jean Baptiste Labat, *Nouveaux voyages aux îles de l'Amérique* (Fort-de-France, Martinique: Éditions des Horizons Caraïbes, 2nd ed., vol. 4, 1742), 463–70; Père Jean Baptiste Labat, *Voyage aux Iles: Chronique aventureuse des Caraïbes 1693-1705* (Paris: Édition Phébus, 1993 [1722]), 230–32. For pertinent discussions of colonial dancing, see Noel Allende-Goitía, "The Mulatta, the Bishop, and Dances in the Cathedral: Race, Music, and Power Relations in Seventeenth Century Puerto Rico," *Black Music Research Journal* 26, no. 2 (2006): 137–64, 11–34; Josefina Elósegui and Graciela Chao, *Apreciación de la danza* (Havana: Editorial Pueblo y Educación, 1982), 149; Tomás Olivera Chirimini, "Candombe, African Nations, and the Africanity of Uruguay" in *African Roots, American Cultures, Africa in the Creation of the Americas*, ed. Sheila Walker (Lanham, Md.: Rowman and Littlefield, 2001), 261–262.

13. Lavinia Williams Yarborough, *Haiti: Dance* (Frankfurt am Main, Ger.: Bronners Druckeri, ca. 1958), 9.

14. Ibid.

15. Compare dance descriptions in Maria del Carmen Hernandez, *História de la danza en Cuba* (Havana: Editorial Pueblo y Educación, 1980), 25–26; Carbonero and Lamerán, *Folklore Cubano*, 91–92; Elósegui and Chao, *Apreciación*, 166–69; Bárbara Balbuena Gutierrez and Graciela Chao Carbonnero, *Apúntes para la enseñanza de las danzas cubanas: história y metodología* (Havana: Editorial Adagio and Ediciones Cúpulas, 2010), 64–65.

16. In addition to already-cited discussions of dance descriptions, see André Pierre Ledru, *Viaje a la isla de Puerto Rico* (San Juan: Ediciones del Instituto de Literatura Puertorriqueña, Universidad de Puerto Rico, 1957 [1797]), 39, 47; for a rare dance description (although not firsthand, but graciously shared by African History professor John Thornton) in seventeenth-century Congo/Angola territory, see Giovanni Antonio Cavazzi da Montecucco, *Istorica Descrizione de' tre regni Congo, Matamba ed Angola* (Bologna, 1678), 166–69.

17. For combat dance research, see Rene Rosalia, *Tambu: De legale en kerkelijke*

repressie van Afro-Curaçaose volksuitingen (Zutphen, Neth.: Uitgeversmaatschappij Walburg Pers, 1997); Gabri Christa, "Tambu: Afro-Curaçao's Music and Dance
of Resistance" in *Caribbean Dance from Abakuá to Zouk*, ed. S. Sloat (Gainesville:
University Press of Florida), 291–304; M. Thomas J. Desch-Obi, *Fighting for Honor:
A History of African Martial Art Traditions* (Columbia: South Carolina Press, 2008);
Daniel, *Caribbean and Atlantic*, 159–69; Julio de Tavares, *Dança de Guerra, Arquivo
e Arma: Elementos para uma teoria da Capoeiraagem* (Belo Horizonte: Nandyala,
2013).

18. These terms refer to flat-footed, stilted, or minimalist locomotor progressions.

19. See Revival Zion ceremony, 2012, https://www.youtube.com/watch?v
=YQ27bfh2Q2w; see also McDaniel, *Big Drum*, 24–28; Daniel, *Caribbean and Atlantic*, 136–41.

20. See Dianne Stewart, "Africa-Derived Religions in Jamaica: Polyvalent Repertoires of Culture and Identity in the Black Atlantic," *Contours* 3, no. 2 (2005): 77, 91–98,
103–5. I thank Professor Stewart for sharing her research on United States African
American influence in Caribbean rituals; this forwarded my previous analyses of
Protestant-influenced drum/dances (Daniel, *Caribbean and Atlantic*) with distinct
divisions within Congo/Angola style (personal communications, August 9, 2015, and
February 13, 2016).

21. For Latin dance history, see Angel Quintero Rivera, *Cuerpo y cultura: Las músicas "mulatas" y la subversión del baile* (Madrid: Iberoamericana, 2009); Chasteen,
National Rhythms; Daniel, *Caribbean and Atlantic*, 123–28, 147–58.

22. See Sheila S. Walker, ed., *Conocimiento desde adentro: Los afrosudamericanos
hablan de sus pueblos y sus historias*, vols. 1 and 2 (La Paz: PIEB [Programa de Investig-
ación Estratégica en Bolivia], 2010), republished as one volume (Popayan, Colombia:
Universidad del Cauca-Popayan, Colombia, 2013). Also see Margot P. Loyola and
Osvaldo V. Cádiz, *Me niegan pero existo* (Santiago, Chile: Consejo Nacional de la
Cultura y las Artes, 2013).

23. Walker, personal communication, August 4, 2015; Walker, personal communication, July 2015.

24. For dance in Suriname, see Sally and Richard Price, *Afro-American Arts of
the Suriname Rain Forest* (Los Angeles: Museum of Cultural History, University of
California / Berkeley: University of California Press, 1980), 171–74; Yvonne Daniel,
"Dancing Down River: A Presentation on the Dance of Suriname," in *Dance Eth-
nologists* (Los Angeles: University of California, 1983), 24–39; Corinna Campbell,
"Sounding the Body, Dancing the Drum: Integrated Analysis of an Afro-Surinamese
Performance Genre," panel presentation, SEM/CORD joint meeting, November 2011.

25. Dance artist/researcher Nia Love presented a comparison of Ghanaian and
hip-hop gestures in "Deconstructing Body Poses in the Diaspora," unpublished paper
within a Contemporary Issues Panel at the ASWAD (Association for the Study of
Worldwide African Diaspora) Conference, Northwestern University, 2003.

26. Olivera Chirimini, "Candombe," 261, 256–74; Daniel, *Caribbean and Atlantic*,
150–53.

27. The UNESCO Conference in Montevideo: "Dance in the Americas, the African Roots," featured *candombe*, November 14–16, 2003.

28. See Daniel, *Dancing Wisdom*, 104–62.

29. Carmen Roman, "The Danced Spirituality of African Descendants in Peru," *African Performance Review* 7, no. 1: 158–72.

30. See Daniel, *Caribbean and Atlantic*, 189–93, and "Dance Artistry," 39–69; See also: Renato Rosaldo, "Cultural Citizenship, Inequality, and Multiculturalism," in *Identities: Race, Class, Gender, and Nationality*, ed. Linda Alcoff and Eduardo Mendieta (Hoboken, N.J.: Wiley-Blackwell, 2003), 336–41; Lucía Suarez, "Citizenship and Dance in Urban Brazil: Grupo Corpo, a Case Study," in *Rhythms of the Afro-Atlantic World*, ed. M. Diouf and I. Kiddoe Nwankwo (Ann Arbor: University of Michigan Press, 2010), 95–120; Camee Maddox, "Drum, Dance, and the Defense of Cultural Citizenship: Bèlè's Rebirth in Contemporary Martinique" (PhD diss., University of Florida, Gainesville, 2015); Yolanda Covington-Ward and Jeanette S. Jouili, eds., *Embodying Black Religions in Africa and Its Diasporas: Memory, Movement, and Belonging through the Body* (in press, Durham, N.C.: Duke University Press).

31. See Lynne F. Emery, *Black Dance in the U.S., 1619 to 1970* (Hightstown, N.J.: Dance Horizon (1988 [1972]); Kariamu Welsh Asante, "Commonalities in African Dance: An Aesthetic Foundation," in *African Culture: Rhythms of Unity*, ed. Molefi Asante and Kariamu Welsh Asante (Westport, Conn.: Greenwood, 1985), 71–82; Brenda Dixon Gottschild, *Digging the Africanist Presence in American Performance: Dance and Other Contexts* (Westport, Conn.: Greenwood, 1996); Brenda Dixon Gottschild, *Waltzing in the Dark: African American Vaudeville and Race Politics in the Swing Era* (New York: St. Martin's, 2000); Brenda Dixon Gottschild, *The Black Dancing Body. A Geography from Coon to Cool* (New York: Palgrave MacMillan, 2003); see also Thomas F. DeFrantz, *Dancing Many Drums: Excavations in African American Dance* (Madison: University of Wisconsin Press, 2002), among many others.

32. For me, the sources already cited are reliable, especially Gerstin, "Tangled Roots," 11–34, for very early dances; but I have found other attempts at early African dance history in the United States both disappointing and unreliable.

33. Ethnomusicologist C. K. Ladzekpo, Collages de la culture africaine Conference, "State of African Performing Arts Panel," organized by Esailama G. A. Diouf, Malonga Center, Oakland, March 5, 2015.

34. See "Two Takes on Tap," a 1992 video by dance historian Sharon Arslanian, sharonarslanian@yahoo.com.

35. I am not aware of how women's formidable arrival on the African drumming scene in Cuba, Puerto Rico, and the United States has affected this knowledge transfer.

36. Notice the work of Oakland's dancer/arts administrator Denise Pate in Osumare, chapter 10 in this volume.

37. Yvonne Daniel, "African Diaspora Dancing Body Power," Rebento Special Edition, Performing Arts Journal, 6 (Sao Paulo: UNESP Institute of the Arts, June 2017): 17–50.

PART III

Perpetual Motion in the Aesthetics of Africa

Embodying Rhythm

Improvisation as Agency in African Dance

Abby Carlozzo

Introduction

In 2014 I conducted research in Burkina Faso, West Africa, collaborating with a Burkinabe dancer to uncover how our sociocultural backgrounds influence our approaches to dance. My collaborator was Awa Nikiema, a tall, slender Mossi[1] woman in her late twenties, who welcomed me into her apartment for the duration of my eight-week stay. According to Awa, as a child she would wander into dance classes in her neighborhood and was allowed to stay because of her charm and curiosity. Although her family questioned her choice to pursue dance as a career, she continues to choreograph, teach, and perform in music videos and live television productions.

I had a similar attachment to dance, having started with ballet lessons as a child and, in college, discovering modern concert and African and Diaspora forms, like West African and *hip-hop* dancing. Later, I dedicated myself to dance research and to fathoming the relationships between Africanist and other performance values within a university research grant. As a young adult, I had encouraging support from my family to study dance and enter university teaching of dance, as well as to journey to Burkina Faso.

In addition to living with and experiencing everyday life alongside my Burkinabe colleague, I took dance classes with her and began an interchange of cultural ideas surrounding dance performance and practices. Together, we taught one another on a daily basis. She wanted to teach me various traditional dances from the ethnic repertoires she knew; in return, she wanted me to teach her about ideas and practices within ballet and modern dance. Although we ventured out to several villages at times, we spent the majority of our time in Ouagadougou, the capital of Burkina Faso, a bustling and vibrant metropolis full of life and art.

Initially, I intended to utilize improvisation as a common ground from which we could reflect, discuss, exchange movement, and learn about our individual tendencies and preferences. I was working with the assumption that improvisation is "of the moment" and needs no more than a willing and able body and mind, a notion that is itself a result of my own cultural biases. In assuming these premises, however, I hoped to use dance improvisation as a tool to reckon with our past and present bodies and tease out how the history within us affected our current approach to movement. While I was eager to reflect and analyze, my collaborator was not as interested in such methodologies. For her, improvisation was so interwoven into her creative process that one could not be extracted from the other; it seemed to be inherent in the movement itself.

We quickly discovered the immense differences in our approaches to improvisation. While mine stems from a postmodern aesthetic in the United States, hers derived from the rhythmic play and "innovation within form" that define the neotraditional West African dances in which she trained.[2] Improvisation arose out of her deep respect and knowledge of dance/music traditions and her understanding that such traditions cannot live without innovation. Although I utilize the term "tradition," I acknowledge its ever-evolving nature with respect to changing contexts and lifestyles.[3] On the other hand, in a European or North American dance context, dance improvisation is often a separate practice, a personal exploration used to gain bodily awareness.[4] With such apparent differences, it became necessary to negotiate carefully and communicate delicately to find a shared place from which to work.

Despite my preliminary research efforts, I had not considered the fact that I was working within a very specific and limited framework of movement improvisation, albeit one that has roots in African aesthetics. As I obsessed over tracing my dancing history using improvisation as a research tool (and expected her to do the same—a mistake on my part that I have learned from), I neglected to consider where each of our experiences of improvisation fell on the historical continuum. And although I briefed her on the goals of my research and she briefed me on the goals of her research, at that time I had not taken into account what tracing her dance history meant to her, if anything—yet another young researcher's mistake from which I have since learned. Once I realized my biases and the assumptions I had made prior to working with Awa, I was able to go with the flow of learning new conceptions of improvisation and potentially of exploring what these mean in the context of the African Diaspora. We spent time in the studio, attended different classes, danced at night clubs, went to many performances, and rehearsed for music videos (I even got to be on set for the filming of several). Through all of our experiences together, I was able to learn more about the inner workings of dance improvisation in these contexts.

The research conducted in 2014 exposed my limited view of dance improvisation. In sharing my experiences in Burkina Faso here, I first present the launching point from which the desire to expand my considerations of improvisation arose. After acknowledging my own cultural biases, I trace the African influences on improvisation in the United States and expand upon the aesthetic and philosophical similarities and differences of improvisation within African dance forms. With this chapter, I define the philosophical and aesthetic characteristics of Africanist approaches to improvisation compared with those of the postmodern dance aesthetic. I work to problematize the existing binaries between these contexts. In a globalized world, cultures do not exist in isolation from one another; information circulates across nations and borders and is transformed in the process.[5] I also work to challenge my initial biases as a dancer who has trained, performed, and created within the postmodern idiom.

Due to the paucity of literature surrounding the uses of improvisation in African dance contexts, I present an intertextual approach to uncovering improvisation as an Africanist aesthetic. I comb through scholarship written on the use of improvisation in African diasporic contexts, such as *jazz dance*, *tap*, and *hip-hop* dances, in order to unearth the intersecting histories of an "Africanist" approach to improvisation. Using this methodology as a launching point, I hope to carve a space for further research on improvisation in African dance forms. I also establish the scope of this research: to focus on Africanist and postmodern improvisational contexts in the African Diaspora. In doing so, I recognize that this excludes a vast range of cultures and dance forms that utilize improvisation for a variety of purposes.

Additionally, throughout this chapter, I acknowledge my own positionality as a white U.S. American woman. As such, I carry with me a set of privileges and biases that I attempt to challenge as I engage with and research Africanist understandings. Moreover, although I make references to "African" music and dance and "Africanist" approaches to improvisation over the course of this exploration, I do not essentialize the diversity of traditions and perspectives that exist inside these blanket terms. I reference dance historian and critic Brenda Dixon Gottschild to clarify that "the term 'Africanist' refers to concepts, practices, attitudes, or forms that have roots/origins in Africa and the African diaspora"[6] while acknowledging the diverse range of practices that this term encompasses.[7]

With that in mind, I seek to illuminate the "invisibilized"[8] Africanist approaches to improvisation that specifically exist in the United States, one of the largest centers of the African Diaspora and the site of tremendous influence from continental West African dance. While Africanist approaches are prevalent in both traditional and vernacular dance forms, such modes of improvising are often absent from considerations of improvisation as a choreographic tool and otherwise. Thereby, I posit several aesthetic and philosophical characteristics of improvisation in African dance contexts, a specific set of concerns that include a deep connectivity to rhythm, improvisation as performance, communication between audience and performers, a mutual knowledge and understanding of tradition among participants, and individual agency within tradition. Ultimately, I argue that it is this individual agency that allows for innovation and transformation of dance/music traditions.

Defining the Africanist Aesthetic

Before I focus on the role of improvisation in African dance contexts, it is crucial to acknowledge the body of existing scholarship surrounding the physical and philosophical aesthetics of African dance forms. Several scholars and dance specialists have laid a groundwork for formally defining characteristics common to dances of Africa and the African Diaspora, including Dolores K. Cayou, Brenda Dixon Gottschild, Katrina Hazzard-Donaldson (formerly Hazzard-Gordon), Jaqui Malone, Marshall and Jean Stearns, Robert Farris Thompson, and Kariamu Welsh (formerly Welsh Asante).

In *African Art in Motion: Icon and Act*, art historian Robert Farris Thompson presents ten defining canons of African art forms. Although Thompson has been critiqued for attempting to universalize an entire continent, his work has laid the foundation from which other scholars have built substantive dance understandings. He points to:

> (1) ephebism: the stronger power that comes from youth; (2) "Afrikanische Aufheben": simultaneous suspending and preserving of the beat; (3) the "get-down quality": descending direction in melody, sculpture, dance; (4) multiple meter: dancing many drums; (5) looking smart: playing the patterns with nature and with line; (6) correct entrance and exit: "killing the song," "cutting the dance," "lining the face"; (7) vividness cast into equilibrium: personal and representational balance; (8) call-and-response: the politics of perfection; (9) ancestorism: the ability to incarnate destiny; (10) coolness: truth and generosity regained.[9]

Notably, although Thompson does not explicitly mention improvisation as a definitive characteristic, he alludes to the improvisational nature of African dance in his discussion of several canons. Thompson speaks to the addition of "personal style" and "demonstration of virtuosity" as markers of a good dancer.[10] He indicates that a skilled dancer knows precisely when to enter and exit the dance ring or cipher, in relation to the drums; the dancer may improvise but always "strikes the last gesture of his dance timed to the last syllable of the master drummer's phrase."[11] A connectivity to rhythm is evident here, as is a mutual understanding of tradition between dancer and drummer. It becomes clear that a knowledge of traditional drum rhythms is necessary in order to begin to play within the dance form.

Additionally, Thompson posits the notion of "an aesthetic of the cool" that permeates African and African American social contexts.[12] As he explains, coolness is an attitude that reflects the moral underpinnings of many African societies, and its significance varies from culture to culture. Among many things, the term "cool" represents an all-embracing sense of composure and self-control that permeates various aspects of society.[13] It is used to describe the act of maintaining a sense of calmness and ease in moments of both stress and pleasure. Specifically, dancers and musicians may wear a mask-like, detached face even as they exert themselves physically.[14] Although Thompson only briefly mentions dance in his work, he acknowledges the interconnectivity of art and life that exists in many African cultures. I argue that these blurred boundaries between life and art contribute to the shared knowledge of tradition among dancing participants, which also helps explain, in part, why an outsider might miss the inner workings of improvisation at a dance event in these contexts.

While Thompson contributes a set of defining characteristics with which we can speak about African art forms, dance scholars such as Welsh and Gottschild provide a closer look at the physical and philosophical underpinnings of African dance. I stand upon the shoulders of these two scholars in particular when I assert that discussions of the role of improvisation in African dance are often missing from scholarly texts.

Choreographer and scholar Kariamu Welsh takes a decidedly dance perspective in examining African arts and posits a thorough listing of characteristics of African dance. In her original essay, "Commonalities in African Dance: An Aesthetic Foundation" (1985), she acknowledges the fact that cultural anthropologists and ethnomusicologists generally "lack the perspective of a trained dancer, choreographer, or dance historian to properly analyze the movements and steps found in [African] dance."[15] Welsh highlights a shortcoming in much of the then-existing literature on African dance: attention to the intricacies of movement. I build on this critique to argue that these shortcomings have occurred, in part, because continental Africans' understandings of improvisation are either unknown or not fully discussed by U.S. American and European dance researchers.

Welsh's work on the oral tradition in African art has also significantly contributed to my assertion of improvisation as agency in African dance contexts concerning matters of ownership. She explains the oral principle that comprises African art, then outlines seven senses that act as a framework through which to view the diverse span of African dances: polyrhythm, polycentrism, curvilinear, dimensional, epic memory, repetition, and holism. According to Welsh, the oral tradition is both an art and a form of documentation. Further, she alludes to the issue of ownership and the fluidity of ownership in African oral traditions:

> The "oral" becomes the property of the speaker to reshape or to retell within a shape. The boundaries are there in plot, structure, outline, and form, but it is the dancer who breathes new life into the dance and it becomes hers/his for the moment. There are no permanent stamps of the creators, only the changing designs, rhythms, movements that change with the performers.[16]

A dancer always performs in relationship with the musicians, audience, and other dancers, thus blurring the lines of ownership. The "oral" is constantly passed around, moving fluidly between the individuals who contribute to the performance. Moreover, Welsh alludes to the agency a performer has over cultural information that is perpetually passed from body to body in a dance event. Welsh's discussion of the fluid nature of ownership within oral traditions supports my assertion that dance improvisation in African contexts not only perpetuates dance traditions but also grants individual artists the agency to contribute to the evolution of dance traditions.

Brenda Dixon Gottschild is another dance scholar whose work greatly contributes to my own, specifically concerning the illumination of Africanist influences on the postmodern aesthetics that define much of my experience with improvisation. Gottschild expands upon Thompson's work, focusing on Africanist aesthetics as they relate to practices of dance. In her seminal work, *Digging the Africanist Presence in American Performance: Dance and Other Contexts* (1996), she contributes significantly to the uncovering of Africanist influences on U.S. American culture that have been invisibilized by dominant European perceptions. She illuminates the racialized history of dance in the United States that privileges Eurocentric thinking. In addition to exposing a history of cultural appropriation and "invisibilization," her text outlines five premises of an Africanist aesthetic, which include embracing the conflict, polycentrism and polyrhythm, high-affect juxtaposition, and, drawing from Thompson, ephebism and especially "the aesthetic of the cool."[17] Once again, there is no direct mention of improvisation; however, improvisation contributes to and is implied by many of Gottschild's premises.

Furthermore, Gottschild acknowledges that Africanist aesthetics pervade dance forms in the United States, though they are not always credited as such. The "invisibilized" Africanist presence in the United States is due in part to the "whitenizing" of black cultures to please European American ideals.[18] Thus, when white America borrowed African-derived traditions, they transformed certain facets of black culture that disagreed with their own, while other aspects remained. This may have been, in part, why I was not originally aware of the shared roots of my friend, Awa, and my approaches to dance improvisation. According to Gottschild, white Americans have adopted everything from African American culture—from hairstyles to physical and verbal mannerisms. They have been drawn to that which was perceived as "exotic" or "sexual" in nature, indicating a reflection of white privilege and cultural biases. The urge to improvise is another example of a borrowed aesthetic that persisted.[19]

Anthropologist Jane C. Desmond also speaks of the changes that occur with the transmission of ideas between cultures. She describes how the dominant culture "refined," "polished," and "often desexualized" the dances of nondominant cultures, which can be seen in the way they "toned down," "tamed," and "whitened" such popular social dances as the *turkey trot* and the *charleston*.[20] Additionally, performance theorist Thomas F. DeFrantz reinforces these concepts in his essay "The Black Beat Made Visible: Hip-Hop Dance and Body Power." DeFrantz speaks of the dangers that occur when nonparticipating, immobile white audiences attempt to reproduce and commodify black social dances.[21] Although DeFrantz raises more questions than he provides answers, his essay serves as a catalyst for important discussions about cultural appropriation. I mention these scholars to clarify that the issue of dominant cultures borrowing without crediting the source is not a new phenomenon; the concept of improvisation in dance is no exception.

The Africanist Aesthetic in Dances of the Diaspora

Various scholars in the fields of musicology and dance studies have written specifically about dances of the African Diaspora in the United States. They have helped illuminate a deep connectivity to rhythm and performative aspects of improvisation in African and Diaspora dance contexts. Musicologists

Marshall and Jean Stearns were two of the first to write at length about the African origins of African American vernacular dance (1968).[22] Focusing on *jazz dance*, the Stearnses revealed a co-mingling of both European and African influences; however, it is the African influence that gives *jazz dance*, in general, its "rhythmic propulsion" and "swing."[23] Moreover, much can be gained from comparing the Stearnses' six characteristics of African dance to those that Thompson, Welsh, and Gottschild offered later. The Stearnses identify: (1) bare feet and the accompanying flat-footed gliding, dragging, or shuffling; (2) bent knees and body bent at the waist; (3) animalistic imitations; (4) importance of improvisation; (5) centrifugal pelvic region; and (6) propulsive rhythm and swing as characteristic elements.[24] Most notable is the problematic essentializing and superficiality of the Stearnses' list, which is arguably more superficial and essentializing than those of scholars such as Thompson and Welsh, who dig deeper into the inner workings and philosophies of many African dances. However, despite their limitations, the Stearnses reinforce an important concept that I explore in this research: the integration of improvisation and rhythm in African dance. My research and fieldwork experiences show that rhythmic play is inextricable from improvisation in African and Diaspora dance contexts, but not without the deep understanding of rhythmic tradition can an artist begin to play within the form.

For instance, my friend Awa's body possessed a sensitivity to rhythm that enabled her to negotiate within a particular dance form. I noted during a *warba*[25] lesson how my collaborator exhibited a sense of freedom confined by the limitations of tradition and style. As she added footwork and arm gestures to the isolated hip movement of the *warba*, she would explicitly declare that she was experimenting with the arms and feet or that she was performing a traditional variation. During my time there, on the other hand, I was only beginning to grasp the *warba*'s perpetual hip twist; neither my mind nor body could fathom embellishing the basic step, illustrated by the discomfort and frustration I experienced within *warba* form. Attempting to isolate my pelvic girdle, I would feel a deep burning in my core; yet despite my efforts, the movement would reverberate up through my torso, refusing to be contained. As I "played," the rhythm pushed through my body.

Dance artist and revered teacher Dolores K. Cayou has written about the historical development of modern *jazz dance*, focusing on its origins in African dance forms.[26] In her discussion of characteristics that define African dance, Cayou presented several important qualities: "Individualism of style within the group style" and "functionalism—becoming what you dance—the art of real life."[27] First, it is important to note that while there are individuation and virtuosic moments in African dance, these are often in the context of the individual's relationship to the group, musicians, and others, including the audience. Referring back to Welsh's discussion of the fluidity of ownership, an individual has room to play, but only within the structures of tradition. Second, because art is often such an integral part of African and Diaspora life, the entire community becomes enmeshed in the performance, blurring the boundaries between audience and performer.[28] Here, I begin to formulate that communication between audience and performers, as well as a mutual understanding of dance traditions among participants, are key philosophical underpinnings of dance/music improvisation in African and Diaspora contexts.

Sociologist and dance practitioner Katrina Hazzard-Donald has also written about the history of dance in the African Diaspora, focusing on secular social dances.[29] Both Cayou and Hazzard-Donald briefly discuss the role of enslavement in bringing African influences to the United States, and they both speak of the integral role of music and movement in everyday life. However, Hazzard-Donald argues that the strongest link to African dances can be found in African American social dances. Within social dances—such as the *jook*—lies a sense of community and of personal identity within the group. Hazzard-Donald also mentions a shortcoming of much of the literature on African American culture: the central role of dance in life is largely ignored.[30] I return once again to my argument that these shortcomings may be a result of North American and European scholars who lack the cultural understanding of those practicing dance in African and Diaspora contexts.

Dance historian Jacqui Malone also contributes to the understanding of the sociocultural history and African roots of African American vernacular dance.[31] Echoing the work of previous scholars in her book, *Steppin' on the Blues*, Malone explores the interconnectivity of music, song, and dance in African American culture. She reaffirms that dances of Africa and the African Diaspora render visible the rhythms of the music; one does not exist without the other. She emphasizes the sign of a good dancer, which is the ability to converse with the music and to utilize various parts of the body to create visualizations of rhythm.[32] Malone describes the qualities of polyrhythmicity and polycentricity.[33] Additionally, she reasserts the idea that art is an integral part of life in African cultures, and that dance events are communal, involving the audience as participants alongside the dancers and musicians.[34] Implied here is a mutual understanding of the inner workings of a given dance event such that an outsider might be unaware of particular characteristics, like improvised rhythmic responses to music.

Finally, as DeFrantz reminds us, "these categories of Africanist tendencies are broad enough to accommodate several generations of music and movement styles."[35] Indeed, Africa's music and dance styles are as diverse as the continent itself.[36] Additionally, the nature of tradition is ever evolving in and of itself. Thus, while the specific nuances across genres and differences across cultures cannot be ignored, my compiled set of characteristics serve as an all-encompassing platform from which more specific and in-depth discussions can take place. In the process of recalling scholars and their findings in the field of dance studies and beyond, I have established a framework through which to speak more specifically about the aesthetics of African dance. While Welsh and Gottschild in particular have led to my desire to uncover philosophical and aesthetic characteristics of improvisation that are often missing from writings on dance, others, such as Cayou, Malone, and DeFrantz, have reiterated the importance of considering what a given dance event means to its practitioners.

Improvisation as an Africanist Aesthetic

It is important to note the skill and knowledge that are required in order to improvise. As defined by the *Oxford English Dictionary*, improvisation is "the action or fact of composing or performing music, poetry, drama, etc., spontaneously, or without preparation."[37] The word *improvisation* has been used to describe music, poetry, and theater, generally in European and North American contexts. Both the definition and origin of the word reveal its inherent limitations, which involve a focus on extemporaneous actions in European and Euro-American art forms. Indeed, the use of the term "improvisation" is largely a "Western" phenomenon; thus, I argue here that the phrase "stylistic innovation within form" is better suited to represent the act of "spontaneous" creation that occurs in the context of this discussion.[38] Even then, to consider improvisation as "spontaneous" creation raises a number of concerns. As performance studies theorist Danielle Goldman elaborates, "spontaneous acts" disregards the skill set that is necessary to perform such acts, relegating the innovation that exists within traditional forms to thoughtless acts. In her introduction to *I Want to Be Ready: Improvised Dance as a Practice of Freedom*, she writes:

> A more serious problem with many discussions of improvisation is that their emphasis on spontaneity and intuition often implies a lack of preparation, thereby eliding the historical knowledge, sense of tradition, and the enormous skill that the most eloquent improvisers are able to mobilize.[39]

Many scholars utilize the term "spontaneous" to describe the of-the-moment composition of embellishments[40] that take place in African dance and the music on which it relies. Temporally, the word works to highlight the moment-to-moment decision-making ability of the performer; however, one cannot ignore the skill set behind each decision. The agency individuals have to spontaneously add their own stylistic nuances is fueled by a deep-seated knowledge and mastery of dance traditions and the steps, rhythms, and connotations that these traditions entail. Thus, I distinguish between "spontaneous" and "spontaneity," two terms that tend to be central to conversations surrounding improvisation. To describe improvised movement as *spontaneous* connotes a sense of unpremeditated, untrained, or "natural" behavior, which disregards a dancer's training and skill sets. However, to speak of an improvised dancer's *spontaneity* is to recognize the dancer's mastery of impulse and moment-to-moment decision making. Though there is only a subtle difference between the two terms, the latter term clarifies what many scholars and artists, including myself, actually mean when they use the former.

One of my best memories and best lessons in *azonto*, a popular dance from Ghana that relies greatly on improvisation, was on the side of the road in the village of Arbolé. Waiting with several friends in the hot sun for a bus back to the city, we began dancing to pass time, which progressed into an *azonto* dance party. (Awa always had a portable speaker prepared for dance classes, rehearsals, and random acts of dancing.) I realized through this roadside event that this was not simply a "spontaneous" cultural exchange; the underlying knowledge of the movements and rhythms of the *azonto* were required before we could "spontaneously" add our own individual flair. Thus, I became more sensitive to the import of this characteristic in African dance improvisation.

African and European Forms of Improvisation

While notable research exists concerning the role of improvisation in various African-derived art forms such as jazz music and hip-hop creations,[41] scholarship focusing solely on improvisation in African dance is sparse, often buried within writing on African music and African American vernacular forms.[42] Despite such limitations, I have formulated a set of characteristics that define the philosophy and aesthetics of improvisation in African-derived movement forms. Such characteristics include: a deep connectivity to rhythm; improvisation as performance; communication and participation between audience and performers; a mutual knowledge and understanding of dance/music traditions among participants; and agency of the individual within dance/music traditions.[43]

African artist and scholar Alphonse Tiérou speaks briefly of improvisation in his book *Dooplé: The Eternal Law of African Dance*. He argues that because African dances rely on the repetition of fundamental movements, dancers are free to improvise within the structures of dance/music traditions. As dancers develop the skills and knowledge necessary for improvisation, their sense of rhythm, coordination, and perception of space and style become evident. Additionally, Tiérou discusses collective improvisation as a highly refined skill. Not only must each dancer possess a knowledge of rhythm and mastery of the dance, but they must also be able to listen to one another and the music (including song improvisation and drum or other instrument cues) with acuity, taking into account the dance actions of their partners. Tiérou alludes to the fact that both participants and spectators require a standard of knowledge in order to fully appreciate the improvisation that is embedded into traditional African dances.[44] Thus, the agency of the individual requires a shared knowledge and understanding of tradition among participants, including dancer, musician, and audience members who, I argue, cannot fully appreciate the inner workings of a dance event without a basic level of underlying knowledge.

In *Yoruba Ritual: Performers, Play, Agency* anthropologist Margaret Thompson Drewal argues that ritual involves a dialogue between past traditions and present practitioners, and she posits that "ritual practitioners as knowledgeable human agents transform ritual itself through play and improvisation."[45] Drewal clarifies that in Yoruba cultures, the words "ritual" and "play" are used interchangeably, emphasizing that they are not discrete categories but interconnected, inclusive concepts. She notes first that "play," in this sense, does not represent frivolous, idle leisure as it does to most average Canadian, U.S. American, or European capitalists; instead, it acknowledges the skilled effort of trained artists whose knowledge contributes to the transformative nature of ritual. Thus, improvisation as "play" does not denote an absentminded, off-the-cuff creation but refers to a performer's thoughtful modification of tradition. Improvisation is implicit in tradition: performers do not break free from the rituals of their ancestors but contribute to the continuation of the spirit of improvisation.[46] In this sense, improvisational agency within the dance/music tradition serves as a respectful honoring of the past, even as the dance or music artist contributes individual style in the present.

Moreover, improvisational play takes on diverse forms. Among many things, performers may reinterpret, recontextualize, intervene, or interrupt in a ritual event, not frivolously but with intention as an homage to tradition. According to Drewal, ritual is not rigid, it is continuously under revision;

that is, the past is not static but constantly evolving, a notion posited by other scholars, such as Welsh, who have contributed to my analyses. Through improvisation, performers are able to transform ritual structures while adhering to the practices of their ancestors. In her discussion, Drewal highlights the agency of performers and their role in perpetuating ever-evolving traditions. Additionally, Drewal emphasizes that Yoruba performance is participatory:

> The relationships between spectators and spectacle are unstable, one always collapsing into the other. Participatory spectacle does not set up fixed unequal power relationships between the gazer and the object of the gaze; rather, the participatory nature of Yoruba spectacle itself means that the subject and object positions are continually in flux during performance.[47]

Digging a bit further into the concept of performance and spectacle (and examining another Eurocentric perspective), I outline anthropologist and cultural performance theorist John MacAloon's four criteria for spectacle:[48] visual sensory and symbolic codes are primary; the event is grand and monumental; spectacle engenders excitement in the audience through its heightened dynamism; and it institutionalizes separate roles between audience and performer, thereby establishing a distance between them.[49] Drewal recognizes that Yoruba improvisatory performances meet these criteria save for the separate roles between audience and performer.[50] Unlike Eurocentric viewing conventions that position the audience as distanced observers,[51] there is no division between spectator and spectacle in Yoruba performance; both viewers and performers possess a knowledge of the improvisation at play in performance—which contributes to the notion that those who do not possess the key cultural information are unaware of the improvisation taking place. I argue that it is the individual's ability to navigate the ever-shifting role of audience and performer that creates space for agency within dance/music traditions, thus allowing ritual transformation to occur.

Art historian Patrick McNaughton affirms my convictions in his discussion of performer-audience relationships in West African masquerade rituals:

> Performers provide entertainment for audiences. But their interaction is by no means one-way. In fact, the symbolic relationship between the performers and the audience is nothing short of artistic co-dependence. Performers feed off audiences, who often share a familiarity with the characters, ideas, and values the performers put at play. This mutual familiarity fuels the excitement of anticipation, the evaluation of execution, and the appreciation of improvisation, and all of that together takes the event out of the realm of mere spectatorship and into the realm of created experience.[52]

On the other hand, I reassert that non-African or nonlocal observers who lack the cultural knowledge necessary for participation are often unaware of the improvisation that takes place in African performances. Drewal, among other scholars previously mentioned, suggests that this is in part responsible for the dearth of writing on the subject.[53]

In her essay, "Improvisation as Participatory Performance: Egungun Masked Dancers in the Yoruba Tradition," Drewal expands upon her statements concerning the improvisational practices that are characteristic of the Yoruba traditions found in southwestern Nigeria and southern Benin. It is interesting to note that this essay is embedded in the larger anthology, *Taken by Surprise: A Dance Improvisation Reader*, which claims to cover a wide variety of dance contexts but is mostly concerned with the U.S. postmodern idiom.[54] Once again, Drewal describes the improvisational nature of Yoruba performance:

> Periodically repeated, unscripted performance, including ritual, music, and dance in Africa, is improvisational. Most performers—maskers, dancers, diviners, singers, and drummers—have been trained from childhood in particular techniques enabling them to play spontaneously with learned, in-body formulas.[55]

Once again, it is evident that a mutual knowledge of cultural traditions is necessary to allow for individual agency within these dance/music and/or ritual traditions. It is a constant cycle: the process of individuals learning and communicating dance/music traditions lends itself to the transformation of those traditions. This knowledge is then passed forward, and so on.

Additionally, Drewal also speaks to the interconnectedness of dance (specifically improvisation) and everyday life. Because dance is so prevalent in many African cultures, children who are surrounded by dance from an early age are able to assimilate specific dance and music traditions via observation and participation during ritual events.[56] In contrast, improvisation in contexts of modern concert dance has historically been used as a compositional tool for choreography; typically, there is a generation of ideas through improvisation and a subsequent honing of material.[57] Therefore, in a modern dance culture that values set choreography, improvisation is part of a compositional process, but not always part of the finished product.[58] In an attempt to challenge these norms, postmodern artists have often utilized improvisation in performance to expose the process of dance making.[59] Thus, although both context sites utilize improvisation in performance, each does so for different, culturally specific reasons, and until now, the African usage in the Diaspora has rarely been fathomed.

Influence of Music in Dance Improvisation

It is important to discuss the role of music within improvisation practices because rhythm is integral to the Africanist conception of improvisation. African drumming often "involves acts of spontaneous creation, unique and impermanent, but it is . . . bounded by strictures of style and by the training, technique, experiences, and habits of a given performer."[60] Just as drummers must work within a standard rhythm before adding embellishment or variation, dancers must first embody the rhythms of the drum before adding personal flair or experimenting with innovation. Rhythm is integral to the relationship between dancer and musician, and improvisation then becomes a conversation among participating parties.

Margaret Thompson Drewal references how dancers "catch the rhythm" in Yoruba traditions: "The idea is that the dance 'catches' the dancer as the dancer begins to 'catch' the nuances of the music."[61] A Yoruba dancer "catches" external rhythms that are so internalized by training that it's almost as if they originate from within. This connection to rhythm contrasts heavily with the postmodern urge to strip dance of theatrical elements such as music and lighting.[62]

Dance scholar Francesca Castaldi expands upon the idea that rhythm is inherent in Africanist understandings of improvisation when she speaks to the polyrhythmic nature of African dance. In *Choreographies of African Identities*, she writes:

> A polyrhythmic model presents us with differentiated layers (nonhomologous relationships) within which different rules of improvisation apply (degrees of freedom) as well as with a circular (nonlinear) mode of connections that refer to each other without claiming an absolute point of origin.[63]

Castaldi posits that the polyrhythmic Africanist aesthetic lends itself to the improvisational nature of African dance and music styles. According to Castaldi, the polyrhythms give the master drummer the power to occasionally break from established patterns and improvise. Echoing previous scholars, Castaldi clarifies that improvisation requires a deep knowledge of tradition in order to remain within the harmony of established interactions; thus, an inexperienced drummer does not usually possess the necessary skills to improvise, nor does an inexperienced dancer. Castaldi, like Drewal, mentions that dancers and drummers, as "masters of their own traditions," contribute to the ever-evolving nature of dance/music traditions. She reaffirms my assertion that improvisation is a skill that grants the artist agency to contribute to the evolution of dance/music traditions.

Castaldi also speaks to the issue of ownership. Polyrhythms lend themselves to a circular logic that resists an absolute point of origin. This aspect of Africanist philosophy contradicts European and Euro-American conceptions of improvisation. In the latter, ownership continues to permeate conversations surrounding dance; the focus is on what one artist can or cannot do, has or has not done, in relationship to another. On the other hand, improvisation as an Africanist aesthetic rejects the notion that there is a single creator, owner, or point of origin. Instead, the participants contribute to the improvisation, and the improvisation contributes to the dance event and tradition at large.

As I mentioned earlier, during my time in Ouagadougou, I had the opportunity to perform on a live television show called *L'Emission Cocktail* that presents local music and dance. Awa choreographed a basic outline for our presentation alongside several other dancers, but there were moments for individual improvisation and interaction with the audience, thus contributing to and evolving the event at large. This also demonstrates improvisation as performance.

Also, regarding improvisation from a musical standpoint, ethnomusicologist Paul F. Berliner analyzes the *mbira* traditions of the Shona in Zimbabwe.[64] Berliner confirms that improvisation is part of African performance and that it relies on both the knowledge and the skill of the musician, as well as the character of a given piece. He provides a glimpse into *how* improvisation occurs in an Africanist context. According to Berliner, artists "have a storehouse of basic patterns and musical formulae from which they draw patterns and combine them in different ways during a performance."[65] Because there is no prescribed order in which to play variations, no two musical events are identical.[66] Thus, not only do we get a sense of the parameters in which improvisation takes place, but we are able to see the ways in which skilled artists innovate within the structures of tradition.

As a result of the merging of many African and several European cultures, so foundational within the United States, the continuity of improvisation can be found in the diasporic forms of jazz music (and dance), *tap*, and *hip-hop* dances, among others. Improvisation is so prominent in jazz music that it has become a seminal construct and primary goal within the art form, used to establish the distinct and emerging voices within the music tradition. In the context of jazz music, two recurring themes surface: innovation-within-tradition and the necessity of deep traditional knowledge before improvisation can occur. Berliner confirms that the popular definition of improvisation as spontaneous and intuitive "belies the discipline and experience on which [jazz] improvisers depend."[67] He also extends improvisation past the individual to a group experience in his discussion of jazz bands. He says: "The operations of improvisation involving more than one person require the instant assimilation of ideas across the band's membership . . . band members endeavor to interact flexibly in order to accommodate one another."[68]

The concept of an "improv jam," associated with contact improvisation in the modern concert dance world, is taken from "jam sessions" in the jazz music world, where jazz musicians come together to create and explore through improvisation.[69] This is yet another example of how a dominant culture asserts the power of propagation while less economically powerful cultures often become marginalized.

Dance scholar Cheryl Willis augments this discussion in her essay "Tap Dance: Manifestation of the African Aesthetic." She affirms that "tap dance, comparable to jazz music, and African music and dance, employs improvisation" in such a way that no two performances are identical.[70] Dancers work within the vocabulary and rhythmic style of *tap* but have the liberty to play with artistic expression and musical structures, such as syncopation. Willis also points out that solos are rich opportunities for improvisation; however, the dancer is not completely "free" to take off in a flight of self-expression and must remain in constant conversation with the musician, which is a direct reflection of African influence.

Dancer/theorist Goldman further elaborates on the word "freedom" and its associations with improvisation and speaks about improvisation in a variety of contexts. Indeed, her study covers topics such as collaborations between dancers and jazz musicians and contact improvisation as a form of nonviolent protest, among others. Through her discussions, both the complexities and the circulation of influences that inform different understandings of dance improvisation become clear.

U.S. Vernacular Dance and Improvisation

Turning to improvisation in African American vernacular dance, the analysis of improvisation encompasses a wide range of social dances, dating from the plantation era to twentieth century *hip-hop*; these dances also adhere to the Africanist aesthetic of improvisation. Reinforcing a direct link between continental and diasporic African forms, artist and scholar Jonathan David Jackson asserts that a thorough knowledge of social dance forms is necessary in order to begin improvising within a given form. He suggests that, much like in both jazz music (and *jazz dance*) and also in *tap* dance, where improvisation largely determines the structure of a performance, "in African American vernacular dancing, improvisation *is* choreography."[71] While

European and North American art forms tend to value composition above improvisation and see these concepts as two separate entities, in African and diasporic forms this dichotomy does not exist. Jackson reaffirms the "inseparability between sound and movement" in African American vernacular forms, which is another clear reflection of African traditions.

In his analyses, Jackson also posits two interrelated symbolic fields that are useful in uncovering the purpose of improvisation. He identifies "individuation" and "ritualization" in vernacular contexts. Individuation constitutes the dancer's negotiation of her/his/their personal style, inviting the viewer to witness his/her/their assertion of physical prowess and inventiveness and promoting the evolution of dance traditions. Individuals can use tools, such as repetition and layering, to enhance their performance and organize movement, emphasizing the composition that takes place in the moment of movement. Entwined with individuation is ritualization, which establishes the community organization of an ongoing and/or repeatable event.[72] Whether the event involves working together or competing, ritualization implies the negotiation of group dynamics.

One such ritual event, the freestyle *hip-hop* battle, exemplifies the recurring theme of individual and group relationships. To participate in such a battle "is to put one's name on the line and test one's self" in the spirit of competition and one-upmanship.[73] Participants perform physical displays of prowess, attempting to prove themselves through inventive, challenging moves in order to gain status within the community. The freestyling artist's desire to create an individual style and the jazz improviser's life pursuit for a unique artistic voice are prime examples of Jackson's premise of individuation. It is from competition with the self and others that innovation arises. Improvisation is assumed to be partly responsible for the evolution of these social dances, both across time and through interaction with other cultures.

Carving a Space for Future Research

I have learned much since my initial, sociocultural, and biased assumption, which emerged with improvisation as "of the moment" movement. Improvisation frequently profits from more than a willing and able body and mind. Recognizing improvisation as an aesthetic of African dance forms permits comprehension of the immense intricacies of different culturally informed approaches to improvisation. Through the dissection and comparison of related dance, music, and cultural scholarship, the aesthetic and philosophical underpinnings of dance improvisation in Africanist contexts have emerged.

While much has been said about the defining characteristics of African dance, much of the writing on improvisation in African dance forms is intertextual and, as we have seen, is buried within texts that focus on African music and dances of the African Diaspora, especially in the United States. Here, such limitations have been minimalized; the examination of dispersed texts and almost-hidden understandings, which I have gathered for close scrutiny, have revealed the participatory, inclusive nature that connects dancer, musician, and spectator in wondrous and learned dance movements. Additionally, the agency of performers and their sensitivity to structured innovation, which define improvisation as an Africanist aesthetic, have been clearly analyzed for broad understanding—for observers, critics, and other researchers. Distinctions have been made between words ("spontaneous" and "spontaneity") and among contexts (African, Diaspora, and European or North American). Thus, this chapter has provided a launching point for future research in improvisation as an Africanist aesthetic.

My focus on identified characteristics of dance improvisation within an Africanist aesthetic broadens contemporary understandings of dance improvisation. Although much work has yet to be done, I have here illuminated important voices that are often absent from current considerations of dance improvisation in U.S. American academia. In doing so, my hope is that we gain a more inclusive understanding of improvisation as it pertains to the field of dance. Starting with this analysis of improvisation as agency in African dance, a next step may be to look closer at existing dance curricula to ensure that a multitude of approaches and understandings of dance improvisation are included. We must honor and validate the vast range of experiences and perspectives that contribute to dance improvisation. It is my ultimate wish that the rhythm of these words may catch hold for future research on dance improvisation within the Africanist aesthetic.

Notes

1. The Mossi are the largest ethnic group in central Burkina Faso, but they also live in Mali, Cote d'Ivoire, Ghana, Benin, and Togo. Although my collaborator was born and raised in the capital, only half of her family is from Burkina Faso; the other half is from Ghana.

2. Over the course of this research, I turn to artist/scholar Kariamu Welsh (formerly Welsh Asante) to clarify the concept of "tradition." In her book (cited below), Welsh distinguishes between traditional and neotraditional, acknowledges the ever-changing nature of tradition, and, referencing dance scholar Peggy Harper, addresses the fact that changes in lifestyle, due to factors such as colonization and urbanization, have resulted in neotraditional dance form. Meanings and movements may not nec-

essarily change, but the context in which the dance is learned and performed does. Kariamu Welsh, *Zimbabwe Dance: Rhythmic Forces, Ancestral Voices: An Aesthetic Analysis* (Trenton, N.J.: Africa World, 2000), 25–28.

3. See also Margaret Thompson Drewal, *Yoruba Ritual: Performers, Play, Agency* (Bloomington: Indiana University Press, 1992), 12–28.

4. See Sally Banes, *Terpsichore in Sneakers: Post-Modern Dance* (Middletown, Conn: Wesleyan University Press, 2011 [1987]); Ramsey Burt, *Judson Dance Theater: Performative Traces* (London: Routledge, 2006); Susan Leigh Foster, *Dances that Describe Themselves: The Improvised Choreography of Richard Bull* (Middletown, Conn.: Wesleyan University Press, 2002).

5. Jane C. Desmond, ed., "Embodying Difference: Issues in Dance and Cultural Studies," *Meaning in Motion: New Cultural Studies of Dance*, ed. Jane C. Desmond (Durham, N.C.: Duke University Press, 1997), 29–54.

6. Brenda Dixon Gottschild, *The Black Dancing Body: A Geography from Coon to Cool* (New York: Palgrave Macmillan, 2003), xiii.

7. Although I cite dance scholar, Brenda Dixon Gottschild, who adapted and used the term inside of a dance context (see *Digging the Africanist Presence in American Performance: Dance and Other Contexts* [Westport, Conn.: Greenwood, 1996] and *The Black Dancing Body*), the term "Africanist" was first used by anthropologist, Melville J. Herskovits in his work *The Myth of the Negro Past* (New York: Harper and Row, 1958 [1941]), 1–32. It has since been used by contemporary African American scholars Joseph Holloway (see *Africanisms in American Culture* [Bloomington: Indiana University Press, 1990]) and Toni Morrison (see *Playing in the Dark: Whiteness and the Literary Imagination* [Cambridge, Mass.: Harvard University Press, 1992]), among others.

8. See Gottschild, *Digging the Africanist Presence.*

9. Robert Farris Thompson, *African Art in Motion: Icon and Act* (Los Angeles: University of California Press, 1974), 5–45.

10. Ibid., 17–18.

11. Ibid., 18. I will elaborate on this in the next section. Discussions of improvisation are often presented as subtexts within texts, though several scholars do explicitly discuss the improvisational nature of African performance.

12. Ibid., 43–45.

13. Ibid., 41.

14. See also Gottschild, *Digging*, 13.

15. Kariamu Welsh Asante, "Commonalities in African Dance: An Aesthetic Foundation," in *African Culture: Rhythms of Unity*, ed. Molefi Asante and Kariamu Welsh Asante (Westport, Conn.: Greenwood, 1985), 72; reprinted in *Moving History / Dancing Cultures: A Dance History Reader*, ed. Ann Dils and Ann Cooper Albright (Middletown, Conn.: Wesleyan University Press, 2001), 144–51.

16. Ibid. (2001), 145.

17. Gottschild, *Digging*, 11–19.

18. Ibid., 25.

19. Gottschild, *Digging*, 31.

20. Desmond, "Embodying Differences," 34.

21. DeFrantz, "The Black Beat Made Visible: Hip Hop Dance and Body Power," in *Of the Presence of the Body: Essays on Dance and Performance Theory*, ed. Andre Lepecki (Wesleyan University Press, 2004), 75.

22. See Marshall Winslow Stearns and Jean Stearns, *Jazz Dance: The Story of American Vernacular Dance* (New York: Schirmer, 1979).

23. Ibid., xiv.

24. Ibid., 14–15.

25. *Warba* is the primary celebration dance of the Mossi, the largest ethnic group in central Burkina Faso, and the national dance of Burkina Faso. *Warba* is characterized by a constant, vigorous shaking of the hips along the transverse plane of the body (that which separates the upper and lower halves of the body). The hips move in isolation of the rest of the body as the dancer performs a variety of footsteps and arm gestures. The buttocks are allowed to release and shake in response to the movement of the hips. A short skirt of braided cotton and bells worn at the waist, ankles, and held by hand are part of the traditional costume for this dance. This percussive adornment accentuates the polyrhythms that permeate this dance.

26. See Dolores Kirton Cayou, *Modern Jazz Dance* (Palo Alto, Calif.: National Press Books, 1971); Dolores Kirton Cayou, "The Origins of Modern Jazz Dance," *Black Scholar* 42, no. 2 (1970): 8–13.

27. Cayou, "Origins," 9; Cayou, *Modern Jazz Dance*, 6.

28. Cayou, "Origins," 12.

29. See Katrina Hazzard-Gordon (later Hazzard-Donald), *Jookin': The Rise of Social Dance Formations in African-American Culture* (Philadelphia: Temple University Press, 1990).

30. Ibid., xi–3.

31. See Jacqui Malone, *Steppin' on the Blues: The Visible Rhythms of African American Dance* (Urbana: University of Illinois Press, 1996).

32. Ibid., 1–15.

33. See also, Gottschild, *Digging*; Thompson, *African Art*; Welsh, "Commonalities."

34. Malone, *Steppin'*, 10–11.

35. DeFrantz, "Black Beat," 69.

36. Malone, *Steppin'*, 9–10.

37. *Oxford English Dictionary*, "improvisation" (2nd ed. Oxford; Oxford University Press: Clarendon, 1989).

38. Drewal, *Yoruba Ritual*, 119.

39. Danielle Goldman, *I Want to Be Ready: Improvised Dance as a Practice of Freedom* (Ann Arbor: University of Michigan Press, 2010), 5.

40. See Kofi Agawu, "African Music as Text," *Research in African Literatures* 32, no. 2 (2001): 8–16.

41. See Paul Berliner et al, *Thinking in Jazz: The Infinite Art of Improvisation* (Chicago: University of Chicago, 1994); Cayou, *Modern Jazz Dance*; William Jelani Cobb,

To the Break of Dawn: A Freestyle on the Hip Hop Aesthetic (New York: New York University Press, 2007); Gottschild, *Digging*; Jonathan David Jackson, "Improvisation in African-American Vernacular Dancing," *Dance Research Journal* 33, no .2 (2001): 40–53.

42. For example, see Kofi Agawu, *African Rhythm: A Northern Ewe Perspective* (New York: Cambridge University Press, 1995); Kofi Agawu, "The Invention of African Rhythm," *Journal of the American Musicological Society* 48, no. 3 (1995): 380–95; Paul Berliner, *The Soul of Mbira: Music and Traditions of the Shona People of Zimbabwe* (Chicago: University of Chicago Press, 1993); Berliner et al., *Thinking in Jazz*.

43. See Agawu, *African Rhythm*; Agawu, "The Invention of African Rhythm," 8–16; Agawu, "African Music as Text," 380–95; Drewal, *Yoruba Ritual*; Margaret Thompson Drewal, "Improvisation as Participatory Performance: Egungun Masked Dancers in the Yoruba Tradition," in *Taken by Surprise: A Dance Improvisation Reader*, ed. Ann Cooper Albright and David Gere (Middletown, Conn: Wesleyan University Press, 2003), 119–32; Alphonse Tiérou, *Doople: The Eternal Law of African Dance*, 2 Vol. (Chur, Switzerland: Harwood Academic, 1992).

44. Tiérou, *Doople*, 19.

45. Drewal, *Yoruba Ritual*, xiii–23.

46. Ibid., 12–28.

47. See also Drewal, "Improvisation," 119–21.

48. John J. MacAloon et al., *Rite, Drama, Festival, Spectacle: Rehearsals Toward a Theory of Cultural Performance* (Institute for the Study of Human Issues, 1984), 243–44.

49. See also Drewal, *Yoruba Ritual*, 15, and "Improvisation as Participatory Performance," 121.

50. Drewal, *Yoruba Ritual,* 15

51. Drewal, "Improvisation," 119.

52. Patrick R. McNaughton, *A Bird Dance Near Saturday City: Sidi Ballo and the Art of West African Masquerade* (Bloomington: Indiana University Press, 2008), 53.

53. Drewal, "Improvisation," 119.

54. See Ann Cooper Albright and David Gere, eds., *Taken by Surprise: A Dance Improvisation Reader* (Middletown, Conn: Wesleyan University Press, 2003).

55. Drewal, "Improvisation," 119.

56. Ibid., 120.

57. See Sally Banes, "Spontaneous Combustion: Notes on Dance Improvisation from the Sixties to the Nineties," in Albright and Gere, *Taken by Surprise*, 77–85; Foster, *Dances That Describe*; Cynthia J. Novack, *Sharing the Dance: Contact Improvisation and American Culture* (Madison: University of Wisconsin, 1990).

58. Novack, *Sharing the Dance*, 23.

59. Banes, *Terpsichore in Sneakers*, xii–19.

60. Drewal, "Improvisation," 123–24.

61. Ibid.

62. Francesca Castaldi, *Choreographies of African Identities: Negritude, Dance,*

and the National Ballet of Senegal (Urbana: University of Illinois Press, 2006), 8; see also Robert Farris Thompson, "An Aesthetic of the Cool," *African Arts* 7, no. 1 (1973): 41–91.

63. Castaldi, *Choreographies of African Identities*, 10–11.

64. Commonly referred to as a "finger piano," "thumb piano," or "hand piano," the mbira is a popular traditional instrument throughout Africa. Here, the mbira is located among the Shona, a Bantu-speaking people in parts of Mozambique and Zambia. Although a great variety of mbira exist, each consists of "a soundboard, a method of amplifying the sound, usually some device for producing the buzzing quality that characterizes mbira music, and, of course, a set of keys" (Berliner, *Soul of Mbira*, 9–10, 18).

65. Ibid., 119.

66. Ibid., 95–111.

67. Berliner et al., *Thinking in Jazz*, 497.

68. Ibid., 492.

69. Gottschild, *Digging*, 55.

70. Cheryl Willis, "Tap Dance: Manifestation of the African Aesthetic," in *African Dance: An Artistic, Historical and Philosophical Inquiry*, ed. Kariamu Welsh Asante (Trenton, N.J.: Africa World, 1996), 151.

71. Jackson, "Improvisation," 42.

72. Ibid., 41–46.

73. Cobb, *To the Break of Dawn*, 78.

From Village to International Stage

Baamaaya and the Politics of Adaptation

Steven Cornelius and Habib Iddrisu

> Dance is a liqueur which is
> distilled of the stuff of culture.
> —Ted Polhemus, 1998

Sankofa (Go Back and Retrieve)

In West Africa, in the late 1950s, as the colonial era gradually came to an end, the performing arts were utilized to support and encourage the development of national consciousness and also to promote African artistic presence beyond the continent. Traditional music and dance genres were evaluated, restructured, and even revived for staged folkloric performance.[1] Senegal's Léopold Sédar Senghor, Guinea's Ahmed Sékou Touré, and Ghana's Kwame Nkrumah established national dance companies that would give voice to nationalist and Pan-African agendas.[2] Such staged performances sought to mitigate ethnic barriers and highlight common heritage. While these initiatives were initially conceived on a national scale, the notion of presenting folkloric music and dance quickly took hold at regional and local levels, thereby laying the groundwork for independent folkloric ensembles across West Africa. These politico-artistic movements affected African dance in national and continental settings, as well as African performance practices in the Diaspora.[3]

What happens when traditional dance is pulled from its indigenous set-ting and adapted for staged performance? Although the specific "folkloric" trajectory of any particular piece is sure to be unique, we believe certain char-acteristics of the general transformation process will be universal. With that idea in mind, we present an in-depth case study of *baamaaya*, a music and dance genre of the Dagbamba ethnic group from Ghana's northern region. This chapter describes, compares and contrasts *baamaaya* in traditional and folkloric performance settings within differing regions of Ghana and then shifts to examine *baamaaya* performance in the United States. We explore how perceptions and markers of aesthetic efficacy and meaning have shifted with physical as well as social distance, as measured by performer/audience expectations, understandings, economics, and politics.

Vivacious choreography, provocative costumes, and a wealth of linguistic formats (spoken, sung, drummed, or song melodies played on flutes) make *baamaaya* a favorite dance among the Dagbamba. Although most closely bound to Dagbamba cultural sensibilities, *baamaaya* is now performed by folkloric music and dance ensembles across the nation, as well as university and independent ensembles in the United States and Europe. While tradi-tional *baamaaya* performances meet ethnically homogeneous local needs, folkloric performances—in which traditional elements have been selectively adopted, transformed, or deleted altogether—serve heterogeneous social groups with diverse ideologies and interests.

What happens along the journey from village to international stage? What do these various audiences experience? What are the commonalities and dif-ferences? What is lost or gained? Where does meaning reside? These simple questions have complex answers.

Dance ethnologist Sondra Fraleigh contends that in understanding a per-formance, audience members construct meaning through the "conscious integration of the work."[4] This is certainly true. We believe, however, that understandings, artistic or otherwise, unfold in myriad ways and are often formed with little conscious thought. For insiders, expressive acts are un-derstood and accepted according to how they fit naturally within their own cultural system.[5] When recontextualization challenges norms, insiders may be pushed to reexamine and even reassess basic understandings. Engagement unfolds differently for outsiders. As a performance is witnessed by outsiders *prima facie*, "understanding" is constructed from the outside in, according to local understandings, imaginations, and even ambitions.

The Roots of *Baamaaya*

Baamaaya is performed, with regional variations, across Ghana's Northern Region, which spreads from the nation's eastern to western borders; its performance home is in and around the territory of Dagbon. *Baamaaya* is secular, but like much music and dance in sub-Saharan Africa, spiritual beliefs and artifacts are often laced into otherwise secular events. *Baamaaya* performances are filled with joking, merrymaking, and ribald sexual references. Underneath these activities reside moral understandings that uphold collective values and communal ideals.

There are a variety of well-known stories regarding *baamaaya*'s origin. Elders in the community might refer to the dance as *tubankpele*, a name that recalls the custom of *wa wariba* (dancers) performing with cornhusks in their belts. As for the origin of *tubankpele*, one account says it was popular at night in family compounds because dancing kept mosquitoes at bay. Another says the dance was done to tease women. Yet another says that children repeated the word after receiving a nourishing meal of *tubaani*, a bean dish.[6] Other origin tales come with the name *baamaaya*. One account can be found in the archives of the northern capital, in Tamale's Center for National Culture:

> Calamity befell the people of Dagbon. The gods were consulted through oracles and sooth-saying. It came to light that the people had gone against the gods. The gods therefore ordained that the men should lampoon themselves and dress like women, so that their womenfolk could see how odd they looked. The men therefore clad themselves in raffia skirts and wore women tops with breast and head gears. They were advised to dance around the town. Lo and behold, when they danced round the town once, rain fell. Before this it was known as *Tuubaan Kpili*—but when it rained the name was changed to *baamaaya*—the valley has become cool.[7]

As a child, co-author Habib Iddrisu participated in programs sponsored by Tamale's Center for National Culture. He learned a similar story from his grandfather, Manguli-Lana Adam Alhassan. Other versions of the story place the drought's cause on a man committing a crime against a woman.

Baamaaya in Context

At some time in the past, the dance became associated with final funeral rites, where performances generally begin sometime after midnight and last until shortly after dawn. Shorter versions of *baamaaya* are also performed on a variety of other occasions, including political gatherings, public openings, the instillation of a chief, and for cultural tourism. Traditional *baamaaya* troupes are informally organized. Membership is open to anyone (although women's roles are limited), but one generally has to be an actual member of the group in order to dance. Troupes vary widely in size and makeup. Membership might be drawn from a village, a community within a village, or even a complex of villages. Dancers might range in numbers from just a handful to as many as fifty.

The music is casual, free-wheeling, and open to innovation. By imitating the inflections and rhythms of speech, a *luŋa* (an individual drummer, and the term for the drum itself) may perform *salima*, which are formal praise verses associated with specific families. More often, however, the *luŋa* plays standardized phrases highlighting social relationships or community values. He may also drum various inside jokes that are understood only by group members. Song texts are drawn from heritage or current events.

Spoken recitation, as performed by a *baanga* (male verbal artist) and/or *kpalinkpaandiba-luŋpaba* (female verbal artists), tends to focus on genealogical heritage. The presentation is designed to honor and inspire the dancers, although audience members may also be singled out. The baanga performs in a chant-like fashion that generally fits with the musical timeline. His performance is spontaneous and occurs at irregular intervals. *Luŋpag'a*, or praise songs, sound independently from the drums' timeline.

Reflecting the music's focus on inclusiveness, for a large event multiple *baamaaya* ensembles may be invited to perform. Sometimes groups combine to create a single performance. Other times, two separate performances take place in adjoining rings. Intergroup rivalries—generally friendly, but sometimes not—are common.

Interpersonal rivalries may also develop. Because gifted dancers accumulate social prestige, they often feel the need to protect themselves from jealous onlookers. To insulate themselves from debilitating spells (*sotim*), dancers generally wear protective belts or armbands (*sabli* or *saba*) packed with protective herbs, animal parts, or even Koranic verses. Additional protection may be worn around the neck or attached to clothing.

The Costume

In accordance with the associated origin stories, *baamaaya* dance costumes are designed to echo women's fashion or femininity in general. Dancers often wear a monkey-skin hat (*mman suluga*). The sides of the hat extend downward with colorful beads and earrings, and are held in place with a woman's hair wrap. This headgear is unique to the *baamaaya* costume. Dancers sometimes wear blouses, though today they generally leave their upper bodies uncovered or partly covered with a tank-top shirt or perhaps wear pairs of strung beads across the shoulders to opposite armpits so as to form an "X."

In order to accentuate and feminize the hips, dancers wear a belt (*yabsa* or *loma*) adorned with colorful beads, cowries, and threaded pompon balls. A skirt is worn under the adorned belt (one far shorter than a traditional Dagbamba woman would wear), and heavy metal jingles (*chagla*) are worn around the ankles and add a rhythmic layer.

Finally, a goat- or sheep-tail switch (*zuli*) is carried in the right hand. There are two types of zuli, decorative and efficacious. The first is used to add beauty to the costume, the second for protection or other power-related functions, including charming the audience. Sometimes dancers carry fans, which provide a breeze in the heat as they also embellish the costume.

Formal Musical and Dance Sections

A traditional *baamaaya* performance consists of up to seven separate sections.[8] The first four are fundamental and will be heard all across Dagbon. The remaining three were developed by members of the Tamale-based cultural troupe, Anakulyada, while they were part of the Arts Council of Ghana.[9]

Invariably, performances begin with *baamaaya so chɛndi*, or the *baamaaya* "procession."[10] *Baamaaya so chɛndi* is an introductory rhythm that the drummers play and the name of the dance, as the ensemble moves into the performance site. To this rhythm, dancers move in stylized walking steps. Further, the percussive sound of the chagla provides a framework for upper-torso sway and pulsation. This gives dancers the opening to demonstrate "self-coolness" (*golisugu*), an expression just short of what might be negatively perceived as showing off. In terms of the story presented by Tamale's Center for National Culture, this section is said to relate to the men as they approached a shrine on their way to begin their dance of penitence. Upon arrival, dancers form a circle and drummers switch their beat to the quicker *baamaaya mangli* ("principal" *baamaaya*, both the drum rhythm and dance name). Dancers switch gears also, moving their hips in a quick and compact twisting motion. With faster footsteps comes a denser chagla rhythm, which imitates the phrase, "Cheli kan wa" (Let me dance). When performed at a funeral, this is by far the longest musical section, lasting from the early hours after midnight until nearly dawn. As related to the myth, this is where the men danced in front of a shrine to appease the gods.

The following sections are brief. Around first light the drummers shift to the rhythm, *shikalo*, during which individual expression is highlighted. Rich

FIGURE 13.1. Dakoli Kutoiko Rhythm

in improvisatory possibilities, *shikalo* dance is a favorite section for dancers, musicians, and the audience. Dancers move naturally between rhythmic densities. The flexibility of this section allows dancers to add spontaneous "carefree," in-the-moment ideas, which are often quickly forgotten. Since this dance is performed at dawn, a time when the community is up and preparing for the workday, dancers have every incentive to show off their talents to a growing audience. In terms of the myth, the men are noticing that the air has cooled; the wind is blowing; and rain is imminent.

Part four is *nyagboli*, the rhythm and the dance for the beginning of the rain. In *nyagboli*, the jubilant dancers take care in their movements, lifting their legs high and placing them down carefully in a manner that will not splash mud, but always in time with the last beat of the drum phrase. Unlike *shikalo* dance, where dancers have endless openings to improvise, the *nyagboli* section restricts improvisation to a minimum so as to fortify the section's portrayal of dancers moving gracefully upon the wet ground.

The following rhythm and dance sections are Anakulada additions. Sometimes *nyagboli* is extended with a variation style called *abalembe*. Rhythmically, *abalembe* dancing bears resemblance to *nyagboli*, but with different lyrics. Dancers hold their hips while executing the movements. Eliminated entirely are "non-splash" gestures performed in *nyagboli*. Here, drums repeat again and again the following warning to sexual braggarts: "Abalembe ka o yamaaya ka o wagsineng" (Abalembe has lost his strength due to an orgasm).

This is followed by two additional dance sections. *Madzo madzo* (or *madje madje*), like *shikalo*, offers considerable room for dancers to improvise. *Dakoli kutoiko* ("A bachelor cannot be a good farmer"), which follows, is tightly choreographed. Arranged in a circle, dancers walk freely for the first part of the rhythm (to the words *dakoli kutoiko*, repeated once). Then words are abandoned and a rhythmic cadence figure concludes the sequence. Dancers now stomp both feet in sync with the main drum strokes of measure 1 (see figure 1). Then they bump butts at the downbeat of measure 2.

After a number of repetitions of the full cycle, the event comes to a close with *baamaaya mangli*–style movements. In some performances, the baamaaya mangli rhythm briefly returns.

The Musical Ensemble

The *baamaaya* instrumental ensemble is made up of drummers (one luŋ'a player and one or more *guŋgɔŋ* players), *calamboo* (flute), and a *sayali* (rattle) player. Supporting them may be praise singers, a male baanga and/or the female kpalinkpaandiba-luŋpaba.

The *luŋ'a* is a flexible-pitched pressure drum that "speaks" by imitating the rhythms and pitch inflections inherent in Dagbanli, the Dagbamba language. The luŋ'a player (*luŋ'a m'mera*) is normally the leader of a performance. He is responsible for directing section changes. Through the drum language, he will use proverbs or contemporary speech to comment on community developments, recite lineages, and praise dancers.[11]

The guŋgɔŋ, a double-headed cedar-shelled drum with a gut snare, sustains characteristic rhythms. Generally speaking, a *baamaaya* ensemble will have two guŋgɔŋ players. While one musician keeps the basic timeline-like rhythm, to which the other instruments and dancers must relate, the other player enlivens and enriches the musical texture through improvisation.

The calamboo is a four-tone-holed end-blown wooden or metal flute. Just as drums "talk," the calamboo "sings" about life events that have been remembered through song, both old and modern. Some songs are associated with proverbs relevant to the entire community. Other songs are directed toward specific individuals.

Finally, there are sayali, hand-held rattles made of gourd and straw. These instruments keep a constant rhythm that serves to fill in spaces in the musical texture. *Baamaaya* ensembles outside Dagbon often omit these.

Now fortified with descriptions of *baayaama's* origin and general performance context, its regular costuming, basic dance sections, and musical structure, we proceed to a discussion of historical events and figures that specifically influenced African dance/music performance practices from the 1960s forward.

Nationalist Visions for the Performative Arts

Two influential philosophical concepts that emerged during Africa's nationalist era were Negritude in Francophone West Africa and African Personality in Anglophone West Africa. Senegalese poet and politician Leopold Cedar Senghor was West Africa's most influential proponent of Negritude. For Senghor, cultural performance allowed a society to visualize, dramatize, and fundamentally transform ideology by "upgrading the image of African dance from one of sexual debauchery and mindless instinctualism to religious mysticism and abstract interpretation of the cosmos."[12] Senghor's vision was fashioned for export. In 1948, more than a decade before Senegal's independence, Maurice Sonar Senghor, Leopold's nephew, became the first to bring staged performances of West African music and dance to Europe.

Kwame Nkrumah, the first president and prime minister of Ghana, understood both the importance of the performing arts and that Ghana, as the first sub-Saharan European colony to achieve independence, was uniquely positioned to serve as a model for the rest of the continent. To do so, Ghana would need to develop and project a distinct national identity. Central to that was the ideal of "African Personality," or what Nkrumah came to call "African genius." Nkrumah envisioned the establishment of a unifying national cultural heritage, one that would celebrate a traditional past while progressing to an international future. By instilling pride in African ways of thinking and being, Nkrumah worked to pull the psychological reins of power away from Europe and wield them—first locally, then internationally.

In 1962 Nkrumah established the National Dance Company (NDC)—soon renamed the Ghana Dance Ensemble (GDE)—to serve as a research laboratory for the preservation and development of Ghanaian national music and dance. The task of collecting repertoire for the NDC primarily fell to musicologist and composer J. H. Kwabena Nketia and dancer/choreographer Mawere Opoku, the ensemble's first artistic director. These two led a team that traveled the country in search of a broad ethnic sampling of music and dance that was visually appealing, sonically dynamic, and narratively appropriate for staged performance. Having spotted a viable genre, they went to work documenting the material, adopting and then adapting it. Nketia wrote, "It is our hope that we can share these with all those who love the dance, both here and abroad, for we know that artists all over the world as well as patrons of the arts love to see and enjoy quality in any dance, no matter its language."[13]

GDE's early stagings were distillations of a culture in the midst of reassessment and redefinition. Music and dance genres, once relevant only within the ethnic confines of village life, were reconceived as "art," with national, even universal, appeal intended. Choreography was designed to fit the proscenium stage. Ring dances were opened into horseshoes or straightened into lines. Dances were condensed into ten-to-fifteen-minute presentations. Athleticism was emphasized. Leaps were higher and gestures more dramatic. Tempos increased.

Today, many of those original dances remain virtually unchanged in the repertories of both national companies: the GDE, housed in Legon at the University of Ghana, and the National Dance Company of Ghana, housed in Accra at the National Theatre. The troupes serve as performing archives "for Ghanaian music and dance as well as the nation's political history."[14] Of course, it is important to remember these are embodied archives of reconceptualized works moved from village to the professional stage. Transplants though they are, the notion of authenticity is central.

Now we return to *baamaaya* to show how these nationalist, philosophical, and political changes affected a single genre.

National Performance Analyses

Tamale: Example 1

The northern Ghanaian sky is filled with dust from dry Harmattan winds blowing southward from the Sahara. Twenty-some members of Anakulada pack themselves into an open-air trailer hooked up to a dusty Massey Ferguson tractor. Their destination is Gushiegu, a village some fifty kilometers northeast of Tamale, where the group will perform *baamaaya* at the funeral for a prominent chief. Although Anakulyada is sponsored by the Center for National Culture and, therefore, technically a folkloric ensemble, we consider the following description to be traditional performance (so, too, would a full-blown funeral *baamaaya* performance by the Suglo N'mali Dang Ensemble, a group that we discuss presently.)

With all aboard, the principal luŋa m'mera opens the day's music by sounding the salima phrase, "Namogu yili mali kpeng pam" (There is strength and wisdom in the house of our ancestors). Next, he drums the phrase, "Bieg'ni n'sa nye chug'u. Katidi sag'm ka ngb nimdi" (Tomorrow is the big festival celebration [the Muslim *Eid-ul-Fitr*]. We will eat a lot of food and meat). *Baamaaya* calls are spontaneous, not based on preconceived notions of what must be said. Unlike when drumming the praise names of chiefs, where the call from the luŋa is very specific, in *baamaaya* it is the prerogative of the luŋa to use a wide variety of language to call in the rest of the ensemble. The chosen call could relate to a situation at the moment or might spring from the memory of things past.

The lead guŋgɔŋ drums a response, which also establishes the processional rhythm baamaaya so chɛndi. He is supported by a second guŋgɔŋ and the sayali. The *calamboo pebra*[15] now introduces a song melody to honor M'ba Abukari, the late respected Tamale elder and supporter of traditional Dagbamba music and dance, "Abukari waa m'buŋu. Abukari yoo yie. Abukari waa m'buŋu" (Abukari, this is your dance and it is your time to shine). This melody is followed by another, "Di mahila Jaŋg'a ka o kpara obia. Din ti mee na oni sheego lab" (Monkeys love carrying their young ones in times of peace, but are hesitant to do so in the midst of chaos). This song is based on one of M'ba Abukari's favorite proverbs, which advises young men to work hard instead of depending on the support of their parents. M'ba Abukari reaches up from the ground to tip the calamboo pebra for bringing his praise name.

As the tractor pulls away, children run alongside—cheering, singing, stumbling, and falling in the middle of the vehicle's dust cloud as it travels the short distance from the National Center to the main road. As the tractor reaches the paved road, the calamboo pebra sounds another melody, "Dagorili ka yaa. A maa pag'la miri ka ozori dabiem Dagorili ka yaa" (A playboy is not physically strong; therefore, a woman should never fear him). The troupe's women exuberantly sing the melody's words.

Virtually besieged by the ardent choir is Azindo, an excellent dancer, who is also known as a *dagorili* (playboy or womanizer) and a *doh loo* (a man who strikes women). Azindo's latest transgression occurred just two days earlier, when he struck a female member of the troupe, who is also riding in the trailer. When she fought back, he got the beating. For the time being, there is nothing for Azindo to do, but take the troupe's criticism.[16]

Hours later, however, during the performance in Gushiegu Azindo musters a musical response.[17] In answer to "Dagorili kaa yaa," Azindo commissions the troupe's second calamboo pebra[18] to play "Jagimelo kpe looree, oka charjee, kazang gb'na ti durova, ka oning nabaaya" (A prostitute boarded a lorry, but could not afford the fee, so she offered him sex in return). The song was directed at a woman who had been intimate with various group members. Salvos expand into new territories when one of Azindo's male adversaries, asks the principal calamboo pebra to play his proverbial song, "N'dagori kpei nyama kpug noli, Kaman mini sankpang n'moro" (My rival frowns upon seeing me, but I mistake his ugly frown as though he is suffering from a toothache). The song does double duty by demonstrating that the adversary does not fear Azindo and by further suggesting that Azindo's character is as commendable as a rotten tooth.

Although under siege on multiple fronts, Azindo counterattacks by asking the second calamboo pebra to play a song that criticizes his enemy's dance skills, "Soo, soo warila jilima kan kinkansi" (Soul, soul is danced with elegance, not with excessive vigor or exaggeration). Further jabs and parries are set loose over the next five hours, but the evening also explores a great many other topics.

Because this story is so dicey, the reader might suspect that this particular event somehow stands apart from other, perhaps more mundane *baamaaya* performances. Not so. This performance was typical. It began with pertinent and timely social commentary designed to engage and animate the troupe's members. No one knew in advance how the various actors might respond and, consequently, how the narrative would unfold. It is the unpredictability and surprises that make such an event entertaining. Such is the case for a performance by cultural insiders, at least.

Continental Folkloric *Baamaaya*

We divide our discussion of folkloric *baamaaya* into various sections. First, we consider another performance in the Tamale area. Next, we turn to Accra to look at *baamaaya*'s treatment at the hands of the GDE and NDCG, and other area folkloric troupes. Finally, we discuss selected performances in the United States.

Generally speaking, the following holds true: the closer a folkloric ensemble's repertoire is to its cultural roots, the richer that repertoire will be in terms of insider meaning. Once removed from its cultural and linguistic home, however, rich layers of insider understandings are shed. Focus moves away from social interaction towards the creation of staging that satisfies a diverse audience consisting mostly of cultural outsiders.

Tamale: Example 2

With modernization and urbanization has come decreasing calls for traditional dance performed in traditional settings. What this means for *baamaaya* performers, even in Tamale, is a reliance on folkloric events. Not surprisingly, Tamale folkloric ensembles are "heavy" on northern dances, but a performance will almost certainly contain *baamaaya* and other Dagbamba dances, as well as repertoire from other ethnic groups from Ghana and elsewhere on the African continent. Today's performers treat these music and dance forms as cultural commodities, sources of financial livelihood.

Tamale-area luŋa drummers fill their folkloric performances with proverbs and other languages. A calamboo pebra is likely on hand to add a song component. Often missing altogether are the praise singers; Tamale-area folkloric performances remain rich with language, however. A twenty-minute performance in May 2002 by the Tamale-based troupe Suglo N'mali Dang Ensemble (Patience Maintains Family Ensemble) included the following drum language and flute songs, all just within the first two minutes:

Luŋa phrases:
> *Jarigu ziem bin barigu.*
> *Ka bin barigu gbago.*

A stupid person underestimates a trap.
He becomes caught himself.

Yam ni yam kutoi kpe.
Jarigu mini yam dan be.
Two wise people cannot live together.
One must be stupid, the other one wise.

Jerigu ziem peto.
So di bori lala o daa bi nya.
A stupid person refuses pants.
Another wants them and cannot have them.

Biegu ni n'sa nya chugu.
Kadi sagm ka ŋubi nimdi.
Tommorow is Chugu [a festival day].
We will eat lots of cornmeal and meat.

Calamboo songs:
   A dinbei, a dinbei ayiŋa.
   Your bad deeds will end in your home.

   Ay lag paga ko ti lanjaa,
   Nimi tuba naa lanjo.
   If you fall in love with a woman and she proves fickle,
   You should never go back to her.

(Luŋ'a was played by Fatawu Karimu. Calamboo was played by
Alhassan Bla.)

Accra

A complete GDE or NDCG performance may feature traditional and newly
created compositions from across the country or across West Africa. Taken
out of its cultural and linguistic area, however, luŋ'a drum language dissolves
into melodious rhythms. Today, just a tiny percentage of an audience in Accra will understand luŋ'a speech, including those Dagbamba not steeped in
traditional ways. According to anthropologist Deborah Pellow, for Dagbamba
cosmopolitan professionals living in Accra, "the distance and difference between the hometown areas in the Northern Region and the suburbs of Accra—societal and spatial—are great, so much so that residents of each operate
in an environment they perceive as being worlds apart from the other."[19]

This includes most members of the GDE and NDCG, which draw membership from ethnic groups across the nation. Drums have occasionally taken
on added importance within the NDCG. Dagara xylophonist and former

NDCG principal musician Bernard Woma has reported that while dance cues are given by the xylophonist in traditional Dagara performances, in NDCG performances they are given by the drummer, whose cues, for the non-Dagara dancers at least, are easier to decipher.[20] In fact, NDCG dancers have told us that they value predictability and straightforward drum cues that move them through the choreographic pathways. Using drum language adds a layer of rhythmic complexity, possibly even confusion. Thus, while drum language provides structural and social order to *baamaaya* when performed among cultural insiders in Dagbon, the same material obfuscates in Accra. Standardized musical cues are preferred to the in-the-moment flow of social ideas.

With Accra's local troupes, *baamaaya* looks and sounds even less like its northern parent. Distance—both cultural and physical—is a factor, but there are others. Local troupes constantly borrow material one from the other and then reshape the music and dance according to their own understandings, their strengths, and a desire to differentiate themselves from their competition.

These factors make for mercurial developments. In the early 1990s, for example, co-author Iddrisu taught a Tamale-style version of *baamaaya* to Nananom, a popular Accra-based folkloric troupe. For the ensemble, the endeavor meant learning new rhythms, dance movements, and acquiring new costumes. Northerners who saw the new dances were delighted, even occasionally mistaking the ensemble as being from their home region. Southerners familiar with *baamaaya* only through the various Accra versions were initially disappointed. They judged the new arrangement inauthentic because it was so dissimilar to the local style. Soon, however, Nananom's arrangements set changes in motion. Troupes, anxious that they, too, should "get it right," began to adopt aspects of the new version. As they copied, they also invented. Within a short time, alterations so permeated performances that Iddrisu barely recognized his own choreographic and musical contributions.

Members of the NDCG are aware that their repertoire, too, may appear inauthentic, at least when seen with the eyes of a genre's home ethnicity. For some, this is troubling. A number of current and former members expressed discomfort when performing staged repertoire in front of their own ethnic group.

Focal shifts from local to regional, from singular to generic, and from personal to impersonal are true of folkloric performances elsewhere. Ethnochoreologist Anca Giurchescu noted that Eastern European folk dances are "characterized by variation and individualization," whereas, "staged performances are based on homogeneity and synchronism, on self-control, and on the integration of the individual into the group" and often praised as "true artistic achievements."[21]

Yet NDCG performances are far more than artistic achievements or spectacles. They are cultural currency. Their dances may no longer be tied to calendar, life-cycle, or spiritual events, but they continue to summon the national vision Nkrumah, Opoku, and Nketia originally envisioned.[22]

Medie, Ghana

The Saakumu Dance Troupe, a folkloric ensemble housed in *the* Dagara Music Center in Medie, performs for an audience of American college students and their professors. Most of the music and dance works are Dagara, but they also perform *kpanlogo*, a Ga social dance, and *baamaaya*, choreographed by Sulley Imoro, an internationally renowned Dagbamba dancer. As one would expect of an Accra-region performance, this *baamaaya* performance includes no drum language, no calamboo, no praise singer, and limited costuming. For the dance's climax, the troupe opens the traditional circle into visually appealing lines. At performance's end, the American audience, mostly new to African dance and Africa itself, shout hoots of approval.

Here, we suggest, yet another transformation has occurred. For these students, who had traveled across an ocean to expand their social and cultural spheres, this performance offers a palpable opportunity to witness the "real" Africa. Later, when invited onstage to dance with the performers, students take first steps (literally and figuratively) toward living within that world.

Diaspora Folkloric Performance

As artist-researchers and teachers with multiple positionalities, we are particularly interested in the stylized approximations of African traditional forms as they are adapted over time and throughout the Diaspora. While providing entertainment and educating in ways appropriate to specific times, places, and audiences, these performances also map cultural change.

Habib Iddrisu's experiences in facilitating understandings and performances of Ghanaian music and dance to the Diaspora have been extensive, geographically from New England to the West Coast. In the almost two decades he has lived in the United States, his teaching and stagings have drawn inspiration from his Ghanaian roots, recent developments in African dance, international stage presentations by African troupes, and modifications and representations of African music and dance as they are developing outside the continent—in the United States and elsewhere in the Diaspora.

As educators, through our Diaspora teachings and performances, both authors work to define, and thereby expand, the peripheries of African cultural sensibilities and aesthetics. We both work, generally, in the Diaspora, but our positions are different. Iddrisu works as a culture bearer; Cornelius serves as a cultural outsider, as a life-long student and advocate.

Beginning in the late 1990s, the authors worked together for five years at Bowling Green State University in Ohio. Cornelius was a faculty member, Iddrisu a student (at both undergraduate and master's levels). Yet, when it came to teaching the African dance and music ensemble, Iddrisu was unquestionably in charge. Cornelius's role was to facilitate, then listen and learn along with other students.

We occasionally struggled with the following questions: What is "African" performance? What functions, or needs, should our performances fulfill? What skills and ideas should our students take away from the class? What forms should our performances take?

There were also pragmatic questions. Can printed cloths from the local fabric store reasonably replace African batik? Should women dance in male roles? Should drum parts be doubled? Even tripled? Do goals regarding the breadth of student experience outweigh attendant compromises in a public performance? In each case, the answer was almost always, yes.

A more complex question was the following: Is it proper to include sacred dance in the repertoire of a university ensemble? We experimented with different levels of involvement, and authenticity. Ultimately, we abandoned the initiative because it was both impractical and too unsettling for students.

Let us now consider in depth a current ensemble. Dema is a University of Oregon–based music-and-dance ensemble Iddrisu formed and directs. The troupe's performances are specifically designed to educate and entertain American audiences by introducing them to the multilayered aesthetics of African dance and music. Even the troupe's name, a Dagbamba word meaning "total performance experience," reflects that mission, which combines instruction in and presentation of music, dance, storytelling, costume making, and set design.

What makes Dema's performances particularly meaningful are the invitations extended to exceptionally talented African artists who (like Iddrisu) were former members of Ghana's national premier ensembles, including the Ghana Dance Ensemble, Abibigromma, the Ghana National Dance Company, and other top amateur troupes in Ghana. Because these artists all live outside of their home country (or spend considerable time abroad), participation in Dema also helps these guests to hold onto African traditions and cultural values, even as they adjust to new communities and lifestyles. For Iddrisu, these reunions are reinvigorating. Because some of the dance relationships extend back to early-childhood participation in Tamale folkloric troupes, Iddrisu's Dema-related collaborations with his Ghanaian colleagues function as reunion spaces that not only evoke memories of a shared past but also provide a supportive environment for sharing understandings about the experience of teaching and performing African dance in the Diaspora.

Importantly, these experiences may be even more powerful for guests than for Iddrisu himself. For many, their personal and professional choices since immigrating to the United States have limited their ability to practice their art. Participation in Dema's annual reunion concert offers a rare opportunity for them to pursue and thereby galvanize their artistic understandings and memories.

We cannot forget the students. For them, Dema provides a unique and generative space in which to have one-on-one interaction with seasoned artists, some of whose dance techniques and approaches to performance may be quite different from Iddrisu's. Through multiple lenses, students witness bodily what they need to learn. They see African performers interact and how they teach; they hear the rhythmic camaraderie between drum and the dance; they internalize the uniting power of song. Dema-sponsored reunions provide space to experiment with standard, and emerging, music/dance forms while broadening performance practices uniquely relevant to diasporic times and places.

The reunion creates a productive space for all. Here everyone can experiment with new and old music/dance forms. This is space in which boundaries are expanded, space in which performance practices adapt to fit new time and places. And of course, this unfolds in an atmosphere in which all participants—master performers or neophytes are free to negotiate among their multivocal identities: as Africans, as diasporan immigrants, and as teachers and students.

Many of the dances performed during Dema's annual concerts are based on an approximation of what the African artists did back home as well as new additions they have developed while living in the Diaspora. Performances adapt to performers' skills, needs, or developing contexts and interests.

Consider a *baamaaya* performance by Dema. Some guest artists understand the Dagbamba drum language in depth. Others do not. Students will understand a couple of carefully introduced phrases. This combination presents opportunities for Iddrisu to innovate. As the troupe's choreographer and producer, as well as a participating dancer and musician, he arranges—through presentation and style—two different productions fused as one. The first focus includes and highlights choreographic and musical elements as they are performed in Ghana. Preparing this material requires only minor adjustments and little rehearsal to produce an exciting and "authentic" stage performance. The second focus introduces new choreography that has emerged as a result of shared experiences with producing *baamaaya* in the Diaspora. These innovations may have only limited cultural relevance to the African guests, but they accommodate and fortify emerging New World understanding, skills, and interests. To the extent to which participants (African masters and students) are willing to accommodate and embrace change, perspectives enlarge and new vitalities are infused. Everyone learns. Because the art form is adapting and putting down new roots, everyone wins.

Boston Comparisons

Now we consider two Boston, Massachusetts–based performances of *baamaaya*. The first, in 2012 at Boston University, was directed by co-author Steven Cornelius. The second performance included co-author Habib Iddrisu at Tufts University for the World Damba Festival 2012.

This was Cornelius's fourth involvement in a university-level staging of *baamaaya*. The first three were at Bowling Green State University in Ohio, and directed by Ghanaians: Iddrisu, Kwesi Brown, and Imoro respectively. All three directors taught slightly different choreography and drumming patterns, which were often simplified to match students' technical skills.

The Boston University performance, which featured mostly female dancers (and two female drummers), primarily drew from Iddrisu's and Imoro's choreographies. Although the luŋa cued the rhythm baamaaya so chɛndi, subsequent section changes were called by the guŋgɔŋ. There was some drummed improvisation. Choreographic flourishes that did not require rhythmic transitions were called by Cornelius's eldest daughter, who had danced in all three Ohio performances and twice worked with Imoro in Ghana. Dancers sang the song "A dinbei," but that song only. There was no calamboo, but a student played traditional melodies and "birdsong" on a Boehm concert flute. The performance lasted approximately twelve minutes. Seven sections were included. Despite many shortcomings, the performance was well received. As far as we know, there were no Ghanaians in the audience.

Although there were two important differences in this event from the previous performances guided by Ghanaian teachers in Ohio, these differences were neither in the music (although it was simplified still further) nor the choreography. Instead, this event lacked both the spontaneity and sense of "rising energy" that develop when seasoned Ghanaian performers engage with their audiences. In the three previous performances, with one or more

Ghanaian musicians or dancers onstage, the final minutes of the performance opened for dance solos, which were spontaneous to the extent that they were neither previously discussed (at least with the students) nor rehearsed. The Ghanaian dancers were featured, but in two of the three performances adventurous ensemble members also took solos.

Here we turn to a brief, but powerful, *baamaaya* performance at the World Damba Festival 2012. That event featured three drummers, a luŋpaga, and just three dancers, but fully embodied the Dagbamba ideals of spontaneity and rising energy. Imoro led the dancers (which included Iddrisu), called the songs, initiated a number of musical breaks, and ultimately invited audience members to dance onstage. The artists did not rehearse before the performance, nor did they need to.

Conclusion

Ethnomusicologist Tamara Livingston convincingly argues that revivalists "create a new ethos, musical style, and aesthetic code in accordance with their revivalist ideology and personal preferences."[23] The transformations of *baamaaya*, as they unfold in the many contexts presented above, support Livingston's general observations with specific details. As our chapter testifies, Ghanaian dance and its attendant meanings, even when choreographies have been relatively standardized, has been on the move—across regions, borders, and continents.

Political exigencies initially sparked West Africa's folkloric dance movement. Today, however, it is local—and even private—interests and needs that inspire performance and change. Ghana's many music and dance ensembles—from the Tamale-based Anakulyada and Suglo N'mali Dang Ensemble to Accra's many competing troupes—strive to infuse the genres they present with new looks and meanings that satisfy existing audiences and develop new ones. Competition is stiff. According to Ghana Dance Association committee member Ricky Adelayta, as of March 2019 there were approximately sixty folkloric troupes in Accra (only twenty-one are officially registered).[24] For a troupe to be successful, it not only has to perform well, but it also has to stand apart, often by showcasing material that other groups do not have. Such an environment encourages the invention and speedy incorporation of new material. Among Accra's lower-level troupes, stage appeal, not authenticity, drives performance decisions.

Yet innovation and change represent only one side of this story. The stabilizing power of tradition, albeit "invented" tradition, is the other. The GDE and NDCG continue to perform Opoku's half-a-century-old "classic" choreography with few changes. This model, though one that, when borrowed, is reconceived, is the standard source for performing groups in Ghana and abroad in the Diaspora.

Finally, the opposing principles of innovation and preservation we have discussed with *baamaaya* hold for all traditional Ghanaian dances. Regardless of where a performance is located, every dance and music genre naturally adapts to needs from within as well as influences and expectations from without. This must be so. An African tradition that remains static becomes irrelevant.

Notes

1. Perhaps these stagings may be likened to "invented traditions," which, as Eric Hobsbawm notes, "attempt to establish continuity with a suitable historic past," in Eric Hobsbawm and Terrance Ranger, *The Invention of Tradition* (Cambridge: Cambridge University Press, 2012 [1983]): 1.

2. This was not the first use of dance to promote national identity internationally. In the late 1920s and 1930s, Uday Shankar (1900–1977) also adopted Indian dance for that purpose. His work, according to dancer/choreographer Jean Erdman, "reflect[ed] the conventions of both the source culture and the culture of translation, [to be] 'from' and yet be 'at' home on a foreign stage," in Joan L. Erdman, "Performance as Translation: Uday Shankar in the West," *Drama Review* 311 (1987): 64–88.

3. For varied descriptions of "folkloric" performance, see Kariamu Welsh Asante, *Zimbabwe Dance: Rhythmic Forces, Ancestral Voices—An Artistic Analysis* (Trenton, N.J.: Africa World, 2000), 9; Theodore S. Gonzalves, *The Day the Dancers Stayed: Performing in the Filipino/American Diaspora* (Philadelphia: Temple University Press, 2010), 27; Mary Masayo Doi, *Gesture, Gender, Nation: Dance and Social Change in Uzbekistan* (Westport, Conn.: Bergin and Garvey, 2002), 10. For discussions of folkloric dance in Africa, see Judith Lynne Hannah, "African's New Traditional Dance," *Ethnomusicology* 9, no. 1 (1965): 280–95, and Peggy Harper, "Dance in Nigeria," *Ethnomusicology*, 13 no. 2 (1969): 280–95.

4. Sondra Fraleigh, "A Vulnerable Glance: Seeing Dance through Phenomenology," in *The Routledge Dance Studies Reader*, ed. Alexandra Carter (London: Routledge, 1998), 137.

5. See A. L. Becker and Judith Becker, "Musical Icon: Power and Meaning in Javanese Gamelan Music," in *The Sign in Music and Literature*, ed. Wendy Steiner (Austin: University of Texas Press, 1981), 203–315, for a convincingly argued Javanese gamelan example of the "iconicity or 'naturalness' of the coherence system" that informs musical structure. Perhaps this is true of all closed aesthetic systems.

6. Warren G. Jones, *Bamaaya: A Study of Dagbamba Drumming*, master's thesis, Tufts University (2002), 19–20.

7. Center for National Culture's Archives, Tamale, Ghana.

8. For greater dance depth, see David Locke's *Dagomba Dance Drumming*, http://sites.tufts.edu/dagomba/the-repertory/baamaaya-baamaaya-2.

9. The ensemble's name is a contraction of Anakuli yara, which translates as "Are you still talking?" This is a proverb to silence gossipers or to criticize the people who talk too much. Many performance troupes draw their names from proverbs.

10. This procession performance is also known as *naa daa* (greetings to trader) or *tuubankp'li* (referring to the bean dish).

11. For overviews of the history of Dagbamba drumming see John Miller Chernoff, *African Rhythm and African Sensibility* (Chicago: University of Chicago Press, 1979), and "Music and Historical Consciousness among the Dagbamba of Ghana" in *Enchanting Powers: Music in the World's Religions*, ed. Lawrence E. Sullivan (Cambridge, Mass.: Center for the Study of World Religions and Harvard University Press, 1997), 91–120; David Locke, *Drum Damba* (Crown Point, Ind.: White Cliffs, 1990); H. I. Abudulai, *Luntali Piligu* (Accra: Bureau of Ghana languages, 1988 [written in Dagbanli/Dagbani]).

12. Francesca Castaldi, *Choreographies of African Identities: Negritude, Dance, and the National Ballet of Senegal* (Urbana: University of Illinois Press, 2006), 54.

13. J. H. Nketia, "A Bold Experiment," in *The Ghana Dance Ensemble* (Legon, Accra: Institute of African Studies, 1967), 10.

14. Paul Schauert, "A Performing National Archives: Power and Preservation in The Ghana Dance Ensemble," *Transactions of the Historical Society of Ghana* 10 (2006–2007): 171–81.

15. The calamboo player. Pebra best translates as blower. Peb'bu is the act of blowing.

16. Azindo is not the transgressor's real name.

17. This development might seem strange to the reader, since the entire troupe seemed to be against Azindo. But in a Dagbamba performance such as *baamaaya*, in which lively, often sexually tinged, musical banter fills the air, no single person or perspective holds a monopoly on the topics of conversation. A baanga, calamboo pebra, or luŋ'a m'mera might take up an opposing viewpoint with the goal of bolstering a performance's emotional energy (or because an opposing party has offered a generous tip). There are endless possibilities for forming allegiances and aggravating oppositions. The controlled protocol of *baamaaya* offers a socially sanctioned format to construct new social relationships and deconstruct old ones.

18. Usually, a *baamaaya* group has only one calamboo, but because Anakulyada was a folklore group committed to promoting cultural heritage and whose repertoire included a variety of genres from across Ghana, members learned many dances and sometimes a variety of instruments.

19. Deborah Pellow, "International Transmigrants: A Dagomba Diaspora," *American Ethnologist* 38 (2011): 133–47.

20. Personal interview with Cornelius, Medie, Ghana, May 22, 2004.

21. Ana Giurchescu, "The Power of Dance," *Year Book for the Traditional Music* 33 (2001): 109–212.

22. Kwame Nkrumah, *The Autobiographpy of Kwame Nkurmah* (Edinburg, N.Y.: Nelson, 1967); Mawere Opoku, "The African Dance," in *Ghana Dance Ensemble*; Ntekia, "Bold Experiment."

23. Tamara Livingston, "Music Revival: Towards a General Theory," *Ethnomusicology* 43, no. 1 (1999): 66–85.

24. Iddrisu, personal communication with Joseph O. Adotey, a long-time executive member of the Greater Accra Dance Association, Accra, Ghana, November 16, 2011.

Men Walk in Parallel!

Dancing in Chuck Davis's "Paths"

C. Kemal Nance

We enter the space from the upstage right corner, walking on the diagonal of the space, side by side with our shoulders touching. I, a six-foot-three-inch, 220-pound man with a muscular build, bald head, and milk chocolate complexion—walk facing the audience while Stafford, a six-foot-five-inch, 210-pound man with long dark brown locks that drape down to the middle of his back, contrasting his cinnamon brown complexion, walks facing the back. Together, we sweep the stage with our long strides, switching position back to front sporadically and simultaneously. As we walk, the path becomes circular, we alternately extend our arms to the side, above our heads, then down in front of our bodies and the melodic sound of the *kora*[1] fills the space. We stop and start; we break away from each other, lapsing into traditional West African and modern dance vocabularies. With long legs and high knees, we dance the signature marching movement of the *doun doun ba*, a "dance of the strong man" originating in Guinea, West Africa. I roll to the floor, and then Stafford descends in a stretch as I run to lift him up from the floor to resume the *doun doun ba*. Our walks become runs and leaps as we separate from each other, each dancing a customized series of walks, jumps, quick and percussive *mendiane*[2]—leg stretches and deliberate high-knee and hip-twisting *sabar*[3] movements. As we dance in concert with the sound of the kora, the ominous voice of "*Baba* Chuck" (as we affectionately refer to him)[4] recites words from Max Erhmann's *Desiderata*:

> Go placidly amid the noise and haste, and remember what peace there may be in silence.

As far as possible, without surrender, be on good terms with all persons.
Speak your truth quietly and clearly; and listen to others,
Even to the dull and ignorant; they too have their story.
Avoid loud and aggressive persons; they are vexatious to the spirit.

If you compare yourself with others, you may become vain or bitter.
For always there will be greater and lesser persons than yourself.
Enjoy your achievements as well as your plans.
Keep interested in your own career, however humble; it is real possession in
the changing fortunes of time.
Exercise caution in your business affairs, for the world is full of trickery
But let this not blind you to what virtue there is;
Many persons strive for high ideals, and everywhere life is full of heroism.
Be yourself. Especially do not feign affection.
Neither be cynical about love, for in the face of aridity and disenchantment, it
is as perennial as the grass.

Take kindly the counsel of the years, gracefully surrendering the things of youth.
Nurture strength of spirit to shield you in sudden misfortune.
But do not distress yourself with dark imaginings.
Many fears are born of fatigue and loneliness.

Beyond a wholesome discipline, be gentle with yourself.
You are a child of the universe,
No less than the trees and the stars;
You have a right to be here.
And whether or not it is clear to you,
No doubt the universe is unfolding as it should.
Therefore, be at peace with God, whatever you conceive Him to be.
And whatever your labors and aspirations, in the noisy confusion of life,
Keep peace in your soul.

With all its sham, drudgery, and broken dreams, it is still a beautiful world.
Be cheerful. Strive to be happy.[5]

As his narration ends, Stafford and I walk to center stage and present ourselves with our long arms extended to the audience and smiles that welcome imagined onlookers into our world. This is the only moment in the dance when our gazes invite. Upon this final gesture, the music has a *decrescendo*, as we gallantly take our bows in an assumed black out.

■ ■ ■

The preceding narrative is a lived-experience description of me and my dancing colleague and friend, Stafford C. Berry Jr. in rehearsal with Charles

"Chuck" Davis, the late artistic director of the African American Dance Ensemble (AADE), as well as the creator of DanceAfrica America. Our rehearsal was at the Durham Arts Council in Durham, North Carolina, on October 16, 2011. Moved by the sight of Davis's strong yet aging body as it represented his tireless years of championing African dance in the United States, Berry and I approached Davis about mounting a new work on us while the three of us were performing at the annual Independence Day Eno River Festival in Durham, North Carolina. With wide-eyed enthusiasm, Davis agreed to choreograph a dance on our bodies, pronouncing, "You two can do everything! There are no limits!" He later called the work "Paths."

While Davis saw the creative process for "Paths" as an opportunity to develop a high level of artistry, Berry and I saw it as an opportunity for him to choreograph his legacy. As mature dancers ourselves and hardly "boundless" as Davis described, we appreciated the temporality of our own dancing bodies and the sanctity of the choreographic offerings our shared mentor could provide.

In this chapter, I focus on a collective discourse of African American men who dance and employ African dance vocabularies for our creative and scholarly work mainly in the African Diaspora. Encyclopedia.com describes African Diaspora in two categories: "First, there are those that discuss the patterns of dispersal of African peoples around the world and the kinds of Diasporic identities these populations developed in their new locations. . . . Second, some studies are concerned with analyzing the various linkages that the diasporas have maintained with Africa."[6] Davis spent his career mining the traditional movement practices of continental Africa and weaving them into his contemporary choreography. In so doing, he not only championed an African identity among African American dancers, but he also developed a diasporic practice of neotraditional African dance that links its participants to an imagined Africa. The research in this chapter reveals that Davis similarly used "Africa" as a resource for constructing a masculinity for his male dancers, one informed by varied cultures throughout Africa's Diaspora.

More specifically, I examine gendered scripts as they emerge from the choreography, "Paths," and as articulated by its choreographer, Chuck Davis. I examine the creative process and its involvement within African dance traditions. In doing so, I posit Berry's and my subjectivity as dancers and researchers within a potential paradigm for the perpetuation of an African American dance culture. In this regard, my analysis underscores the intersection of cultural permanence via gendered scripting.

Method and Methodology

An autoethnography methodology illuminates the linkages between dancing "Paths" and the discourse surrounding African American dancing men. I use the writing of this chapter as a mode of inquiry to deepen an understanding of culture within my specialized field.[7]

At the outset of a two-day rehearsal period during which Davis created "Paths," I interviewed Davis to inquire about his choreographic intentions in light of what he viewed as an evolving African dance tradition in the United States. Midway through the first day of the rehearsal process, both Berry and I wrote our individual field notes, often chatting about some of the poignant moments in the dance while theorizing their connection to the interview. I wrote many of these notes as episodes, with particular attention to lived-experience description.[8]

On the second day of rehearsal, I interviewed Davis again, asking him to revisit some of the issues from the initial interview and to comment on the progress of his choreographic intent. Most important, I asked him to describe "Paths" in light of his contentions about African dance performance. After we finished the dance over the two-day rehearsal period and after my departure, Berry interviewed Davis a final time.

The last part of our inquiry method is the writing of our stories. Sociologist Laurel Richardson, who specializes in gender and qualitative studies, suggests that qualitative researchers write about the writing process to contextualize their work. These *writing stories*, as she coins them, "[remind] us of the continual co-creation of the self and social science."[9]

Men Dance Like This

The Black male body has been a recurring discourse on the American concert stage. Media and communication specialist Ronald Jackson coined the term "*scripts*" to articulate the stereotypes that concertgoers—namely, White audiences—project onto our bodies. His research reveals that the Black male body has been historically inscribed as sexual, violent, and exotic.[10] Dance historian Susan Manning in her examination of danced spirituals found at the turn of the twentieth century that the Black male body was seen as a site of aesthetic failure.[11] According to historian Ramsey Burt's theory about masculinity as a European or Euro-American universal, Black masculinity is "marked" because it differs from that of White male rule.[12] Yet Berry and I still dare to grace the concert stage with our big, Black male bodies in search of our agency and in response to our deep-seated need to express our cultural identities. Fully aware of the theoretical discourse that surrounds our performance presence, we, as researchers, focus our attention on the scripts with which our Baba Chuck has imbued our dancing bodies in "Paths." In our African dancing world, a solace from the strictures of conventional masculinity prescribed by both our American and African American communities, we ask: How would Davis have audiences receive our performance?

Davis's response to this inquiry resides in his description of Berry's and my gendered performance. For him, a visceral heteronormativity resides in the integrity of "Paths." Our performed masculinity, as it is constructed in American contexts, further perpetuates the narrative.

Davis responds:

> If you were some other dancers, it would be a problem. There is no problem with you, as an artist, and Stafford, as an artist, when it comes to masculinity on stage. *We have to be realists.* In what we're doing, there is a masculine side and a feminine side. When I want the feminine side, I will ask for women or very effeminate men. This work is for men—for two men—not for two sissies—not for two homosexuals. I mean flamboyant. (You know what the word is.) The dance is for two masculine men.[13]

Heteronormativity describes the assumption that all people are heterosexual.[14] In the context of this chapter, it refers to the absence of a seemingly queer gender performance. I interpret Davis's terms "sissy" and "homosexual" as his attempt to articulate a particular gender performance for our male bodies, one not eclipsed by queerness. In this context "sissy" and "homosexual" establish an antithesis to Berry's and my masculinity. It is heteronormative in that Davis wants our dancing to obscure the possibility that our sexual desire could be for each other. And Davis's comment, "We have to be realists," is riddled with assumption and worthy of investigation.

Arguably, Davis is drawing on a problematic assumption that a gendered performance necessitates particular sexuality. However, he is addressing the artistic valor of "Paths," which for him requires a particular masculine portrayal. He explains later in the interview that he has both masculine and feminine sides to his personality. "Paths," he asserts, emanates from his masculine consciousness. Performance, he asserts also, is about gender, not sexual preference.[15] Performance studies theorist Judith Butler purports that the repeated acts of our socialized experiences are the substance for the construction of gender.[16] Davis's assertions raise the question of which culture informs the masculine representation he required for Berry's and my dancing in "Paths." In a different interview about men and African dancing in which I asked Davis to compare dancing to sport in terms of both their potentials for masculine behavior, he offered the following.

> They are about equal. Because of the amount of energy and there again, it's the stigma that is associated. Now, we go back to the history, and we look at the classical European dance. There, all men used to dance all the female roles. And one thing led to the other, and they could be masculine as anything, but once they put on the wig and the makeup, et cetera, et cetera, et cetera.
>
> But then I go to Africa, and in Africa, there—men dance because that was part of the culture, and because of the society. Now you look at the—what is it, the men who put on the makeup and they show—they stretch their eyes and show their teeth and they have on lipstick and makeup and everything, because the women have to decide who's the most beautiful man that she wants to sleep with.
>
> You see? So now, someone who did not know the culture, would see these men with all this makeup and the way they're primping and priming, they would swear that they were feminine. But these are some of the fiercest warriors on the continent. . . .
>
> You've got the strong dancers all over the place. . . .
>
> You see? So, it depends on where you are, and how you look at it. They're both fantastic as far as I'm concerned.[17]

Davis's awareness of the various ways in which male behavior is observed in different parts of the world supports the theory that gender is a "scripted" ideology. While he referred to sexual desire, gender specialist John Gagnon's articulation of scripts applies, in that "sexual scripts," too, free sex and sexuality from the stricture of biological determination.[18] In this regard, Davis's answer to the question, definition, and analysis of masculinity in both sport and dance underscores the significance of culture. However, in the situation in which Davis created a new work on two African American men, both of whom were versed in neotraditional African movement vocabularies and familiar with various masculine expressions from locations throughout the Diaspora, what cultural scripts give way to the realism Davis aimed to choreograph in "Paths"?

Berry asserts that Davis's rehearsal process commanded us to embody regionally specific dances from the African continent, as he would bellow in the studio, "Nigeria! Ghana! Senegal!"[19] Yet there were no congruent instruc-

PHOTO 14.1. (Opposite page) *Paths*, choreographed by Chuck Davis. Dancers (left to right): Stafford C. Berry Jr. and C. Kemal Nance. Steve Clarke, photographer (2006).

tions for our gendered performance as it related to the identifiable African cultures he wanted us to access in "Paths." As his comments reveal, Baba Chuck saw Berry's and my dancing as being unproblematic with regard to his gendered vision, a vision that arguably emanates from a U.S. American construction of heteronormativity.

Davis justified his heteronormative conformity by observing Berry's and my physicality. Berry displayed extreme height with a lean 'swimmer's' build, long arms and legs that appeared to extend out to the audience when he performed on stage. I am shorter and heavier, but still tall with pronounced thick legs and longer torso (see figure 1). Thus, for Davis, Berry's body and my body had a physical history that represented a former somatic reality for him. Using a food metaphor, he remarked, "Remember. I didn't always have all this macaroni cheese! There were several times when I was just a lean string bean and boiled potatoes with no butter."[20] He continued:

> All that comes into play. The fact that both of you are tall . . . You see? I can relate. The fact that both of you have big butts . . . I can relate.
> There is, by happenstance, a biological connection that is psychological. You see? Fortunately, neither you nor Stafford is ugly. Thank God! So, I can say that you are my sons.[21]

Our dancing bodies served as script for a masculinity situated in Davis's lived experience. Height, full buttocks, and handsome, Berry and I could dance vestiges of Davis's younger dancing body, a body he considered a masculine body.

In "Paths," Davis would have Berry and me dance in a way that somehow reflected the society out of which both he and we were born (realism). I argue that Davis's proposed realism is steeped in a White American and African American heteronormativity, one in which being tall, dark, and handsome has currency. Yet Berry and I profoundly danced our authentic selves, replete with our physical athletic potential, but with no conscious or reverent regard for what an imagined larger society would expect of us. With laughter, tomfoolery, and impromptu "drag" performances, we took improvisational jabs at heteronormativity during the creative process. During rehearsals, Davis himself performed an unforgettable rendition of "Big Spender" from the musical "*Sweet Chariot*." If our rehearsal process informed our dancing bodies' projection of gender, then our achievement in appearing like "average Joes" is ironic at best. Yet it is our heteronormative portrayal, a gender performance, that is authentic for us and significant for "Paths." As I contend in my doctoral research, Berry's and my gender performance by way of Davis's choreography is the result of our "maleness," a customized recipe of manhood and masculinity that comprises the individual constriction of gender.[22]

Scripts for masculinity and manhood extend into the philosophies that surround Davis's work in preserving and choreographing within African dance traditions. Both in the formal interview and personal conversations, Davis offered what he thought were important lessons for Berry and me as male artists, as keepers of African dance traditions in the Diaspora. The following is an excerpt from one of these conversations about the lessons Baba Chuck Davis thought African American men should learn from their involvement in dance:

> Some of what hinders us when we are on our path?
> In the ancient days, we had rites of passage under the guidance of the elders. They taught us to walk with our faces lifted and our eyes on the horizon. If [your] eyes are on the horizon, you are able to use your peripheral vision to see. When you are walking in that parallel position, you are walking, one step . . . one step . . . one step . . . like this. If there is an object on that path that will cause you difficulty, you see it before you get to it. If you walk in turn out with one foot going this way and one foot going that way—you begin to look down because the body is forced to look down. As you continue with one foot going this way and this foot going that way eventually, your testicles will split.
> And naturally that is . . . (What's the word?) a metaphor.[23]

In his advice to Berry and me, Davis drew a metaphor for feet positioning. African dance is largely performed in parallel, that is, feet facing directly forward, while European and other dance vocabularies are accessed through a 'turned out' position of the feet, generally called "turn-out." Davis's "moral to the story" was that Black men should dance in proper alignment. This is both a cultural and physiological project. A focused attention on the European dance canon or a distraction from what Black males are supposed to do results in castration, a proverbial emasculation. A drastic and painful conceptualization, this metaphor is one that spoke loudly to me as an African American man. The reference to a "horizon" and the integration of elder wisdom have all the components for an Afrocentric paradigm, one that places African phenomena in the center of an analysis of African people.[24] Moreover, Davis's parallel versus turn-out model also provides a useful schema for examining masculinities.

Current trends in masculine studies literature reveal that masculinity is a rhetorical device that codes male behavior for a given society.[25] While such trends are historically situated and informed, masculinities are created all the time; they instruct us on how we are "supposed" to embody our gender role.

According to the masculinities that exist in our United States of America, Davis, Berry, and I, with our tall, muscular physiques and our bodies' heteronormative materiality, should be something other than dancers.

Turn-out. African American masculinities have been largely situated in a problematic comparison with White male rule. Largely, African American masculinity is the stylistic acceptance of being denied the rights and privileges within White patriarchy, thereby essentializing European and North American "Whiteness" as an archetype to which to aspire.[26] As I run the risk of exhausting Davis's metaphor, this unattainable White masculinity is the gravity that forces our hips to turn out and our feet to point away from us. African American masculinity sits in Davis's metaphor as the Black masculinity that pioneering gender theorist Robert Staples argued and that emerged from the emasculation of African people during the enslavement period.[27]

Walk in parallel. Davis admonished us, as African American dancing men, to avoid using standardized European and North American dance nomenclature as tools to project our identities. When we asked him to articulate his message to all African American dancing men, not just those of us who study African dance, he said the following:

> Is there a lesson in the world of dance for Black men? YES! The lesson is to learn your discipline. *Learn who you are.* Be prepared to understand that other worlds might be there for you to use, but not necessarily for you to keep. Dance affords you the opportunity to do whatever you desire. Once you have become disciplined, you choose your course.[28]

Davis uses dance vocabularies to describe a gender role for African American men. "Walking in parallel" encourages us to look to an African ideology when constructing our identities, one that precedes our experience in the United States, one that the "elders" would sanction. Throughout the interview, and the creative process itself, Davis referred to the ways of the elders, prioritizing an ancient African continent for a preferred code of ethics. For Davis, the elders have the code for which we should pattern our lives, much like he served as an elder in Berry's and my life. With dance of ancient Africa, Davis has directed Berry and me on a trajectory toward our African center.

Conclusion

To be the receivers of Baba Chuck's legacy is unfathomable. He stands as the most recognized and accomplished American-born African dance choreographer and teacher since traditional African dances have graced the American concert stage. He has acquired a deep-rooted wisdom without compromising his identity, his ethics, or his mission. He is the example for aspiring male dancers to follow.

Berry and I premiered Chuck Davis's "Paths" at Kwanzaa Fest in Durham, North Carolina, and performed the work at Swarthmore College's Faculty Dance Concert in Swarthmore, Pennsylvania, the Africa Moves Concert at Denison University in Granville, Ohio, and the International Association of Blacks in Dance Conference's Performance Showcase in Washington, D.C.— all in 2012. We wore black-and-white Ghanaian-inspired costumes (Berry in black and me in white) with *bokolafini* trimming[29] and an Adinkra symbol[30] that started on Berry's attire and finished on mine. As Davis demanded in our rehearsals, we provided our audiences with vestiges of Nigerian, Ghanaian, and Senegambian cultures as we danced vocabularies from the *sabar, kplanlogo*, and *jola* dances of those regions. While it was unclear if the concertgoers read our bodies as the masculine images that Davis saw in us, images that he argued contributed to the integrity of the work, it is noteworthy that Berry's and my maleness as portals for our gender performativity had a discernable message. While we danced in the performance in Washington, for example, one audience member shouted over the applause, "All right! Make magic, brothers! Make magic!"

As Davis's paternal advice and choreographic direction required, we walked in parallel. As detailed in the close description of the work that opens this chapter, Berry and I surveyed the performance space, shoulder to shoulder, side by side, with parallel walks, kicks, and jumps, dancing our shared "Dance Father's" message to the world. As a budding scholar, I walk in parallel position as I navigate the field with its dearth of resources that document and analyze the movement systems that Chuck Davis has championed in the United States. While I still argue that a heteronormative ideology is required for African American men to maintain a knowledge of themselves and prevent a proverbial castration (turn-out), that peripheral vision that an African American masculinity requires, the upright walk of parallel footing that Davis advocates, is worthy of exploration as both an aesthetic and philosophical value.

As a research process, "Men Walk in Parallel" afforded me an opportunity to examine Berry's, Davis's, and my shared creative process as a potential portal for the transmission of varied African American masculinities. Unpacking our collective discourse as African American dancing men who employ African dance vocabularies for our creative and scholarly work, and using our subjectivity as a potential paradigm for the continuation of African traditions in an African American dance culture, we land in an important space that underscores the intersection of gendered scripting, cultural permanence, and the creative process. This space of multidimensional understanding requires the critical and—simultaneously—delicate handling of a legacy from our elder(s) that will perpetuate the existence and propagation of men in the African dance arena within an American context.

Notes

1. The *kora* is a twenty-one-stringed West African instrument made with a long wooden stick as the neck and a gourd as the resonating chamber.

2. *Mendiane* is a harvest dance that originated during the Malian Empire. While *mendiane* comprises several movements, it is best identified by its leg stretches, which are done with the body close to the floor.

3. *Sabar* is a traditional African dance from the Senegal region of West Africa; it is characterized by it its rapid knee lifts, twisting hips, and flirtatious performance style.

4. "Baba" is a West African term that means "Father." In African dance communities of the United States it is an honorific title designated for male elders.

5. Max Erhmann, "Desiderata," in *The Journal of Max Erhmann*, ed. Bertha Erhmann (Boston: Humphries, 1952), 2.

6. "African Diaspora," https://www.encyclopedia.com/social-sciences-and-law/anthropology-and-archaeology/human-evolution/african-diaspora.

7. Laurel Richards, "Writing: A Method of Inquiry," in *Handbook of Qualitative Research*, ed. Norman K. Denzin and Yvonna S. Lincoln (Thousand Oaks, Calif.: Sage, 2000), 924.

8. Max van Manen, *Researching Lived Experience* (Albany: State University of New York Press, 1990).

9. Richards, "Writing," 934.

10. Ronald L. Jackson II, *Scripting the Black Masculine Body: Identity, Discourse, and Racial Politics in Popular Media* (Albany: State University of New York Press, 2006), 75.

11. Susan Manning, "Danced Spirituals," in *Of the Presence of the Body: Essays on Dance and Performance Theory*, ed. André Lepecki (Middletown, Conn.: Wesleyan University Press, 2004), 84.

12. Ramsay Burt, "The Performance of Unmarked Masculinity," in *When Men Dance Choreographing Masculinities across Borders*, ed. Jennifer Fisher and Anthony Shay (New York: Oxford University Press, 2009), 154.

13. Chuck Davis, interviewed by C. Kemal Nance, Durham, North Carolina, October 16, 2011. Emphasis added.

14. "Heteronormative," http://queerdictionary.blogspot.com/2014/09/definition-of-gender-essentialism.html; http://queerdictionary.blogspot.com/search/label/hetero.

15. Davis, October 16, 2011.

16. Judith Butler, *Gender Trouble* (Routledge: New York, 1990), 45.

17. Davis interview, Durham, North Carolina, October 2009.

18. John Gagnon, *Interpretation of Desire: Essays in the Study of Sexuality* (Chicago: University of Chicago Press, 2004), 59–87.

19. Stafford C. Berry Jr. and C. Kemal Nance, "Baba to Sons: Chuck Davis Choreographs His Legacy with 'Paths,'" (presentation) Honolulu, Hawaii: International Conference of the Humanities, 2012.

20. Davis, October 16, 2011.

21. Ibid.

22. C. Kemal Nance, "Brothers of the Bah Yah! The Pursuit of Maleness in the Umfundalai Tradition of African Dance" (PhD diss., Temple University, 2014), 49–51.

23. Davis, October 16, 2011.

24. Molefi Kete Asante, *Afrocentricity: The Theory of Social Change* (Chicago: African American Images, 2003), 2.

25. Michael Gard, *Men Who Dance: Aesthetics, Athletics and the Art of Masculinity* (New York: Peter Lang, 2008), 2.

26. See Athena D. Matua, "Theorizing Progressive Black Masculinities," in *Progressive Black Masculinities*, ed. Athena D. Matua (New York: Taylor and Francis, 2006), 20–21; Richard Majors, "Cool Pose," in *Men's Lives*, ed. M. S. Kimmel and M. A. Messner (New York: Macmillan, 1989), 83–84; Marlene Conners, *What Is Cool? Understanding Black Manhood in America* (New York: Crown, 1995).

27. Robert Staples, *Black Masculinity: The Black Male Role in American Society* (San Francisco: Black Scholar, 1982), 2.

28. Davis interview with Berry and Nance, Durham Arts Council, Durham, North Carolina, October 16, 2011 (tape recording). Emphasis added.

29. *Bokolafini* (or *bokolan*) is a Malian mud cloth. The word "trimming" in this phrase refers to the costumes, which were decorated with this mudcloth fabric. The cuffs of the pants and the bottom of the daishiki-shaped top had bokolafini borders.

30. Adinkra symbols are African visual representations of concepts or aphorisms that are situated in Ghanaian culture but have currency in a larger, African worldview. The Adinkra symbols were developed by the Akan people of West Africa.

SELECTED BIBLIOGRAPHY

Abrahams, Roger. "Concerning African Performance Patterns." In *Neo-African Literature and Culture: Essays in Memory of Janheinz Jahn*, edited by Bernth Lindfors and Ulla Schlid, 32–42. Wiesbaden, Ger.: Heymann, 1976.

Abudulai, H. I. *Luntali Piligu*. Accra: Bureau of Ghana Languages, 1998.

Achebe, Chinua. *Things Fall Apart*. 1958. New York: Knopf, 1994.

"African Diaspora." https://www.encyclopedia.com/social-sciences-and-law/anthro pology-and-archaeology/human-evolution/african-diaspora.

Agawu, Kofi. "African Music as Text." *Research in African Literatures* 32, no. 2 (2001): 8–16.

———. *African Rhythm: A Northern Ewe Perspective*. Cambridge: Cambridge University Press, 1995.

———. "The Invention of African Rhythm." *Journal of the American Musicological Society* 48, no. 3 (1995): 380–95.

———. *Representing African Music: Postcolonial Notes, Queries, Positions*. New York: Routledge, 2000.

Ahye, Molly. *Golden Heritage: The Dances of Trinidad and Tobago*. Petit Valley, Trinidad: Heritage Cultures, 1978.

Albright, Ann Cooper, and David Gere, eds. *Taken by Surprise: A Dance Improvisation Reader*. Middletown, Conn.: Wesleyan University Press, 2003.

Alexander, M. Jacqui. *Pedagogies of Crossing: Meditations on Feminism, Sexual Politics, Memory, and the Sacred*. Durham, N.C.: Duke University Press, 2005.

Allende-Goitía, Noel. "The Mulatta, the Bishop, and Dances in the Cathedral: Race, Music, and Power Relations in Seventeenth-Century Puerto Rico." *Black Music Research Journal* 26, no. 2 (2006): 137–64.

Angola Maconde, Juan. "Las raíces africanas en la historia de Bolivia." In Walker, *Conocimiento desde adentro*, 1:145–222.

Anku, Willie. "The Contexts and Meaning in Asante Dance Performance: The Case of Kete." MA thesis, University of Ghana, 2015.

Arslanian, Sharon. "Two Takes on Tap." Video recording. New York: Dance on Camera Festival (honorable mention), 1992; sharonarslanian@yahoo.com.

Asante, Molefi Kete. *Afrocentricity: The Theory of Social Change*. Chicago: African American Images, 2003.

ASWAD. http://aswadiaspora.org.

Ayoade, John A. A. "The Culture Debate in Africa." *Black Scholar* 20 (Summer/Fall 1989): 2–7.

Balbuena Gutiérrez, Bárbara, and Graciela Chao Carbonnero. (2010). *Apúntes para la enseñanza de las danzas cubanas: História y metodología*. Havana: Editorial Adagio and Ediciones Cúpulas.

Banes, Sally. "Spontaneous Combustion: Notes on Dance Improvisation from the Sixties to the Nineties." In Albright and Gere, *Taken by Surprise*, 77–85.

———. *Terpsichore in Sneakers: Post-Modern Dance*. 1987. Middletown, Conn.: Wesleyan University Press, 2011.

Batcher, Melanie, "Song and Dance Nexus in the Africana Aesthetic: My Approach." In *African American Studies*, edited by Jeanette R. Davidson, 224–38. Edinburgh: Edinburgh University Press, 2010.

Becker, A. L., and Judith Becker. "A Musical Icon: Power and Meaning in Javanese Gamelan Music." In *The Sign in Music and Literature*, edited by Wendy Steiner, 203–315. Austin: University of Texas Press, 1981.

Beckford, Ruth. "Celebrating the Dunham Legacy." Speech to the audience at Katherine Dunham Legacy Northern California Memorial, Laney College Theater, Oakland, June 8, 2006.

———. *Katherine Dunham, A Biography*. New York: Dekker, 1979.

"Bed-Stuy: A Very Brief History." *Weekly Nabe*. June 23, 2012. http://www.theweekly nabe.com/2012/06/23/bed-stuy.

Berliner, Paul. *The Soul of Mbira: Music and Traditions of the Shona People of Zimbabwe*. Appendix: Building and Playing a Shona Karimba. Chicago: University of Chicago Press, 1993.

Berliner, Paul, et al. (American Council of Learned Societies). *Thinking in Jazz: The Infinite Art of Improvisation*. Chicago: University of Chicago Press, 1994.

Berry, Stafford C., Jr., and C. Kemal Nance. "Baba to Sons: Chuck Davis Choreographs His Legacy with 'Paths.'" Presentation. Honolulu, Hawaii: International Conference of the Humanities, 2012.

Biancardi, Emília. *Raízes Musicais da Bahia: The Musical Roots of Bahia*. Bahia: Oficina das Artes, Governo da Bahia, 2006.

Bilby, Kenneth, and Bunseki Fu-Kiau. *Kumina: A Kongo-Based Tradition in the New World*. Brussels: Centre d'Études et de Documentation Africaines, 1983.

Birat, Kathie. "The Conundrum of Home: The Diasporic Imagination in the Nature of Blood by Caryl Phillips." In *African Diasporas in the New and Old Worlds: Consciousness and Imagination*, edited by Geneviève Fabre and Klaus Benesch, 195–212. Amsterdam: Rodopi, 2004.

Bond, Karen. "The Human Nature of Dance: Towards a Theory of Aesthetic Community." In *Communicative Musicality: Exploring the Basis of Human Companionship*, edited by Stephen Malloch and Colwyn Trevarthen, 401–22. Oxford: Oxford University Press, 2008.

"Brooklyn Community District 3: Bedford Stuyvesant, 2015." New York City Community Health Profiles 2015. https://www1.nyc.gov/assets/doh/downloads/pdf/data/2015chp-bk3.pdf.

Brown-Danquah, Benita B. "African Diaspora Movement Arts in Philadelphia: A Beginning Resource List." *Philadelphia Folklore Project Working Papers* 1–41, 1994.

Brown, Ronald K. "March: An Excerpt from Lessons." https://www.youtube.com/watch?v=wabf31OC6vY.

Buckland, Theresa, ed. "Dance Authenticity and Cultural Memory: The Politics of Embodiment." In *Yearbook for Traditional Music* 33 (2001): 1–16.

Burt, Ramsay. *Judson Dance Theater: Performative Traces.* London: Routledge, 2006.

———. "The Performance of Unmarked Masculinity." In *When Men Dance: Choreographing Masculinities across Borders*, edited by Jennifer Fisher and Anthony Shay, 150–77. New York: Oxford University Press, 2009.

Burton, Richard D. E. *Afro-Creole: Power, Opposition, and Play in the Caribbean.* Ithaca, N.Y.: Cornell University Press, 1997.

Butler, Judith. *Gender Trouble.* New York: Routledge, 1990.

Cabrera, Lydia. *La Sociedad secreta Abakuá.* 1958. Miami: Ediciones Cabrera y Rojas, 1970.

Campbell, Corinna. "Sounding the Body, Dancing the Drum: Integrated Analysis of an Afro-Surinamese Performance Genre." Panel presentation, SEM/CORD joint meeting, November 2011. Online archive.

Carrico, Rachel, and Esailama G. A. Diouf. "Flying High: Function and Form in New Orleans Second Line Dancing." In *Freedom's Dance: Social Aid and Pleasure Clubs in New Orleans*, edited by Karen Celestan and Eric Waters, 137–42. Baton Rouge: Louisiana State University Press, 2018.

Castaldi, Francesca. *Choreographies of African Identities: Negritude, Dance, and the National Ballet of Senegal.* Urbana: University of Illinois Press, 2006.

Cavazzi da Montecuccolo, Giovanni Antonio. *Istorica Descrizione de' tre regni Congo, Matamba ed Angola.* Bologna, 1678.

Cayou, Dolores Kirton. *Modern Jazz Dance.* 1st ed. Palo Alto: National Press, 1971.

———. "The Origins of Modern Jazz Dance." *Black Scholar* 42, no. 2 (1970): 8–13.

Center for National Culture Archives, Tamale, Ghana.

Chalá Cruz, José F. "Los afrochoteños: Legítimos guardianes de la memoria histórica y del conocimiento." In Walker, *Conocimiento desde adentro*, 2:1–32.

Chao Carbonero, Graciela, and Sara Lamerán, *Folklore Cubano I, II, III, IV.* Havana: Editorial Pueblo y Educación, 1982.

Charry, Eric. *Mande Music: Traditional and Modern Music of the Maninka and Mandinka of Western Africa.* Chicago: University of Chicago Press, 2000.

Chasteen, John C. *National Rhythms, African Roots: The Deep History of Latin American Popular Dance.* Albuquerque: University of New Mexico Press, 2004.

Chernoff, John M. *African Rhythm and African Sensibility: Aesthetics and Social Action in African Musical Idioms.* 1979. Chicago: University of Chicago Press, 1981.

Chernoff, John Miller. "Music and Historical Consciousness among the Dagbamba of Ghana." In *Enchanting Powers: Music in the World's Religions*, edited by Lawrence E. Sullivan, 91–120. Cambridge, Mass.: Center for the Study of World Religions and Harvard University Press, 1997.

Christa, Gabri. "Tambu: Afro-Curaçao's Music and Dance of Resistance." In *Caribbean Dance from Abakuá to Zouk*, edited by S. Sloat, 291–304. Gainesville: University Press of Florida, 2002.

Christie, Maria Elisa. *Kitchenspace: Women, Fiestas, and Everyday Life in Central Mexico.* Austin: University of Texas Press, 2008.

Clark, VèVè A. "Performing the Memory of Difference in Afro-Caribbean Dance: Katherine Dunham's Choreography, 1938–87." In *History and Memory in African-American Culture*, edited by Geneviève Fabre and Robert O'Meally, 188–204. New York: Oxford University Press, 1994.

Cobb, William Jelani. *To the Break of Dawn: A Freestyle on the Hip Hop Aesthetic.* New York: New York University Press, 2007.

Collins, Patricia H. *Black Feminist Thought: Knowledge, Consciousness, and the Politics of Empowerment.* New York: Routledge, 2000.

Conners, Marlene. *What Is Cool? Understanding Black Manhood in America.* New York: Crown, 1995.

Conrado, Amélia. "Afro-Brazilian Dance as Black Activism." In *Dancing Bahia: Essays on Dance, Education, Memory and Race*, edited by Lucía Suárez, Amélia Conrado, and Yvonne Daniel, 17–38. Bristol, U.K.: Intellect; Chicago: University of Chicago Press, 2018.

Covington-Ward, Yolanda, and Jeanette S. Jouili, eds. *Embodying Black Religions in Africa and Its Diasporas: Memory, Movement, and Belonging through the Body.* In press: Durham, N.C.: Duke University Press.

Crehan, Kate. *Community Art: An Anthropological Perspective.* New York: Berg, 2011.

Cudjoe, E. "Drumming among the Akan and Anlo Ewe of Ghana: An Introduction." In *African Music*, 8, no. 3 (2009): 38–64.

Curtin, Philip, Steven Feierman, Leonard Thompson, and Jan Vasina, eds. *African History from Earliest Times to Independence.* 1978. London: Longman, 1995.

Dalili, Efia N. "'More than a Sisterhood': Traditional West African Dance in a Contemporary Urban Setting." PhD diss., University of Pennsylvania, 1999.

Daniel, Yvonne. "African Diaspora Dancing Body Power." In *Rebento Special Edition, Performing Arts Journal* 6:17–50. Sao Paulo: UNESP Institute of the Arts, 2017.

———. *Caribbean and Atlantic Diaspora Dance: Igniting Citizenship.* Urbana: University of Illinois Press, 2011.

———. "Dance Artistry and Bahian Forms of Citizenship: Isaura Oliveira and *Malinké*." In *Dancing Bahia: Essays on Afro-Bahian Dance, Education, Memory, and Race*, edited by Lucía Suárez, Amélia Conrado, and Yvonne Daniel, 39–69. Bristol, U.K.: Intellect; Chicago: University of Chicago Press, 2018.

———. "Dancing Down River: A Presentation on the Dance of Suriname." In *Dance Ethnologists* 7:24–39. Los Angeles: University of California, Los Angeles, 1983.

———. *Dancing Wisdom: Embodied Knowledge in Haitian Vodou, Cuban Yoruba, and Bahian Candomblé*. Urbana: University of Illinois Press, 2005.

———. *Rumba: Dance and Social Change in Contemporary Cuba*. Bloomington: Indiana University Press, 1995.

Davis, Martha Ellen. "Afro-Dominican Religious Brotherhoods: Structure, Ritual and Music." PhD diss., University of Illinois, Urbana-Champaign, 1976.

DeFrantz, Thomas F. "The Black Beat Made Visible: Hip Hop Dance and Body Power." In *Of the Presence of the Body: Essays on Dance and Performance Theory*, edited by Andre Lepecki, 64–81. Middletown, Conn.: Wesleyan University Press, 2004.

———, ed. *Dancing Many Drums: Excavations in African American Dance*. Madison: University of Wisconsin Press, 2002.

———, ed. *Dancing the African Diaspora*. Durham, N.C.: Duke University Press (forthcoming, 2020).

DeFrantz, Thomas F., and Takiyah Nur Amin, eds. "Talking Black Dance Inside Out/ Outside In." In *Conversations across the Field of Dance Studies*, Fall 2016, 66–67.

DeFrantz, Thomas F., and Tara Aisha Willis. "Black Moves: New Research in Black Dance Studies." *Black Scholar* 46, no. 1 (2016).

Demby, Gene. "I'm from Philly: 30 Years Later, I'm Still Trying to Make Sense of the MOVE Bombing." *National Public Radio*. May 13, 2015. http://www.npr.org /sections/codeswitch/2015/05/13/406243272/im-from-philly-30-years-later-im -still-trying-to-make-sense-of-the-move-bombing.

Desch-Obi, M. Thomas J. *Fighting for Honor: A History of African Martial Art Traditions*. Columbia: South Carolina Press, 2008.

Desmond, Jane C. "Embodying Difference: Issues in Dance and Cultural Studies." In *Meaning in Motion: New Cultural Studies of Dance*, edited by Jane C. Desmond, 29–54. Durham, N.C.: Duke University Press, 1997.

de Tavares, Julio Cesar. *Dança de Guerra, Arquivo e Arma: Elementos para uma teoria da Capoeiraagem*. Belo Horizonte: Nandyala Editora, 2013.

Diop, Cheikh Anta. *The African Origin of Civilization: Myth or Reality*. Edited and translated by Mercer Cook. 1955. Chicago: Chicago Review Press, 1989.

Diouf, Esailama. "Staging the African: Transcultural Flows of Dance and Identity." PhD diss., Northwestern University, June 2012.

"District 3—Bedford Stuyvesant, 2015." *New York City Community Health Profiles*. http://www1.nyc.gov.

Doi, Mary Masayo. *Gesture, Gender, Nation: Dance and Social Change in Uzbekistan*. Westport, Conn.: Bergin and Garvey, 2002.

Dolan, Jill. "Utopia, and the 'Utopian Performative.'" *Theatre Journal* 53, no. 3 (2001): 455–79.

Donne, John. "Meditation 17." http://www.online-literature.com/donne/409.

Drake, St. Clair. *Black Folk Here and There*. 1987. Los Angeles: UCLA Press, 1990.

Drewal, Margaret Thompson. "Improvisation as Participatory Performance: Egungun Masked Dancers in the Yoruba Tradition." In Albright and Gere, *Taken by Surprise*, 119–32.

———. *Yoruba Ritual: Performers, Play, Agency*. Bloomington: Indiana University Press, 1992.

Du Bois, W. E. B. *The Souls of Black Folks*. 1903. New York: Signet Classic, 1994.

Dunham, Katherine. *Dances of Haiti*. Los Angeles: Center for Afro-American Studies, University of California 1984. Originally published In *Acta Antropologica* 2, no. 4 (1947).

———. *Island Possessed*. Garden City, New York: Doubleday, 1969.

———. *Journey to Accompong*. New York: Holt, 1946.

Ebron, Paulla. *Performing Africa*. Princeton, N.J.: Princeton University Press, 2002.

Elósegui, Josefina, and Graciela Chao. *Apreciación de la danza*. Havana: Editorial Pueblo y Educación: 1982.

Eltis, David, Stephen D. Behrendt, David Richardson, and Herbert S. Klein. *The Trans-Atlantic Slave Trade: A Database on CD-ROM*. 1999. http://www.theroot .com/articles/history/2012/10/how_many_slaves_came_to_america_fact_vs _fiction.html.

Emery, Lynne F. *Black Dance from 1619 to 1970*. 1972. 2nd ed., Princeton, N.J.: Princeton Book Company, 1988.

Erdman, Joan L. "Performance as Translation: Uday Shankar in the West." *Drama Review* 31, no. 1 (1987): 64–88.

Erhmann, Max. *The Journal of Max Erhmann*. Edited by Bertha Erhmann. Boston: Humphries, 1952.

Fabre, Geneviève. "The Slave Ship Dance." In *Black Imagination and the Middle Passage*, edited by Maria Diedrich, Henry Louis Gates, and Carl Pedersen, 33–46. New York: Oxford University Press, 1999.

Foster, Susan Leigh. "Choreographies of Gender." *Signs: Journal of Women and Culture and Society*, 24 no. 1 (1998): 1–33.

———. (2002). *Dances That Describe Themselves: The Improvised Choreography of Richard Bull*. Middletown, Conn.: Wesleyan University Press, 2002.

"400 Youth Join Brooklyn Brawl: Police Break Up Fighting in Bedford-Stuyvesant." *New York Times*, July 9, 1966.

Fraleigh, Sondra. *Dance and the Lived Body: A Descriptive Aesthetics*. Pittsburgh: University of Pittsburgh Press, 1996.

———. "A Vulnerable Glance: Seeing Dance through Phenomenology." In *The Routledge Dance Studies Reader*, edited by Alexandra Carter, 134–43. London: Routledge, 1998.

Gagnon, John. *Interpretation of Desire: Essays in the Study of Sexuality*. Chicago: University of Chicago Press, 2004.

Gard, Michael. *Men Who Dance: Aesthetics, Athletics, and the Art of Masculinity*. New York: Lang, 2008.

Gerstin, Julian. "Tangled Roots: Kalenda and Other Neo-African Dances in the Circum-Caribbean." *New West Indies Guide* 78, nos. 1 and 2 (2004): 5–41. Reprinted in *Making Caribbean Dance*, edited by S. Sloat, 11–34. Gainesville: University of Florida Press, 2010.

Gilroy, Paul. *The Black Atlantic: Modernity and Double Consciousness*. Cambridge, Mass.: Harvard University Press, 1993.

Giurchescu, Anca. "The Power of Dance." *Yearbook for Traditional Music* 33 (2001): 109–212.

Glesne, Corrine. "That Rare Feeling: Re-presenting Research through Poetic Transcription." *Qualitative Inquiry* 3, no. 2 (1997): 202–21.

Goldman, Danielle. *I Want to Be Ready: Improvised Dance as a Practice of Freedom*. Ann Arbor: University of Michigan Press, 2010.

Gonzalez, Anita. *Jarocho's Soul: Cultural Identity and Afro-Mexican Dance*. Lanham, Md.: University Press of America, 2010.

———. "Urban Bush Women: Finding Shelter in the Utopian Ensemble." *Modern Drama* 47 (2004): 249–68.

Gonzalves, Theodore S. *The Day the Dancers Stayed: Performing in the Filipino/ American Diaspora*. Philadelphia: Temple University Press, 2010.

Gottschild, Brenda Dixon. *The Black Dancing Body: A Geography from Coon to Cool*. New York: Palgrave Macmillan, 2003.

———. *Digging the Africanist Presence in American Performance: Dance and Other Contexts*. Westport, Conn.: Greenwood, 1996.

———. *Waltzing in the Dark: African American Vaudeville and Race Politics in the Swing Era*. New York: St. Martin's, 2000.

Graham, Martha. *Blood Memory: An Autobiography*. New York: Doubleday, 1991.

Gross, Terry. "The Great Migration: The African American Exodus North." Interview with Isabel Wilkerson. *Fresh Air*, NPR, September 13, 2010. http://www.npr.org /templates/story/story.php?storyId=129827444.

Halbwachs, Maurice. *On Collective Memory*. Edited, translated, and with an introduction by Lewis A. Coser. Chicago: University of Chicago Press, 1992.

Hamera, Judith. *Dancing Communities: Performance, Difference, and Connection in the Global City*. New York: Palgrave Macmillan, 2011.

Hamlet, Janice D. "Word! The African American Oral Tradition and its Rhetorical Impact on American Popular Culture." *Black History Bulletin* 74, no. 1 (2011): 271–89.

Hanna, Judith Lynne. "Africa's New Traditional Dance." *Ethnomusicology* 9, no. 1 (1965): 13–21.

Harper, Peggy. "Dance in Nigeria." *Ethnomusicology* 13, no. 2, (1969): 280–95.

Harris, Joseph. "The African Diaspora in World History and Politics." In *African Roots/American Cultures: Africa in the Creation of the Americas*, edited by Sheila Walker, 104–17. Lanham, Md.: Rowman and Littlefield, 2001.

Hast, Dorothea. "Performance, Transformation, and Community: Contra Dance in New England." *Dance Research Journal* 25 (1993): 21–32.

Hazzard-Donald, Katrina. "Dance in Hip Hop Culture." In *Droppin' Science: Critical Essays on Rap Music and Hip Hop Culture*, edited by William Eric Perkins, 220–37. Philadelphia: Temple University Press, 1996.

———. *Jookin': The Rise of Social Dance Formations in African-American Culture.* Philadelphia: Temple University Press, 1990.

Heard, Marcia, and Mansa K. Mussa. "African Dance in New York City." In DeFrantz, *Dancing Many Drums*, 143–53.

Hernández, María del Carmen. (1980). *Historia de la danza en Cuba.* Havana: Editorial Pueblo y Educación.

Herskovits, Melville J. *The Myth of the Negro Past.* 1941. New York: Harper and Row. 1958 [1941].

Herzfield, Michael. *Cultural Intimacy: Social Poetics in the Nation-State.* New York: Routledge, 1977.

"Heteronormative." *Queer Dictionary.* http://queerdictionary.blogspot.com/2014/09 /definition-of-gender-essentialism.html.

Heywood, Linda, ed. *Central Africans and Cultural Transformations in the American Diaspora.* Cambridge: Cambridge University Press, 2002.

Heywood, Linda, and John Thornton. *Central Africans, Atlantic Creoles, and the Foundation of the Americas 1585–1660.* Cambridge: Cambridge University Press, 2007.

"History of Bedford Stuyvesant Restoration Corporation." Bedford Stuyvesant Restoration Corporation. Accessed July 15, 2016. http://www.restorationplaza.org /about/history.

Hobsbawm, Eric, and Terence Ranger. *The Invention of Tradition.* Cambridge: Cambridge University Press, 1983.

Holloway, Joseph E., ed. *Africanisms in American Culture.* 1990. Bloomington: Indiana University Press, 2005.

Hurston, Zora Neal. *The Sanctified Church.* Berkeley, Calif.: Turtle Island, 1981, 60.

———. *Tell My Horse.* Philadelphia: J. B. Lippincott, 1938.

Inikori, Joseph E. "Africans and Economic Development in the Atlantic." *African Roots/American Cultures: Africa in the Creation of the Americas*, edited by Sheila Walker, 123–38. Lanham, Md.: Rowman and Littlefield, 2001.

Jackson, Jonathan David. "Improvisation in African-American Vernacular Dancing." *Dance Research Journal* 33, no. 2 (2001): 40–53.

Jackson, Ronald L., II. *Scripting the Black Masculine Body: Identity, Discourse, and Racial Politics in Popular Media.* Albany: State University of New York Press, 2006.

Jaffe, Hosea. *The History of Africa.* London: Zed, 2017.

Johanson, Donald C., and Maitland Edey. *Lucy: The Beginnings of Humankind.* 1981. New York: Simon and Schuster, 1990.

Johnson, Patrick E. *Appropriating Blackness: Performance and the Politics of Authenticity.* Durham, N.C.: Duke University Press, 2003.

Jones, Warren G., Jr. "Bamaaya: A Study of Dagbamba Drumming." Unpublished master's thesis, Tufts University, 2002.

Jordan-Smith, Paul, and Laurel Horton. "Communities of Practice: Traditional Music and Dance." *Western Folklore* 60 (2001): 103–9.

King, Martin Luther, Jr. "Nobel Lecture." December 11, 1964. http://www.nobelprize .org/prizes/peace/1964/king/lecture.

Kisselgoff, Anna. "Dance: 'Dance and Music of Africa' at Jacob's Pillow." *New York Times*, July 22, 1987. https://home.comcast.net/~dzinyaladzekpo/Ensemble.html.

———. "Dance View: What Is Repetition Doing to Choreography?" *New York Times*, October 19, 1986. http://www.nytimes.com/1986/10/19/arts/dance-view-what-is -repetition-doing-to-choreography.html?pagewanted=all.

Kivenko, Sharon Freda. "Mobile Bodies: Migration, Performance and Social Belonging in Malian Dance." PhD diss., Harvard University, Graduate School of Arts and Sciences, 2016.

Kodish, Debora, Lois Fernandez, and Karen Buchholz. "The African American Festival of Odunde: Twenty Years on South Street." *Pennsylvania Folklife* 45, no. 3 (1996).

Kringelbach, Hélène Neveu, and Jonathan Skinner, eds. *Dancing Cultures: Globalization, Tourism, and Identity in the Anthropology of Dance*. Oxford: Berghahn, 2012.

Labat, Père Jean Baptiste. *Nouveaux voyages aux îles de l'Amérique*. Vol. 2. 1724. Fort-de-France, Martinique: Éditions des Horizons Caraïbes, 1972.

———. *Voyage aux Iles: Chronique aventureuse des Caraïbes 1693–1705*. 1722. Paris: Édition Phébus, 1993.

Ladzekpo, C. K. "State of African Performing Arts." Panel presentation, Malonga Center, Oakland, March 5, 2015.

Ladzekpo, Kwaku. "Organizational History and Purpose." Program, 2nd Annual African Dance Season at San Francisco, Cowell Theater, Fort Mason Center, February 8–9, 1991.

Ledru, André Pierre. *Viaje a la isla de Puerto Rico*. 1797. San Juan: Ediciones del Instituto de Literatura Puertorriqueña, Universidad de Puerto Rico, 1957.

Livingston, Tamara. "Music Revivals: Towards a General Theory." *Ethnomusicology* 43, no. 1 (1999): 66–85.

Locke, David. "Dagomba Dance-Drumming." https://sites.tufts.edu/dagomba.

———. *Drum Damba: Talking Drum Lessons*. Crown Point: White Cliffs Media, 1990.

Long, Richard A. *The Black Tradition in American Dance*. New York: Rizzoli International, 1989.

Lorde, Audra. *Sister Outsider: Essays and Speeches by Audre Lorde*. Berkeley, Calif.: Crossing, 1984.

Love, Nia. "Deconstructing Body Poses in the Diaspora." Unpublished paper. Contemporary Issues Panel of Association for the Study of Worldwide African Diaspora Conference, October 3, 2003.

Loyola, Margot P., and Osvaldo V. Cádiz. *Me niegan pero existo*. Santiago, Chile: Consejo Nacional de la Cultura y las Artes, 2013.

MacAloon, John J., ed. *Rite, Drama, Festival, Spectacle: Rehearsals Toward a Theory of Cultural Performance*. Philadelphia: Institute for the Study of Human Issues, 1984.

MacGaffey, Wyatt. *Religion and Society in Central Africa*. Chicago: University of Chicago Press, 1986.

Maddox, Camee. "Drum, Dance, and the Defense of Cultural Citizenship: Bèlè's Rebirth in Contemporary Martinique." PhD diss., University of Florida, Gainesville, 2015.

Majors, Richard. "Cool Pose." In *Men's Lives*, edited by M. S. Kimmel and M. A. Messner. New York: Macmillan, 1989.

Malone, Jacqui. *Steppin' on the Blues: The Visible Rhythms of African American Dance*. Urbana: University of Illinois Press, 1996.

Malonga, Kiaszi. "Fua Dia Congo—Oakland Based Drum and Dance Group—Interview Excerpts with Kiazi Malonga." https://musicethnographybayarea.wordpress.com/bay-area-musics/fua-dia-congo-oakland-based-congolese-drum-dance-group.

Malonga, Muisi-Kongo. "Malonga: The Spirit of a Master Teacher." *Movement Stories: I've Known Rivers; The MoAD Stories Project*. Museum of African Diaspora, San Francisco, January 2006. http://www.iveknownrivers.org/read-2.0.php?id=56.

Mama Kariamu | Umfundalai. "Raaahmona Revisited." Video. http://ww.mamakariamu.com/portfolio.

Manning, Susan. "Danced Spirituals." In *Of the Presence of the Body: Essays on Dance and Performance Theory*, edited by André Lepecki, 82–96. Middletown, Conn.: Weslyan University Press, 2004.

Mannix, Daniel P., and Macolm Cowley. *Black Cargoes: A History of the Slave Trade, 1518–1865*. New York: Viking, 1962.

McDaniel, Lorna. *The Big Drum Ritual of Carriacou: Praisesongs in Rememory of Flight*. Gainesville: University Press of Florida. 1998.

McNaughton, Patrick R. *A Bird Dance Near Saturday City: Sidi Ballo and the Art of West African Masquerade*. Bloomington: Indiana University Press, 2008.

Miller, Ivor. *Voice of the Leopard: African Secret Societies and Cuba*. Jackson: University of Mississippi Press, 2009.

Mobonda, Honoré. "Les Joutes Musicales Dominicales de Congo Square ou Devoir Délibéré de Mémoire." In *Héritage de la musique africaine dans les Amériques de les Caraïbes*, edited by Alpha Noël Malonga and Mukala Kadima-Nzuli, 117–24. Brazzaville, Congo: Festival Pan-Africain de la Musique [FESPAM], and Paris: l'Harmattan, 2007.

Molina, Lucía Dominga, and Mario Luis López. "Afro-Argentineans: 'Forgotten' and 'Disappeared'—Yet Still Present." In Walker, *African Roots/American Cultures*, 332–47.

Monti, Franco. *African Masks*. New York: Hamlyn, 1969.

Mooney, Jake. "Star Power, Still Shining 40 Years On: In Bedford Stuyvesant, Robert F. Kennedy's Work Lives On." *New York Times,* January 29, 2009.

Moore, Alex. "Cross-cultural Perspectives on the Creation of American Dance." Senior thesis, Hofstra University, December, 2010.

Moreau de Saint-Méry, Médéric Louis Elie. *de la Danse*. 1798. Parma: Bodoni, 1803.

Morrison, Toni. *Playing in the Dark: Whiteness and the Literary Imagination*. Cambridge, Mass.: Harvard University Press, 1992.

Moss, Katherinea "Adowa: Funeral Dance of Asante as A Vehicle to Express Ethnic Identity." *African Diaspora ISPS 62* (1998). http://digitalcollections.sit.edu/african_diaspora_isp/62.

Mudimbe, V. Y. *The Idea of Africa*. Bloomington: Indiana University Press, 1994.

Mutua, Athena D. "Theorizing Progressive Black Masculinities." In *Progressive Black Masculinities*, edited by Athena D. Matua, 3–42. New York: Taylor and Francis, 2006.

Mwakikagile, Godfrey. *The People of Ghana: Ethnic Diversity and National Unity*. Dar es Salaam, Tanzania: New Africa, 2017.

Nance, C. Kemal. "Brothers of the Bah Yah! The Pursuit of Maleness in the Umfundalai Tradition of African Dance." PhD diss., Temple University, 2014.

Nelson, Matthew. "Polycentrism in Contemporary Dance." http://mail.bodysensate .com/bodysensation.

Ness, Sally. "Being a Body in a Cultural Way: Understanding the Cultural in the Embodiment of Dance." In *Cultural Bodies: Ethnology and Theory*, edited by Helen Thomas and Jamilah Ahmed, 123–44. Oxford: Blackwell, 2004.

Nettleford, Rex. *Dance Jamaica: Cultural Definition and Artistic Discovery; National Dance Theater Company of Jamaica, 1962–1983*. New York: Grove, 1985.

———. *Roots and Rhythms: Jamaica's National Dance Theatre*. New York: Hill and Wang, 1970.

Nicholls, Robert W. "African Dance: Transition and Continuity." In *African Dance: An Artistic, Historical and Philosophical Inquiry*, edited by Kariamu Welsh-Asante, 41–62. Trenton, N.J.: Africa World, 1996.

Nketia, J. H. (Joseph Hudson) Kwabena. "A Bold Experiment: The Ghana Dance Ensemble." 1967. Repr. in International Reviews of the Ghana Dance Ensemble, edited by A. M. Opoku, 12–14. Legon: University of Ghana Press, 1993.

Nkrumah, Kwame. *The Autobiography of Kwame Nkrumah*. Edinburgh, N.Y.: Nelson, 1957.

Nora, Pierre. *Les Lieux de Mémoire*. Paris: Gallimard, 1984.

Norris, Rebecca. "Embodiment and Community." *Western Folklore* 60 (2001): 111–24.

Novack, Cynthia J. *Sharing the Dance: Contact Improvisation and American Culture*. Madison: University of Wisconsin, 1990.

Odom, Maida. *Ramona Africa Given Jail Term for Siege Role*. Philadelphia Inquirer, April 15, 1986.

Olivera Chirimini, Tomás. "Candombe, African Nations, and the Africanity of Uruguay." In Walker, *African Roots/American Cultures*, 256–74.

Opoku, Mawere. "The African Dance." In *The Ghana Dance Ensemble*, 12–16. Legon: Institute of African Studies, 1967.

Ortiz, Fernando. *Contrapunteo cubano del tabaco y el azúcar*. 1940. Havana: Consejo nacional de Cultura, 1963.

Osumare, Halifu. "Dancing the Black Atlantic: Katherine Dunham's Research-to-Performance Method." In *AmeriQuests* 7, no. 2 (2010): *Dance the Americas*. http:// www.ameriquests.org/index.php/ameriquests/article/view/165.

Oxford English Dictionary. "Improvisation." 2nd ed. Oxford: Oxford University Press:, 1989.

Pate, Denise. "Fua Dia Congo: Dancing Malonga Casquelourd's Legacy." *Dancer's*

Group—Bay Area Dance Service Organization, December 2007. http://dancers group.org/2007/12/fua-dia-congo-dancing-malonga-casquelourds-legacy.

Pellow, Deborah. "Internal Transmigrants: A Dagomba Diaspora." *American Ethnologist* 38, no. 1 (2011): 132–47.

Philadelphia Folklore Project. "Honoring Ancestors: Notes from an Exhibition." *Works in Progress* 26 (summer 2014): 1–25.

Pierce, Wendell. *The Wind in the Reeds: A Storm, a Play, and the City That Would Not Be Broken.* New York City: Riverhead, 2015.

Pogrebin, Robin. "New York Arts Organizations Lack the Diversity of Their City." *New York Times*, January 28, 2016.

Polhemus, Ted. "Dance, Gender and Culture." In *The Routledge Dance Studies Reader*, edited by Alexandra Carter, 171–79. London: Routledge, 1998.

Price, Sally, and Richard. *Afro-American Arts of the Suriname Rain Forest.* Los Angeles: Museum of Cultural History; University of California, Berkeley, University of California Press, 1980.

Primus, Pearl. "African Dance." In *African Dance: An Artistic Historical and Philosophical Inquiry*, edited by Kariamu Welsh Asante. Trenton, N.J.: Africa World, 1996.

Purnell, Brian. *Fighting Jim Crow in the County of Kings: The Congress of Racial Equality in Brooklyn.* Lexington: University Press of Kentucky, 2013.

Quintero Rivera, Angel. *Cuerpo y cultura: Las músicas "mulatas" y la subversión del baile.* Madrid: Iberoamericana, 2009.

Reich, Steve, and Paul Hillier. "Gahu—A Dance of the Ewe Tribe in Ghana (1971)." *Writings on Music 1965–2000.* Oxford Scholarship Online, 2004. DOI:10.1093/ac prof:oso/9780195151152.003.0009.

Richards, Laurel. "Writing: A Method of Inquiry." In *Handbook of Qualitative Research*, edited by Norman K. Denzin and Yvonna S. Lincoln. Thousand Oaks, Calif.: Sage, 2000.

Robinson, Danielle, and Jeff Packman. "After-School *Samba*: Cultural Memory and Ownership in the Wake of UNESCO Recognition as Intangible Heritage of Humanity." In *Dancing Bahia: Essays on Dance, Education, Memory and Race*, edited by Lucía Suárez, Amélia Conrado, and Yvonne Daniel, 117–36. Bristol, U.K.: Intellect; Chicago: University of Chicago Press, 2018.

Rodriguez, Romero Jorge. "The Afro Populations of America's Southern Cone: Organization, Development, and Culture in Argentina, Bolivia, Paraguay, and Uruguay." In Walker, *African Roots/American Cultures*, 314–31.

Roman, Carmen. "The Danced Spirituality of African Descendants in Peru." *African Performance Review* (African Theatre Association, Goldsmiths, University of London), 7 no. 1: 158–72.

Rosaldo, Renato. "Cultural Citizenship, Inequality, and Multiculturalism." In *Identities: Race, Class, Gender, and Nationality*, edited by Linda Alcoff and Eduardo Mendieta, 336–41. Hoboken, N.J.: Wiley-Blackwell, 2003.

Rosalia, Rene. *Tambu: De legale en kerkelijke repressie van Afro-Curaçaose volksuitingen.* Zutphen, Neth.: Uitgeversmaatschappij Walburg Pers, 1997.

Salaam, Kalamu ya. "Second Line: Cutting the Body Loose." In *Wavelengths* 21 (1982): 26–30.

Salgado Henriquez, Marta. "El legado africano en Chile." In Walker, *Conocimiento desde adentro*, 1:223–70.

Sandri, Sarah. "Performance, Politics, and Identity in African Dance Communities in the United States." PhD diss., University of Oregon, 2012.

Santiago, Chiori. "Lessons Learned at Alice Arts Center: Art and Politics Don't Mix at New Arts-Based Charter School." *Dance Magazine*, February 1, 2003. https://www.thefreelibrary.com/Lessons+learned+at+Alice+Arts+Center%3A+art+and+politics+don%27t+mix+at . . . -a097174133.

Schauert, Paul. "A Performing National Archive: Power and Preservation in The Ghana Dance Ensemble." *Transactions of the Historical Society of Ghana, New Series* 10 (2006–2007): 171–81.

Shay, Anthony. *Choreographing Identities: Folk Dance, Ethnicity and Festival in the United States and Canada.* Jefferson, N.C.: McFarland, 2006.

Shillington, Kevin. *History of Africa.* New York: Palgrave Macmillan, 2012.

Shils, Edward. *Tradition.* Chicago: University of Chicago Press, 1981.

Sklar, Deidre. *Dancing with the Virgin: Body and Faith in the Fiesta of Tortugas, New Mexico.* Berkeley: University of California Press, 2001.

Snipe, Tracy D. "African Dance: Bridges to Humanity." In *African Dance: An Artistic, Historical and Philosophical Inquiry*, edited by Kariamu Welsh Asante, 63–78. Trenton: Africa World, 1996.

Sondervan, Karien, and Schouwenaar, Sophie. "Sabar dancing in Senegal." https://www.youtube.com/watch?v=RTDC7hJEqT4.

Staples, Robert. *Black Masculinity: The Black Male Role in American Society.* San Francisco: Black Scholar.

Stearns, Marshall Winslow, and Jean Stearns. *Jazz Dance: The Story of American Vernacular Dance.* 1968. New York: Schirmer, 1979.

Stewart, Dianne. "Africa-Derived Religions in Jamaica: Polyvalent Repertoires of Culture and Identity in the Black Atlantic." In *Contours* 3, no. 2 (2005): 74–122.

———. *Three Eyes for the Journey: African Dimensions of the Jamaican Religious Experience.* London: Oxford University Press, 2005.

Stuckey, P. Sterling. "Christian Conversion and the Challenge of Dance." In DeFrantz, *Dancing Many Drums*, 39–58.

Suarez, Lucía. "Citizenship and Dance in Urban Brazil: Grupo Corpo, a Case Study." In *Rhythms of the Afro-Atlantic World*, edited by M. Diouf and I. Kiddoe Nwankwo, 95–120. Ann Arbor: University of Michigan Press, 2010.

Sunkett, Mark Ellis. *Mandiani Drum and Dance: Djembe Performance and Black Aesthetics from Africa to the New World.* Tempe: White Cliffs, 1995.

Sweet, James Hoke. *Recreating Africa: Culture, Kinship, and Religion in the African-Portuguese World, 1441–1770.* Chapel Hill: University of North Carolina Press, 2003.

Tamisari, Francesca. "The Responsibility of Performance: The Interweaving of Politics and Aesthetics in Intercultural Contexts." *Visual Anthropology Review* 21 nos. 1–2 (2005): 47–62.

Taylor, Rob. "Bringing the Message: Naomi Diouf and Diamano Coura West African Dance Company." *Dancers Group: Promoting the Visibility and Viability of Dance*, July 2014. http://dancersgroup.org/2014/07/bringing-message-naomi-diouf-diamano -coura-west-african-dance-company.

Thompson, Robert Farris. "An Aesthetic of the Cool: West African Dance." In *Signifyin(g), Sanctifyin' and Slam Dunking: A Reader in African American Expressive Culture*, edited by Gena Caponi, 72–86. Amherst: University of Massachusetts Press, 1999.

——. *African Art in Motion: Icon and Act*. Los Angeles: University of California Press, 1974.

Thompson, Robert Farris, and Joseph Cornet. *Four Moments of the Sun: Kongo Art in Two Worlds*. Washington, D.C.: National Gallery of Art, 1981.

Thornton, John. *Africa and Africans in the Making of the Atlantic World, 1400–1800*. 1992. Cambridge: Cambridge University Press, 1998.

Tiérou, Alphonse. *Dooplé: The Eternal Law of African Dance*. Choreography and Dance Studies Series. Philadelphia: Harwood Academic, 1992.

UNESCO. Intangible Culture List. 2009. https://ich.unesco.org/en/RL/candombe -and-its-socio-cultural-space-a-community-practice-00182.

Van Collie, Shimon-Craig. "What Is African Dance in America?" *Dance Teacher Now*, July/August 1992, 63.

van Manen, Max. *Researching Lived Experience*. Albany: State University of New York Press, 1990.

Vaughan, Umi. *Rebel Dance, Renegade Stance: Timba Music and Black Identity in Cuba*. Ann Arbor: University of Michigan Press, 2012.

Vaz, Kim Marie. *Baby Dolls: Breaking the Race and Gender Barriers of the New Orleans Mardi Gras Tradition*. Baton Rouge: Louisiana State University Press, 2013.

Walker, Sheila S., ed. *African Roots/American Cultures: Africa in the Creation of the Americas*. Lanham, Md.: Rowman and Littlefield, 2001.

——, ed. *Conocimiento desde adentro: Los afrosudamericanos hablan de sus pueblos y sus historias*. Vols. 1 and 2. La Paz: PIEB (Programa de Investigación Estratégica en Boivia), 2010; republished as one volume, Popayan, Colombia: Universidad del Cauca-Popayan, Colombia, 2013.

Washington, Giovanna. "Performing Africa: Memory, Tradition, and Resistance in the Leimert Park Drum Circle." PhD diss., University of California, Los Angeles, 2008.

Welsh, Kariamu. Interview by Laura Katz Rizzo. August 8, 2012.

——. Unpublished interview by Indira Etwaroo. May 2016.

Welsh Asante, Kariamu, ed. *African Dance: An Artistic, Historical and Philosophical Inquiry*. Trenton, N.J.: Africa World, 1996.

Welsh-Asante, Kariamu. *The African Aesthetic: Keeper of the Traditions*. Westport, Conn.: Praeger, 1994.

——. "Commonalities in African Dance: An Aesthetic Foundation." In African Culture: Rhythms of Unity, edited by Molefi and Kariamu Welsh Asante, 71–82. Westport, Conn.: Greenwood, 1985; reprinted in *Moving History / Dancing Cultures:*

A Dance History Reader, edited by Ann Dils and Ann Cooper Albright, 144–51. Middletown, Conn.: Wesleyan University Press, 2001.

———. "The Jerusarema Dance of Zimbabwe." *Journal of Black Studies* 15, no. 4 (June 1985): 381–403.

———. *Zimbabwe Dance: Rhythmic Forces, Ancestral Voices; An Aesthetic Analysis.* Trenton, N.J.: Africa World, 2000.

Wilkerson, Isabel. *The Great Migration: The African American Exodus North.* NPR, *Fresh Air*, September 13, 2010. http://www.npr.org/templates/story/story .php?storyId=129827444.

———. *The Warmth of Other Suns: The Epic Story of America's Great Migration.* New York: First Vintage, 2010.

Willis, Cheryl. "Tap Dance: Manifestation of the African Aesthetic." In Welsh Asante, *African Dance*, 145–59.

Wilson, Sule Greg C. "The Story of Fanga." As told to *Rhythm Bridge*. N.d. https:// www.rhythmbridge.com/fanga.

Yarborough, Lavinia Williams. *Haiti: Dance.* Frankfurt am Main, Ger.: Bronners Druckeri, ca. 1958.

Videos

Brown, Ronald K./Evidence. "March: An Excerpt from *Lessons*." https://www.youtube .com/watch?v=wabf31OC6vY.

"Fua Dia Congo—Oakland Based Drum and Dance Group—Interview Excerpts with Kiazi Malonga." Music Ethnography of the Bay Area. https://musicethnogra phybayarea.wordpress.com/bay-area-musics/fua-dia-congo-oakland-based -congolese-drum-dance-group.

"Fusion: *Lambarena* by Val Caniparoli." https://www.youtube.com/watch?v=ohV2z Vhq8bI.

"The Jacob's Pillow Story." https://www.jacobspillow.org/about/pillow-history/jacobs -pillow-story.

Mama Kariamu: Umfundalai. http://www.mamakariamu.com.

"The Real Mandiani" (video of a traditional *mandiani*: "*Mendiani à Koumana*"). https://www.youtube.com/watch?time_continue=194&v=2EiTQjNJU90.

Revival Zion ceremony, 2012. https://www.youtube.com/watch?v=YQ27bfh2Q2w.

Sondervan, Karien, and Sophie Schouwenaar. "Sabar Dancing in Senegal." January 16, 2007. https://www.youtube.com/watch?v=RTDC7hJEqT4.

CONTRIBUTORS

Ausettua Amor Amenkum is a native of New Orleans, Louisiana, whose name means "Giving thanks to God who gives stability to be devoted." She is director of Kumbuka African Drum and Dance Collective, co-director of the Drama Club and Graduates of the Louisiana Correctional Facility for Women in St. Gabriel, adjunct professor of dance at Tulane University, and the Big Queen of the Washitaw Nation Black Indian Tribe.

Esailama G. A. Diouf, PhD, is founder of Bisemi Foundation and Arts and Anchoring Communities Specialist at the San Francisco Foundation. Dr. Diouf's findings come after twenty years of work as a professional dancer, researcher, and arts administrator. She serves on the board of directors for the Alliance for California Traditional Arts (ACTA) and the Silicon Valley African Film Festival, and she is the working group advisor to actor Danny Glover for the United Nations International Decade for People of African Descent. As a scholar and performing artist, she has lectured throughout the United States and conducted long-term residencies in India, Senegal, South Africa, Barbados, and Trinidad-Tobago.

Abby Carlozzo graduated with a BFA in dance from Ohio State University before completing an MA in Dance from Temple University. In 2014 she conducted cross-cultural research and studied various neo-traditional and contemporary West African dance forms in Ouagadougou, Burkina Faso. Inspired by her collaborative fieldwork, Carlozzo's current research focuses on the diverse approaches to dance improvisation that exist in the United

States. Presently, Carlozzo is working as an assistant director at a preschool in Austin, Texas, where she incorporates elements of dance into the creative-curriculum classroom.

Steven Cornelius received a PhD from the University of California, Los Angeles; he currently teaches at University of Massachusetts, Boston. His previous teaching positions include Boston University (2008–2012), Bowling Green State University (1991–2008), Bruckner-Konservatorium Linz (adjunct faculty, 1992–97), and University of Wisconsin-Madison (1984–86). His published books include: *Music: A Social Experience* (with Mary Natvig, 2012/2018), *Music of the Civil War Era* (2004), and *The Music of Santería: Traditional Rhythms of the Batá Drums* (with John Amira, 1991). From 1996 to 2006 Cornelius authored some twelve hundred articles as music and dance critic for *The Blade*, Toledo, Ohio's daily newspaper. His performance credits as a percussionist include the Metropolitan Opera, New York City Opera National Company, Radio City Music Hall, Oklahoma Symphony, and other venues.

Yvonne Daniel, PhD, is Smith College's professor emerita of dance and Afro-American studies. She has worked as a choreographer, performer, and anthropologist, specializing in Circum-Caribbean societies. Her publications include *Rumba* (1995), *Dancing Wisdom, Embodied Knowledge in Haitian Vodou, Cuban Yoruba, and Bahian Candomblé* (Society of Dance History Scholars' de la Torre Bueno prize, 2006), *Caribbean and Atlantic Diaspora Dance: Igniting Citizenship* ("Choice" award, 2011); she was co-editor of *Dancing on Earth* (with Kimerer LaMothe and Sally Hess, 2017) and *Dancing Bahia: Essays on Dance, Education, Memory and Race* (with Lucía Suárez and Amélia Conrado, 2018). Additionally, she is credited with more than forty published articles, chapters, and encyclopedia entries, and four documentary videos. In January 2018 Dr. Daniel received the scholar's award for lifetime achievement in research on black dance from the International Black Dance Association (IABD).

Indira Etwaroo, PhD, is an educator, scholar, and nonprofit arts leader. She has worked with institutions across the country to explore the complex intersections among community, performing arts, and the topics of our time, furthering models of institutional diversity and sustainability. She received a PhD in dance from Temple University and was awarded a Fulbright scholarship in 2003 to conduct research in Addis Ababa, Ethiopia. Dr. Etwaroo is a recipient of several awards and has published articles and chapters on the arts and community. She resides in Bed-Stuy, Brooklyn, where she is the executive director of RestorationART and the historic Billie Holiday Theatre.

Habib Iddrisu, PhD, is an assistant professor of dance and musicology/ethnomusicology at the University of Oregon. His research interests include African music and dance practice and performance, cultural studies, oral history, African Diaspora music, and dance aesthetics. He has received Ghana's Best Traditional Dancer Award and is a scholar-practitioner; he is currently working on a book manuscript, "The Myth of Authenticity: Global Hybridization of African Music and Dance."

Julie B. Johnson, PhD, completed her doctoral studies at Temple University, where her research focused on meanings and experiences of "community" in a West African Dance class in Philadelphia. She is a dance artist and educator who works at the intersections of creative practice and research on African Diaspora movement aesthetics, community interaction, and social justice. Dr. Johnson is a co-founding editor of *The Dancer-Citizen*, an online, peer-reviewed, open-access dance journal that explores the work of socially engaged artists. She is also executive artistic director of Moving Our Stories LLC, a multifaceted creative practice that explores embodied memory and personal narratives through dance workshops, collaborative choreographic practice, interactive performance, creative and scholarly research, and community dialogues. Currently, she is at Spelman College in the Department of Dance Performance and Choreography and in the African Diaspora and the World Program.

Naomi Gedo Johnson Diouf, MAOM, is the artistic director of Diamano Coura West African Dance Company, which began in 1975 with the Emmy Award–winning musician Dr. Zakaraya Diouf. She has done extensive research and comparative analysis of dance forms from around the world and has consulted and choreographed for several performing companies throughout the United States, Netherlands, Singapore, and South Africa. She has a master's degree in organization management with an emphasis on change management. She is a strong advocate for arts in education and has conducted and organized various projects that introduce the arts to youth and in presentations that merges academics, music, and dance.

C. Kemal Nance, PhD, is a performer, choreographer, and scholar of African Diaspora Dance and assistant professor in the Departments of Dance and African American Studies at the University of Illinois, Urbana-Champaign. He is a master teacher of the Umfundalai technique of contemporary African dance, and in 2013 he was awarded the Katherine Dunham Award for Creative Dance Research. Dr. Nance is also artistic director of the Nance Dance Collective, a dance initiative composed of dancing men throughout the African Diaspora who produce choreographies that centralize Black maleness. Additionally, he is a member of the executive board of the Collegium for African Diaspora Dance (CADD).

Halifu Osumare, PhD, is currently professor emerita of African American and African Studies (AAS) from the University of California, Davis. She has been a dancer, choreographer, arts administrator, and scholar of black popular culture for more than thirty years. She is recognized as one of the foremost scholars of global hip-hop, publishing *The Africanist Aesthetic in Global Hip-Hop: Power Moves* in 2007 and *The Hiplife in Ghana: West African Indigenization of Hip-Hop* in 2012, after her 2008 Fulbright fellowship at the University of Ghana, Legon. She has published many articles and chapters on hip-hop, dance, and Katherine Dunham. She received the Scholar's Award for 2019 from the International Association of Black Dance (IABD).

Amaniyea Payne is the artistic director of Muntu Dance Theatre of Chicago. She studied extensively with Senegalese dance companies, including the National Dance Company of Senegal, International Afrikan-American Ballet, Ballet D'Afrique Noire De Toubacouta and Djolibah, and Les Ballet Africans from Guinea. Additionally, she studied with African American dance experts including Frankie Manning, Micki Davison, Lenwood Sloane, Pepsi Bethel, and Norma Miller, as well as international dance artists from Costa Rica, Brazil, Columbia, Cuba, and South Africa. Her choreographic credits are abundant; highlights include the production "Black Heroes and the Hall of Fame," which later toured the United States and England, and the restaging of Oscar Brown Jr.'s award-winning musical "The Great Nitty Gritty." She is included in several dance documentaries produced by the BBC and has received the prestigious Ruth Page Award twice, in 1994 for Dance Achievement and in 2001 for Lifetime Service.

William Serrano-Franklin is a musician, writer, and editor based in San Antonio, Texas. He holds bachelor's degrees in government and music from Wesleyan University and a master's degree in public administration from Georgia State University's Andrew Young School of Policy Studies. As a writer, Mr. Serrano-Franklin's perspective is rooted in his wide-ranging passions for African Diaspora history, ethnomusicology, cultural studies, and social justice.

Kariamu Welsh, PhD, is a contemporary dance choreographer and scholar whose awards include a National Endowment for the Arts Grant and a Guggenheim fellowship. Dr. Welsh serves as the director of the Institute for African Dance Research and Performance in Philadelphia. She is the author of

Zimbabwe Dance: Rhythmic Forces, Ancestral Voices: An Aesthetic Analysis (2000) and *Umfundalai: An African Dance Technique* (2003). She is the editor of *The African Aesthetic: Keeper of Traditions and African Dance; An Artistic, Historical and Philosophical Inquiry* (1994) and co-editor of *African Culture: Rhythms of Unity* (1985). She is currently professor emerita of dance, Temple University.

INDEX

Page numbers in italic indicate charts, maps, and photographs.

AADE (African American Dance Ensemble), 75, 76, 77, 78–79, 80, 83, 83nn3–4, 96, 250–51
Abakuá (Carabalí), 182, 184, *184*, 185, *187*
Abrahams, Roger, 155
Abukari', M'ba, 236, 237
academic approach, 104–5, 106, 107, 110, 116–17
ACE (Arts for Community Empowerment), 116
achebekor (*atsiagbekor*), 153, 155, 164n18, 168, 169
Acogny, Germaine, 15
activists, Black, 144, 150, 161–62 (*see also* artists/activists; social justice adaptation of tradition dance); about, 11–12, 245–46; African dance performances in Diaspora, 228, 241–45; audience/performer expectations/understandings, 229, 230, 238, 239, 240, 241, 243, 244, 246n5; authentic African culture, 236, 240, 242, 244; cultural systems and, 229, 238, 240, 246n5; Dema and, 242–43; folklore, 228, 229, 238, 240, 241, 245, 246n1; innovation and, 231, 243, 244, 245–46; nationalism/national identity, 228, 234–36, 246n2; Pan-Africanism, 228; philosophical characteristics of African dance, 234, 236; politics and, 229,

230–31, 235–36; transformations and, 229, 241, 245; West Africa and, 228, 234–35, 239, 245. *See also baamaaya*; Ghana, and dance companies
Adelayta, Ricky, 245
ADF (American Dance Festival), 78, 79, 80
adowa, 88, 153, 164n19
aesthetic, Black, 117–18, 155. *See also* African/Africanist aesthetic; African/Africanist aesthetic, and improvisation
affranchi, 2
Africa: as term of use, 85, 91–93, 112; cultural connection with, viii, 26–32, 143–44, 162–63; definition of, viii, 4–5; Diaspora's symmetry with, 6; independence of nations, 93; invention of, 24; postcolonial era, 3, 148, 153; precolonial era, 91, 92, 108, 175–76. *See also* African/Africanist aesthetic; African culture; African culture, and African Americans; African descendants; African Diaspora; African Diaspora dance; African ritual practices; African(s); Africa tropes; authentic African culture; Central Africa/Central African dance; East Africa; enslaved Africans; Southern Africa; traditional African dance; West Africa/West African dance; *and specific countries, and peoples*
Africa, Ramona, 44
African/Africanist aesthetic: about, 7, 43, 46–51, 208–11; "aesthetic of the cool,"

209, 210–11; African American culture as invisible and, 208, 210–11, 213; African Americans, 22, 24–25, 26–27, 29, 30–31; African-derived dance practice, 65, 155; African descent artists, 52–53; in African Diaspora dances, 206–7, 211–14; "Africanist" as term of use, 181, 207–8, 224n7; agency, 210; call and response, 43, 49, 52, 65, 75, 83n1, 117, 129; cultural appropriation, 210–11; cultural memory, 90–91, 94–95; entrance and exit of dancer, 43, 50, 52, 209; fluidity, 101, 210, 213; get-down quality, 43, 48; masks/masquerade, 86, 92, 94, 171–72, 218; multiple meter, 47, 50; oral technique, 39, 43, 46–48, 51–52, 210; Pan-Africanism, 33, 122n1, 149, 150, 162, 228; philosophical characteristics of African dance, 208, 209, 212, 213, 214; polycentrism, 43, 48–49, 51, 52, 210–11; polyrhythm, 210–11, 219; postmodern aesthetic, 210; repetition, 43, 47, 49–50, 51, 210; social/vernacular dance, 2, 13, 29, 184, 210, 211–12, 213; stilt walking, 91–92, 136; text-like performance, 155; transatlantic slave trade, 52; *warba*, 212, 225n25; Whites' transformation of Black cultures, 207, 211. *See also* traditional African dance

African/Africanist aesthetic, and improvisation: about, 214–15; African/Africanist aesthetic described, 208–11; "Africanist" as term of use, 207–8, 224n7; audience/performer relationship, 213, 215; cultural appropriation, 211; polyrhythm, 219; Whites' transformation of Black cultures, 207, 211. *See also* African/Africanist aesthetic; improvisation; polyrhythm

African American Dance Ensemble (AADE), 75, 76, 77, 78–79, 80, 83, 83nn3–4, 96, 250–51

African Americans (Black Americans): African/Africanist aesthetic, 22, 24–25, 26–27, 29, 30–31, 208, 210–11; Africa tropes, 108–9; Bed-Stuy and African dance, 40, 41; Black dancers/dance, viii; Black hippies, 128–29, 142n6; Black popular culture, ix, 34; choreographers, 121; Civil Rights Movement, 32, 33, 43; cultural healing of, 108, 112, 113; and culture in United States as invisible, 208, 210–11, 213; Diamano Coura members, 149; freedom narrative, 37–38, 43; Fua

Dia Congo members, 160; *funga*, 130; Hawaiian/Polynesian dance, 150; "Mama" as title of endearment/respect for, 38; Mardi Gras Indians, 124, 129, 135; Muntu, 114, 121; performance of African dance in Diaspora, *107*, 109, *109*, 112, *113*; politics, viii, 116, 117; polyrhythm, 28–29; popular culture, ix, 34; "shouting," 42–43; statistics, 41, 54n13; West African culture, 104–5, 106–7, 108, 111–12. *See also* dance/dance vocabularies, for African American male dancers; social/vernacular dance, of African Americans

African culture: connection with, viii, 26–32, 143–44, 162–63; culture transmission and, 23, 25, 27; marginalization of, 34, 69, 193; performing/teaching African dance, 170–71; West Africa, 104–5, 106–7, 108, 111–12. *See also* African heritage; authentic African culture

African culture, and African Americans: about, 7, 32–34; aesthetic characteristics, 22, 24–25, 26–27, 29, 30–31; African dance, 34; African heritage, 22, 27, 29, 30–31, 33; Africanness (*Africanité*), 29, 30–31, 33; Africa tropes, 24; Afrocentricity, 30; authentic African culture, 22, 30–31, 104–5; in California, 22, 35–36n17; choreographers, 22–23, 24, 25, 26; creole performance culture, 25–26; cultural connection, 26–32; cultural values, 31, 32, 33–34; culture transmission, 23, 25, 27; drumming, 23, 24, 28; embodiment, 21, 24, 28–29, 33; epic memory, 27–28; ethnography, 24–25, 29, 30–31; folklore, 22–23; globalization, 32, 33–34; migration of artists, 28, 33; "SAUCE!," 23–24, 34; spirit, 21–22, 23–24, 34, 34n1; traditional African dance, 22–23, 25–26; traditional African music, 22–23, 34. *See also* African Americans (Black Americans); African culture

African dance: colonial era, 85–86; definition of, 21, 38; "Father" of, 77; "no such entity as," 85. *See also* African Diaspora dance; traditional African dance; West African dance class; *and specific dances*

African descendants: choreographers/choreographies, 90; cultural memory, 93; marginalization of, 34, 189; in New Orleans, 125, 141n4; performing and teaching African dance, 169–70

African descent artists: about, 13; African aesthetic, 52–53; African American popular culture, 34; Bed-Stuy, 39, 40, 46, 48; blues music, 52–53; choreographers, 90; dance companies, 1–2; documentation of African dance, 13, 14; drumming, 3; International Decade for People of African Descent, xi, xii, *xii*, 12; jazz music, 52–53; oral technique, 46; performing/teaching African dance, 169–70; titles of endearment/respect for, 3, 16n5, 38, 66, 75, 83n2, 104, 131, 249, 260n4. *See also* West African (WA)-derived music and dance

African Diaspora: about, xi-xii, 4, 5, 16n6, 251; adaptation of tradition dance for staged performance, 228, 241–45; CADD conference, ix, 3–4, *4*; folkloric music/dance, 229, 243–44; International Decade for People of African Descent, xi, xii, *xii*, 12; movement arts, 58; performance of traditional African dance, 88, 95, 99–100, 109, *109*, *113*; transatlantic slave trade, 5. *See also* African Diaspora dance styles; American African Diaspora; religions, in African Diaspora

African Diaspora dance: about, 1, 5, 7, 15; African/Africanist aesthetic, 206–7, 211–14; African and Diaspora dancer comparison, 166–67, 168, 169; audience/performer relationship, 213, 215; documentation, 12–13, 14; future of, 178; "Gospel" of traditional African dance, 85, 91, 98–101; improvisation, 205, 211, 212, 215, 220, 221–22; Muntu, 116, 117, 119, 120; Pan-, 33; Pan-Africanism, 33; social/vernacular dance, 52–53, 207, 215. *See also* American African Diaspora; dance companies; *and specific artists*

African Diaspora dance styles: about, 10–11, 180–81; African heritage, 180, 182, 193; American African Diaspora, 181–82, 185–86, 192–93, 197; commonalities among, 185–86; continuity/mentoring for continuity, 14, 194–98; Creole identities (*transculturación*), 186, 188, 190, 192–93; distinctions between, 181–82, 188–89, 201n18; Native/African/Creole/European continuum, 186, *187*, 188, 190, 191, 192–94; rhythm, 183–84, 191. *See also* Afro-Latin America and dance; Caribbean/Afro-Caribbean dance; Cuba/Afro-Cuban dance; Haiti/Afro-Haitian

African heritage: African Americans, 22, 27, 29, 30–31, 33; African Diaspora dance styles, 180, 182, 193; the Americas, 186; the Caribbean, 180, 186, 188–89; cultural memory, 86, 88, 89–90, 91, 95, 98; Kankouran, 104, 107–8, 111; Kumbuka, 131; Mandeleo Institute, 155–56, 161; marginalization of, 193; Muntu, 116–17, 118, 119; Native/African/Creole/European continuum, 186, *187*, 188, 190, 191, 192–94; West African dance class, 63–64. *See also* African culture, and African Americans; African descent artists

African Heritage Drummers and Dancers, 97

Africanist aesthetic. *See* African/Africanist aesthetic; African/Africanist aesthetic, and improvisation

Africanity, 2, 119

African music. *See* drummers/drumming; traditional African music

Africanness (*Africanité*), 29, 30–31, 33

African Personality, 234, 235

African ritual practices: about, 1, 13; Arará ritual communities, 182, 184, 190; *dobale*, 15, 50, 58, 68–69, 70; life-cycle rituals, 172–73, 174; traditional African dance, 86, 87; traditional African dance in Diaspora, 100. *See also* spirit/Spirit

African(s): marginalization of, 34, 69, 193; as "slaves"/"captives," 175–76; as term of use, 101n4. *See also* Africa; African/Africanist aesthetic; African culture; African descendants; African Diaspora; African Diaspora dance; African ritual practices; Africa tropes; authentic African culture; enslaved Africans; traditional African dance

"Africans Are Coming!" (African Cultural Festival), 156, 161

Africa tropes: African Americans, 108–9; cultural memory, 84, 85–86, 88–89; drumming, 13, 21; Europe, xi, 7, 24, 85–86; Kumbuka, 128; national dance companies, 106; New Orleans, 127–28; North America, xi, 7, 24

Afro-Latin America and dance: about, 3, 180, 181, 189; African dance heritage, 189–90, 193; *Afrosuramericanos*, 190; Argentina, 15n2, 189; *atajos/hatajos de negritos*, 186, 191, 192; *bastonero/el escobero*, 190–91; Bolivia, 3, 189, 190; Canada, 146, 180;

candombe, 2, 15n2, 190, 191, 192, 193; Catholicism, 190, 191, 192; Central America, 3, 180, 189–90; Chile, 1, 3, 189; Christmas celebrations, 190, 191; *cofradías*, 190, 191; Congo/Angola style, 182–84, *184*, *187*, 188, 189, 191, 193; Creole identities, 190; dance styles chart, *184*; drum batteries (*llamadas*), 190; Ecuador, 3, 190; elders/cultural leaders/pioneers of African dance, 3; enslaved Africans; ethnography, 190–91; *gramillero*, 191; *La mama vieja*, 191; marginalization, 3, 189; Maroon nation/dances, 190, 192; Mexico, 3, 118–19, 180; Native/African/Creole/European continuum, *187*, 190, 191, 192–94; *Orisha* dances, 58, 59, 135, 181; Peru/Afro-Peruvians, 186, 189, 191, 192; spirit/Spirit, 183, 190–91; Suriname, 2, *184*, 190, 192; *tango*, 189; transatlantic slave trade, 191; Uruguay/Afro-Uruguay, 2, 15n2, 189, 190–91; Winti, 2, *184*; Yoruba/Anago style, 184, *184*, *187*; *zapateo*, 191. *See also* the Americas; Brazil and Afro-Brazilian dance; Central Africa/Central African dance; South America

Afrosuramericanos, 190

agbadza, 153, 164n18

agency: about, 14; Black male bodies, 252–53; improvisation, 208, 215, 219, 223; traditional African dance, 215, 216, 217, 218, 219

Ago! Ame!, 75, 83n1

Ahye, Molly, 15

Ailey, Alvin, 14, 33, 39, 51

"The Aims of Modzawe" school of dance, 96

Ain, Baderinwa (Baderinwa Roland), 131, 133, *134*, 136, 137

ajaja, 136

Akan/Asante, *184*, *187*, 190

Akon, 34

Alafia, Gaidi, 131

Alamin, Saladeen, 121

Alexander, Dee, 121

Alexander, M. Jacqui, 21

Alhassan, Manguli-Lana Adam, 230

Alternate Roots, 140

"*Amai*" as title of endearment/respect, 78, 83n2. *See also* "Mama" as title of endearment/respect

Amenkum, Ausettua, 3–4, *4*, 15, 97, 131, *134*, 137. *See also* Kumbuka African Drum and Dance Collective, New Orleans, Louisiana

American African Diaspora: about, 1, 2–3, 5; American culture, 1, 2, 211; commonalities, 185–86; dance styles, 181–82, 185–86, 192–93, 197; mentoring for continuity, 14, 197; Native/African/Creole/European continuum, *187*, 192–93; in Philadelphia, 58. *See also* African Diaspora dance; Afro-Latin America and dance; dance/dance vocabularies, for African American male dancers

American India Foundation, 121

The Americas: African dance, 6, 7, 8, 9, 186, 188; African dance heritage, 186; enslaved Africans, 35n4. *See also* North America; South America; United States

Amevuvor, Kwashi, 153

Amin, Takiyah Nur, ix

Amor Amenkum, Ausettua, 3–4, *4*, 15, 131, *134*, 137. *See also* Kumbuka African Drum and Dance Collective, New Orleans, Louisiana

"And the Children Are Watching" (Davis), 79

Angell, Ferolyn, 164n28

Angola: Congo/Angola, 182–84, *184*, *187*, 188, 189, 191, 193; in West Africa, 93, 160, 173, 182–83, *183*

"Angola" (Louisiana State Penitentiary), 138. *See also* Kumbuka African Drum and Dance Collective, New Orleans, Louisiana

anthropologists, 25–26, 39, 209, 224n7

Arará ritual communities, 182, 184, 190

Argentina, 15n2, 189

Arslanian, Sharon, 164n28

Artist as Activist Fellowship, Robert Rauschenberg Foundation, 140

artists/activists: about, 43; Bay Area African dance, 161–63; Bed-Stuy, 43–44, 47, 48–49, 50, 51, 52, 55n32; continuity/mentoring for continuity, 14, 136, 194–98; *dobale* and musicians, 68; documentation, 13–14; marginalization, 44, 70; Oakland, 158–63; traditional African music, 96. *See also* social justice

Artry-Diouf, Esailama, 149, 162

Arts for Community Empowerment (ACE), 116

ArtSpot Productions, 138, 140

Asante, Molefi Kete, 30

ase/ache/ashe/axe, 21, 34n1

Ashe, Amauunet, 131, *134*

atajos (*hatajos de negritos*), 186, 191, 192
atsiagbekor (*achebekor*), 153, 155, 164n18, 168, 169
audience/performer relationship: African Diaspora dance, 213, 215; audience/performer expectations/understandings, 229, 230, 238, 239, 240, 241, 243, 244, 246n5; cultural outsiders, 229, 238; improvisation, 213, 215, 217, 220
authentic African culture: adaptation of tradition dance, 236; African Americans, 22, 30–31, 104–5; Bay Area African dance, 144, 149–50, 160; Kumbuka, 130, 132–33; New Orleans, 125, 129
azonto, 215

baamaaya: about, 229, 230–31, 236; Anakulyada, 232, 233, 236–39, 245, 247n9, 247nn15–18; audience/performer expectations/understandings, 230, 238, 239, 240, 241, 243, 244; authentic African culture, 240, 244; *baanga*, 231, 234, 247n17; *calamboo/calamboo pebra*, 234, 236, 237, 238, 239, 247n15, 247n17; costumes, 231–32; cultural insiders, 238, 240; Dagbamba/Dagbanli, 229, 232, 234, 241, 243, 245, 247n17; dance costumes for women dancers, 231–32; Dema music-and-dance ensemble, 243–44; formal musical and dance sections, 232–33, 247nn9–10; Ghana Dance Ensemble (GDE), 236, 238, 239, 245–46; *guŋgɔŋ*, 234, 236, 244; innovation, 231, 244, 246; *kpalinkpaandibaluŋpaba*, 231; *luŋa/luŋa m'mera*, 231, 234, 236, 238–39, 244, 247n17; *luŋpag'a*, 231; modernization of performances of, 238–41; musical ensemble, 231, 234; National Dance Company of Ghana (NDCG), 238, 239–40, 241; performances in Diaspora, 229, 243–44; performances in Ghana, 229, 236–41, 247nn15–18; politics, 230–31, 236; rhythm, 231, 232–33, 233, 234, 236, 239, 240, 243, 244; Saakumu Dance Troupe, 241; *salima*, 231, 236; *sayali*, 234, 236; spontaneity, 244–45; Suglo N'mali Dang Ensemble, 236, 238–39, 245; Tamale area, 230, 232, 236–39, 247nn15–18; transformations, 241, 245; World Damba Festival 2012, 244, 245
baanga, 231, 234, 247n17
"Baba" as title of endearment/respect, 3, 16n5, 131, 249, 260n4

Bach, Johann Sebastian, 151
Baegne, Mabiba, 150
Baker, Alfred, 121
ballet/ballet companies, 105, 121, 132, 147, 148, 151, 157, 159
BAM (Brooklyn Academy of Music), 77, 80, 96
bamboula/bambula, 186
"Bamboula" conference, 199n9
Bamboula 2000 (dance company), 133
banda, 135
Bangour, Moustapha, 121
Banks, Marilyn, 81
Bantaba circle, vii–viii, x, 58, 66–67, 69, 71n21
Baptista, Mercedes, 15
Baptista, Milton, and The Olympia Brass Band, 121
Baraka, Amiri, 43
Barnes, Elendar, 148
Barth, Fredrik, 197
basket dance, 130
Bass, Michael, 148
Basse-Wiles, Marie, 15, 82, 121, 132
bastonero/el escobero, 190–91
Bates Dance Festival, 120
Baxter, Ivy, 15
Bay Area, California. *See* Oakland-San Francisco Bay Area, California
b-boying, 1
Bears, Kim, 121
Beckford, Ruth: Afro-Haitian dance classes, 144, 145; Bay Area African dance, 144, 148; *Cabin in the Sky* (musical), 146; cultural memory, 145; *dobale*, 15; Dunham legacy, 144, 146, 161–62; embodiment of African heritage, 145; as Katherine Dunham Dance Company member, 146; Pan-Africanism, 33; protégés, 145, 156; socialization of female dance students, 144; UCB, 146
Bedford Stuyvesant (Bed-Stuy), Brooklyn, New York, and African dance: about, 7–8, 38, 39–40, 52n2; aesthetic characteristics of Europe, 46, 49; African aesthetic, 39, 42, 43, 46–51, 52–53, 55n40; African Americans, 40, 41; African descent artists, 39, 40, 46, 48; artists/activists, 43–44, 47, 48–49, 50, 51, 52, 55n32; Bedford Stuyvesant Development Service Corporation, 41–42; Bedford Stuyvesant Restoration Corporation, 42, 53n4; Black Arts

Movement, 43; CORE, 43–44; *djembe*, 50, 51; freedom narrative, 37–38, 43; "March" (Ronald K. Brown), 44, *46*, 47, 48, 50, 51, 55n32; memories of, 39, 40–41, 50; neotraditional African movements, 42–43; "Raaahmona Revisited" (Welsh), 44, *44–45*, 47, 48–49, 50. *See also* Brown, Ronald K.; Welsh, Kariamu (Kariamu Welsh-Asante)

Bell, Latashia, *171*

Benin, 92, 173, *185*, 190, 218, 223n1

Berkeley, California, 146, 147, 148, 152, 153. *See also* Oakland-San Francisco Bay Area, California

Bernard, Kunute, 121

Berne, Michelle, 164n28

Berry, Stafford C., Jr., 81, 82, 249, 250–51, 253, *254–55*, 256

Bey, James Hawthorne, 15, 121

Bey, Yasiin (formerly known as Mos Def), 39

Birch, Ivy, 76

Black activists, 144, 150, 161–62. *See also* artists/activists; Oakland-San Francisco Bay Area, California; social justice

Black aesthetic, 117–18. *See also* African/ Africanist aesthetic

Black Americans. *See* African Americans (Black Americans)

Black artists. *See* artists/activists; Black male dancers; choreographers and choreographies; dancers; traditional African dance; women; *and specific dancers, and dance companies*

Black Arts Movement, viii, 7–8, 14, 33–34, 43, 61, 90, 97, 129, 143, 150

"Black," as term of use, 90

Blackburn, Darlene, 29

Black Caucus, 116

Black choreographers. *See specific choreographers, and companies*

Black Liberation Movement, 14, 30

Black male dancers: gender performativity, 7, 11, 253, 254, 256–57, 258; "March" (Ronald K. Brown), 44, *46*, 47, 48, 50, 51, 55n32; parallel position versus turn-out model, 257, 258, 259. *See also* dance/dance vocabularies, for African American male dancers; "Paths" (Davis); *and specific male dancers*

Blackman, Bakari, 137

Blackman, Chemwapuwa, 137

Black Nationalism, 43

Black Panther (film), 112

Black Panthers, 150, 161–62

Black Power Movement, viii, 7–8, 14, 43, 61, 90, 122n1, 129

Black women dances/dancers. *See* women; *and specific women artists*

Blake, Eubie, 39

Blitz the Ambassador, 34

bodies, Black male, 252–53, 256, 258, 259. *See also* embodied practice

bokolafini, 259, 261n29

Bolivia, 3, 189, 190

Borde, Percival, 15

Boston, Massachusetts, 244–45

Braddix, Daryl, 30, 32

Braimah, Weedie, 34

Branch, Billy, 121

Brazil/Afro-Brazilian dance: African American dance, 117; artists and companies, 120, 121, 158; Candomblé, 120, 183, 184; *capoeira*, 188; *congada*, 182–83; enslaved Africans, 92–93; Fogo Na Roup Bay Area dance company, 150; Jeje, 184; *maculêlê*, 188; Nago or Ketu/Nago nation and tradition, 184; *Orisha* dances, 58; *samba*, 160; *samba da roda*, 186; West African communities, 184

breakdance, 125

Brooklyn, New York. *See* Bedford Stuyvesant (Bed-Stuy), Brooklyn, New York, and African dance

Brooklyn Academy of Music (BAM), 77, 80, 96

Brown, Camille, 90

Brown, Clayola, 33

Brown, Jerry, 158, 159

Brown, Kwesi, 244

Brown, Maggie, 121

Brown, Oscar, Jr., 121

Brown, Oshun Taye, 133

Brown, Ronald K.: about, 38, 42, 53n4, 121; aesthetic characteristics, 42; African tradition dance, 42; artists/activists, 43, 44, *46*, 47, 48, 50, 51, 52; Bed-Stuy, 42, 53; Black Arts Movement, 90; "blood memory," 39; get-down quality, 48; Green, Pam Martin, 79; "March," 44, *46*, 47–48, 50, 51, 55n32; multiple meter, 50; Muntu, 121; neotraditional African movements, 42; oral technique, 46, 47, 51; Pan-Africanism, 33; polycentrism, 51; polyrhythm, 47–48, 50, 51; repetition, 50, 51

Brown, Sannyu, 133
Burgess, Jacqueline, *171*
Burkina Faso, 164n19, *185*, 205, 206, 207, 223, 223n1, 225n25
Burney, Skip, 121
Bush, George W., 109
bush/forest dance styles, 168–69, 178n1
Butler, Judith, 253
Byrd, Henry Roeland "Roy," 128

Cabin in the Sky (musical), 146
Cabuag, Arcell, *46*
CADD (Collegium for African Diaspora Dance) conference, ix, 3–4, *4*
calamboo/calamboo pebra, 234, 236, 237, 238, 239, 247n15, 247n17
calenda/kalenda/calinga/caringa, 186
California, 22, 35–36n17, 152. *See also* Oakland-San Francisco Bay Area, California
calinda, 135
"Calinda" (Destiné), 135
call and response, 43, 49, 52, 65, 75, 83n1, 117, 129
Calloway, Regina, 160
Camara, Abdoulaye "Papa," 15, 115, 119–20, 121, 132, 133
Camara, Ladji, 15, 28, 35n17, 93, 96
Cameroon, *183*, 184, 185
Canada, 1, 146, 180
candombe, 2, 15n2, 190, 191, 192, 193
Candomblé, 120, 183, 184
Caniparoli, Val, 151
capoeira, ix, 58, 188
Carabalí (Abakuá), 182, 184, *184*, 185, *187*
Carey, Teja, 131
Caribbean/Afro-Caribbean dance: about, 2, 5, 180, 181; African heritage, 180, 186, 188–89, 193; artists, 162; "Bamboula" conference, 199n9; Big Drum dances/nations, 184, 188, 192; Carriacou, 183, 188, 193; Catholicism, 189; Congo/Angola style, 182–84, *184*, *187*, 188, 189, 193; consultants and choreographers, 121; Creole identities, 186, 188; cultural memory, 145–46, 186; dance styles chart, *184*; elders/cultural leaders/pioneers of African dance, 3; Etu, 184; Grenadines, 183, 184, 192; Guadeloupe, 188; Jamaica, 121, 146, 182–83, 184, 188, 192, 193; *konpa*, 181; Mardi Gras, 189; Martinique, 146, 188; *mereng/merengue*, 181; Muntu, 121; Myal/Revival Zion/Poco dances, 182–83, 188; Native/African/

Creole/European continuum, *187*, 192–94; networking, 116; polyrhythm, 189; Protestantism, 188–89, 193, 201n18; *reggae*, 181; *salsa*, 181; "shouting," 42–43; *soca*, 181; spirit/Spirit, 183; Spiritual Baptist dances, 188; stylistic distinctions, 182, 188–89, 201n18; transatlantic slave trade, viii, 42, 53n1; Trinidad-Tobago, 29, 146, 183, 184, 188, 192; Yoruba style, 184, *184*, *187*; *yuka*, 188; *zouk*, 181. *See also* Cuba/Afro-Cuban dance; Haiti/Afro-Haitian
Carlozzo, Abby, 11, 205–6. *See also* improvisation
Carmichael, Stokley (Sekou Touré), 128
Carnival (Mardi Gras) celebrations, 124, 129, 135, 142n8, 189
Carriacou, 183, 188, 193
Carver, George Washington, 122
Casa Samba, 133
Casquelourd, Boueta, 160
Casquelourd, Lungusu, 160
Casquelourd, Malonga: about, 144, 157–58, 159; Alice Arts Center, 159; as artists/activists, 158, 159; Bay Area African dance history, 144; children of, 157, 160, 161, 162; Congolese dance teacher, 157; as dancer-drummer, master, 146–47, 160; *dobale*, 15; Fua Dia Congo, 154, 156, 160; legacy of, 160, 161, 162; Malonga Casquelourd Center for the Arts, 150, 158, 161
Castaldi, Francesca, 219
Catholicism, 182, 188, 189, 190, 191, 192
Cayou, Nontsizi Dolores Kirton, 148, 208, 212, 213, 214
CDDC (Chuck Davis Dance Company), 78, 79–80, 96
CEC (Community Education Center), 58, 61, 62, 66
Central Africa/Central African dance: about, 14; African dance heritage, 193; African Diaspora, 3, 104; Angola, 160; Cameroon, *183*, 184, 185; Caribbean West African dance, 2; Congo/Angola, 182–84, *184*, *187*, 188, 189, 191, 193; Congo/Bantu, 182, 198n1; creole performance culture, 2, 26; Cuba/Afro-Cuban dance, 184, 186; dance companies, 143, 157, 160; Democratic Republic of Congo, 160; Gabon, 151, 160; map, *183*; *simbi*, 34n2; *tambú*, 188. *See also* Angola; Congo (Congo-Brazzaville)
Central America, 3, 180, 189–90
Chakra Dance Theater, 133

charleston, 1, 211

Chernoff, John Miller, 58

chica, 186, 188

Chicago, Illinois, 41, 54n13. *See also* Muntu Dance Theatre of Chicago

Chigamba, Julia Tsitsi, 150

Chile, 1, 3, 189

ching, 175

Chinyakare, 150

Chiweshe, Stella, 162

choreographers and choreographies: about, 3, 8, 12, 13; African Americans, 22–23, 24, 25, 26, 121; African descendants, 90; contemporary African dance, 89, 121; embodied practice, 167, 169; future of African dance, 170; Kankouran, 104–5, 110; Kumbuka, 133; multidimensional/ multidisciplinary dance, 99–100; Muntu, 115–16, 118, 119–20, 121; Pan-Africanism, 33; West African-derived music and dance, 28, 29–30. *See also* performing and teaching African dance; *and specific choreographers, and dances*

Christie, Maria Elisa, 35n6

Chuck Davis Dance Company (CDDC), 78, 79–80, 96

Ciss, Idy, 121, 150

Cissoko, Katbah, 121

Cissoko, Tacko, 121

Civil Rights Movement, 32, 33, 43

Clark, Vèvè A., 145

Cohran, Phil, 121

Collegium for African Diaspora Dance (CADD) conference, ix, 3–4, *4*

Collins, Janet, 14

Colombia, 189

community: dance companies, 178; Diamano Coura and, 178; Dimensions Dance Theater, 148, 159, 162; Kankouran, 110, 111; Kumbuka, 130–31, 133, 137; Muntu, 117; West African dance class, 57–59, 62, 65–66

Community Education Center (CEC), 58, 61, 62, 66

Congo (Congo-Brazzaville): aesthetic characteristics, 160; artists, 121, 150, 157, 160; *basket dance*, 130; Fua Dia Congo, 154, 156, 160; *funk*, 160; musician/dancer relationship, 161; national Congolese Dance Company, 157; *ngoma bakongo*, 160; *zebola*, 160. *See also* Central Africa/Central African Dance

Congo/Angola, 182–84, *184*, *187*, 188, 189, 191, 193. *See also* Angola

Congress On Racial Equality (CORE), 43–44

Conjunto Folklórico Cutumba (Santiago de Cuba), 121

contemporary African dance, 1, 25–26, 89–90, 121, 133. *See also* modern dance; neotraditional African movements

Contemporary Arts Center, 134, 135

contemporary dance forms, 1. See also *specific dances*

contemporary issues, and performing and teaching African dance, 169–71

Coogler, Ryan, 112

CORE (Congress On Racial Equality), 43–44

Cornelius, Steven, 242, 244. *See also* adaptation of tradition dance; *baamaaya*

Cote d'Ivoire (Ivory Coast), 105, 149, 169, 190, 223n1

Covington, Ameen Muhammed-Sonny, 121

Crehan, Kate, 69–70

Creole: Creole identities (*transculturación*), 186, 188, 190, 192–93; creole performance culture, 25–26; Native/African/Creole/ European continuum, 186, *187*, 188, 190, 191, 192–94

Crowder, Robert, 15, 59

Cuba/Afro-Cuban dance: about, 58, 181, 182, 186; Abakuá (Carabalí), 182, 184, *184*, 185, *187*; African heritages/dances, 2, 182, 183, 198n1; Akan/Asante, *184*, *187*, 190; Arará, 182, 184, 190, 193; artists, 121, 162; Catholicism, 182; Central African dance, 184; Congo/Angola style, 182–84, *184*, *187*, 188, 189; cultural memory, 145–46; enslaved Africans, 92–93; Ewe/Fon, 184, *184*, *187*; Lukumí (Santería), 2, 184; *makuta*, 188; masks/masquerade, 185; New Orleans culture, 125; Palo/Palo Monte, 181, 183; *rumba*, 160, 186; stylistic distinctions, 182, 183–84, 185; *tumba francesa*, 2; West Africa, 184; Yoruba style, 184, *184*, *187*; *yuka*, 188

cultural memory: about, 9, 98–101; aesthetic of traditional African dance, 90–91, 94–95; "African" as term of use, 85, 101n4; African descendants, 93; African heritage, 86, 88, 89–90, 91, 95, 98; Africa tropes, 84, 85–86, 88–89; articulated memory, 89; artists, 95–98; Bay Area African dance,

145, 148–49; "Black" as term of use, 90; "blood memory," 39; the Caribbean, 145–46; Caribbean African dance, 186; colonial era in Africa, 85–86, 89, 91–93; contemporary African dance, 89–90; culture transmission, 85; *djembe*, 84, 96; embodied practice, 85, 93–94, 98; epic memory, 27–28, 61, 210; "Gospel" of traditional African dance in Diaspora, 85, 91, 100–101; identity, 85, 86, 89, 100; Kumbuka, 123, 129, 130; national dance companies of Africa, 87–88; neotraditional African movements, 86–89; performance of traditional African dance in Diaspora, 88, 95, 99–100; philosophical characteristics of African dance, 90, 98; precolonial era, 91; social justice, 90, 96, 97; songs sung in local languages in Diaspora, 88; spirit, 87, 94–95; "trace," 85, 98, 100; traditional African dance described, 84–86, 98–99
cultural nationalism. *See* nationalism/national identity (cultural nationalism)
cultural systems, 59, 218, 229, 238, 240, 246n5
cultural values: African Americans, 31, 32, 33–34; African dancers as compared with Diaspora dancers, 166; Kankouran, 104–5, 106, 107, 109, 110–11, 113; performing/teaching African dance, 167; socialization of dance students, 144
Culu and N'Kafu Traditional African Dance, 133
Curry, Mariama, 15, 131, 133, *134*, 137

Dafora, Asadata: biography of, viii, 1, 14, 15, 95–96; *Kykunkor* (Broadway show), 1, 96
damba, 153, 244, 245
dance. *See* African Diaspora dance; African Diaspora dance styles; dance companies; ethnography/ethnologization; traditional African dance
DanceAfrica, 71n21, 77, 79, 81, 82–83, 96, 121, 132, 250–51
dance companies: about, 1–2; Bay Area African dance, 146; collaborations with, 133; community, 178; funds for, 78–79, 81, 114, 121, 122, 134, 135, 150, 195–96; leadership/guidance, 81, 82, 136–37; lecture demonstrations ("lec dems"), 79, 83n5; members/personnel of, 80, 153; mentoring relationship with, 136; multiethnic model, 153; "paid per" performance, 79, 83n4;

salaries for dancers, 79, 80, 83n4. *See also* African Diaspora dance
dance/dance vocabularies, for African American male dancers: about, 12, 251, 259–60; African Diaspora described, 251; autoethnography methodology, 252; Black male bodies, 252–53, 256, 258, 259; gender performativity, 253, 254, 256–57, 258; heteronormativity, 253, *254–55*, 256; masculinity, 252, 253–54, 256–58, 259; neotraditional African movements, 254; parallel position versus turn-out model, 257, 258, 259; sexuality, 252, 253, 254; traditional African dance, 254, 256; Whites, 252, 256, 258. *See also* "Paths" (Davis)
danced gender (gender performativity), 7, 11, 75, 253, 254, 256–57, 258. *See also* Black male dancers; women; *and specific male dancers*
dance ethnography. *See* ethnography/ethnologization
dance improvisation. *See* improvisation
dance in Brooklyn, New York. *See* Bedford Stuyvesant (Bed-Stuy), Brooklyn, New York, and African dance
dancers: African and Diaspora dancer comparison, 166–67, 168, 169; Black dancers/dance, viii, 5, 39; dancer/musician relationship, 59, 64–65, 68–69, 129, 164n18, 166, 219; gender performativity, 7, 11, 75. *See also* Black male dancers; dance companies; embodied practice; traditional African dance; women; *and specific dancers, and dance companies*
Daniel, Yvonne, 3–4, *4*, 33, 86. *See also* African Diaspora dance styles
Davidson, Mickey, 121
Davis, Charles "Chuck": about, 3, 90; AADE, 75, 76, 77, 78–79, 80, 83, 83nn3–4, 96, 250–51; artists/activists, 43; "Baba" as title of endearment/respect, 3, 16n5, 249, 260n4; BAM, 77, 80; *Bantaba* circle, 71n21; Black Arts Movement, 90; CADD conference, ix, 3–4, *4*; on cultural connection with Africa, 26–27; DanceAfrica, 71n21, 77, 79, 81, 82–83, 96, 121, 250–51; as elder/cultural leader/pioneer of African dance, 3, 15; Kumbuka, 132; legacy of, 77–78, 96, 251, 258–59; on masculine behavior, 254; Muntu, 121; Pan-Africanism, 33. *See also* interview with Davis; "Paths" (Davis)

Dawkins, Diedre, 121
Dawkins, Ernest, 120
Deal, Melvin, 15, 97, 108
Dee, Ruby, 43
Deeply Rooted Dance Theater, 121
DeFrantz, Thomas F., 3, 15, 211, 213–14
Democratic Republic of Congo, 160
Desmond, Jane C., 211
Destiné, Jean-León, 15, 132, 134–35
Diabankouezi, Sandor, 160
Diakite, Abdoulaye, 156
Diamano Coura West African Dance Company: African American dance members, 149; African dance styles, 169, 178; Alice Arts Center, 159; artistic co-directors of, 97, 149, 169; ballet companies, 151; Bay Area African dance history, 151; Collages des Cultures Africaines, 97, 150, 156, 161; community, 178; "Diamano Coura" or "those who bring the message," 97, 149, 172; funds for, 150; photographs of, 106; West African dance, 149; youth company, 151. See also Jusat (Naomi Diouf)
"Diaspora" defined, 104. See also African Diaspora; American African Diaspora
Dickson, Shireen, ix
Dimensions Dance Theater, 146, 148, 150, 151, 156, 158, 159, 161, 162
Dinizulu, Alice, 96
Dinizulu, Kimati, 132
Dinizulu, Nana Yao Opare, 15, 96
Diop, Cheikh Anta, 148
Diop, Souleymane, 15, 121, 132
Diop, SuQuan, 15, 132
Diop, Vieux, 121
Diouf, Esailama G. A., 3–4, 89
Diouf, Ibrahima O., 149, 171
Diouf, Kine, 149
Diouf, Madiou, 34, 149
Diouf, Naomi (Gedo Johnson): about, 22, 97, 149; as artistic co-director of Diamano Coura, 97, 149, 169; as artists/activists, 158; authentic African culture, 149–50; Bay Area African dance community, 149; CADD conference, 3–4, 4; children of, 34, 149; dobale, 15; photographs of, 4, 171. See also Diamano Coura West African Dance Company; Jusat (Naomi Diouf); performing and teaching African dance
Diouf, Zakarya "Zak" S.: about, 22, 28, 32, 144; as artist/activist, 97, 148, 158; as artistic co-director of Diamano Coura, 97,

149, 169; Bay Area African dance, 144, 148–50; children of, 34, 149; Dimensions Dance Theater, 151; dobale, 15; as drummer-dancer, master, 146–47, 148–49; embodiment, 28; higher education, 147, 148, 152; Lambarena (ballet), 151; on modern dance training, 151; as musical producer, 34; national ballet companies, 31, 148; national dance companies, 148; Performing Arts Training Center, 147, 148; "trickster" role, 31; UCB, 147, 148, 152; Wajumbe Cultural Institution and, 151; World Black and African Festival of Arts and Culture (FESTAC), 148. See also Diamano Coura West African Dance Company
djembe: about, 35n17, 129; Bed-Stuy, 38, 50, 51, 52; cultural memory and, 84, 96; hip-hop, 34; Kumbuka and, 129, 130; master drummers, 146–47, 148–49; polyrhythm, 129
djouba/juba/yuba, 135, 186, 188
dobale (ritual to honor), 15, 50, 58, 60, 68–69, 70
Donkor Asante, 121
Donne, John, 47, 55n32
Dos Santos, Inaicyra Falco, 15
Drewal, Margaret Thompson, 216–17, 218, 219
drum batteries (llamadas), 190
drummers/drumming: African Americans, 23, 24, 28; African dancers as compared with Diaspora dancers, 166; African descent artists, 3; Africa tropes, 13, 21; Afro-Haitian dance, 144; agency, 219; embodied practice, 125; Ewe, 153; Ghana, 153; musician/dancer relationship, 59, 64–65, 68–69, 129, 161, 164n18; New Orleans, 124, 125, 128; philosophical characteristics of African dance, 130; spontaneous acts, 219; text-like performance, 155. See also djembe
Dumaeke, Thuli, 121
dunduns, 61
Dunham, Katherine: Cabin in the Sky (musical), 146; career in dance and film, 145, 148; Caribbean fieldwork, 145–46; cultural memory, 145; dobale, 15; drumming, 147; Dunham technique, 10, 28, 29, 145, 151; East St. Louis, Illinois community, 147; embodiment of African heritage, 145; Haitian dancing, 147; Katherine Dunham Dance Company, 144, 146, 147; Kumbuka, 135; legacy of, viii, 14, 51, 97, 144–46,

161–62; master musicians Africa, 147; mentoring for continuity, 197; modern dance, 147; multidimensional/multidisciplinary dance, 147; Pan-Africanism, 33; Performing Arts Training Center, 147–48; spirit of the dance, 21, 24; West African artists, 35–36n17

Durham, Mark, 120

Durham, North Carolina: African American Dance Ensemble, 75, 76, 77, 78–79, 80, 83, 83nn3–4, 96, 250–51; "Paths" (Davis) premier in, 259. *See also* interview with Davis

earth dance styles, 168–69, 178n1

East Africa: African aesthetic, 39; cultural connection with dance, 29; Ethiopia, 39, 92, 170, 173; independence history of nations, 93; precolonial era, 92; savannah dance style, 168; Zambia, 227n64; Zimbabwe, 91, 150, 162, 220

East St. Louis, Illinois, 147

Ebron, Paulla, 31

Ecuador, 3, 190

education, and mentoring for continuity, 196, 197–98

Egypt, 27, 93, 172, 173

elders/cultural leaders/pioneers of African dance, 3, 6–7, 8–9, 14, 15, 260. *See also* African Diaspora dance styles; cultural memory; interview with Davis; Kankouran West African Dance Company (KWADC or Kankouran), Washington, D.C.; Kumbuka African Drum and Dance Collective, New Orleans, Louisiana; Muntu Dance Theatre of Chicago; Oakland-San Francisco Bay Area, California; performing and teaching African dance

Elzy, Lula, 131

embodied practice: of African culture by African Americans, 21, 24, 28–29, 33; African dancers as compared with Diaspora dancers, 166, 168, 169; Bay Area African dance, 145; Black male bodies, 252–53, 256, 258, 259; body/mind, xii; choreographers/choreographies, 167, 169; cultural memory, 85, 93–94, 98; dancing in New Orleans, 127, 129; drumming, 125; Kumbuka, 137; New Orleans culture, 125, 127, 129; West African dance class, 60, 63–64, 65, 66, 69

The Emerging Philanthropists of New Orleans, 140

enslaved Africans: about, 92–93; Afro-Latin America, 191; freedom, 37–38, 43; masculinity, 258; in Mexico, 118; New Orleans, 123, 124, 125, 128; performing/teaching African dance, 176, 213; "shouting," 42–43, 49, 67; traditional African dance, 85, 88, 93; in United States, 40, 92. *See also* transatlantic slave trade

epic memory, 27–28, 61, 210

Erdman, Jean, 246n2

Erhmann, Max, 249–50

espri, 21

Ethiopia, 39, 92, 170, 173

Ethnic Dance Festival, 147, 169

ethnography/ethnologization, 24–25, 29, 30–31, 58, 190–91

Etwaroo, Indira, 39. *See also* Bedford Stuyvesant (Bed-Stuy), Brooklyn, New York, and African dance

Europe: as term of use, 6; aesthetic characteristics of, 25, 46, 49, 211; African dance performances, 229, 235; Africa tropes, 7, 24, 85–86; colonial era boundaries in Africa, 85–86, 89; documentation of African dance, 12; improvisation, 213, 214, 216, 217, 220, 221–22; Native/African/Creole/European continuum, 186, *187*, 188, 190, 191, 192–94; secular materialism versus spirit in dance, 21; transatlantic slave trade, 92

"family": Kumbuka, 130; Muntu, 115–16; titles of endearment/respect, 3, 16n5, 38, 66, 78, 83n2, 104, 131, 249, 260n4; West African dance class, 59, 66

fanga/funga, 88, 130

Farr, Gloria, 121

Faye, Mariama/Mareme, 121, 150

Faye, Oumou, 150

Fidel, Malonga, 157

finances, and dance companies, 78–79, 81, 114, 121, 122, 134, 135, 150, 195–96

folklore: about, 1; adaptation of tradition dance, 228, 229, 238, 240, 241, 245, 246n2; African Americans, 22–23; Bay Area African dance, 157, 164n28; Caribbean West African dance, 2; Kumbuka, 132, 138, 139; Mandeleo Institute, 155–56; Muntu, 115; Philadelphia Folklore Project, 61–62. See also *baamaaya*

forest/bush dance styles, 168–69, 178n1

Forte, Syvilla, 29
Foster, Susan Leigh, 29–30
Fraleigh, Sondra, 65, 229
freedom, 37–38, 43, 44, 219, 221
Free Spirit Network, 133, 136
funds, for dance companies, 78–79, 81, 114,
    121, 122, 134, 135, 150, 195–96
funga, 130
funk, 160

Gabon, 151, 160
Gagnon, John, 254
gahu, 88, 153, 164n18
Gambia, 5, 35n4, 105, 149, 154, 259
Ganyo, C. K., 132, 133
gender performativity (danced gender), 7,
    11, 75, 253, 254, 256–57, 258. *See also* Black
    male dancers; women; *and specific male
    dancers*
genealogical heritage. *See* African heritage
George-Graves, Nadine, ix
Gerstin, Julian, 188
Ghana: Accra, 164n19, *185*, 235, 239–40;
    Adinkra symbols, 259, 261n30; aesthetic
    characteristics, 29; African Personality,
    234, 235; *agbadza*, 153, 164n18; *Ago! Ame!*,
    83n1; Akan/Asante heritage, 190; artists,
    121, 144, 152; Arts Council of Ghana, 152,
    232; Ashanti, 153, 164n19; *atsiagbekor/
    achebekor*, 153, 155, 164n18, 168, 169;
    azonto, 215; Center for National Culture
    in Tamale, 230, 232; Dagara Music Center,
    Medie, 241; Dagbamba and Dagbanli,
    229, 232, 234, 238, 239, 241, 242, 243, 245,
    247n17; Dagomba, 153, 164n19; dance and
    music, 88, 153; dance/dance vocabularies
    for African American male dancers, 254,
    259; Ewe, 21, 34n2, 85, 88, 152, 153, 155,
    164n18, 184, *184*; folkloric ensembles, 238;
    gahu, 88, 153, 164n18; *hip-hop*, 201n25;
    history and independence of, 52, 92, 93,
    235; *kete*, 88; Kumbuka, 133; Medie, 241;
    Mossi, 223n1; Nananom troupe, 240;
    precolonial era, 92; Tamale area, 230,
    232, 236–39, 238, 247nn15–18; University
    of Ghana, Legon (UG-Legon), 152, 153,
    164n19, 235. *See also* adaptation of tradi-
    tion dance; *baamaaya*
Ghana, and dance companies: about,
    35n4, 129, 228; Abibigromma, 242; Ac-
    cra, 235, 239–40; amateur troupes, 242;
    Anakulyada, 232, 233, 236–39, 245, 247n9,
    247nn15–18; Ghana Dance Ensemble

(GDE), 235–36, 238, 239, 242, 245–46;
    National Dance Company of Ghana
    (NDCG), 235–36, 238, 239–40, 241,
    242, 245–46; Saakumu Dance Troupe,
    241; Suglo N'mali Dang Ensemble, 236,
    238–39, 245; Tamale, 238–41, 245. *See also
    baamaaya*; Ghana
Gibson, Michelle, 133
Gilroy, Paul, 145
Gittens, Fatou, 15
Giurchescu, Anca, 240–41
globalization, 32, 33–34, 115, 207
Goff, Greer, 131
Goldman, Danielle, 214, 221
Gonzales, Richard, 132
"Gospel" of traditional African dance, in
    Diaspora, 85, 91, 100–101
Gottschild, Brenda Dixon, 15, 33, 42, 207–8,
    209, 210, 224n7
gramillero, 191
Gray, Luther, 131, 133
Green, Doris, 15
Green, Pam Martin, 79
Grenadines, 183, 184, 192
Guadeloupe, 188
Guerra, Ramiro, 15
Gueye, Medoune Dame, *113*
"Guias" (choreographed dance), 120
Guinea: artists, 121, 150; Ballet Africaine de
    Diebel Guee, 105; Les Ballets Africains
    of Guinea national dance company of,
    22, 87–88, 96, 129; dance styles, 169;
    Diamano Coura, 149; *kassa*, 68; *koukou*,
    177; Mali Dance Ensemble company, 148;
    Malinke/Maninka, 68, 71n21, 85, 149, 168,
    175; *mandiani/mendiani/majani*, 87–88,
    130, 133, 149, 175; migration and, 5
Gullah Sea Islands, the Carolinas, 93, 194
gungɔŋ, 234, 236, 244

Haiti/Afro-Haitian: *affranchi*, 2; African
    dance/African heritages, 2, 184; *banda*,
    135; *calinda*, 135; *congo*, 2, 182, 183; cultural
    memory, 145–46; dance/drumming, 144,
    145, 147; *djouba/juba/yuba*, 135, 188; *kon-
    pa*, 181; *mayí/mayi*, 2, 135; *Nago*, 135; Nago
    or Ketu/Nago nation and tradition, 184;
    Native/African/Creole/European contin-
    uum, *187*; New Orleans culture, 125; Rada,
    184; rhythm, 145; Vodou, 2, 183, 184, 188;
    yenvalú/yenvalou/yanvalou, 2, 135, 145
Hall, Arthur, 121
Hamera, Judith, 62

Hamilton (musical), 195
"Hard Times Blues" (choreographed dance), 119–20
Haridon, Asiel, 121
Harlem and Harlem Renaissance, 33, 38, 40
Harper, Peggy, 223n2
Harrison, Safiya, 128, 129, 130, 131
hatajos de negritos (*atajos*), 186, 191, 192
Hayes, Charles, and The Spiritual Warriors, 121
Hazzard-Donald, Katrina (Katrina Hazzard-Gordon), 208, 213
Heard, Marcia, 15, 95
Herskovits, Melville J., 224n7
Herzfeld, Michael, 99
heteronormativity, 253, *254–55*, 256
Higgins, LaDonna, *171*
hip-hop: African Diaspora dance, 52–53, 207, 215; dance in African Diaspora, 58; *djembe*, 34; forms of, 1, 125; Ghanaian dance, 201n25; *Hamilton* (musical), 195; improvisation, 220, 221, 222; *sabar*, 34
Hispanic Caucus, 116
Holder, Geoffrey, 29, 43
Holland, Antoinette, *171*
Holloway, Joseph E., 224n7
Horne, Lena, 39
Horton, Laurel, 62
Huff, Light Henry, 120
Hurston, Zora Neale, 33, 51

Iddrisu, Habib, 230, 240, 241, 242–43, 244, 245. *See also* adaptation of tradition dance; *baamaaya*
identity, and cultural memory, 85, 86, 89, 100
Ifel, Elise, 15
Ile Aiye Ballet Folclorico Do Brasil, 121
Illinois, 41, 54n13, 147. *See also* Muntu Dance Theatre of Chicago
Imoro, Sulley, 241, 244, 245
improvisation: about, 11, 206–8, 222–23, 223n2, 224n7, 224n11; African Diaspora dance, 205, 211, 212, 215, 220, 221–22; agency, 208, 215, 219, 223; audience/performer relationship, 217, 220; cultural biases, 206, 207, 211; cultural knowledge, 218; culture transmission, 211; Europe, 213, 214, 216, 217, 220, 221–22; freedom, 219, 221; improvisation as term of use, 214; innovation of dance/music techniques, 208, 219, 220–21; jazz music, 220–21, 222; live television pro-

duction, 205, 220; modern dance, 218; neotraditional African movements, 11, 206, 223n2; Nikiema, 205, 207, 211, 212, 215, 220; North America, 213, 214, 220, 221–22; philosophical characteristics of African dance, 213, 214, 222; postmodern aesthetic, 206, 207, 210, 218, 219; research and methodology, 205–7; social/vernacular dance of African Americans, 207, 208, 212, 215, 220, 221–22; spontaneity, 214, 215, 223; spontaneous acts and, 214–15, 218, 220. *See also* African/Africanist aesthetic, and improvisation
India, 92, 246n2
innovation: adaptation of tradition dance, 231, 243, 244, 245–46; of dance/music techniques, 208, 214, 219, 220–21, 222; marginalization, 221; neotraditional African movements, 206
International Decade for People of African Descent in 2015–2024, xi, xii, *xii*, 12, 101
interview with Davis: about, 8–9, 75–78; AADE, 75, 76, 77, 78–79, 80, 83, 83nn3–4; African dance history, 82; African Diaspora, 77; "And the Children Are Watching" (Davis), 79; BAM, 77, 80; CDDC, 78, 79–80; characteristics and personality described, 77, 80, 82–83; DanceAfrica, 77, 79, 81, 82–83; funds for dance companies, 78–79, 81; gender performativity, 75; leadership/guidance, 81, 82; lecture demonstrations ("lec dems"), 79, 83n5; legacy, 77–78, 81; members/personnel issues, 80; "paid per" performance, 79, 83n4; period for growth, 83; *Porgy and Bess* (Gershwin), 81; salaries for dancers, 79, 80, 83n4; *Umfundalai* technique, 82; Welsh and, 75, 82–83. *See also* Davis, Charles "Chuck"
Ipi Tomb (musical), 156
Ishangi, Kwame, 15, 132, 133
Israel, Michal, 133
Israel, Zohar, 15, 128, 131, 133, *134*, 137
"I've Known Rivers" (choreographed dance), 119–20
Ivey, Cachet, 59, 60, 61, 62, 63
Ivory Coast (Cote d'Ivoire), 105, 149, 169, 190, 223n1

Jackson, Jonathan David, 221, 222
Jackson, Ronald L., 252
Jamaica, 121, 146, 182–83, 184, 188, 192, 193
Jamison, Judith, 14
Jamison, Theodore, 121

Javanese gamelan, 246n5
Jay-Z, 39
jazz dance, 207, 212, 215, 220, 221, 222
jazz music, 28–29, 52–53, 96, 220–21, 222
Jidenna, 34
Johnson, Bernice, 96
Johnson, Charmaine, *134*
Johnson, Efuru, 131, 133
Johnson, E. Patrick, 30
Johnson, Janeen, 160
Johnson, Jasmine, ix
Johnson, Kito, 137
Johnson, Linda Faye, 15
Johnson, Momudu, 95
Johnson, Rashidi, 137
Johnson, Sherille, 121
Johnson, Suzette, 148
jola, 259
Jones, Bill T., 14
jook, 213
Jordan-Smith, Paul, 62
Jubilate Children's Choir, 121
Jusat (Naomi Diouf): African culture, 170–
    71; African descent population, 169–70;
    "The Birth," 170, 173; *ching*, 175; chore-
    ographers/choreographies, 170; "Civil-
    ization," 172, 173; contemporary issues,
    169–71; "The Division," 175–76; "Division
    and Grief," 176; enslaved Africans, 176;
    Ethiopia archeological remains, 170; Eth-
    nic Dance Festival, 169; Gio people, 177;
    "The Harvest," 170, 175; "The Initiation,"
    170, 174–75; "Jusat" as title, 178n2; *kora*,
    177; *koukou*, 177; Liberian civil war, 170,
    176; life-cycle rituals, 172–73; masks/mas-
    querade, 171; multidimensional/multidis-
    ciplinary dance, 170; *nyaka*, 175; photo-
    graph, *171*; pop music, 169–70; Prologue,
    172; *sabar*, 177; "slaves"/"captives," 175–76;
    spiritual and natural worlds, 170; "Unity
    and Final Strength," 177; Vai people, 177;
    youth, 170, 172, 175, 177

Kahey, Sherral, 140
Kai, Val, 153
kakilambe, 133
Kalapriya Foundation, 121
Kamau, 128
Kane, Alassane, 156
Kankouran West African Dance Company
    (KWADC or Kankouran), Washington,
    D.C.: about, 9, 97, 108, 113; academic, cul-
tural and spiritual approach, 104–5, 106,
107, 110; African Americans and, 104–5,
106–7, 108, 111–12; African heritage, 104,
107–8, 111; authentic African culture, 104–
5; choreographers/choreographies, 104–5,
110; co-founders of, 97, 104, 108, *113*; community, 110, 111; cultural values, 104–5,
106, 107, 109, 110–11, 113; culture transmission, 109; "Diaspora" defined, 104; members of, 110; performances in Africa, 112;
performances in Diaspora, *107*, 109, *109*,
112, *113*; photographs of, *105*, *107*, *109*, *111*,
113; spirit guide or "Kankouran," 109–10;
Unity Conferences, 110–11, 132; "A Visit to
Africa" (Konte), 108; youth dance/music
classes, 107, *107*, *111*, 112. *See also* Konte,
Assane
Karenga, Maulana (Ron), 30, 122n1
kassa, 68
Keita, Sundiata, 132
Kennedy, Robert F., 41–42
kete, 88
Ketu/Nago or Nago nation and tradition,
    184
King, Martin Luther, Jr., 44, 47–48, 51–52
King, Mestre, 15
King, Obba, 121
Kisselgoff, Anna, 49, 154, 155
kitchenspace defined, 23, 34, 35n6
klakan, 168, 169
Knight, Kai, 133
Knox, Fay, 160
konpa, 181
Konte, Assane (Baba Assane): about, 9,
    97, *105*, 106, 107; academic, cultural and
    spiritual approach, 104–5, 106, 107, 110;
    African Americans and West African cul-
    ture, 104–5, 106–7, 108, 111–12; on African
    dance, 104; Africa tropes, 108–9; as artist,
    121, 150; authentic African culture, 104–5;
    CADD conference, 3–4, *4*; as co-founder
    of Kankouran, 97, 104, 108; commu-
    nity, 110, 111; cultural healing of African
    Americans, 108, 112, 113; dance critics, 110;
    as dancer, 105, *106*, *113*; *dobale*, 15; future
    of African dance, 113; Kounta, 97, 108,
    111; legacy of, 107; multivalent practices,
    106–7; pedagogy, 104, 110–11, 112; perfor-
    mance of African dance in Diaspora, *106*,
    107, 109, *109*, 112, *113*; as spirit guide or
    "Kankouran," 110; technological products,
    112; on technology products and youth,

112; "A Visit to Africa," 108; youth dance/music classes, 107, *107*, *111*, 112. *See also* Kankouran West African Dance Company (KWADC or Kankouran), Washington, D.C.

kora, 34, 177, 249, 260n1

"Kosonde" ["Balante"] (NDiaye), *118*

koukou, 177

Koumbassa, Youssouf, 15, 121, 150

Kounta, Abdou, 97, 108, 111

Kouyate, Amadou, 34

Kouyate, Djimo, 15, 34, 121

Kouyate, Mori Keba, 121

kpalinkpaandiba-luŋpaba, 231

kpanlogo, 153, 164n19, 241

krahn, 169

Kringelback, Hélène Neveu, 84

krumping, 125

Kulu Mele African Dance and Drum Ensemble, 59

Kumbuka African Drum and Dance Collective, New Orleans, Louisiana: about, 10, 123, 131, 141; African dances and styles, 132; African heritage, 131; Africa tropes, 128; authentic African culture, 130, 131, 132–33; *calinda*, 135; "Calinda" (Destiné), 135; choreographers/choreographies, 133; collaborations with dance companies, 133; community, 130–31, 133, 137; conferences for African dance, 130, 132; Congo Square, 130, 131, 134, 135; contemporary African dance, 133; cultural memory, 123, 129, 130; *djembe*, 129, 130; embodied practice, 137; "family," 130; folklore, 132, 138, 139; founding members of, 130, 131, *134*; funds for, 134, 135; Haitian dances, 135; leadership/guidance, 136–37; Louisiana Correctional Facility for Women (LCIW) prison project, 137–40, 141; Louisiana State Penitentiary ("Angola"), 138; Mardi Gras Indians, 135; members of, 130, 131, 133; mentoring relationships, 136; mission of, 136; New Orleans culture, 130, 131; philosophical characteristics of African drumming/dancing, 130; "to remember" or "Kumbuka," 123, 130; Skull and Bone Gangs, 135, 142n8; spirit/Spirit, 130–31, 137; stilt walking, 136; teachers, 130, 132; traditional African dance, 130, 131, 133, 138, 142n7; West Africa, 133; youth classes, 131. *See also* New Orleans, Louisiana

kutiro, 148–49

Kwabene, John Darkay, 121

Kwanzaa, 83n1, 117–18, 122n1, 259

Kykunkor (Broadway show), 1, 96

Ladji Camara African Drum and Dance Company, 96

Ladzekpo, Betty, 153

Ladzekpo, C. K.: about, 144, 152; African Music and Dance Ensemble, 150, 152, 153, 154, 155, 156; "Africans Are Coming!" (African Cultural Festival), 156, 161; Bay Area African dance and music, 144, 152; cultural values, 154; *dobale*, 15; as drummer-dancer, master, 146–47, 153–54, 155; Ewe, 152, 153, 164n18; Ghanaian music and dance, 152; legacy of, 162; Mandeleo Institute, 155–56, 161; members/personnel of company, 153; multiethnic model, 153; on organization, 194; pedagogy, 152–53; UCB faculty, 152, 153; University of Ghana Legon (UG-Legon), 153

Ladzekpo, Kobla, 152, 155

Ladzekpo, Kwaku, 154, 155–56, 161

lamban, 132, 133

Lambarena (ballet), 151

Larkins, Erica "Famata," 133

Latimore, Jonita, 121

Latin America. *See* Afro-Latin America and dance; South America

LCIW (Louisiana Correctional Facility for Women), St. Gabriel, Louisiana, Drama Club and Graduates of, 137–40, 141

leadership/guidance, 81, 82, 136–37, 195

Liberia: artists, 22, 28, 32, 144, 149; civil war, 170, 176; consultants and choreographers, 121; dance and music, 35n4, 88, 97, 168, 169, 177; Diamano Coura, 149; *fanga/funga*, 88, 130; Gio, 149, 177; *klakan*, 168, 169; *krahn*, 169; Kru, 149, 169; national dance company of, 22, 35n4, 149; Vai, 88, 149, 177

life-cycle of artists, 197

life-cycle rituals, 172–73

lindjien/lenjengo/lindjiang/lindjien, 149

The Lion King (musical), 77, 178

Livingston, Tamara, 245

llamadas (drum batteries), 190

local histories: about, 7–8; Chicago, Illinois, 41, 54n13; Washington, D.C., 14, 82–83, 97, 109, *109*, 110–11, 132, 259. *See also* African culture, and African Americans; Bedford Stuyvesant (Bed-Stuy), Brooklyn, New

York, and African dance; Durham, North Carolina; New Orleans, Louisiana; Oakland, California

Lorenzo, Jose, 156

Louisiana Correctional Facility for Women (LCIW) prison project, 137–40, 141. *See also* Kumbuka African Drum and Dance Collective, New Orleans, Louisiana; New Orleans, Louisiana

Louisiana Divisions of the Arts, 140

Louisiana State Penitentiary ("Angola"), 138

Love, Nia, 201n25

Lucus, Buddy, 121

luŋa/luŋa m'mera, 231, 234, 236, 238–39, 244, 247n17

luŋpag'a, 231

maculêlê, 188

makuta, 188

Malcolm X, 51–52

male dancers. *See* Black male dancers; dance/dance vocabularies, for African American male dancers; *and specific male dancers*

Mali: artists, 150; Bamana people, 87–88; *bokolafini*, 259, 261n29; dance styles, 169; Diamano Coura, 149; *djembe*, 129; "internal diaspora," 5; Kumbuka, 133; *lamban*, 132, 133; Malinke/Maninka, 149; *mandiani/mendiani/majani*, 87–88, 130, 133, 149, 175; *mendiane*, 249, 260n2; migration and, 5; Mossi, 223n1; national ballet companies, 105, 148; national dance company of, 22, 35n4, 87–88, 129; pop music, 169–70; precolonial era, 92; *Wolofsodung/Wolosodon*, 88

Malone, Jacqui, 208, 213

Malonga, Kiazi, 160, 161, 162

Malongo, Muisi-Kongo, 157, 160, 162

"Mama" as title of endearment/respect, 38, 66, 131. *See also* "*Amai*" as title of endearment/respect

La mama vieja, 191

mambo, 2

mandiani/mendiani/majani, 87–88, 130, 133, 149, 175

"Manifest" (Walker), 119

Manning, Frankie, 121

"March" (Ronald K. Brown), 44, 46, 47–48, 50, 51, 55n32

Mardi Gras (Carnival) celebrations, 124, 129, 135, 142n8, 189

marginalization: activists against, 44, 70; of African descendants, 34, 189; of Africans/African culture, 34, 69, 193; in Afro-Latin America, 3; innovation of dance/music techniques, 221; mentoring for continuity, 180, 197

Martinique, 146, 188

Maryland, 104, 108

masks/masquerade: African aesthetic, 86, 92, 94, 171–72, 218; audience/performer relationship, 217; Cuba/Afro-Cuban dance, 185; Kumbuka, 136; Mardi Gras Indians, 124, 135; performing/teaching African dance, 171

Mason, Judah, 137

Mason, Solomon, 137

Massachusetts, and African Dance and Music at Jacob's Pillow, 154–55

Matthews, Edsel, 158

Mauritania, 92, 175, *185*

mayí/mayi, 2, 135

mbira, 162, 220, 227n64

Mboup, Serigne Babacar, 132

McAlpine, Efuru, 131, 133, *134*, 137

McAlpine, Shangobumi, 137

McBurnie, Beryle, 15

McIntyre, Dianne, 51, 90

McKayle, Donald, 51

McKee, Stephanie "Qena Tchass," 133

McNaughton, Patrick, 217

memories of Bed-Stuy, and African dance, 39, 40–41, 50. *See also* cultural memory

mendiane, 249, 260n2

mentoring, and continuity, 14, 136, 180, 194–98

mereng/merengue, 2, 181

Mexico, 3, 118–19, 180

Middle Passage. *See* transatlantic slave trade (Middle Passage)

Miller, Bebe, 14, 77

Miller, Joan, 96

Miller, Norma, 121

Mills, Stephanie, 39

Milon, Mosheh, Sr., 15, 156

Mitchell, Arthur, 14

Mobonda, Honoré, 186

modern dance: African dance, 132, 151; African Diaspora, 58; Bay Area African

dance, 158, 164–65n28; dancers and schools for, 131, 147, 205–6; improvisation, 218. *See also* contemporary African dance
Monroe, Raquel, ix
Moody, Frances Pace, 121
Moore, Arthur, 24, 28–29
Moore, Charles, 15
Moore, Ella, 15
Morrison, Toni, 224n7
Mos Def (now know as Yasiin Bey), 39
Mouton, Kufaru, 131
MOVE event, 44
Mozambique, 227n64
Mudimbe, V. Y., 24–25
Muhammad, Jamilah, 133, *134*
multidimensional/multidisciplinary dance, 99–100, 170, 195
Muntu Dance Theatre of Chicago: about, 9–10, 97, 114, 121–22; academic approach, 116–17; ACE, 116; African Americans, 114, 121; African Diaspora dance/music, 116, 117, 119, 120; African heritage, 116–17, 118, 119; Africanity, 119; Africans/African dance and music, 116; artistic directors of, 97, 114–15, 121; artists' relationships with, 120–21; Black aesthetic, 117–18; Caribbean dance, 116; choreographers/choreographies, 115–16, 118, 119–20, 121; community collaboration, 117; cultural diversity, 117–18; "family," 115–16; folklore, 115; funds for, 114, 121, 122; "Guias" (choreographed dance), 120; "Hard Times Blues" (choreographed dance), 119–20; "I've Known Rivers" (choreographed dance), 119–20; "Kosonde" ["Balante"] (NDiaye), 118; Kwanzaa, 117–18, 122n1; "Manifest" (Walker), *119*; multicultural communities, 116, 117, 118–19; Muntu (The Essence of Humanity), 114; musicians, 114, *118*; "No More Trouble" (Stacy Letrice Smith), *120*; Payne, P. Amaniyea, 97, 115, 118–19; photographs of, *115*, *118*; politics, 116, 117; UHCC, 114; "Yanga" (Payne), *118*; youth, 115, 116–17
music/musicians: blues music, 28–29, 38, 52–53, 128; gospel music, 52–53; jazz music, 28–29, 52–53, 96, 220–21, 222; *kora*, 34, 177, 249, 260n1; *mbira*, 162, 220, 227n64; Muntu, 114, *118*; musician/dancer relationship, 59, 64–65, 68–69, 129, 161;

166; pop music, 169–70; songs sung in local languages in Diaspora, 88. *See also* traditional African music; West African (WA)-derived music and dance
Mussa, Mansa K., 95

Nago, 135
Nago or Ketu/Nago nation and tradition, 184
Naima (Gwen) Lewis Dance Experience, 146
Nakid, Giselle, 133
Namsa, Rehema, 132
Nance, C. Kemal, ix, 75, *254–55*. *See also* dance/dance vocabularies, for African American male dancers; interview with Davis; "Paths" (Davis)
Napla, Nimely, 121, 149
nationalism/national identity (cultural nationalism): adaptation of tradition dance for staged performance, 228, 234–36, 246n2; African Personality, 234, 235; national dance companies, 3, 22, 31, 35n4, 87–88, 106, 129, 131, 148, 153; national dances, 2–3, 15n2; Negritude and, 33, 234–35
Native Americans: Mardi Gras Indians, 124, 129, 135; Native/African/Creole/European continuum, 186, *187*, 188, 190, 191, 192–94; Native Caucus, 116; New Orleans, 123, 124, 129, 135
n'dep/ndepp/ndëp, 169, 178n1
NDiaye, Babacar, *118*, 121
N'Dong, Mame Diara, 121
N'dounda, Regine, 160
Neely, Zakiya, 130, 131
Negritude, 33, 234–35
Nelson, Mathew, 48
neotraditional African movements: about, 5, 42, 54n19, 87, 223n2; aesthetic characteristics of, 88–89; cultural memory and, 86–89; dance/dance vocabularies for African American male dancers, 254; innovation, 206; rhythm, 206; "shouting," 42–43, 49, 67; traditional African dance as compared with, 54n19, 87, 88. *See also* contemporary African dance
Nettleford, Rex, 15
Neville, Namdi, 137
New Orleans, Louisiana: about, 123; Afri-

can American Black Indians, 124, 129, 135; African culture, 125, 129; African descendants, 125, 141n4; Africa tropes, 127–28; Black hippies, 128–29, 142n6; call and response, 129; Congo Square, 124, 125, 128, 130, 131, 134, 135; contemporary companies, 133; culture and heritage of, 123, 124, 127, 128, 129; dance/music, 124, 125–27, 129, 141; drumming, 124, 125, 128; embodied practice, 125, 127, 129; enslaved Africans, 123, 124, 125, 128; Mardi Gras celebrations, 124, 129, 135, 142n8; musician/dancer relationship, 129; music/musicians, 121, 128–30; national dance companies Africa, 131; Native Americans, 123; politics, 128; polyrhythm, 129; *second line*, 124, 125–27, 129; "second liners," 124, 126; spirit/Spirit, 124, 125, 129; Tremé Community Center dance classes, 128, 129, 131, 135; "Won't Blow Down" project, 140; World's Fair in 1984, 131. *See also* Kumbuka African Drum and Dance Collective, New Orleans, Louisiana

New York, New York: "The Aims of Modzawe" dance school, 96; ballet companies, 151; Brooklyn, 38, 40, 43–44; CDDC, 78, 79–80. *See also* Bedford Stuyvesant (Bed-Stuy), Brooklyn, New York, and African dance

ngoma bakongo, 160

Nicholls, Robert W., 25–26

Nigeria: about, 185, *185*; Africanness, 30; artists, 95, 96, 121; "Betelehemu" carol, 121; dance/dance vocabularies for African American male dancers, 254, 259; Kumbuka, 133; masks/masquerade, 185; national dance company, 35n4; *patakato*, 88; World Black and African Festival of Arts and Culture (FESTAC), 148; *yemoja*, 169, 178n1; Yoruba style, 218

Nikiema, Awa, 205, 207, 211, 212, 215, 220

Nimely Pan-African Dance Company, 149

Nketia, J. H. Kwabena, 235, 241

Nkrumah, Kwame, 52, 220, 235, 241

"No More Trouble" (Stacy Letrice Smith), *120*

Nora, Pierre, 145

North Africa, 92

North America: as term of use, 6; aesthetic characteristics, 25, 211; Africanity, 119; Africa tropes, 7, 24; Canada, 1, 146, 180; documentation of African dance, 12, 13;

improvisation, 213, 214, 220, 221–22; secular materialism versus spirit in dance, 21; transatlantic slave trade, 53n1, 101n4. *See also* Afro-Latin America and dance; the Americas; United States

Notorious B.I.G., 39

Nuamah, Auntie Grace, 153

nyaka, 175

Oakland, California: and activists, Black, 150, 161–62; African and African Diaspora dance, 156; Alice Arts Center, 157, 158–59, 162; Alliance for California Traditional Arts, 150; artists/activists, 14, 158–63; AXIS Dance Company, 158, 159; Batucaje Dance Company, 156; Black cultural legacy, 157; Ceedo Senegalese Dance Company, 156; CitiCentre Dance Theater (CDT), 158, 160; Dance a Vision Entertainment, 158; Dimensions Dance Theater, 146, 148, 150, 151, 156, 158, 159, 161, 162; Everybody's Creative Arts Center (ECAC), 157, 158, 164n28; Every Body's Dance Studio, 157, 164n28; "From Africa to America," 162; Koncepts Cultural Gallery, 158; Malonga Casquelourd Center for the Arts, 150, 158, 161; Oakland Ballet, 159; Oakland School of Arts, 158, 159, 162; population statistics, 147; "Project Panther," 161–62; Zulu Dance Theatre of South Africa, 156. *See also* Oakland-San Francisco Bay Area, California

Oakland-San Francisco Bay Area, California: about, 10, 143–44, 147, 161–63; and activists, Black, 144, 150, 161–62; African and African Diaspora community, 156, 157–58; African Dance and Music at Jacob's Pillow, 154–55; African Music and Dance Ensemble, 150, 152, 153, 154, 156; "Africans Are Coming!" (African Cultural Festival) event, 156, 161; Afro-Haitian dance classes, 144, 145; Alice Arts Center, 157, 158–59, 162; artists/activists, 161–63; authentic African culture, 144, 149–50, 160; ballet training, 151; Bantaba Dance Ensemble, 156; Berkeley, 146, 147, 148, 152, 153; Black cultural history, 150, 156, 160–61; Collages des Cultures Africaines, 97, 150, 156, 161; cultural connection with Africa/African dance, 143–44, 162–63; cultural history, 151, 156; cultural memory, 145, 148–49; cultural values,

154; and dance, traditional African, 144, 148–49, 152, 153, 154, 155; dance companies, 146; and dancers-drummers, master, 146–47, 148–49, 156, 160; Dimensions Dance Theater, 146, 148, 150, 151, 156, 158, 159, 161, 162; *djembe*, 148–49; Dunham legacy, 144–46, 161–62; embodiment of African heritage, 145; Ethnic Dance Festival, 147, 169; Fogo Na Roupa, 150; folklore, 157, 164n28; Ghanaian music and dance, 152, 153–54; Malonga Casquelourd Center for the Arts, 150, 158, 161; modern dance, 151, 158, 164–65n28; and music, traditional African, 148, 151, 152–53; Pan-Africanism, 150, 162; rhythm, 154, 162; Wajumbe Dance Ensemble, 148; World Black and African Festival of Arts and Culture (FESTAC), 148. *See also* Oakland, California; San Francisco, California; *and specific artists/activists, and dance companies*

Obba King of South Africa, 121

ocean/water dance styles, 168–69, 178n1

odunde, 88

Ohio, 242, 244, 259

Okok, Efrom, 95

Olatunji, Babatunde (Michael), 15, 77, 96, 121, 132, 133, 136

Olivera Chirimini, Tomás, 190

Opah Resurrection Dance Ensemble, 121

Opare, Kwame, 121

Open Society Foundation, 140

Opoku, Mawere, 235, 241, 245–46

oral technique, 5, 39, 43, 46–48, 51–52, 86, 210

Orisha dances, 58, 59, 135, 181

Owens, Gary Jamil, 131

Page, Jeffrey, 121

Pan-Africanism, 33, 122n1, 149, 150, 162, 228

"Papa" (as title of endearment), 104

Paris, Carl, ix

Passawe, Kai Pau, 121

Pat, Sis Denise, 134, 158, 159, 160

patakato, 88

PATC (Performing Arts Training Center), 147–48

"Paths" (Davis): Berry, 249, 250–51, 253, 254–55, 256; Black male bodies, 252–53, 256, 258, 259; costumes, 259, 261nn29–30; gender performativity, 253, 254, 256–57; heteronormativity, 253, 254–55, 256; *jola*, 259; *kora*, 249, 260n1; *kplanlogo*, 259; masculinity, 253–54, 256–57; *mendiane*, 249, 260n2; narration, 249–50; parallel position versus turn-out model, 257, 258, 259; photograph, 254–55; premier and performance locations for, 259; rehearsals for, 249–50, 252, 254, 256, 260nn1–3; *sabar*, 249, 259, 260n3; sexuality, 253, 254; traditional African dance, 254, 256. *See also* dance/dance vocabularies, for African American male dancers

Payne, Duke, 120

Payne, P. Amaniyea, 15, 97, 115, 118–19. *See also* Muntu Dance Theatre of Chicago

Pellow, Deborah, 239

Percussion Inc., 133

performance practices: African Diaspora dance, 88, 95, 99–100, 107, 109, 109, 112, 113; cultural systems, 229, 238, 240, 246n5. *See also* audience/performer relationship

performing and teaching African dance: about, 10, 177–78; African and Diaspora dancer comparison, 166–67, 168, 169; African culture, 170–71; African descendants, 169–70; *ching*, 175; community, 178; contemporary issues, 169–71; cultural values, 167; embodied practice, 168–69; enslaved Africans, 176, 213; Ethiopia archeological remains, 170; Ethnic Dance Festival, 169; forest/bush, earth, savannah, and ocean/water styles, 168–69, 178n1; future, 167, 170, 178; Gio people, 177; *kora*, 177; *koukou*, 177; Liberian civil war, 170, 176; life-cycle rituals, 172–73; masks/masquerade, 171; multidimensional/multidisciplinary dance, 170; musician/dancer relationship, 166; *nyaka*, 175; philosophical characteristics of African dance, 167; photograph, 171; pop music, 169–70; *sabar*, 177; "slaves"/"captives," 175–76; spiritual and natural worlds, 170; STEM-based curricula, 178; Vai people, 177; youth, 170, 172, 175, 177. *See also* Diamano Coura West African Dance Company; *Jusat* (Naomi Diouf); performance practices

Performing Arts Training Center (PATC), 147–48

Perpener, John O., III, ix, 15

perpetual motion in aesthetic of Africa, 7, 11–12. *See* adaptation of tradition dance; *baamaaya*; dance/dance vocabularies, for

African American male dancers; improvisation
Peru/Afro-Peru, 186, 189, 191, 192
Peters-Muhammad, Jamillah, 131
Philadelphia, Pennsylvania, 14, 44, 58, 59,
61–62, 66, 88, 88. *See also* West African
dance class
philosophical characteristics of African
dance: adaptation of tradition dance,
234, 236; African/Africanist aesthetic,
208, 209, 212, 214; African Americans
and West African culture, 111–12; cultural
memory, 90, 98; drumming versus dancing, 130; improvisation, 213, 214, 222;
performing/teaching African dance, 167;
polycentrism, 48; social justice, 7
Pickens, Willie, and The Willy Pickens
Quintet, 121
Pierce, Wendell, 37
Pierre, Bomani, 137
Pierre, Curtis, 131, 133, 137
politics: African Americans, viii, 116, 117;
African dance, 7; Bay Area African
dance, 144, 150; Black activists, 144, 150,
161–62; Black dancers/dance, viii; Black
Liberation Movement, 14, 30; Black
Power Movement, viii, 7–8, 14, 43, 61, 90,
122n1, 129; Muntu, 116, 117; New Orleans,
128; politico-artistic movements, 228;
politico-cultural figures, 7; West African
performers and, 31. *See also* artists/activ-
ists; social justice
polycentrism, 43, 48–49, 51, 52, 55n34,
210–11
polyrhythm: about, 43, 50, 55n40; African/
Africanist aesthetic, 210–11, 219; African
Americans, 28–29; Bed-Stuy and, 52;
Caribbean African dance, 189; improvisation, 219; "March" (Ronald K. Brown),
47–48, 50, 51; New Orleans culture, 129;
"Raaahmona Revisited" (Welsh), 50
Pomare, Eleo, 43, 77, 90, 96
Porgy and Bess (Gershwin), 81
postcolonial era, 2, 3, 148, 153. *See also* adaptation of tradition dance
postmodern aesthetic, 206, 207, 210, 218, 219
Pratt, Ron, 90
Primus, Mama Pearl: African Dance and
Music at Jacob's Pillow, 154; on cultural
connection with Africa/African dance,

viii, 143–44, 162–63; *dobale*, 15; embodiment, 29; *fanga/funga*, 88, 130; "I've
Known Rivers" (choreographed dance),
119–20; legacy of, 14, 51; Liberian dance,
88; Pan-Africanism, 33; spirit of the
dance, 21
prison project, Louisiana State Penitentiary
("Angola"), 137–40, 141
professional dance companies. *See* dance
companies
Protestantism, 188–89, 193, 201n18

"Raaahmona Revisited" (Welsh), 44, *44–45*,
47, 48–49, 50
Rafael, Matingou, 160
Rashida, Sister, 131
Reagun, Rosita, 121
Redd, Douglas, 130
Reed, Theophilus, 121
reggae, 181
religions, in African Diaspora: Akan,
96; Candomblé, 120, 183, 184; Catholicism, 182, 188, 189, 190, 191, 192; Lukumí
(Santería), 2, 184; Protestantism, 188–89,
193, 201n18; Vodou, 2, 181, 183, 184, 188;
women and, 138
repetition, 43, 47, 49–50, 51, 210
research and methodology: about, 3, 4, 5–6,
7, 12, 13, 14; autoethnography methodology, 252; improvisation, 205–7
Reynolds, Pearl, 51
rhythm: African/Africanist aesthetic, 90,
145; African Diaspora dance styles,
183–84, 191; *baamaaya*, 231, 232–33, *233*,
234, 236, 239, 240, 243, 244; dancer/musi-
cian relationship, 219; social/vernacular
dance, 212, 213; traditional African dance,
154, 155, 219
Richardson, Laurel, 252
Ricouer, Jean Paul, 100
ring shout, 67
rituals, and *dobale*, 15, 50, 58, 60, 68–69, 70.
See also African ritual practices
Rivera, Eduardo, 15
Roach, Max, 39
Robert Rauschenberg Foundation, Artist as
Activist Fellowship, 140
Roberts, Alfred "Uganda," 128
Robinson, Cleo Parker, 121
Robinson, Reginald, 121

Rockefeller Foundation, 134, 135
Rodrigues, Nereyda, 15
Rojas, Isiais, 162
Roland, Baderinwa (Baderinwa Ain), 131, 133, *134*, 136, 137
Rolfe, John, 101n4
Romaine, Marshall, 81
Ross, Kwame, 132, 135
Rukiyah, Sister, 131
rumba, 2, 160, 186

sabar/sabaar: about, 133, 249, 260n3; Bay Area African dance, 148–49; *hip-hop*, 34; Senegal, 58, 88, 91, 149, 177, 249, 259, 260n3; Wolof, 26, 149
Sako, Djeneba, 150
Salaam, Abdel, 79, 81, 90, 121
salima, 231, 236
Salongo Production, 133
salsa, 181
samba, 160
samba da roda, 186
Sanchez, Sonia, 43
San Francisco, California, 147, 148, 150, 151, 169. *See also* Oakland-San Francisco Bay Area, California
Santiago, Chiori, 158–59
"SAUCE!," 23–24, 34, 35nn5–6
savannah dance styles, 168–69, 178n1
Savin, Nancy R., 154
Sawyer, Raymond, 96
sayali, 234, 236
second line, 124, 125–27, 129
"second liners," 124, 126
Senegal: artists, 22, 28, 32, 105, 121, 132, 144, 147, 148, 150; Ballet Africaine de Diebel Guee, 105; Ballet De Sengarmoo, 132; *ching*, 175; dance/dance vocabularies for African American male dancers, 254, 259; *djembe*, 129; First World Festival of Negro Arts, 147; forest, earth, savannah, and ocean dance styles, 169; "internal diaspora," 5; Kumbuka, 133; *lindjien/lenjengo/ lindjiang/lindjien*, 149; Mali Dance Ensemble company, 148; National Ballet of Senegal, 147, 148; National Dance Company of Senegal, 22, 31, 35n4, 87–88, 115, 129; *n'dep/ndepp/ndëp*, 169, 178n1; *nyaka*, 175; pop music, 169–70; precolonial era, 92; *sabar/sabaar*, 58, 88, 91, 133, 149, 177,

249, 259, 260n3; Senegambian cultures, 259; Wolof, 26, 97, 149, 169
Senghor, Léopold Sédar, 21, 33, 228, 234–35
Senghor, Maurice Sonar, 235
Service, Carla, 158
sexuality, 94, 167, 211, 234, 252, 253, 254
Shabaka, 128
Shaka, Naimah, 133
Shaka, Zulu, 133, 137
Shankar, Uday, 246n2
Shay, Anthony, 27
Sheriff, Amon, 131
"shouting," 42–43, 49, 67
Sierra Leone, 1, 35n4, 87, 95–96, 169
Sila, Ramon, 15
Silas, Meshach, 15, 132
Silas, Nahgeree (Nahgeree Sutton-Silas), 15, 132
Silimbo Ballet, 121
Silvestre, Roseangela, 121
simbi, 34n2
Simon, Jawara, 137
Simon, Kenyatta, 130, 131, 133, *134*, 137
Simpson, Erica, 160
Singapore, 151
Singleton, Menhati, 131
Skinner, Jonathan, 84
"slaves"/"captives" African system, 175–76
Smith, Judith, 158
Smith, Nailah, 137
Smith, Stacy Letrice, *120*
Snead, Majeeda, 131, *134*
soca, 181
social justice: African dance artists, 6–7, 15; cultural memory, 90, 96, 97; Diaspora communities, 13–14, 15; Philadelphia, 44, 61; philosophical characteristics of African dance, 7; restorative justice, 7, 13; women in prison system, 137, 140. *See also* artists/activists
social values. *See* cultural values
social/vernacular dance, of African Americans: about, 1, 29, 58; African/Africanist aesthetic, 2, 13, 29, 184, 210, 211–12, 213; African Diaspora dance, 52–53, 207, 215; *charleston*, 1, 211; cultural appropriation, 211; improvisation, 207, 208, 212, 213, 215, 220, 221–22; *jazz dance*, 207, 212, 215, 220, 221, 222; *jook*, 213; rhythm, 212, 213; *tap dance*, ix, 28–29, 195, 207, 220, 221; tradi-

tional African dance, 13; *turkey trot*, 211.
See also *hip-hop*
Sompa, Biza, 121
Sompa, Titos, 157
Sorina, Gaynell Anaya, 133
Souso, Mousa, 121
South America: African dances, 1, 2–3, 12;
Africanity, 2; artists, 121; drumming, 3;
Muntu, 116; transatlantic slave trade, 53n1,
150, 191. *See also* Afro-Latin America and
dance; the Americas
Southern Africa: artists, 2; ballet companies,
151; colonial era, 93; *Ipi Tomb* (musical),
156; *mbira*, 162, 220, 227n64; Mozam-
bique, 227n64; precolonial era, 92; Swazi
Women Singers and Dancers, 154; Zulu
Dance Theatre of South Africa, 156
spirit/Spirit: about, 21–22, 23–24, 34, 34n1;
African dance styles, 169; Afro-Latin
America, 183, 190–91; American African
Diaspora, 181–82; Caribbean/Afro-Ca-
ribbean dance, 183; cultural memory, 87,
94–95; "Kankouran" or spirit guide, 109–
10; Kumbuka, 130–31, 137; natural worlds,
170; New Orleans, 124, 125, 129; spiritual
approach to dance, 104–5, 106, 107, 110.
See also African ritual practices
spontaneity, 214, 215, 223, 244–45
spontaneous acts, 214–15, 218, 219, 220
Stearns, Jean, 208, 211–12
Stearns, Marshall Winslow, 208, 211–12
STEM (Science, technology, Engineering,
and Math)-based curricula, 178
step/stepping, 58, 125
Stines, L'Antoinette, 121
Stuckey, P. Sterling, 15
Surdna Foundation, 140
Suriname, 2, 184, 190, 192
Suso, Foday Musa, 154
Sutton-Silas, Nahgeree (Nahgeree Silas),
15, 132
Sylvestre, Roseangela, 120

takai, 153, 164n19
tambú, 188
Tamisari, Francesca, 65
tango, 189
tap dance, ix, 28–29, 195, 207, 220, 221
technologies, production, 99–100, 170, 195
Teish, Luisah, 27, 30

Thiam, Mor, 28, 31, 32, 34, 97–98, 147, 148
Third World, 121
Thomas, Makeda, ix
Thomas, Tamara, *44–45*
Thompson, Liz, 154
Thompson, Robert Farris, 15, 43, 208–9,
210–11, 212
Thurop, Missa, and Ballet De Sengarmoo,
132
Tiérou, Alphonse, 216
titles of endearment/respect, 3, 16n5, 38, 66,
75, 83n2, 104, 131, 249, 260n4
Togo, 105, 164n18, *185*, 190, 223n1
Tolbert, Alyo, 15, 97, 114–15, *115*, 130, 132
Tone Foundation, 121
Touré, Ahmed Sékou, 228
Touré, Sekou (Stokley Carmichael), 128
Tourkwase, Sister, 132
"trace," and cultural memory, 85, 98, 100
traditional African dance: about, viii, ix, x,
xii, 1–2, 6, 12, 42, 54n19, 82, 87, 212, 223n2;
African Americans, 22–23, 25–26, 34; "African" as term of use, 85, 101n4; agency,
215, 216, 217, 218, 219; creole performance
culture, 25–26; cultural memory, 84–86,
98–99; cultural values, 136, 154; dance/
dance vocabularies for African American
male dancers, 254, 256; documented his-
tory/research about, 12–13, 82, 84; forest/
bush, earth, savannah, and ocean/water
styles, 168–69, 178n1; future of, 113, 167,
170, 178; improvisation, 215, 216–18; performance in African Diaspora, 88, 95,
99–100, 109, *109*, *113*; rhythm, 154, 155;
sexuality, 94, 167, 234; social justice, 6;
social/vernacular dance, 13; transatlantic
slave trade, 61, 93, 98. *See also* adaptation
of tradition dance; African/Africanist
aesthetic; African Diaspora dance; cultural memory; neotraditional African movements; West African (WA)-derived music
and dance; *and specific African countries,
and dance companies*
traditional African music: about, viii, ix;
African Americans, 22–23, 34; artists/ac-
tivists, 96; Bay Area, 148, 151, 152–53, 154,
157. *See also* drummers/drumming; West
African (WA)-derived music and dance
transatlantic slave trade (Middle Passage):
about, 150; abolishment of, 92; African/

Africanist aesthetic, 52; "African" as term of use, 101n4; African Diaspora, 5, 104; Afro-Latin America, 191; the Caribbean, viii, 42; narrative of, 37, 150; statistics, 53n1, 93; traditional African dance, 61, 93, 98
transculturación (Creole identities), 186, *187*, 188, 190, 192–93
transformations, 207, 211, 229, 241, 245
Trinidad-Tobago, 29, 146, 183, 184, 188, 192
Tulsa, Oklahoma, 151
tumba francesa, 2
turfing, 1
turkey trot, 211

Uchiyama, Mahea, 150
Umfundalai technique, 14, 53n3, 82, 83n2
UNESCO, 12, 15n2, 101, 202n27
Unifying Humanity through Cultural Creativity (UHCC), 114
United Nations International Decade for People of African Descent in 2015–2024, xi, xii, *xii*, 12, 101
United States: African American culture as invisible in, 208, 210–11, 213; African dance/music, 1, 3, 7, 8, 229, 241, 243; African Diaspora, 5; Berkeley, California, 146, 147, 148, 152, 153; Boston, Massachusetts, 244–45; Congo/Angola style, 193; creole performance culture, 26; cultural appropriation, 210–11; dance history, 82, 210; documentation of African dance, 12, 14; Durham, North Carolina, 3, 75, 77, 78, 96, 251, 259; enslaved Africans, 40, 92; Gullah Sea Islands, 93, 194; Illinois, 41, 54n13, 147; migration of artists to, viii, 3, 33, 107, 166; Native/African/Creole/European continuum, 193–94; Ohio, 242, 244, 259; transatlantic slave trade, 101n4; Washington, D.C., 14, 82–83, 97, 109, *109*, 110–11, 132, 259. *See also* African Americans (Black Americans); African culture, and African Americans; Bedford Stuyvesant (Bed-Stuy), Brooklyn, New York, and African dance; improvisation; New Orleans, Louisiana; New York, New York; Oakland, California; Oakland-San Francisco Bay Area, California; Philadelphia, Pennsylvania; San Francisco, California
Unity Conferences, Washington, D.C., 110–11, 132

University of California, Berkeley (UCB), 146, 147, 148, 152, 153
Uruguay/Afro-Uruguay, 2, 15n2, 189, 190–91
Uthman, JaJa, 132

Valdés, Andrea E. Woods, ix
Van Collie, Shimon-Craig, 155
Vaughan, Deborah, 146, 148, 156, 158, 161, 162
Venezuela, 189
Villard, Sylvia del, 15
Vineset, Ava LaVonne, ix
Virginia, 38, 101n4, 104, 108
"A Visit to Africa" (Konte), 108

Wajumbe Cultural Institution, 151
Wajumbe Dance Ensemble, 148
Wale, 34
Walker, Atiba, 132
Walker, Christopher, 119, 121
Walker, Sheila, 189–90
warba, 212, 225n25
Washington, D.C., 14, 82–83, 97, 109, *109*, 110–11, 132, 259. *See also* Kankouran West African Dance Company (KWADC or Kankouran), Washington, D.C.
Washington, Giovanni, 15
Washington, Lula, 33
water/ocean dance styles, 168–69, 178n1
Watson, Angela, 15
Welsh, Kariamu (Kariamu Welsh-Asante): about, 38, 53n3; African/Africanist aesthetic, 42, 47, 49, 50, 208, 209–10, 212, 214; African dance, 54n19; artists/activists, 43, 44, *44–45*, 47, 48–49, 50, 51; *Bantaba* circle, 71n21; Bed-Stuy, 38, 40–41, 53; "blood memory," 39; CADD, ix, 3–4, *4*; call and response, 49; characteristics and personality of, 82–83; *djembe*, 50; entrance and exit of dancer, 50, 52; epic memory, 27–28, 210; fluidity, 101, 210, 213; multiple meter, 47, 50; neotraditional African movements, 42, 54n19, 223n2; oral technique, 46, 47, 210; Pan-Africanism, 33; philosophical characteristics of African dance, 209, 214; polycentrism, 48–49, 55n34, 210; polyrhythm, 50, 55n40, 210; "Raaahmona Revisited," 44, *44–45*, 47, 48–49, 50; repetition, 47, 49, 210; "shouting," 49; titles of endearment/respect for,

38, 75, 83n2; traditional African dance, 42, 223n2; *Umfundalai* technique, 14, 53n3, 82, 83n2. *See also* cultural memory

West African dance class, Philadelphia, Pennsylvania: about, 8, 56–60, 69–70; African heritage, 63–64; call-and-response, 65; CEC, 58, 61, 62, 66; the circle/*Bantaba* circle, 58, 66–67, 69, 71n21; community, 57–59, 62, 65–66; cultural knowledge, 59; dancing down the floor, 58, 64–66; *dobale*, 58, 60, 68–69, 70; embodied practice, 60, 63–64, 65, 66, 69; epic memory, 61; ethnography, 58; "family," 59, 66; Ivey as dance instructor, 59, 60, 61, 62, 63; the lesson, 58, 62–64; musician/dancer relationship, 59, 64–65, 68–69; *ring shout*, 67; shared practice, 57–58, 59, 62, 65, 66; warm-up, 58, 60–62; white dancers, 60. *See also* West Africa/West African dance

West African (WA)-derived music and dance: about, 22, 32–34; aesthetic characteristics, 26–27, 29, 30; Africanness (*Africanité*), 29; authentic African culture, 30–31; choreographers, 28, 29–30; creole performance culture, 26; cultural connection with Africa/African dance, 27–29; embodiment, 28–29; epic memory, 27–28; ethnography, 25, 29; "SAUCE!" and spirit in, 23–24, 34; West African as term of use, 35n4.

West Africa/West African dance: about, 5; adaptation of tradition dance, 228, 234–35, 239, 245; *adowa*, 88, 153, 164n19; African Americans and culture of, 104–5, 106–7, 108, 111–12; African heritages, 181, 182, 193; Africanness (*Africanité*), 30, 31; African Personality, 234, 235; Akan/Asante heritage, 96, 184, 187, 190; Asante/Ashanti, 85, 88, 153, 164n19, 184, 190; audience/performer relationship, 217; "Baba" as title, 16n5; CAAD, xii; creole performance culture and, 2, 26; Cuba/Afro-Cuban dance, 184; cultural values, 5, 31, 32, 104; Dagari, 153; *damba*, 153, 244, 245; dances/dance companies, xii, 2, 3, 143, 157, 186; Diaspora, 5, 58; *espri*, 21; Fanti, 153; Fon-based techniques, 21, 184, 184, 187; improvisation, 217; "internal diaspora," 5; *jola*, 259; *kakilambe*, 133; *kora*, 34, 177, 249, 260n1; *kpanlogo*, 153, 164n19, 241; Kumbuka, 133; Lobi, 153; maps, 183, 185; migration and, 3, 5; Mossi, 164n18, 205, 223n1;

Negritude, 33, 234–35; New Orleans culture, 125; politics among performers, 31; precolonial era, 92, 175–76; Sierra Leone, 1, 35n4, 87, 95–96, 169; spirit, 21; *takai*, 153, 164n19; Tanawa dance company, 157; transatlantic slave trade, 61, 104; *warba*, 212, 225n25; West African as term of use, 35n4. *See also* Caribbean/Afro-Caribbean dance; Congo (Congo-Brazzaville); *djembe*; Ghana; performing and teaching African dance; West African dance class; West African (WA)-derived music and dance; Yoruba and Yoruba-based technique; *and specific countries*

West Coast of United States, 22, 35–36n17, 241

West Indies, 121

West Philadelphia, Pennsylvania. *See* West African dance class, Philadelphia, Pennsylvania

White-Burrell, Kelly, 133

Whites: African culture/dance/music, 60, 154, 192, 195, 207, 211; dance/dance vocabularies for African American male dancers, 252, 256, 258; as female *chica* dancers, 188; turn-out model, 258

Wiles, Olukose, 132

Wilkes, Corcy, 121

Wilkes, Dorothy, 15

William and Flora Hewlett Foundation, 150

Willis, Cheryl, 221

Wilson, August, 43

Wilson, Cedric, 148

Wilson, Lionel, 158

Wilson, Olly, 152

Wilson, Reggie, 121

Wolofsodung/Wolosodon, 88

women: Black dances/dancers, 7, 11; *chica*, 186, 188; circumcision, 174; mentoring for continuity, 197; prison system and project for, 137–40, 141; socialization of dance students, 144; "Won't Blow Down" project, 140. *See also specific women artists*

World Damba Festival 2012, 244, 245

Xaba, N'diko, 121

"Yanga" (Payne), 118

Yarborough, Camille, 15

Yarborough, Lavinia Williams, 15, 188

yemoja, 169, 178n1

yenvalú/yenvalou/yanvalou, 2, 135, 145

Yoruba and Yoruba-based technique: *ajaja*, 136; *ase/ache/ashe/axe*, 21, 34n1; Cuba/Afro-Cuban dance, 184, *184*; *dobale*, 68; improvisation, 216–17, 218, 219; *odunde*, 88; *Orisha* dances, 58, 59, 135, 181; rhythm, 219; *yemoja*, 169, 178n1

Young, Tyra, 131

youth: Diamano Coura, 151; Kankouran, 107, *107*, *111*, 112; Kumbuka, 131; mentoring for continuity, 194–95; Muntu, 115, 116–17; performing/teaching African dance, 170, 172, 175, 177; socialization of, 144; technology products, 112

yuka, 188

Zadonu African Dance Company, 152

Zambia, 227n64

zapateo, 191

zebola, 160

Zellerbach Family Foundation, 150

Zollar, Jawole Willa Jo, 14, 90, 121

zouk, 181

Zulu, Naimah, 133

Zulu, Shaka, and Zulu Connection, 133

The University of Illinois Press
is a founding member of the
Association of University Presses.

———————————————————

University of Illinois Press
1325 South Oak Street
Champaign, IL 61820-6903
www.press.uillinois.edu

Printed by Printforce, United Kingdom